Contents

Preface

'We do not care for Charles II', Queen Victoria told one of her officials in 1889. This attitude has long persisted. As recently as August 1978, the director of the Victoria and Albert Museum wrote that the reign of Charles II was 'universally condemned as a triumph of vice, an affront to middle-class morality.'

There are several biographies of Charles II already published; there are also volumes of peripheral material and countless books about the extraordinary characters who people his reign. In addition there are extensive contemporary memoirs, pamphlets, diaries and other reminiscences most of which have, at some time, been published for private or public distribution.

You may reasonably ask, therefore, what could possibly be added to this library of historical discourse? As I tramped along the same road as that taken by Charles after his escape from Worcester, saw something of his places of exile, stood where he was humiliated by the Scots, visited those parts of England in which he sought refuge when King, and was entertained by some of his living descendants and those of his chief ministers, it seemed there was little I would unearth that had not been noted somewhere before. Yet, after looking through a mountain of documents in much the same way as every writer about Charles had done, and having the image of Queen Victoria clearly before me, it became apparent that a fresh look at the man and the age which he transcended was in order.

There is the view that many of the changes which occurred in mid-seventeenth-century England, were a result of Cromwell's military triumph; that the Civil War was in effect a class struggle between the Royalists who wished to maintain economic and social privileges, and the Puritans, who wanted freedom of trade and conscience; that progress was achieved by sudden and bloody political events, rather than by 'the accumulated wisdom of generations.' It has become increasingly clear, however, that the Civil War was not decisive. Its principal legacy was a countryside wasted and a people embittered. Puritanism, far from being an angel of enlightenment, became for many a harbinger of darkness. It attempted to discipline a society bursting with activity, by means inimical to the times.

The extent to which Oliver Cromwell's 'revolution' failed can be seen after 1660, when England breathed again. Many theatres re-opened, the arts were encouraged. Trade prospered, investment soared. Science made prodigious advances, and new territories opened up in far distant regions. Paradoxically, as Parliament became increasingly autocratic, the beginnings of party politics engendered an involvement in government. The dreariness of Puritan manners was replaced by an exuberant and colourful flamboyance. Above all this, towered King Charles II. Magisterial yet familiar, dazzling yet earthy. He could hunt, fish, swim, sail and swear as well as any man. That he had more mistresses than most, was a source of envy rather than disdain; that he was more intelligent, and unscrupulous, than his political opponents, more a source of wonder than distrust. He was father and hero to his people, possibly the last English monarch who could justifiably claim to be so.

His reign was shaken by a series of cataclysmic events, of which his own Restoration was but the first. Plague, fire, the destruction of the Fleet in the Medway, bankruptcy, wars with the Dutch, the Popish Plot – these were events as dangerous as any which had confronted his father before 1649. Men thought the civilized world was about to end. It was argued that Charles's apparent inactivity encouraged absolutism, and condoned (for instance a form of Anglicanism damaging to the State. But Charles came to view the numerous crises through which he lived as merely regrettable, if useful. The absurdities of human behaviour never ceased to amuse, nor distress him.

This book seeks to understand how such a man restored the Crown, attempted to establish a constitutional monarchy, witnessed the beginnings of a two-party system of democratic government, guided a bankrupt community toward prosperous and dynamic nationhood, and translated into public policy the social and economic changes gathering momentum during the previous fifty years. That he did so without bloody revolution, is witness to his genius as a politician and his wisdom as a man. If the triumph was personal rather than constitutional, it is no less extraordinary and no less exciting. It was perhaps Charles, rather than Cromwell, who fashioned modern Britain, and this in spite of Queen Victoria.

I have relied as far as possible on eyewitness accounts. Although in many ways these contemporary writings do not provide a balanced picture of the events they describe, they are a clue toward understanding the mood of their times. As my purpose is avowedly popularist, I have avoided burdening the reader with endless footnotes. At the end of the book I have appended a select bibliography, including most of the sources I have consulted. Apart from published works, those who have helped me are too numerous to mention. However, I should like to thank particularly the Duke of Grafton and the Lord Clifford who between them provided me with many insights; The Goodwood Estate Office; John Drummond, now Director of the Edinburgh Festival, for textural suggestions; David Machin, John Cushman, Diana Crawfurd, Eric Warne and Julian Watson for patient encouragement; and Sheila Thompson, Evelyne Lewiston and Patricia Evans for typing it all out.

A word about spelling. As Carolean spelling was variable, I have modified it for clarity. Likewise references to the Dutch provinces which, through various constitutional changes, adopted various names. That part which was Catholic, and owed its allegiance to France or Spain, I have referred to as the Spanish Netherlands; that part which was Protestant, and eventually became the territory of William of Orange, I have referred to as Holland or the United Provinces. Dates in the text are old style, but I have taken the year as beginning on 1 January. In Charles's numerous financial transactions with Louis XIV, I have translated the livre as being approximately 8p. As a rough guide, £1 in 1660 would be worth £11 in 1978, although present-day inflation makes such a calculation comparatively meaningless.

Kensington Park Gardens 1974–8

Chapter One
Lurking behind the hangings

The scene could scarcely be imagined. The Lord Mayor and over one hundred thousand citizens of London stood amazed as the procession approached. First came a dozen gilded coaches, accompanied by squadrons of horse in silver doublets. Then rode the Earl of Cleveland with a thousand buff-clad soldiers. Next, the sheriffs in gold lace, their footmen in red cloaks and green scarves. Trumpeters in black velvet and cloth of gold, followed by the Life Guards, the City Marshal and the heralds. Next, General Monck and the Duke of Buckingham . . . surrounded by five regiments of foot. In all, 'a triumph of above twenty thousand horse and foot, brandishing their swords and shouting with inexpressible joy; the ways strewed with flowers, the bells ringing, the streets hung with tapestry, fountains running with wine . . . and myriads of people flocking the streets. And was as far as Rochester, so as they were seven hours in passing the city, even from two in the afternoon till nine at night.'

Near the end of the procession came the 'black boy' himself, tall, dark and slim, riding bare-headed, dressed in a plain, dark suit with a crimson plume in his hat, 'looking to all, raising his hat to all in the most stately manner ever seen, amid the acclamations and blessings of the people,' 29 May, 1660.

In Whitehall, the Lords awaited their King. 'Dread Sovereign', boomed the orator, 'I offer no flattering titles, but speak words of truth. You are the desire of these kingdoms, the strength and stay of the tribes of the people, for the moderating of extremities, the reconciling of differences, the satisfying of all interests, and for restoring the collapsed honour of these nations.' Charles smiled, some thought mysteriously, answering that he was 'disordered by my journey, with the noise still sounding in my ears which I confess was pleasing to me because it expressed the affections of my people.' He then proceeded, amid acclaim, to the Banqueting Hall of the Palace for yet another loyal address, this from the Speaker of the Commons. His reply to them was direct. 'The laws and liberties of my people, with the Protestant religion – next to my life and crown – I will preserve.' By now he was exhausted. 'I am so weary', he told the Speaker, 'that I am scarce able to speak.' It was suggested that the new

King might go to Westminster Abbey for an immediate service of thanksgiving, but he declined. As the Earl of Leicester later recalled, 'there was so great disorder and confusion that the King scarce knew or took notice of anybody.' Leicester was mistaken. As he left Whitehall, Charles was mobbed by a crowd of Lords anxious to assert their loyalty. 'I doubt it has been my own fault I have been absent so long', he told them, 'for I see nobody that does not protest he has ever wished for my return.' There was a moment of silence, followed by some forced laughter. Charles added, again with a smile: 'Where are all my enemies?' Again, there was silence. A few looked sheepish, others drifted away. Charles tipped his hat, and walked on.

Nonetheless, the welcome given to Charles was in many quarters heartfelt. The diarist Evelyn remembered how, waiting in the Strand, he had 'beheld it and blessed God . . . for it was the Lord's doing, and such a restoration never mentioned in any history, ancient or modern, since the return of the Jews from the Babylonish captivity.' And in Buckinghamshire, the rector of Maid's Moreton wrote in his register; 'This day, by the wonderful goodness of God, his Sacred Majesty . . . was peacefully restored to his martyred father's throne, the powerful armies of his enemies being amazed spectators and in some sort unwilling assistants to his return . . . And from this day ancient orders began to be observed. Laus Deo!'

* * *

From the first, Charles was not quite what had been expected. His dress was sombre. He preferred brown, ochre and dark blue velvets. Nor did he bother to hide his greying hair with a wig, at least not until three years after his Restoration. He wore few rings and said he was only comfortable in long, close-fitting coats. His laces were unbleached. Although much concerned with the dignity of royalty, he did not care for the pastel satins or glittering brocades of his courtiers.

For many, he was also too familiar. He desired 'nothing but to be easy himself and that everybody else should be so; and would have been glad to see the least of his subjects pleased, and to refuse no man what he asked.' One courtier later observed the King at Newmarket 'mixing himself among the crowd.' Charles, remembered a shocked Sir John Reresby, even went to plays 'acted in a barn, and by very ordinary Bartholomew-fair comedians.' Some thought this familiarity denoted lack of purpose. Sir William Temple, later ambassador to Brussels and The Hague, thought Charles's behaviour betrayed a 'softness of temper [which] made him apt to fall into the persuasions of whoever had his confidence and kindness for a time, however different soever from the opinions he was of before.' Temple added with disappointment; 'he [Charles] was very easy to change hands when those he employed seemed to have engaged him in any difficulties; so that nothing looked steady in his conduct of affairs nor aimed at any certain end.' Bishop Burnet, one of Charles's more loyal supporters, noted that although the King was 'the best bred man in the world, . . . he talks too much and runs out too long and too far.'

Burnet and Temple were shrewd enough, however, to recognize Charles's knack of softening hostility in others with his casual humour. They acknowledged Charles possessed a careful memory and sharp intuition, and it became obvious to both that he trusted no one. 'He has a strange command of himself', Burnet noted, and had 'the greatest art of concealing himself of any man alive, so that those about him cannot tell when he is ill or well pleased.' Clarendon, Charles's first Chancellor, complained to Secretary Nicholas that 'the King loves both you and me, and thinks us very honest and useful servants; but he will sometimes use another, of whom he hath not so good an opinion, as well or better than either of us.'

Such unease grew with Charles's familiarity. 'He lived with his ministers as he did with his mistresses . . . he used them, but he was not in love with them . . . he tied himself no more to them, but they did to him, which implied a sufficient liberty on either side.' This informality often bred insolence.

> We have a pretty witty King,
> Whose word no man relies on;
> He never said a foolish thing,
> And never did a wise one.

Charles replied: 'That is very true, for my words are my own; my actions are my ministers'.'

Charles's contemporaries did not know what to make of him. Evelyn, not the most impressionable of diarists, records four successive conversations with the King early in his reign. At one, Charles talked excitedly about astronomy. At a second, he spoke of the need for cleaner air in the cities, of the legislation necessary to enforce smoke abatement, and of the benefits thereby to architecture and gardening. At a third, he chatted enthusiastically about his private collection of 'brave pictures' by those 'new masters', Raphael, Titian and Holbein, passing later to his book of maps and his growing assortment of chiming clocks and model ships. At a fourth, he discoursed about bee-keeping.

What were his subjects to make of a monarch who wished that 'Whitehall was like a fair all day'? 'The eagerness of men, women and children to see his Majesty and kiss his hands', recalled one eyewitness, 'was so great that he had scarce leisure to eat for some days, coming as they did from all parts of the nation. And the King being as willing to give them that satisfaction, would have none kept out.' Could a King sit up all night, with a party of mathematicians from the Philosophical Society, watching an eclipse of Saturn through his telescope? Could a King be so concerned to stock his lake in St James's Park with 'melancholy water-fowls – between a stork and a swan' brought by the Russian ambassador from Astrakhan (their progeny, incidentally, still inhabit

11

the lake today), or fill his parks with antelopes, an elk, guinea goats and Arabian sheep? The King kept a pet monkey, and the Royal bedroom was cluttered with dogs, including a breed of spaniels that soon took his name.

Charles also spoke fluent French and knew sufficient Italian and Spanish to comprehend the verbal procrastinations of various foreign ambassadors. He was a brilliant yachtsman, and Evelyn relates how the King raced his brother James from Greenwich to Gravesend for a wager of £100. Charles won. Inspired by success, he then challenged all-comers to a race round the Isle of Wight. When, finally, Charles took to wearing a wig, it was more frequently off than on because (he said) it got sticky in the heat. 'The King and Duke of York play bowls in the Park', an official complained, 'while the guns [of the Dutch] could be plainly heard.' The King 'hates the very sight or thought of business.'

And then, of course, there was the matter of Charles's illegitimate children. There were eventually fourteen whom he publicly acknowledged and liked to have about him at Court, and God knows how many mistresses. One estimate was thirty-nine; when asked why this number, Charles replied that it reminded him of the Articles of Faith.

He was over six foot tall, brown-eyed and broad shouldered; his left eye had a slight cast. He had no illusions about his looks; 'odd's fish, I am an ugly fellow', he remarked more than once. His mother agreed. When the lad was only nine, she had written to a Parisian friend, Madame St George: 'he is so ugly that I am ashamed of him.' However, she added, 'he is so serious that I cannot help fancying him far wiser than myself.'

He had a wide mouth and long, drooping cheeks. His stride was elegant, his arms rarely still. No one turned their backs on him, and not merely because he was King. When angered, his eyes sunk into deep pits of flesh. His adversaries sweated; their knees shook. They were being mocked and they knew it.

'His good looks, kind words and fair promises', remembered Burnet to his cost, 'charmed all who came near him, till they found how little they could depend [on them].' Temple grimly acknowledged that Charles was possessed of a 'great variety of knowledge and true judgment of men.' For all his charm, Charles could be vicious and lethal. He 'knew men to a hair', and never let them forget it.

*   *   *

At his birth, 29 May, 1630, the astronomical signs had been confusing. A constellation was seen shining about St Paul's Cross before midday; 'to behold this babe in heaven, seemed to open one more eye than usual, from which most men presaged that the Prince should be of high understandings and of no common glory among Kings.' Others noticed that it was the planet Venus that shone so brightly, the rest being ominously absent. Such a loneliness in the

Charles I and his Queen, Henrietta Maria, in 1634, by Daniel Mytens. Charles I had succeeded on 27 March, 1625, aged twenty-five. Although well-read and a competent linguist, he stammered. In his youth, he had been thought weak-kneed and undersized; he could not walk until he was seven. As King, he was neat, quiet, apologetic, and graceful. He would dismiss a loyal address with the phrase: "by your favour, I think otherwise." Henrietta Maria, however, was rude, peevish and given to hysterical rages in which she smashed plates, windows and coxcombs. Born in 1609, the youngest daughter of Henry IV of France, she married Charles by proxy on 1 May, 1625. After the civil war, she lived in France, founding a convent at Chaillot. After her son's Restoration, she received a pension of £60,000 a year, and died near Paris on 31 August, 1669, unaware of the harm she had caused. Charles II was the second son of Charles and Henrietta Maria; their first, also called Charles, had died soon after birth.

Heavens, it was argued, did not promise good companionship on earth. After numerous miscarriages, Queen Henrietta Maria had at last given birth to a screaming, lusty lad – the 'son of our love.' He was a solemn baby who slept a lot. 'The nurses told me', the Venetian ambassador reported, 'that after his birth he [Charles] never clenched his fists but always kept his hands open. From this they augur that he will be a prince of great liberality.' The boy's horoscope was equally optimistic. He would, of course, be handsome with 'hair and eyes somewhat tending to black, thin beard, shrill voice, a mincing gait and will live either to 108 or 66 years, be very fortunate . . . attain wealth by marriage and war and be particularly fond of mathematicians, sailors, merchants, learned men, painters and sculptors.' Bonfires were lit, bells were rung. Only the Puritans 'showed their sorrow.' But not so Archbishop Laud at the Prince's baptism. 'Double his father's graces upon him', he intoned – adding, almost as an afterthought, 'if it be possible.'

It is as well that the Archbishop's wish was granted. Charles I stammered. Although loving, he always seemed remote. Doubtless remembering his own father, James I, a brilliant, amusing, slobbering drunk, Charles I was formal and austere. He neglected his young son abominably, while his wife, Henrietta

Maria, was a spoiled, silly woman, given to hysterical outbursts. When the old Duke of Buckingham had told her that 'Queens of England have had their heads cut off before now', she had thrown a 'fit of temper that lasted for several weeks.' She was also a bully with an 'immoderate desire for power.'

Instead of family affection, Charles I and Henrietta heaped on the lad an entourage, including a Welsh wet-nurse, two chamberlains, two physicians, an apothecary, a lawyer, eight rockers and a large number of needlewomen, cooks, pages and ushers; in all nearly 250 people costing £5,000 per annum and everyone of them camping somewhere in St James's Palace. Charles was dressed in white satin frocks and a tight cap and paraded like a prize doll. 'It was no wonder if England was thought secure', Clarendon wrote later, 'the Court in great plenty, or rather . . . excess and luxury; the country rich and . . . fully enjoying the pleasure of its own wealth.' All Charles lacked was parents.

Once he was taken violently ill and began vomiting blood, the result (it was thought) of a boil on his neck. The young Prince was made to swallow ladles of chicken broth followed by an aperient of senna and rhubarb. The windows of his bedroom were shut; the stench was unbearable. Only his mother failed to visit him. Nor did she tend him during his subsequent recurring bouts of nausea and diarrhoea. Instead she took him to her Catholic Chapel in Somerset House and organized parlour games with the courtiers for which the rewards were relics and crucifixes.

When he was almost two, a sister, Mary, was born. When three, a brother, James. A year later, another sister, Elizabeth; and when he was five and a half, a third sister, Anne. (Later, there would be two other sisters, Mary and Minette, and another brother, Gloucester.) When Anne was born, the household moved to Richmond, and was joined by George and Francis Villiers, the orphaned sons of the Duke of Buckingham. George, two years older than Charles, was clever and handsome and immediately became like an elder brother. They giggled at the ladies in chapel, breakfasted on beer, mutton, chicken, bread and buttermilk. Dinner was equally lavish. They had a choice of four different kinds of fish, custards and often one of Charles's favourite dishes – pigs' and chickens' livers with ginger and hard-boiled eggs. Each dish was tasted for poison, and served on silver-gilt platters by a procession of kneeling pages.

At six, Charles was given a French tutor, whom he detested, much preferring the advice and company of the 46-year-old Earl of Newcastle, newly appointed Charles's governor. It was a fortunate appointment. Newcastle was a devoted monarchist. He was also cynical, and despised pedantry, priggishness and fanaticism. Being a considerable horseman, he encouraged the Prince in athletic pleasures. Before long, Charles could dance, fence and ride 'leaping horses, and such as would overthrow others – with the greatest dexterity.' Nor did the Earl neglect Charles's other training. Homilies about courtesy to women, prayers, good government, the nature of Kingship and the necessity of reading, abounded. Above all, Newcastle urged, study history 'that [you] might so compare the dead with living; for the same humours is now as was then; there is no alteration but in names.'

Before his eighth birthday, Charles was made a Knight of the Garter and Prince of Wales. That he 'hastens apace out of his childhood' proved an understatement. Parliament was being dissolved, the Archbishop of Canterbury impeached, and the Scottish chieftains were demanding the King's death. Charles was sent to the Commons to plead for the life of his father's friend, the Earl of Stafford, lately condemned to death by Charles I himself. It was all very puzzling. In the Commons, Charles 'made the strongest representations' but was sent away 'with scant civility.' The King tried to hide the growing chaos from his son, but the Prince became moody, refusing to speak to his father. Eventually, he was asked what was the matter. 'Your Majesty should have asked me that sooner', came the bitter reply. 'My grandfather left you four Kingdoms, and I am afraid your Majesty will leave me never a one.' His two youngest sisters had died, the second, Anne, in much pain. Anne had held Charles's hand as he knelt by her bedside. 'I am not able to say my longer prayer' (the Lord's Prayer), she told him, 'but I will say my short one.' Folding her hands, she went on: 'Lighten mine eyes, O Lord, lest I sleep the sleep of death.' Then, she died.

As opposition to his father increased, it became necessary for the young Charles to move constantly from house to house for safety. When his father failed to arrest various members of the House of Commons who were defying Royal authority, it was even suggested that Charles be taken as hostage for the King's good faith. The King replied by moving Charles to Hampton, while the Queen fled to Holland, taking with her Charles's favourite sister, Mary. With Civil War now threatening, the King and his son went north. At York, Charles was made Captain of the Guard and given a regiment of cavalry. Within weeks, he had to endure the humiliation of seeing the Royal standard trampled in the mud at the Battle of Edgehill. One minute Charles was forced to hide in a barn among wounded cavaliers screaming for help. Next, the boy stood facing an enemy troop of horse shouting, 'I fear them not, I fear them not', as they charged down upon him. He was forcibly removed from the battlefield by his cousin Rupert and taken to Oxford where the Royalists set up their headquarters. 'When are we to go home?' Charles asked Rupert. Came the reply: 'We have no home.'

Six weeks later, Parliament discontinued all the Royal revenues. The Queen, back from Holland with promises of aid, was pregnant again. She proposed marrying the young Charles to Louis XIV's first cousin, the wealthy Anne-Marie de Montpensier, but the King wanted Charles to rally political support for the Crown, and suggested that the Prince become head of a new West of England Alliance. Despite protests from Rupert, who considered the West his responsibility, Charles, now 12, was despatched to organize what assistance he could.

But nothing seemed to stop Parliament's advance. At Marston Moor, Charles's father was again defeated, on this occasion by a redoubtable cavalry officer, Oliver Cromwell; Charles's mother once more fled to France. York was seized by the Parliamentary Army, while the Prince of Wales toured Dorset, Devon and Cornwall in an attempt to recruit a reluctant populace. The King lost again at Naseby in 1645, although it took six weeks for the news to reach the Prince. Even then the full extent of the disaster was not realized. When a letter finally arrived from his father, Charles can have been in little doubt as to what was now in store. 'It is very fit for me now to prepare for the worst', his father wrote with self-pity. 'Wherefore know that my pleasure is, whensoever you find yourself in apparent danger of falling into the rebels' hands, that you convey yourself into France and there be under your Mother's care; who is to have the absolute full power of your education in all things, except religion; in that, [she is] not to meddle at all . . .'

As General Fairfax, Cromwell's lieutenant, advanced westwards, the fifteen year old Charles retreated to Launceston where he spent a 'tedious, cold winter.' The inactivity galled him and he urged his council to let him attack Fairfax. Rupert, meanwhile, surrendered Bristol – the last effective Royalist stronghold – and Charles appealed to Parliament for peace. Parliament ignored him. He retreated further west to Pendennis Castle, overlooking Falmouth Bay, where he passed the time strengthening the fortifications. The local people criticized him for seeming too lenient with the Roundhead prisoners being kept there. Fairfax wrote suggesting that he and the Prince join forces and depose the King, to which, in a fury, Charles replied: 'Rogues! Rogues! Are they not content to be rebels, but would have me in their number?' Rashly, he launched a furious assault on Fairfax's well-entrenched army near Truro. Defeat was inevitable. There was nothing for it but to leave the country; just three months before his sixteenth birthday, Charles set sail for the Scilly Isles, twenty-six miles off the coast, in a boat called the *Phoenix*.

The weather now added to his depression. In St Mary's Castle, where the Royal refugees lodged, water came in through the roof. There was no fuel and Charles slept in a loft among dried herrings. 'We begged our daily bread of God', wrote Lady Fanshawe, a fellow exile, 'for we thought every meal our last.' Parliament tried to seduce Charles back to the mainland and sent a 'loving and tender appeal', promising he could 'reside in such a place and have such attendants and counsellors . . . as should be approved by both Houses.' To ensure that Charles understood what was intended, Fairfax despatched a fleet of two dozen ships to surround St Mary's; luckily a storm dispersed them. But the Prince realized he would have to move on. Ireland was considered, but Jersey, off the French coast, was thought safer. Charles sent a characteristic reply to Fairfax: 'We have a great and earnest desire to be amongst you', he wrote, '. . . if we might have an assurance that it might prove an expedient towards a blessed peace . . . We are . . . removing to Jersey, as being nearer to you and fitter for corresponding.' In fact, Jersey was six times further away from the mainland than the Scillies. The House of Commons thought Charles's letter 'artful.'

*   *   *

Charles arrived in Jersey aboard the *Proud Black Eagle*. To the islanders, who had not seen a Stuart Prince before, he was a hero. To Charles, the island, although safe, was far from home. Its chief occupation, moreover, was knitting. Charles learned to sail and ordered himself a 12-oared yacht. With the ladies he was a success, particularly when he recommended that they wear their jewels, previously hidden for fear of invasion. But despite a troop of some three hundred Royalists who had followed him to Jersey, Charles felt redundant. The King wrote from Newcastle, urging the Prince to France to enlist support there. Edward Hyde, the future Chancellor and Earl of Clarendon, and by now Charles's closest adviser, thought otherwise. The French, he said, 'talk but do not act'. Digby, later Earl of Bristol, wanted Charles to go to Ireland and from there invade England. From Paris came a letter saying that 'the Queen can no longer support his Highness where he is. If he comes into France he will be given 14,000 pistoles for his maintenance . . .' Again Hyde objected. 'If the Prince should put himself under a foreign power, the Kingdom will apprehend a new embroilment [with Catholicism] and thus your Majesty will render yourself irreconcilable to the whole nation.' Remote though Jersey might seem, it was at least 'a corner of His Majesty's Kingdom. In France . . . you will be a foreigner, begging your bread . . . It will be said that [you go] to mass with the Queen, even if [you do] not.' Yet, as Hyde admitted, 'no man in his wits can think fit that the Prince should bury himself in this obscure island from action . . .' News arrived that Parliament was planning to invade neighbouring Guernsey. That settled it. Charles announced: 'I shall be gone tomorrow by five o'clock in the morning' – to France.

This time he sailed aboard his own yacht. Unfavourable winds delayed his departure for several days, but finally he arrived at St Malo on 26 June 1646. He was greeted by less than a Royal welcome; over two months passed before 'the least message [came] from the Court [of Louis XIV] to congratulate his arrival there.' Charles was soon informed, moreover, that the eight-year-old King of France was not about to finance an invasion of England; the only immediate solution, as his mother had already argued, was to marry a rich heiress as quickly as possible. Fortunately, there was no shortage of candidates. Negotiations had been proceeding for some time with the richest of all, Anne-Marie de Montpensier, Sovereign of Dombes, Princess of Joinville and Laroche-sur-Yon, Duchesse of Châtelleraut and St Fargeau, Dauphine of Auvergne and Countess of Eu, in short La Grande Mademoiselle. Alas, she had certain disadvantages. She was fat, and her face was dominated by an

Charles dancing at a ball in The Hague during his exile, in an engraving by A. Bosse. Charles was at The Hague when news was brought to him by his brother-in-law of his father's execution. It was also there, nine years later, that Charles received a £50,000 grant from Parliament in anticipation of the King's Restoration. Note Charles's ridiculous clothes in the engraving. Who was fooling whom? Contrary to popular belief, Charles's taste in clothes was, in comparison to that of his sycophants, austere.

enormous nose; her favourite occupations were picnics, cards and guessing games. Despite his fluent French, Charles pretended not to understand a word this absurd lady said, a habit which, as Madame de Motteville observed, 'was most inconvenient.'

Eventually, Charles was allowed to meet cousin Louis, 'as if by chance', while walking in the forest at Fontainebleau. (Louis's grandfather, Henry IV of France, was also Charles's mother's father.) This carefully stage-managed meeting did not promise much for Royal co-operation. Yet, after many delays, the French treasury granted the penniless exile a small pension which Henrietta promptly grabbed for her out-of-pocket expenses. Her bullying of Charles increased, as did her unpopularity with the French.

The Prince also made a bad impression at the socially conscious French Court. He was thought shy, lacking in wit, inclined to stammer and impervious to the advances of La Grande Mademoiselle. 'I thought no longer of the Prince of Wales except as an object of pity', she wrote, piqued. Only his courtesy was favourably received. 'His gallantry was carried to such lengths

18

that it caused great comment', noted his mother. 'During the three days at Fontainebleau', wrote one who had benefited from Charles's gallantry, the Prince 'enjoyed the pleasures of the chase, and any others there available; he visited *all* the princesses.' His reputation had preceded him.

In Jersey, it was rumoured, he had already fathered a child, later called James de la Cloche. Evidence for this is sketchy, and the Parliamentary spies who followed Charles everywhere to gather whatever evidence they could against him and the Royal family, never mention such a child. The arrival in Paris of George Villiers, now Duke of Buckingham, who had already 'got into all the vices and impieties of the age', apparently completed Charles's 'corruption.' Buckingham was witty and gay. Monarchy, he told Charles, is a 'perpetual subject for raillery.' He introduced Charles to his tutor, Thomas Hobbes, who 'under the pretence of instructing him with mathematics, laid before him [Charles] his schemes both as to religion and politics, which made a deep and lasting impression on [Charles's] mind, so that the main blame of [his] . . . bad morals was owing to the Duke.' In adversity, the young refugees found consolation in each other's company, a companionship which, despite many provocations, Charles never forgot.

From England, the news grew worse. The King had been imprisoned in Edinburgh, and Parliament declared it would 'make Prince Charles repent' for having joined the Papists. Such was Parliament's distaste for Henrietta Maria that £100,000 was offered by Parliament on condition she never set foot in England again. Then word came that the Marquis of Argyll had delivered the King to Parliament. The Queen pawned her jewels in Amsterdam, while her son moved first to Calais, thence to Helvoetluys to meet his brother James, who had recently escaped from England dressed as a woman. In Holland the brothers were joined by eleven ships of the Navy although, as Charles realized, these were probably more discontented with the Parliamentary republicans than loyal to the King. As usual, there was indecision as to the most profitable course of action – whether to attempt a rescue of the King from the Isle of Wight where he was now imprisoned, whether to sail north to Scotland and ally themselves with those Scots still at war with Cromwell, or whether merely to sail up the Thames in search of booty. The decision was not made easier by disagreements among the Scots. The Earl of Lauderdale was sent over by one faction with the offer of support, provided Charles agreed that, upon his Restoration, he would establish Presbyterian worship with the consequent abolition of the Prayer Book and all 'episcopal ceremonies.' Buckingham told Charles not to trust Lauderdale as he was a 'man of blundering understanding.' Lauderdale and his ally Hamilton may well have the support of the Scottish Parliament, Buckingham said, but not of the Scottish people.

Irritated by the delays, Charles set out for England in July 1648 aboard the *Satisfaction* and sailed up and down the Thames estuary looking for the Earl of Warwick, Parliament's new naval commander. En route, the tiny fleet captured several merchantmen, selling them subsequently to Parliament for £12,000. Hamilton, meanwhile, not waiting for Lauderdale's return, invaded England on his own initiative. Aboard the *Satisfaction*, supplies were low although, surprisingly, the seamen offered to go on half-rations rather than retreat. Warwick finally set out to meet them. As the two fleets approached, Charles was urged to go below for safety. 'I will not hear of it', he shouted. 'My honour is more to me than my safety. Do not speak of it any more.' Seizing a gun, he went on: 'I am confident with this piece today to shoot Warwick through the head if he dares in person to appear in the fight.' Alas, his threats were in vain as the two fleets separated in a storm, Charles returning to Holland much disappointed. In port, the unpaid sailors drifted away and the royal fleet disbanded. News came that Hamilton's forces had been destroyed by Cromwell at Preston, and Parliament announced that 'the office of a King is unnecessary, burdensome and dangerous to the liberties of the English people.' Warwick's fleet appeared off the Dutch coast and Charles was obliged to retreat once more to the comparative safety of Paris, where he got smallpox. All seemed lost.

* * *

Charles's resolution, however, remained unshaken. Recovering from his illness, he wrote to the crowned heads of Europe asking for money and support – to the Queen of Sweden, the Prince de Conde, the King of Denmark and the Queen Dowager of France, Anne of Austria. He appealed to the Dutch, and two Dutch ambassadors were sent to plead with the Commons for the King's safety. He wrote to Fairfax. He wrote to Parliament, asking them not to be the authors of 'misery unprecedented by contributing to an action . . . repugnant . . . to the principles of religion . . . and destructive of all security.' When word came that the King was to be tried and, if found guilty, beheaded, it was rumoured that Charles sent Parliament a blank sheet of paper bearing only his signature begging them name whatever terms they wished in return for his father's life, although no evidence has been found for this bravado. Charles received a 20,000 word letter from his father full of advice about religion, duty, misfortune and the likelihood of his martyrdom. Be forever faithful to the Church of England, the King urged, for which (he believed) he was about to die. 'I had rather you should be Charles le bon', he wrote, 'than le grand.' If ever the Prince be restored to the throne, advised the King, 'use it humbly and far from revenge. If He restore you to your right, upon hard conditions, whatever you promise, keep.'

Two months later, on 30 January, 1649, Charles I was beheaded. One earnest young Roundhead declared that if he were asked to preach that day, his text would be: 'And the memory of the wicked shall rot.'

Confirmation of the King's execution was brought five days later. Charles

The Execution of Charles I in a contemporary engraving. Some of these engravings show the King's blood spouting from his severed neck; this version is more decorous. Charles I's last words were full of religious and political contradictions and paradoxes; his son came to understand what his father had merely hinted at, and to live and act with this knowledge. "For the people", Charles I had said, "truly I desire their liberty and freedom as much as anybody whomsoever. But I must tell you, their liberty . . . consists in having government . . . It is not for their having a share in the government; that is nothing pertaining to them. A subject and a sovereign are clean different things."

burst into tears and shut himself in his bedchamber where he remained for several hours. His estate was now desperate. George Winram, a Scottish commissioner sent to inform the new King that he had been proclaimed in Edinburgh – provided, that is, he 'gave satisfaction' about his religion – noted that Charles was 'brought very low. He has not bread both for himself and his servants, and betwixt him and his brothers not one English shilling.' Parliament confiscated all his property in England, condemning him to death *in absentia*. In Europe, his friends melted quietly away, apparently overawed by the 'powerful devils in Westminster.'

But the eighteen-year-old Charles was determined not to give up. He sent Rupert to Ireland to see what support could be rallied there, particularly from the Earl of Ormonde. He wrote to Virginia asking the colonists for help, and encouraged the Scots to invade England once more. Having discovered that Argyll had made a secret pact with Cromwell promising to stop Charles landing in Scotland, however, he was a little surprised when the devious Marquis sent emissaries offering the hand of his daughter in return for the Crown of Scotland. The offer was rejected. Instead, Charles wrote again to Spain and to Holland where Parliament had now sent a deputation demanding Charles's extradition. To Charles's horror, its leader was seized by over-zealous cavaliers and his head 'cleaved... with a broadsword.' Diplomatically, but firmly, Charles was told to leave, and Parliament issued a warrant for the arrest of 'Charles Stuart, eldest son of the late King, by name Charles II', while a group of Puritan fanatics set off from London planning his assassination. Charles fled back to Jersey, narrowly avoiding a small Parliamentary squadron when at sea.

*   *   *

Worse was to come. Ormonde was crushed by Cromwell and wrote pathetically to Charles that it was pointless for him to come to Ireland. Only the Scots seemed anxious to have Charles, but on their own terms. He found some consolation among the island's women, who pitied rather than loved him. But he was neither wanton nor promiscuous. As Charles himself wrote, with unfortunate irony, 'I do not understand how it is that a man who has a sensible wife can love another woman. For myself, when I do marry, there will be no one else.' In Paris, he had frequently proclaimed his love for one Lucy Walter, a 'bold, brown, beautiful, but insipid' lady (according to Evelyn) from Haverfordwest in Pembrokeshire. He had even promised to marry her, and she was frequently to assert that he had done so. In March 1649, she had given birth to James Scott, the future Duke of Monmouth, later acknowledged by Charles to be his eldest son. Charles was also believed to have fathered another child, this by a certain Lady Shannon.

In fact, throughout his exile Charles rarely deviated from what he conceived as his duty. He insisted at first on a permanent retinue of forty or fifty with never fewer than three or four chaplains. Buckingham, who was much better placed financially, had only two. Accordingly, swallowing his pride, Charles agreed to the terms imposed on him by Argyll in return for his Crown. Both the Queen of Sweden and the King of Denmark told him he had chosen sensibly, but Charles had few illusions. 'I perfectly hate the Scots', he wrote, 'but I may have to give in to them.'

Charles said he would agree to dismiss his chaplains, allow the establishment of Presbyterianism throughout his kingdom and enforce the penal laws against the Catholics. Some thought him weak to have given away so much. 'He hath not resolution enough to discountenance those he knows to be false', wrote Nicholas. Hyde thought Charles's weakness was 'not publicly to detest what privately he abhors.' Ormonde's judgment of Charles's attitude is more perspicacious. 'So early was he embarked in a course of hypocrisy', wrote the Earl. 'This seems to have laid the foundation of that unthinking kind of life which afterwards His Majesty observed too much.' Unthinking? Certainly, his behaviour accorded with one sensible piece of advice that his mother had given him. 'You must not think it necessary to keep any treaties, further than may serve your ends.' Or, as a Cromwellian spy reported at the time and with equal foresight: 'They must not be ashamed to beg that cannot dig – they needs must go whom the fates drive. Charles Stuart will stroke them till he is in the saddle, and then will make them feel his spurs.' Charles set out for Scotland.

*   *   *

The Scots made the most of their present victory over Charles. En route, Charles was told that Argyll now demanded more comprehensive terms: the Marquis of Montrose, recently appointed lieutenant-general of Scotland by Charles in defiance of Argyll, had been captured while attempting an invasion of England, executed and his dismembered limbs sent throughout northern England as a warning to other would-be supporters of Charles. Eventually, in a thick mist, Charles landed at Garmouth, near Elgin, in the mouth of the River Spey. He was ordered by Argyll to dismiss all his courtiers except Henry Seymour and Buckingham, and, as he entered Aberdeen, was shown the right hand of Montrose nailed to the kirk door. Later, he saw Montrose's skull in Edinburgh. 'Yes', he said, 'the scenery reminded him of old England.'

'It was a miserable life', Charles recalled later. 'I saw no women, and the people were so ignorant they thought it sinful to play the violin.' He was forced to condemn publicly the sin of his father having married into an 'idolatrous family'. He was told to apologize publicly for his own 'ill-education and former wickedness'. Even in his bedroom he was nagged continuously by theologians about his own iniquities and those of his father, mother, brothers, sisters, companions and soldiers. He was threatened with betrayal – unless he obeyed, he would be handed over to the English. After all, what had been done to his father could as easily be done to him.

At Dunfermline he signed another confession acknowledging, again, 'his own sins and the sins of his father's house, craving pardon and hoping for mercy and reconciliation through the blood of Jesus Christ.' Unfortunately, he was caught by a member of the kirk 'toying and fondling with one of his fair mistresses', and was threatened with exposure of his 'indecent sinful' behaviour unless he agreed to yet more conditions. He told Dr King, a chaplain rescued from the purge: 'The Scots have dealt very ill with me, very ill.' When Charles was restored to the English throne, political necessity prompted him to forgive them; but he never forgot.

Irked by Argyll and his bullying, Charles attempted to escape, but was 'recaptured' near Perth, hiding in a hay loft. Argyll had him 'put away' to 'prepare for the ceremonies in Gowrie House on the Tay', a building in which, as Argyll never ceased reminding Charles, some fifty years earlier the Earl of Gowrie and his brother, Alexander Ruthven, had tried to murder Charles's grandfather, James I.

Cromwell, meanwhile, had advanced against the Scots up the east coast and on Christmas Eve had occupied Edinburgh Castle. Charles's sister Elizabeth had died from tuberculosis and his youngest brother Gloucester had been imprisoned. Cromwell's massive defeat of the Scots at Dunbar, however, gave Charles one last opportunity. Amid wild cheering, and to Argyll's furious annoyance, he addressed the Scottish Parliament direct, telling them that God had moved him 'to enter into a covenant with his people, a favour no other King could claim.'

As a result, Charles was crowned at Scone on 1 January 1651 in a mood of relative euphoria, and he always chronicled his reign from this date. The ceremony began, inevitably, with a sermon lasting over three hours, during which the preacher suggested that Charles underwent further humiliation for his own and his family's sins. Charles then said: 'I declare on the word of a King that I agree to all the terms of the Covenant.' And later: 'I believe the Covenant to be the true Church of God.' These declarations were followed by a further three hours of sermons. Argyll later recalled how, after the ceremonies, he went to Charles's bedchamber and the two of them cried for joy. Argyll's wife was more astute. She told her husband: 'They are crocodile tears . . . and this night will cost you your life.'

Illness forced Cromwell and his troops to retreat from Edinburgh, so Charles determined to capitalize on his current popularity and advance on Cromwell as King and commander of the army. His esteem was high. One admirer wrote: 'his judgment and activity, both in civil and martial affairs, are to a degree as you would not imagine . . . adventuring his person upon every show of danger.' Dr King reported with satisfaction that 'the King's power is absolute, all interests are received, all factions composed, the ambitious defeated, the army cheerful, accomplished, numerous.' In fact, the army numbered only 8,000 foot, 2,000 horse, and 16 antiquated leather cannon. There were also squabbles with Buckingham who had wanted to command the troops. As he marched south through Carlisle, Lancashire and the Welsh marches, however, Charles was confident that many Englishmen, loyal to the Crown, would rally to the flag. Indeed, they did. At Stoke, a contingent, all 310 of them, under the Earl of Derby, joined the Royal forces. By the time Charles arrived at Worcester on 29 August, his army was smaller than when it had left Scotland, but he was greeted in the Guildhall by the Mayor and Sheriff as King of Great Britain, France and Ireland; his forced march of over three hundred miles in just three weeks even impressed General Cromwell, who hurried to surround the encamped King.

The expected nationwide rebellion failed to materialize. 'I am sure the King omitted nothing that might encourage the country to rise with him', wrote one of his companions on the long trek south, 'or at least to lie still as neuters. But they, on the contrary, rose against us.' Cromwell merely had to wait until Charles was sufficiently far south and away from his power base in Scotland before attacking.

24

The ensuing battle was short and brutish. Worcester was a sorry place for Charles to have finished up: 'it was neither fortified nor victualled', wrote one Royalist soldier. Cromwell's siege was methodical, and complete. Charles had to break out or starve. 'The King was very active and sent often very strong parties', Hyde remembered. 'But [Cromwell's] army was so watchful and lay so strong that though our men behaved themselves courageously, they could get no advantage of them.' The Duke of Hamilton had his head blown off, and Charles, having watched proceedings from the Cathedral tower and despairing of the Scots, took command. His first horse was shot from under him, as was his second. Half the Scots refused to charge at all. 'I command you – upon your honour and loyalty – charge!' he screamed at them. But they did not. Cleveland, a Cavalier veteran of the Civil War, shouted that Leslie (the Scottish commander) 'hath betrayed you [Charles]. You must shift for yourself . . . else you will be delivered up, as your father was.' 'All was confusion', recalled Hyde. 'There were few to command and none to obey.' 'The King', wrote an amazed Royalist officer, 'was forced to quit his horse and climb up over half-raised mounts, and there so encouraged our foot that the enemy retired with loss.' Later, the officer continued, 'taking a fresh horse, [Charles] rides to the cavalry with the intention to rally them and secure the foot from the walls. But it was in vain . . . for they were so confused that neither threats nor entreaty would persuade them to charge with His Majesty.'

The streets of Worcester were soon choked with shrieking horses and wounded men. Charles tore off his breast-plate and charged round the streets collecting his troops. He refused to flee – 'I would rather be shot', he said. Leslie seemed paralysed, and Charles became convinced that his inactivity was on direct orders from Argyll. Cromwell finally broke in and Charles had to be forcibly removed. Two thousand Royalist soldiers were killed and 3,000 taken prisoner. Some said 9,000 had been taken. Cromwell's 'business' had been accomplished, although, as he himself admitted, it was 'as stiff a contest for four or five hours as ever I have seen.' One eyewitness reported: 'a braver Prince never lived, having in the day of fight hazarded his person much more than any officers of his army, riding from regiment to regiment, and leading them upon service with all the encouragement (calling every officer by his name) . . . showing as much steadiness of mind and undaunted courage, in such continual danger, that had not God covered his head and wonderfully preserved his sacred person, he must, in all human reason, needs have perished that day.'

*   *   *

The truth of Charles's escape from Worcester was, if anything, more remarkable than the many legends. He wandered about England for forty-three days, living mostly on sherry and biscuits. He darkened his face with walnut juice, had his hair cut with a pair of shears, and donned green breeches, a leather doublet and a felt hat. He even imitated a country accent. After his Restoration, he used to bore friends and sycophants alike with tales of his 'miraculous escape.' Numerous pamphlets commemorated every last detail of the odyssey. The anonymous *Extract Narrative and Relation* began: 'Fortune had now twice counterfeited and double-gilt the trophies of rebellion.' Another called his account simply *The Royal Oath*. A third was entitled *England's Triumph*. Each was a best seller, and there were some forty other versions of the story prior to the official account, dictated by Charles himself during a drunken weekend at Newmarket racecourse almost thirty years after the event.

Certainly the journey was hazardous. Charles's first refuge was at a house named Boscobel, north of Worcester, where he spent a day hiding in an oak tree consuming large quantities of beer, bread and cheese, and praying he would escape detection from the pursuing Roundheads. Befriended by a local squire, Colonel Lane, Charles was disguised as the manservant of the Colonel's sister, Jane, and given the passport of one William Jackson. On the journey south, his shoes cracked, his feet blistered and more than once he collapsed in agony. His nose bled, his head throbbed and his legs trembled. 'But his stout guide [Jane Lane] still prevailed with him to make a new attempt, sometimes promising him that the way should be better, sometimes assuring him that he had but a little farther to go.' A reward of £1,000 was offered for his recapture – 'Charles Stuart, a long dark man, above two yards high' read the Parliamentary 'Wanted' notices. He met a soldier who claimed he had been in the King's regiment and 'knew him well.' He hid in Moseley Hall where he was given comfort by one Father Huddleston. 'If it please God to restore me', he told the Catholic Father, 'you shall never need more privacies. Both you and all of your persuasion shall have as much liberty as any of my subjects.' When his horse shed a shoe, a blacksmith told him: 'if that rogue [Charles] were taken, he deserves to be hanged more than all the rest for bringing in the Scots.'

Charles sought an escape ship in Swansea, Lyme and Southampton, but none seemed available. In Charmouth, the local parson in his Sunday sermon declared that 'Charles Stuart is somewhere in this [district]. You will merit from Almighty God', he told his congregation, 'if you find him out . . .' Charles moved on, this time to Bridport where he insisted on staying at the best inn in town posing as an ostler. In Broadwindsor, he stopped at the same tavern as forty Roundheads. Calling himself Barlow, Charles boasted that he too was a Roundhead. He visited Stonehenge and eventually heard of a cargo boat in Shoreham, captained by one Nicholas Tattershall. Unaware of his passengers, Tattershall was told that Charles and his companions were merchants in debt needing to escape. He demanded £60 in advance and £200 insurance. Charles arrived at Fécamp on the north coast of France on 15 October 1651.

The return to Paris could not have been more forlorn. Charles's finances were so bad that no one would advance him money. France, now preoccupied with its own Civil War, had little time for Charles. 'I do not know that any man is yet dead for want of bread', Hyde wrote to Nicholas the following summer, 'which I really wonder at . . . I am sure the King himself owes for all he hath eaten since April, and I am not acquainted with one servant of his who had a pistole [the smallest French coin] in his pocket.' In desperation, Charles wrote to the Pope asking for £5,000 as the price of his conversion. Innocent X did not believe him. Spain sent thirty boxes of chocolates.

Charles stayed in Paris for three years, pawning his jewels and those of his friends. He hunted, played tennis and billiards, went to parties and danced. He was still hounded by his mother to marry a rich heiress, but he was not tempted. La Grande Mademoiselle had been scared off by the prospect of having to finance Charles's restoration; Jersey surrendered to Parliamentary forces. Only Hyde took a more positive view of Charles's enforced idleness. 'God', began Hyde self-importantly, 'by subjecting Your Majesty to these dangers, hath instructed you in much knowledge which could not have been purchased but at that price; your own fate, and that of your three kingdoms, depends now on your virtue.' Charles busied himself writing letters. He offered his services to the Dutch, now at war with the English; he promised the Scillies as payment for their help. The Dutch declined, fearing that his presence in their camp might further exacerbate relations with Cromwell. Charles then suggested that the Dutch provide him with enough arms and ammunition to equip those in Scotland still loyal to the Crown. A fresh invasion from the north, he argued, might filter off some of Cromwell's resources. He even offered to sell the Orkneys in return. But the Dutch were defeated at sea and forced to conclude an humiliating peace with Cromwell. Charles had to look elsewhere. He despatched emissaries to Spain, Persia, Moscow, Morocco and Brussels, and kept a permanent representative in Vienna.

In France, the fourteen-year-old Louis wanted to help his cousin (he said) and in 1652 granted Charles 6,000 livres (about £500) a month. But Mazarin, the effective ruler of France, was concluding a treaty with the English republicans, in which context Charles's continued presence in France would be an embarrassment. Indeed, his behaviour in Paris was again causing comment; he was 'so absorbed in pleasures', it was said, 'especially women, that the whole town rings of them.' It was rumoured that he had secretly married the Duchess of Châtillon, although according to Buckingham Charles was 'apt to be persuaded into debauchery for the satisfaction of others.' 'For all his dancing', a Cromwellian spy reported, 'I think he [Charles] has a heavy heart.' An atmosphere of plot and counter-plot against Cromwell, uncomfortable for the French, continued to surround him. One proclamation, circulating in Paris, described Cromwell as 'a certain mechanic fellow' whom anyone has His Majesty's 'free Leave' to kill for a reward of £500.

Charles constantly received deputations from England bringing news of anti-Cromwellian conspiracies. 'Command them that they shall be quiet', Charles warned one such visitor, 'and not engage themselves in any plots – which will prove ruinous to them and not do me any good.'

For all his caution, Charles was outstaying his welcome. 'Everybody is weary of him', Hyde recorded. He sent Lucy 40 pistoles for the care of his son, apologizing that his 'beggary [was] extreme, unheard of and intolerable.' Hyde's room was so cold he could not hold a pen. Mazarin informed Charles he would be paid the arrears of his pension, plus a six month advance, provided he leave France within ten days. Even his mother did not intercede. 'Your disrespect to me is notorious to all men', she said haughtily. 'You never come where I am, though you lodge under the same roof.' Charles left France by night, believing there to be neither sincerity nor charity in the world.

*   *   *

He made first for Spa in Germany to meet his sister, Mary. There he was joined by Henry Bennet, another of Charles's messengers to Spain. Together they moved to Aix where Charles saw Charlemagne's skull and sword which he measured against his own. Hyde wanted Charles to go once more to Scotland, but Charles refused. 'I should in a short time be betrayed and given up', he said. The Scots were being persistent, however. 'At the King's command I would go to Japan!' declared one Scottish emissary, Sir James Turner. 'Japan would be out of your way', Charles observed politely. On they went to Cologne where 'the poor King and his train live, feeding on hopes'; thence to Düsseldorf where Charles was met by the Duchess of Neuberg; 'she confirms me in my aversion from ever marrying a German', said Charles.

Relations with his mother deteriorated further when he learned that she intended to convert his brother Gloucester to Catholicism. 'If you proceed in this', Charles wrote furiously to Henrietta, 'I cannot believe that you either believe or wish my return to England . . . remember the last words of my dead father, who charged my brother upon his blessing never to change his religion.' Gloucester was told by Henrietta: 'if you do not become a Catholic, your brother will never succeed'; and was then despatched to a secret hiding place. Even his little sister, Minette, was forbidden to speak to him because 'he had committed such a great sin.' Ormonde, who had also by now joined Charles in Germany, sold his last possessions (he had already lost a million pounds in the Royalist cause) to raise money for the rescue of Gloucester in the middle of the night. Henrietta, in tears, said that if only she had been trusted Charles would now be back in England. 'If it had not been for Your Majesty', replied Ormonde, 'he would never have been *out* of England.'

Lucy Walter arrived demanding support, and word came of another rebellion being planned in England. Charles was sceptical of its chances: 'I know very well they will be deceived. There is too much division and lack of trust.' Nonetheless, he wrote to the newly formed Action Party saying he had been 'so tender of my friends that I have deferred to call upon them till I could find myself able to give them good encouragement from abroad . . . Since I find that comes on so slowly, I will no longer restrain those affections which I most desire to be beholden to.' To risk defeat so soon after Worcester was foolish, yet a group called the Sealed Knot, most of whose members were younger sons of the aristocracy, swore loyalty to Charles and rose in rebellion.

Charles's instinct was right. The 'rebellion' was a fiasco. In Nottinghamshire, a cartload of arms was driven round and round in the middle of the night by a Royalist sympathizer, but nobody knew what to do with it. The 'simultaneous' revolt in Yorkshire consisted of 150 horsemen also riding around wondering where to go. On Hexham Moors, the Royalist forces dispersed almost before they had assembled, 'strangely frightened by their own shadows.' In Hampshire, a small number tried to seize Winchester but were not surprisingly overwhelmed and shot. In all, some twenty Royalist leaders were executed and hundreds sold as slaves to Barbados. 'Charles's heart is almost broken', wrote Hyde. Buckingham was less diplomatic. 'The failing of the King's designs', declared Buckingham, was 'through his own default.'

What neither Buckingham, Hyde nor Charles knew was that all the King's correspondence was being copied and sent to Cromwell by one of Charles's more trusted courtiers, Henry Manning. Manning was also sending detailed reports of Charles's movements three times a week to Parliament. Cromwell had thus been forewarned of the Sealed Knot rising. Manning was later discovered and arrested. Charles insisted upon a fair trial, at which Manning admitted that, while pleading great poverty as part of Charles's entourage, he had been receiving an enormous salary of £1,200 per annum as a Cromwellian spy. He sobbed for mercy, but was found guilty, taken to a wood, and shot. He was, said Charles, 'one of the greatest villains that ever was.' The entire proceedings were reported to Cromwell by another member of Charles's entourage, John Adams.

Other diversions were few. Thurloe, the Cromwellian spy-master, observed: 'The poor King of Scots who lies lurking behind the hangings, having no part to act upon the theatre of the world.' Spain offered help, but only if Charles declared himself Catholic, married one of the Infantas and abandoned the French. To Nicholas, Hyde wrote: 'if you knew the miserable life the King leads, and how he is used, you would believe that he acts his part not amiss.' 'Many light foolish persons propose wild things to the King which he civilly discountenances', Hyde added later. 'The truth is the King thinks there are some honest men who will do what is possible and stir when it is fit.' In fact, there was little to be done, except wait.

The waiting was often misinterpreted. Hyde began to think Charles unwilling to work, 'which vexes me exceedingly.' Charles's 'inactivity and habitual neglected business' irritated many. 'The King is exceedingly fallen in reputation', wrote one of his supporters, 'which cannot be recovered but by some bold attempt . . . He is so much given to pleasure that if he stays here he will be undone.' In fact, Charles did try. He went to Bruges and there organized three regiments of English, Irish and Scottish troops. But, according to yet another Cromwellian spy, these were in poor condition. Charles could only afford to pay the troops six pence (6d) a day, and before long most had mutinied. Nor was the King's reputation helped by the loud mouthed Lucy, now a prostitute. Rebuffed by Charles, she set off for England where, although she claimed to be the widow of a Dutch sea captain, Cromwell knew well who she was and put her and her son in the Tower. One Catherine Pegge appeared claiming that Charles was the father of her son, Don Carlos; Charles did not deny it. (Later, Don Carlos was made Earl of Plymouth.)

Only Charles's good humour, it seems, kept the exiles together. 'We now have as good as can be', Charles wrote to Henry Bennet, 'and pass our time as well as people can that have no more money, for we dance and play as if we had taken the Plate fleet.' One visiting Irish aristocrat, Lord Taafe, found the same high spirits. 'May I never drink wine', he wrote boisterously, 'if I had not rather live at six sous a day with him, than have all the pleasures of this world without him.' Those who chided Charles with his apparent loose behaviour, then, as later, misunderstood the man. Hyde remembered: 'there are and always will be some actions of appetite and affection which cannot be separated from the age of twenty-one' (actually Charles was now twenty-five), 'and which we must all labour by good consent to prevent and divert. And when we have done our duty, we must make the best of what we cannot help.' To the Earl of Bristol, however, Charles wrote: 'If this winter pass without any attempt on my part, I shall take very little pleasure in living till the next.' At dawn on 26 February 1656, accompanied by only two servants and a dozen horsemen, Charles slipped away from Cologne and headed for Brussels and the Spanish Netherlands.

*   *   *

The mists and fog of Northern Europe, together with the etiquette which dominated the social life of Brussels, increased the sense of futility. Charles wrote a defiant letter to Cromwell – 'I know I shall live to see the day when you shall bow before your King.' An astrologer, Lilly, who had correctly predicted Charles I's death, foretold that 1657 was to be the year of Charles's restoration, whereupon there were wild celebrations in Charles's tiny camp. Thurloe reported maliciously: 'fornication, drunkenness and adultery are esteemed no sin amongst them.' The reality was different. From England came news that another pro-Royalist plot, headed by one Miles Syndercombe, had been discovered and the conspirators hanged.

Charles in Scotland; or, the Scots holding their young King's nose to the grindstone. Another contemporary engraving.

> "In Scotland, where they seem to love the lad
> If he'll be more obsequious than his Dad . . ."

"Nothing," Charles wrote to Sir Edward Nicholas, "could have confirmed me more to the Church of England than the treachery and hypocrisy of the Kirk." "For the present," advised the Marquess of Argyll, "it is necessary to please these madmen." On 27 May, 1661, Argyll was beheaded for his collaboration with Cromwell and, possibly, for having kept his King's nose . . . to the grindstone.

A large quantity of expensive armaments purchased by Royalist supporters in preparation for an invasion was shipwrecked and lost. Charles was again badly in debt. There were rumours that Cromwell had offered a gang £2,000 each for Charles's assassination. His sister Mary sent him more jewels to pawn; Lucy died 'of a disease incident to her profession.' Worst of all, Buckingham deserted, marrying Fairfax's heiress and thus regaining all his estates. James was received into the Catholic Church, to Charles's horror, and in March 1657, Parliament offered Cromwell the Crown.

* * *

Despite these disappointments, Charles continued to seek support in the

31

capitals of Europe. The King of Spain again promised Charles 6,000 soldiers toward an invasion force, but only in return for certain 'concessions' including the restoration of those Spanish West Indian possessions seized by Cromwell. As Cromwell now policed the channel, an invasion would be unlikely to succeed, although Charles did reassemble his small mercenary troop, 'all ragged miserable creatures', according to Thurloe. He was momentarily cheered by news of an assassination attempt by the Levellers against Cromwell, 'that ugly tyrant who calls himself Protector', but a firework left in Cromwell's hand-basket at Whitehall failed to go off, and Cromwell lived on.

Charles begged his new sponsors, the Spaniards, to be allowed into the field, but soon realized that his only chance would be as a pawn in other people's war games. Alliances forged out of present necessity might be to his future disadvantage, so again, the Royal party waited.

Charles went to hunt at Hoogstraeten; alas, 'the standing corn imped'd sport and few partridges were found for the hawks.' Nearby Dunkirk fell to Franco-English forces and Charles was obliged to move on again. Another pro-Royalist revolt collapsed; Hyde urged Charles to write to Cromwell's military ruler in Scotland, General Monck. Monck, although a Parlimentarian, was known to have Royalist sympathies, had actually fought for Charles I at the beginning of the Civil War, and been captured and imprisoned. 'I am confident', one Royalist informer had told Hyde, 'that the person . . . able alone to restore the King is Monck.' Charles wrote to Monck promising him 'a title of honour . . . upon the word of a King.' Monck did not reply.

*   *   *

Then, suddenly, in September 1658, during a game of tennis, a messenger from Dunkirk brought unexpected news. Cromwell, 'that beast, whom all the Kings of the earth worship', was dead. Charles could hardly believe it. 'As for this tow', wrote Culpepper, another of Charles's secretaries, from Amsterdam, 'they are mad with joy. No man is at leisure to buy or sell; the young fry dance in the street at noon-day.' Louis sent a message to Charles that with the death of Cromwell all French obligations to the Protectorate were annulled. 'It was', confirmed Evelyn, 'the joyfullest funeral I ever saw, for there were none that cried but dogs.' Charles was cautiously optimistic.

The celebrations were short lived; Cromwell's son, Richard, was 'cheerfully proclaimed' and the terror in England increased. At Gresham College in London, a young mathematician called Christopher Wren was stopped from lecturing by an armed guard. 'The King's condition never appeared so hopeless, so desperate; for a more favourable conjecture his friends could never expect than this, which blasted all their hopes.' Charles lived on one meal a day eating off wood and pewter. 'We have not yet found that advantage by

Cromwell's death as we reasonably hoped', said Hyde; 'nay, rather we are the worse for it, and the less esteemed, people imagining by the great calm that hath followed that the nation is united and that in truth the King hath very few friends.' 'If we continue longer as we are', Charles noted sadly, 'we must perish.' The best he could do was advise his friends in England to 'lie still and be quiet till a good opportunity offered.'

But his friends would not lie still. The predictable uprising resulted in the predictable chaos. The 'battle' of Winnington was more a picnic. 'In short, sir', reported Cavalier Mordaunt, 'twas never fought. The foot saved themselves in the enclosures, the horse trotted away, which is the civilest term.' Charles had expected it. 'Sure, never people went so cheerfully to venture their necks as we do', he wrote to Hyde. Charles's troupe moved on to Dieppe and then to Rouen where it was learned that violent arguments had broken out between Richard Cromwell and the army. Both wanted exclusive power. The army's unpaid troops began to mutiny and the army chiefs forced Richard to dissolve Parliament. The younger Cromwell was retired into private life, with the Speaker appointed temporary head of the army. The new members of Parliament were even more critical of the military government than their predecessors, however, and the unrest continued. Again Charles wrote to Monck. 'If you once resolve to take my interest to heart', said Charles, 'I will leave the way and manner of it entirely to your judgment, and will comply with the advice you shall give me.' No reply came. Once again, foreign aid seemed the only hope.

Charles set off for the Pyrenees to raise support from either the French or the Spaniards or both. 'Our journey hath hitherto been very lucky', he wrote, 'having met with many pleasant accidents and not one ill to any of our company . . . we have found the beds, and especially the meat, very good. The only thing I find troublesome is the dust . . .' But when Charles arrived in the Pyrenees, Mazarin, on behalf of the French, refused to see him. Instead he suggested that Charles marry his niece, Hortense Mancini, by repute a lesbian. The Spanish ambassador offered to pay Charles all the pension still owing from his previous grant, provided the King stayed well clear of Madrid.

The trip had one good result. As Hyde wrote to Ormonde, 'the King's dexterity and composedness (of which there is very good mention in many letters hither) hath removed the fatal misfortune which you say follows us, of not being believed', although this can have been poor consolation to Charles. In his heart, he knew the Spaniards had lost interest in his cause. Unwelcome in France and Holland, his brother James suspected of being a Catholic, his mother a tyrant and his brother Gloucester lazy (Gloucester was by now a tennis instructor), Charles even agreed to marry the wealthy and Protestant Henrietta of Orange; fortunately, both mothers refused their consent and the 'engagement' was broken off. Only his youngest sister, Minette, seemed loyal.

*   *   *

Then, as if from nowhere, a letter arrived from General Monck seeking the King's pardon. Hyde was sceptical; after all, Monck had been unreliable in the past. 'I will spend the last drop of my blood rather than that the Stuarts should come into England', he was reported to have told a Royalist agent, for which Parliament had 'rewarded' him with £20,000. Known to his soldiers as 'old George', he was a 'dull, heavy man' with a pronounced Devonshire accent. He had married his wife, known as 'Dirty Bess', bigamously, and acquired a fortune through the sale of commissions. Charles replied to Monck, 'I trust you absolutely', and waited. Before long, it seemed, Monck reverted to his Parliamentary allegiance.

Monck was not political; his primary concern was for stable government. From Scotland he had watched with growing suspicion the absurd goings-on in London, or at least that is how they seemed to him, what with Parliament cashiering Cromwell's ex-second in command, Major-General John Lambert, and Lambert cashiering Parliament. Monck assembled his troops and told them he intended to march into England and assert 'the freedom and rights of those Kingdoms from arbitrary and tyrannical usurpations.' With 7,000 puzzled men, he marched south. 'It was the Lord's Day too, and it was His doing', noted Mr Price, Monck's chaplain. In London, some apprentices rioted, clamouring for a 'free Parliament', whatever that was. At Southampton, the townsmen locked the gates. Eleven years almost to the day after Charles I was executed, General Monck marched into London.

*   *   *

No one knew quite what to expect; Monck insisted first that the moderate members lately excluded from Parliament be readmitted. Parliament refused, so Monck dissolved it. A painter, Michael Darby, smeared over the inscription 'Exit Tyrannus, Regum Ultimus', cut into a corner of the Royal Exchange where previously had stood a statue of Charles I. 'The tyrant is gone, the last of the Kings' was obliterated. Darby blurted out: 'God bless King Charles the Second', at which 'the whole Exchange joined with the greatest shout.'

In Flanders, Charles remained curious, but calm. He had been disappointed before. Once more he was hopelessly in debt, by £80,000 it was reckoned. It was rumoured that Spain was planning to arrest him as a hostage for the return of Dunkirk and Jamaica. Unmoved, he wrote to the City of London saying that he desired 'to recover [his] power rather for the protection and benefit of good men than to satisfy any appetite of [his] own.' Two envoys, a Mr and Mrs Palmer, were sent from London; again, Charles waited. 'I will not buy my crown on conditions that would make me ashamed of wearing it.'

Monck, meanwhile, was recommending Presbyterianism as a national religion; it was also reported he had told his confidant and cousin William Morice: 'I find most gentlemen of quality and interest inclined to call in the

General George Monck, 1st Duke of Albemarle; from the studio of Lely. Born 1608, at Potheridge in Devon, he had fought against the Spanish at Cadiz and in the Netherlands in 1637, against the Scots in 1640, and against the Irish in 1642. He had supported Charles I against the parliamentarians and been imprisoned in the Tower, where he wrote "Observations upon Military and Political Affairs" (published posthumously in 1671) which show him to have been a thoughtful and skilful professional soldier. Cromwell admired him and formed a foot regiment especially for him which later became the Coldstream Guards, named after the site of his headquarters prior to his march on London, February 1660. He died in Whitehall, 3 January, 1670, having "freed his country from the intolerable slavery of a sword government."

35

King.' Charles wrote to Monck indicating that maybe the General relied more on the King's assistance for his continued success than he suspected, and promising that he, the King, would 'take all ways he can to let the world see his entire trust in him.'

Monck now sent Sir John Grenvile as envoy to Charles, asking him to agree mutually acceptable conditions for his Restoration. Fearful of any unforeseen consequences, Monck refused to write down Grenvile's instructions but ordered him to memorize them. Grenvile arrived in Brussels, and advised Charles he should move to Breda and thus away from the Spanish before making any declaration. Sensing that their diplomatic pawn might slip away in the night, the Spanish placed a guard. But it was too late; Charles escaped to Holland. There, in April 1660, he drafted what became known throughout Europe as the Declaration of Breda. 'We have more endeavoured', he wrote in a letter to Monck, 'to prepare and to improve the affections of our subjects at home for our Restoration, than to procure assistance from abroad to invade either of our Kingdoms, as is manifest to the world', although which world Charles had in mind he did not state. In his Declaration Charles assured the Speaker of the Commons that 'in a word, there is nothing you can propose that may make the Kingdom happy, which we will not contend with you to compass.' 'Our opinion of parliaments', he continued blithely, is 'that their authority is most necessary for the government of the Kingdom.' He conceded that they should be summoned regularly. As to religion . . . well, there should be 'a liberty to tender consciences.'

The Declaration, with five covering letters, was taken back to Monck by Grenvile. For three weeks there was silence. Lambert, who had been put in the Tower, escaped and rallied the remaining Republicans; Monck and his soldiers efficiently rounded them up. Fairfax, nominally the Parliamentary Commander-in-Chief, hesitated until he saw which way the majority was inclined, and then declared for the King. William Morice proposed in the Commons that the constitution of England lay in the King, Lords and Commons, and his motion was carried without a single dissident vote. The Commons particularly liked that section of Charles's declaration which affirmed 'we will strive with you to make the Kingdom happy, and we hope that our subjects will be the better for our experience of other countries, and what we have seen and suffered . . . We desire no effusion of blood . . . [and] none shall be reproached for the past.'

And that was that. Parliament voted £50,000 to His Majesty, affirming their belief that 'all the troubles of this realm . . . have been caused by the separation of the head from the limbs', an ironic choice of metaphor. On 9 May messengers reached Breda with the invitation to Charles for his return. 'My head is dreadfully stunned', Charles wrote later from Canterbury to Minette, 'that I know not whether I am writing sense or nonsense.' Back in London, Lady Derby was equally puzzled. 'I can hardly believe it', she noted. 'This passes human wisdom . . . it is beyond our unerstanding.' Such events were 'never read in history, when monarchy laid aside at the expense of so much blood, returned without the shedding of one drop', although Evelyn noted that 'this government was as natural to them (the English) as their food or raiment; and naked Indians dressing themselves in French fashion were no more absurd than Englishmen without a Parliament and a King.'

*   *   *

Everyone now wished to know Charles. Holland sent eighteen deputies laden with presents, invited him to The Hague, and offered £30,000 to cover his expenses. Charles's brother James was appointed Lord High Admiral, and fourteen important London citizens dispatched £10,800 worth of gold in a trunk for the Royal family. The City of London contributed a further £10,000. Holland also sent a complete dinner service in gold plate and a huge bed hung with tapestries. The exiles gathered in Breda; James, Duke of York, Henry, Duke of Gloucester, their elder sister Mary, and her child William. William sat on James's knee admiring the riches. Twenty-eight years later, when James had succeeded Charles as King, William invaded his Kingdom and took his throne.

Charles politely received ambassadors from France, Spain, Sweden, Denmark and Austria, and a deputation arrived from Scotland informing the King 'we have always wished Your Majesty very well', and reminding him he had once promised not to use the Prayer Book. His reply was ominous. 'While I give you liberty', Charles told them, 'I will not have my own taken from me.' To the other ambassadors, Charles was equally firm. 'I have referred all differences to Parliament', he said.

In London, cannon thundered all night and a massive firework display was staged in celebration. The heralds announced Charles's accession, and the Navy, which had already declared for Charles, sent General Edward Mountagu with an escort of thirty frigates to bring back the King.

Charles had already progressed to Scheveningen, and there he embarked upon the *Naseby*, hurriedly rechristened the *Royal Charles*. All hands were in a frenzy, reported Mountagu's cousin and secretary, Samuel Pepys, painting out the Commonwealth Harp, and replacing it with the Royal crest. Others were cutting up yellow cloth for the initials 'C.R.' to be embroidered on all flags. Charles wrote to Monck saying he had great difficulty in getting a quarter of an hour to himself; 'I have resolved, God willing, to land at Dover . . . I pray bring Mrs Monck with you.'

The Royal party set off amid crowds of over 50,000. On board, Charles was 'very active and stirring'; Pepys was put in charge of Charles's guitar. The King chatted to the sailors, sharing their breakfast of pease, pork and boiled beef and telling them of his adventures after Worcester. But Pepys noted how

Charles withdrew when he thought others were not watching, taking solace only from the spaniels which accompanied him. Pepys also noticed they were not house-trained.

*   *   *

Pepys could not know, of course, all that had befallen this strange figure who now sat upon the poop deck watching the cliffs of Dover approach across the skyline. Only a year earlier, one of his followers, the Earl of Norwich, had thought their situation so hopeless that he would have to 'retire into some cave or bush to mend his old breeches.' Now, they had money to buy fifty pairs. The King was obviously likeable, although what he liked was a mystery. He seemed to eat sparingly and drink hardly at all. He tolerated tobacco, but no more. True, there were abundant rumours about his women. It was known that Lucy Walter had tried continuously to blackmail Charles for recognition, money, or both. She had failed, and was now dead. But Catherine Pegge, by whom the King had a son, was not, and was forever pestering Charles for 'rewards'. Charles himself complained vigorously of the 'blind harpers' who had done him 'too much honour in assigning [him] so many fair ladies as if [he] were able to satisfy the half.' It was said that Charles delighted in 'effeminate and vulgar conversation'; 'he was an everlasting talker', who 'told his stories with a good grace.' He 'had a great compass of knowledge', although whether he was to prove 'capable of much application or study' remained to be seen. He was reported to be 'well versed in ancient and modern history', and knew about mathematics. He seemed aloof, although not distant. If his temper was quick, it seemed not to be vengeful. No one could be sure what lay behind those piercing black eyes.

*   *   *

Years earlier, his most influential governor, William Cavendish, the Earl of Newcastle, had drawn up a manual of instruction for the future King's use. Although there is no evidence that Charles had ever read it, its advice was curiously prophetic. Newcastle had been patron of Ben Jonson and Dryden; he had known both Charles's father and grandfather well, and understood the Stuart temperament better than most. Love of subjects, he had told Charles, was of far greater value than learning. Yet 'too much contemplation spoils action. I confess, I would rather have you study things than words, matter than language.' 'Authority doth what it list, I mean power that's the stronger, though sometimes it shifts sides. Therefore, the King must know at what time to play the King, and when to qualify it.' 'Beware of too much devotion, for one may be a good man but a bad King.' 'Reverence to prayers . . . is essential, even were there no heaven or hell . . . for [successful government].' The Papists waste too much time in processions and pilgrimages; accordingly, better to fall in with the Church of England which enjoins only a moderate number of holy days. Beware the Presbyterians who are prodigal of ranting and cause unrest among the common people – 'the Bible in English under every weaver's and chambermaid's arms hath done as much hurt.' Concentrate on history – but not for too many hours a day; foreign tongues – but not so as to become a living dictionary; short prayers and good manners – 'to women you cannot be too civil, especially to great ones. Certainly, sir, you cannot lose by courtesy; and to have consideration for the feelings of all classes – how easy a way is this to have the people.' 'Though you cannot put on too much King, yet even there sometimes a hat or a smile in the right place will advantage you.'

Beware too many students; if there were only half the present number, they would be better taught and fed. There are also too many at grammar schools, with the result that the horse and plough are neglected. Lawyers should be 'lookt to', since their role in the recent troubles ought not to be forgotten. Salaries and profits derived from the offices of State should be reduced. When everything is cheap, there is scarcity of money. But when everything is dear, there is plenty of money. It might be a sensible policy, therefore, to keep prices and rents high. Excise is an ideal tax because it falls on everyone, including tradesmen who hoard money and then loan it out at high rates of interest, thus damaging everyone. Patrol the counties with troopers, and remember it is with the army and not the lawyers or the clergy that the King's power rests.

Parliaments are justifiable only if the King is able to control them, and 'a Parliament which bargains with you is not a free Parliament.' Do not create too many peers – a bad policy for pacifying your opponents. Anyway, it was good to maintain class distinctions if only because 'ceremony and order, with force, governs all and keeps every man and everything within the circle of their own conditions.' And do not allow too many news-sheets which fill the minds of the ignorant with inflammatory domestic and foreign intelligence.

As to Charles himself, he should entertain – at Newmarket, if possible, 'the sweetest place in the world.' For exercise, why not try riding to demonstrate his horsemanship, or tennis, or that new game he himself had invented, goffe?

Newcastle's treatise was weighty, and Charles very sensibly thought it too long to read. Newcastle, for his part, had long ago understood his pupil. 'The purity of his wit doth not spoil the serenity of his judgment', the Earl had noted. 'He [Charles] reads men as well as books...'

*   *   *

Fifty thousand people greeted Charles's arrival at Dover where, at dawn on 25 May, 1660, the King disembarked. As his foot touched the shore, he knelt and gave thanks to God. Few recognized the lean, elegant man in a dark suit with a scarlet plume in his hat to whom the Mayor presented an ornate Bible.

'It is the thing I love above all things in the world', Charles began to say as the saluting cannon deafened both Charles and the Mayor who continued by shouting their compliments at each other. Charles spent the weekend in Canterbury before moving on to London. Monck took the opportunity of giving the King a list of some forty people whom he wished to see elected to the Privy Council; Charles thanked him. At Deptford, a hundred girls threw sweet herbs and flowers at his horse's feet, and at St Paul's School he was presented with another Bible. Along the rooftops, he noticed, effigies of Cromwell waited to be burnt as night fell. Charles passed Whitehall where his father had been executed. He smiled and waved his hand. After all, it was his thirtieth birthday.

Chapter Two
Mercy, indulgence and plenty?

England was not the country Charles had dreamed of in exile. London, for instance, was a rotten, ant-hill of a place. There was a 'horrid smoke' [Evelyn noted], 'which obscures our churches and makes our palaces look old, which fouls our clothes and corrupts the waters.' In winter, smog from the furnaces of brewers, dyers and soap-boilers was often so thick that 'horses ran against each other, carts against carts, coaches against coaches.' The stench was appalling and Pepys, taking an evening stroll during April, repeatedly had to take refuge from the 'stink of shying in a shitten pot.'

Nor was it a land of plenty or joyful opportunity. Child labour flourished, and apprentices were, in effect, slaves. If they tried to escape – and runaway apprentices were accepted as part of the English scene with cash offered for their recapture – they were hanged or transported for absconding. Gregory King, one of the first statisticians, estimated later that, from a population of less than 5 million, 1.3 million were 'cottagers and paupers', 250,000 'labouring people and out-servants', and a further 30,000 'vagrants, or gypsies, thieves, beggars etc'; after a bad harvest or a poor year's trade, almost sixty per cent of the entire population lived in poverty.

It is not surprising therefore that many took consolation in violent sport and drink. Bull-baiting was a favourite pastime, and legally encouraged in the belief that the meat of a bull would be most tender after considerable exhaustion. At Tyburn, human executions, particularly those of children, caused widespread absenteeism every six weeks.

*　　*　　*

These were not Charles's immediate problems, however. There was a stampede of those seeking redress for real or imagined wrongs suffered because of Cromwell; the dispossessed Clerk of the Court of Wards and Liveries claimed a favour before his death. He was already 110 years old, he said, and could not be patient much longer. Twenty Sherborne officers reminded

Charles of a promise made them by his father that, when they had first taken up arms in 1642, their pay would continue in perpetuity. Thousands of petitions poured in – from 600 impoverished Protestants who had lost everything in the Irish rebellion; from cities and boroughs now claiming they had always remained loyal to the new King's father even after such loyalty seemed futile. The widow Carey, whose son Peter had followed Charles I to Oxford and there been bitten by the late King's dog Cupid, sought compensation.

Charles received them all. There was little he could do, he explained, although he recompensed those who had helped him during his flight from Worcester. Tattershall, who had ferried the King across the Channel, received a ship in the Navy. The Lane family, who had engineered his escape, received pensions. And in grateful remembrance of one Colonel George Gounter, now dead, who had supervised the preparations for Charles's sea passage, the King paid for his son's education at Winchester and Oxford.

For the rest, it became apparent there was to be no Royal bounty. Property confiscated by the State, whether belonging originally to the Crown, Church or private individuals, was returned to its rightful owners. But for the majority, including those who had sold everything to pay fines imposed on them by Cromwell, there was nothing. Too many others had profited by these enforced sales, and Charles was compelled to pass an Act confirming all sales and leases of property since the Civil War. Many complained that it had been neither Monck nor the Parliamentarians who had made possible Charles's return, but the continuing loyalty of the squires and local gentry. 'The Royal party, that have endured the heat of the day and become poor', grumbled one bishop, '[are] put off with inconsiderable nothings.'

Charles threw himself into the business of government with astonishing vigour. James I had only gone to meetings of the Privy Council when needed; Charles I had stayed away as often as he could. But Charles II attended meetings almost every third day and missed only twelve out of one hundred and fifteen in the first year; his ministers were terrified of discussing important business when the King was not present. The actual administrative work was completed by various standing committees of the Council. These were known as the 'cabinet', 'junta', or simply as the 'committee'; from 1660 to 1668, for instance, there was a mysterious 'secret committee'. Charles was usually there. There was also a formally appointed council committee of foreign affairs at which the more important or the more secret matters, domestic as well as foreign, were discussed prior to being raised in general Council; Charles was usually there. After the reform of the Privy Council in 1679, the foreign committee was succeeded by a committee of intelligence which often met two or three times a week; Charles was usually there. And all this quite apart from Charles's private meetings with individual ministers or small groups of ministers or representatives from abroad or particular petitioners.

In short, Charles became involved in the detail of government routine far more than either his father or grandfather had been, and more so than almost any of his descendants. 'He grew by age', noted Halifax, 'into a pretty exact distribution of his hours, both for his business, pleasure and the exercise for his health.' The impression given by generations of historical writers – from Hume who thought Charles 'profuse, thoughtless and negligent', to Trevelyan who said that if the King was 'caught and brought in to the Council, he played with his dogs and let the others talk unheeded' – is false. In fact, the King rose by five almost every morning, and put in three hours' work on affairs of state before any of his ministers appeared. Laziness was not his problem, although this was often the impression he wished to give.

Charles turned for assistance first to those who had helped him in exile. Edward Hyde, already appointed Lord Chancellor and Chancellor of the Exchequer two years before the Restoration (although, at the time, there had been no Exchequer to manage), was made Earl of Clarendon and confirmed as Lord Chancellor. 'The Chancellor was generally thought to have the most credit with his master', Clarendon wrote of himself later, 'and most power in his counsels, because the King referred all matters of what kind so ever to him.' Clarendon had few doubts as to his ability. He was, he wrote in his autobiography, a man 'without blemish and believed to be without temptation.' This was not a view shared by all his contemporaries.

Clarendon was soon to find himself uniquely placed in his relations with the Royal Family; his daughter Anne was seduced by Charles's brother James while lady-in-waiting to Princess Mary. She became pregnant and James said he would marry her. Clarendon was furious. The Queen Mother rushed over from France. James's friends told him he was absurd promising to marry a girl whom they had all had anyway. Uncharacteristically, he kept his word and married Anne Hyde in 1661.

Nicholas was made Secretary of State, while Monck himself, created Duke of Albemarle, was appointed Lord Lieutenant of Ireland, replacing Ormonde who returned to London as Lord Steward of the Household. The Earl of Southampton, who had remained in England during the Republic but had consistently refused to have dealings with Cromwell, was made Treasurer. Southampton's nephew by marriage, Antony Ashley Cooper, was, at Clarendon's suggestion, made Chancellor of the Exchequer.

These, with William Morice, comprised the 'secret committee' which, according to Clarendon, 'under the notion of foreign affairs, was appointed by the King to consult all his affairs before they came to the public debate.' The committee was supplemented by two other groupings; there was still an old-style Privy Council numbering some forty or fifty, although twelve of these had been in arms against Charles's father. Charles treated them circumspectly. He made it clear he preferred a group of younger men, such as the Earl of Bristol, whose attraction seemed to be their wit and irreverence. 'There was no companion like the young gallants', noted one who felt excluded from their

P.Lely pinx.   M.Burg sculp.

DEUS NOBIS HÆC OTIA FECIT

Edward Earl of CLARENDON, Lord High CHANCELLOR of England,
and Chancellor of the University of Oxford. Anᵒ Dñi 1667.

44

select gathering. Even Clarendon seemed insecure in their presence, and Pepys was among many who feared their influence. 'My Lord Chancellor', he observed, 'much envied that very great men such as Buckingham and Bristol do endeavour to undermine him.'

* * *

The tasks confronting these groupings, official and unofficial, were monumental. Neither the Army nor the Navy had been paid for several years; yet, as civil unrest was a constant threat, they could not be disbanded. A vast national debt had accumulated, while political and social grievances festered deep. The Presbyterians did not tolerate the Catholics, nor the Catholics the Anglicans. Jealousy of the Dutch caused by what Englishmen considered unfair trading practices, seemed likely to escalate. Technically, England and Holland were still at war, since the peace treaty concluding the Anglo-Dutch war in 1654 had never been ratified. What was to be done about the existing Parliament, which was not a true Parliament in any constitutional sense? It had not been summoned by the King; he had been summoned by it. There was also the problem of those directly responsible for the death of the King's father. 'I find myself set on fire', Bristol told the Lords, 'when I think that the blood of so many virtuous and meritorious peers and persons of all ranks, so cruelly and impiously shed, should cry so loud for vengeance and not find it from us.'

Charles immediately set the tone of his entire administration. He insisted on bringing before Parliament a Bill of Indemnity and Oblivion granting immunity to those who had most feared his return. Surprised by this generosity, the Commons wasted a month in a fever of self-protectionist humbuggery adding names to the list of those to be pardoned. The Lords were less certain about this policy of forgiveness. Charles had to appeal to them himself: 'this mercy and indulgence is the best way to bring men to a true repentance', he told them, 'and to make them more severe to themselves, when they find we are not so to them. It will make them good subjects to me and good friends and neighbours to you.'

Charles was determined, and the Bill received the royal assent on 29 August, 1660. A general pardon was granted for all treasons, felonies and similar

◁ Edward Hyde, 1st Earl of Clarendon, in a portrait by Lely. Born 18 February, 1609 in Dinton, Wiltshire. Educated at Magdalen Hall, Oxford and the Middle Temple. Friend of Ben Jonson. MP for Wootton Basset, and later Saltash. Appointed to the Privy Council by Charles I in 1643, but accompanied the King's son to Jersey in 1646. Eventually, he became Charles II's Lord High Chancellor, and Chancellor of the University of Oxford. He fled in October 1667 and was never recalled, although, after his death at Rouen in 1674, he was buried in Westminster Abbey. He wrote of himself, "he had ambition enough to keep him from being satisfied with his own condition ... he was in his nature inclined to pride and passion and to a humour between wrangling and disputing, very troublesome ..." He was grandfather to two future Queens of England; Mary II and Anne.

offences committed since 1637. All acts of hostility between King and Parliament committed during that time were consigned to perpetual oblivion. Only forty-nine named persons were to be exempt, these 'for their execrable treason in sentencing to death, or signing the instrument for the horrid murder, or being instrumental in taking away the precious life of the late sovereign Lord Charles.' Of these, nineteen had already given themselves up and were granted clemency, two escaped to die in Massachusetts, and of the remaining twenty-eight rounded up and put on trial the following October, only ten were sentenced to death. Two others were executed; Argyll, legally for his brutal murder of Montrose but perhaps for his bullying of Charles in Scotland, and Sir Henry Vane for his continued abuse against the monarchy. Vane acknowledged no power in England except Parliament, he declared at his trial. Charles wrote to Clarendon that Vane was 'too dangerous to live', adding reluctantly: 'if we can honestly put him out of the way.'

Charles himself watched some of the executions. One died facing the very window from which his own victim had stepped out twelve years before. 'The hand of God is powerfully against those cruel murderers', reported another eyewitness, 'and no man pities them.' But Charles was much moved. During a Privy Council meeting, he scribbled to Clarendon: 'I must confess that I am weary of hanging except on new offences . . . Let it sleep.' The people of London, however, wanted sport. The remains of Cromwell, Ireton and Pride were dug up and hanged. 'This day – O the stupendous and inscrutable judgments of God!' recorded Evelyn, 'were the carcasses of those arch rebels . . . dragged out of their superb tombs in Westminster among the Kings, to Tyburn and hanged on the gallows there from nine in the morning until six at night, and then buried under that fatal and ignominious monument in a deep pit, thousands of people who had seen them in all their pride being spectators.'

*   *   *

Clarendon ensured that the House of Stuart became associated with security of persons and possessions. When an extremist sect called the Fifth Monarchy Men threatened to disturb the peace of London in January 1661, for instance, it was speedily put down. In Newcastle, horsemen surrounded the town by night. Old Commonwealth men were seen distributing powder among disbanded troops; one report said that 'pulpits blew sparks.' In Wrexham, 'the most factious town in England', it was thought that an uprising was being planned to coincide with the anniversary of Cromwell's death; at Ferrybridge in Yorkshire, talk of revolution became so insistent that the militia were called out. One plot imagined Whitehall captured, Clarendon seized, sundry taxes abolished, and a 'gospel ministry' restored. The supposed ringleaders, Fairfax and Manchester, were arrested, although they denied knowledge of any plot.

Exiles were continuously 'inquired into.' As many surviving regicides still

The Execution of the regicides, 13–19 October, 1660. A contemporary engraving. Pepys wrote: "I went to Charing Cross to see Major-General Harrison, hanged, drawn and quartered – which was done there – he looking as cheerfully as any man could do in that condition. He was presently cut down and his head and heart thrown to the people, at which there was great shouts of joy. It is said that he said that he was sure to come shortly at the right hand of Christ to judge them that now have judged him . . ." Carew, Cook, Peters, Scott, Axtell, Clements, Hacker, Scroop and Jones were executed in like manner; Vane and Argyll were also executed; the bones of 25 other regicides – including Cromwell, Cromwell's mother, Ireton and Pym – were removed from Westminster Abbey and buried in a pit.

lived on the continent, mail from abroad was opened and checked. Ports were carefully watched. As late as 1671, Richard Cromwell, one of the limper personalities of his age, was reckoned sufficiently dangerous that orders were given to search any house in London where he was believed hiding. Gatherings of all kind were thought suspicious, down to and including apprentices' 'rambles' in the countryside. The new coffee-houses in particular were reckoned hotbeds of dissent. Thomas Player wrote to Sir Joseph Williamson: 'The common people talk anything, for every carman and porter is now a statesman; and indeed the coffee-houses are good for nothing else. It was not thus when we drank nothing but sack and claret, or English beer and ale. These sober clubs produce nothing but scandalous and censorious discourses and at these nobody is spared.' Those who frequented such 'sober clubs' were

> ... raskals in whose tainted veins
> The blood of their religious fathers reign;
> Villains that Faction daily do forment,
> And practise to defame the Government,
> Assembling their cabal, at whose discretion
> The Royal line must prostrate the succession.

That Charles died peacefully in his bed has misled the popular imagination into believing his reign essentially one of inner calm and contentment, marred only by squabbles abroad and the occasional if spectacular catastrophe at home. It was not.

*   *   *

Charles was determined to rule by constitutional means. Accordingly, he dissolved Parliament and ordered fresh elections. The new assembly, known as the Cavalier Parliament, seemed more Royalist than he dared hope, and in a mood of patriotic well-being, the Coronation was finally arranged for St George's Day 1661. The celebrations were intended to promote the idea and fact of a restored monarchy. A 'magnificent train on horseback proceeded through the streets', reported Evelyn, 'strewed with flowers, houses hung with rich tapestry, windows and balconies full of ladies, the London militia lining the ways, and several companies with their banners and loud music in their orders: the fountains running wine, with speeches made at several triumphal arches.' Charles appeared 'in a most rich, embroidered suit and cloak', looking 'most nobly.' 'So glorious was the show with gold and silver', noted Pepys, 'that we were not able to look at it – our eyes at last being so much overcome with it.' In Westminster Abbey, Charles, bare-headed, 'was very fine.' Later, 'the Crown being put upon his head, a great shout begun.' A general pardon was read out by Clarendon and silver coins thrown into the crowd. Pepys records sadly that he failed to get any.

The special commission appointed by Clarendon to supervise the ceremonies had done its job well. Every last detail, from the blue cloth upon which Charles walked from Palace Yard, to the appropriate text upon which the Bishop of Worcester preached, was personally approved by Clarendon. 'For the transgression of a land, many are the princes thereof', the Bishop read from the Book of Proverbs. 'But by a man of understanding and knowledge the state thereof shall be prolonged.' That night the city had a 'light like a glory round it with bonfires', obviously in gratitude for Charles having sworn to maintain religion, Magna Carta and the laws of the land. It was ten years to the month since he had received the 'tottering Crown of Scotland' on a bleak day at Scone, been bullied by the Presbyterians, lectured about his need of 'personal reformation', and gone south in a futile attempt to gain his kingdom by force

The Coronation of King Charles II in Westminster Abbey, 23 April, 1661, St. George's Day. A contemporary engraving. Said Charles: "I doubt it has been my own fault I have been absent for so long – for I see nobody that does not protest he has ever wished for my return." Sixty-eight Knights of the Bath, six earls and six barons were created. In the Abbey, the Bishop of Worcester preached on Proverbs xxviii. 2: . . . "by a man of understanding and knowledge the state thereof shall be prolonged." Charles said later: "I do not desire to be the Head of nothing . . ."

from Protector Cromwell. Charles was optimistic, therefore, as he made ready to face Parliament.

'Let us look forward and not backward', he told the new members, 'and never think of what is past . . . God hath wrought a wonderful miracle in setting us up as He hath done; I pray let us do all we can to get the reputation at home and abroad of being well settled.' He had reason to be confident; he went on: 'I know most of your faces and names, and can never hope to find better men in your places.' He had begun as he intended to continue, he said. Already, under the guidance of the old Parliament, much of the army had been disbanded. With money given him as gifts, plus an additional grant from Parliament, he had settled the army's arrears of pay, with an extra week's money as a bonus. He had also eased the re-entry of many soldiers into civilian life by modifying the strict requirements of the apprenticeship acts. The only remnant of the hated Cromwellian army which remained was a regiment of infantry kept at Monck's request and later called the Coldstream Guards.

Anxious to please his new Parliament, Charles was persuaded to approve numerous penal laws which, he was told, were necessary for the continuance of stable government. They included a bill for regulating corporations, a bill to restore the temporal power of bishops, a bill against tumultuous petitioning and a bill of high treason. Henceforward it was illegal to write, print or preach 'any doctrines subversive of the King's royal estate.' The Corporation Bill ensured that membership of all municipal bodies, including those which controlled the selection of members of Parliament, was restricted to the Church of England. 'Succession in such corporations', the bill stated, 'may be most profitably perpetuated into the hands of persons well affected to His Majesty and the established government.'

By an Act of Uniformity (1662), over two thousand Puritan clergy were expelled from their livings, unless, that is, they could give their 'unfeign'd consent and assent' to the Prayer Book. By the Conventicle Act (1663), all attendance at religious meetings other than those authorized by the Established Church was punishable by imprisonment for the first and second offence, transportation for the third, and death should the criminal return thereafter. By the Five Mile Act (1665), no clergyman or schoolmaster was to come within five miles of any city or corporate town which had had a Puritan minister, unless he avowed he would not 'at any time endeavour any alteration of Government either in Church or State.' As most Puritan congregations were in the towns, this Act cut them and their children from private education and the domestic practice of their faith. These Laws were to be rigorously enforced through a network of paid informers and corruptible Justices of the Peace. Short of burning heretics in the streets, they could not have been more savage.

Charles became alarmed by this intolerance, regretting he had been so open with Parliament. 'I shall concur with you in all things which may advance the peace, plenty and prosperity of the nation', he had said, adding prophetically: 'I shall be deceived else.' He had pleaded for harmony, at least between the Crown and Parliament. 'I need not tell you how much I love Parliaments', he had declared. 'Never King was so much beholden to Parliaments as I have been; nor do I think the Crown can ever be happy without frequent Parliaments.' Privately he began to think otherwise. He told the French ambassador: 'I am not so absolute in my State as the King my brother is in his. I have to humour my people, and my Parliament.' Clarendon said that 'it is the privilege, if you please, the *prerogative* of the common people of England to be represented by the greatest and learnedst and wealthiest and wisest persons that can be chose out of the nation.' Charles realized that the Chancellor spoke less than he knew; wealthiest they may have been, but not necessarily the wisest.

Resentment was also caused by what was described as the land settlement. Those who had lost their estates in the Royal cause had not unnaturally wanted them back. That this was impracticable mattered little; even

Newcastle, who brought a special Act of Parliament to restore his lands, failed to recover all of them. 'Let no man's love, friendship or favour draw thee to forgo thy profits', Sir John Oglander advised his descendants. Charles, it was said, had passed the Act of Indemnity for his enemies, and Oblivion for his friends. 'Presbyterians for their money must be served', complained one bishop. Only in Ireland, with its Acts of Settlement (1661) and of Explanation (1665), were the discontented rewarded. There, adventurers and soldiers were left with two-thirds of what they had grabbed.

The English Act of Settlement was less generous. One pamphlet vigorously asserted that, as a result, 'this island . . . is . . . governed by the influence of a sort of people that live plentifully and at ease upon their rents, extracted from the toil of their tenants and servants, each . . . of whom within the bounds of his own estate acts the prince . . . They sit at the helm in the supreme Council. They command in chief at sea and land; they impose taxes and levy it by commissions of the same quality. Out of this rank select we sheriffs, Justices of Peace and all that execute the authority of a Judge; by the influence of which powers they so order all elections, to Parliament or otherwise.' Sir Edward Chamberlayne added that, because of the Act of Settlement, 'most of the tradesmen and very many of the peasantry' hated, despised or disrespected 'the nobility, gentry and superior clergy.' Another pamphlet was more succinct. It hoped 'all the gentry in the land would kill one another, that so the commonalty might live the better.'

What became known as the Clarendon Code – which was neither a Code nor especially the work of Clarendon – represented a victory of one sect over another, a triumph for the landowners and the squires. Taking advantage of a popular wave of Royalist sympathy, they consolidated their power and imposed on a bewildered and malleable society the hypocrisies of Anglicanism. The class system which still plagues Britain has many of its origins here; in 1641, for instance, there had been one non-Royal Duke (Buckingham), one marquis and sixteen earls, half of whom had been elevated by Charles I. Charles II doubled that number; like his father, he was persuaded to underpin his security by promoting cronies, however worthless their merits. Lacking any specific long-term policy, it seemed, his administration was stumbling from one expedient to another.

Charles began to understand how the Crown's effective powers were being eroded. After all, the freedoms gained during the King's absence were not to be relinquished easily. For nearly twenty years, committees of Parliament had controlled the Army, Navy, Church and foreign trade, all once the prerogative of the Crown. The Civil Service, re-organized by Cromwell, had no intention of being ignored; groups such as the City merchants who had gained direct experience of government, were not going to be overlooked. Charles had to confirm the abolition of the Star Chamber, and acknowledge that the Privy Council, even in the occasional exercise of its remaining functions, could never again be the irresponsible Court of the King. It could no longer set aside, for instance, merely by proclamation. Parliament was steadily gathering unto itself the necessary authority whereby the King's will was irrelevant. As Macaulay wrote later, 'the great English revolution of the seventeenth century, that is to say the transfer of the supreme control of the executive admini- stration from the Crown to the House of Commons was, through the whole long existence of this Parliament, proceeding noiselessly.'

Whatever Charles thought of the repressive legislation, his attitude toward Clarendon changed. The Chancellor's permanent affliction with gout, and steady refusal to speak any language other than English, irritated Charles. Perhaps he grew tired of an older man whom his younger companions dubbed 'His Majesty's schoolmaster'. Maybe he took note of the French ambassador's criticism of his senior advisers – 'they are cold, slow, phlegmatic, motionless, frozen.' Charles hated being nagged. And Clarendon nagged. 'That which breaks my heart', Clarendon wrote later of Charles's apparent slackness in government, 'is that the same affections continue still, the same laziness and unconcernedness in business and a proportional abatement of reputation.' Clarendon nagged about one of Charles's mistresses being appointed a Lady of the Bedchamber; he nagged about Charles's continued, although private, religious ambiguity; he nagged about Charles's political appointments. Maybe Charles felt disgust at measures passed by Parliament in his name that were contrary to his private beliefs and to his publicly declared policy at Breda – 'we do declare a liberty to tender consciences.' He blamed himself for having failed to capitalize on the goodwill of the Restoration. He recognized he had been weak, and reluctantly began to think of Clarendon as his scapegoat. It was little consolation to know that his people were not deceived. 'The King is honest in spite of Parliament', noted one country squire; 'they could not have done more to make him loved and themselves hated.'

At first Charles was amused to observe Clarendon's public taunting. The Earl of Bristol, despite a warning from Charles, tried to impeach Clarendon for treason. The judges knew there was not a scrap of evidence to support Bristol's allegations, and told the Earl that if he continued with his overweening behaviour he would be arrested. Charles's more extremist Royalist supporters maintained that Clarendon was deliberately limiting the King's authority by centering the day-to-day administration on the Privy Council. Worse, Clarendon was refusing to encourage a 'Court interest' in Parliament, arguing that this would be against 'the constitution.' For Bristol and his friends, Clarendon was a country lawyer, a back-bencher, a member of the gentry, a social inferior.

Outraged by Bristol's tormenting of Clarendon, the judges eventually issued a warrant for Bristol's arrest although, lacking a police force, no one could be found to make the arrest. To an outsider, such as the French ambassador, these shenanigans were incomprehensible. 'Here we have a regular suit between a private person and a Chancellor', he wrote to King Louis, 'this last having his high rank, his past services, the good will of the King and of all the Court; but the other walks about the town as if nothing were the matter . . . I confess I am at my wits' end and that it seems to me as if I were transported beyond the spheres of the moon.'

Charles's difficulty was that he was reluctant to accept the changed nature of his authority. Although his natural cynicism prevented him from upholding any claim to Divine Right, except as a useful political weapon, he believed in the ultimate sanction of monarchical power, that his authority was as absolute and as actual as that of the Tudors. This was what kingship was all about. If he wished to send someone to the Tower, he could and would; the problem was that he lacked the resources to do so. Whereas the power of the king had previously depended upon the feudal relationship between the Crown and its subjects, a relationship guaranteed by land and the Crown's ability thereby to inflict economic harm, now the Crown exercised less actual power except in controlling appointments to State offices. Charles came to realize that his authority would need to be personal, rather than constitutional.

Parliament, of course, resisted any attempt made by the Crown to increase its authority. When Charles wanted the commissions appointed under the Corporation Act made permanent, for instance, to ensure that 'persons well affected to his Majesty' were elected, Parliament limited their period of authority to fifteen months. For the next eighteen years, therefore, Charles was constantly obliged to revise town charters in an attempt to give him the right to nominate local officials. Most of these attempts failed.

*   *   *

What kind of country was it that Charles, his Ministers and Parliament were attempting to govern in uneasy alliance? The total population did not exceed 5 million, compared with 19 million in France. The French ambassador travelling westwards from London was surprised at the emptiness of the countryside, in spite of two and a half million agricultural labourers. Another one and a half million were town-dwellers; a third lived in London. Of the other towns, Bristol and Norwich were the largest with approximately 30,000 inhabitants each. Only about 10,000 of the total population were merchants; about the same number were clergy. There were also 10,000 public servants and officials, and nearly 15,000 lawyers; surprisingly, there were some 9,000 employed in the arts. The majority of people were illiterate, despite the foundation of numerous grammar schools during the Protectorate.

The national drink was beer and ale; the average annual consumption was almost two and a half barrels of ale per man, woman and child. Food was fresh, apart from salted beef and cheese; coffee and tea were only just arriving from Turkey and China. It would be wrong to think that only the rich ate well, while the majority starved. The abundance and variety of crops, as well as a plentiful supply of home-grown mutton, milk, beef and poultry, ensured that good eating was one pleasure of Restoration England enjoyed by all.

The nobility stopped at nothing to gratify themselves and their guests. Ormonde and his wife, for example, gave a small dinner party for sixteen at Dublin Castle in 1666. There were seventeen dishes for the first course, seventeen for the second and thirteen for the third. For starters, each guest was given 'a sallet, a fricassee, a boiled meat, a roast meat, a baked meat and a carbonado.' These were accompanied by four kinds of salad, stewed fresh-water fish for the roast meat, and sea-fish for the baked meat. The second course consisted of a choice of mallard, teal, snipe, peacock and quail, served with baked pies and tarts of marrow-bones. To finish, the table was covered with silver circular dishes on which a variety of choice sweetmeats such as quinces, marzipans, comfits and preserves was served.

Charles's tastes were more delicate. He loved jellies, which cooled and refreshed the mouth after hunting or love-making, and syllabubs. He kept a small herd of cows in St James's Park so that whenever he took a stroll in nearby Whitehall, the cows could be freshly milked. New milk, preferably still warm, was thought essential for good liquid syllabubs, especially when mixed into a bowl of spiced or sweetened wine and then stirred.

Visitors from abroad were shocked by the lack of manners which the Englishman, even the cultivated Englishman, displayed; Charles's attempts to lead his Court toward more civilized behaviour seemed to him an uphill struggle. 'When I reflect that this land produces neither wolves nor venomous beasts', the French ambassador wrote, 'I am not surprised. The inhabitants are far more wicked and dangerous.' A pamphlet called *The Rules of Civility* (inevitably translated from the French) gave some indication of what had hitherto been accepted as polite behaviour. 'You must not blow your nose publicly at the table', the pamphlet urged, 'or, without holding your hat or napkin before your face, wipe off the sweat from your face with your handkerchief. To claw your head, to belch, hawk and tear anything up from the bottom of your stomach, are things so intolerably sordid that they are sufficient to make a man vomit to behold them.'

For more serious sport (and sport was considered seriously), hunting was a major preoccupation. Even judges on circuit took days off for the hunt. Game was plentiful, and Charles, by his frequent example, encouraged what was thought to be a healthy activity. He was up at dawn to hunt stag in the forests surrounding London; he would exhaust all his horses and return, muddy but happy.

Charles loved horse racing, prohibited during the Commonwealth. 'The King is highly pleased with all his Newmarket recreations', wrote one of his attendants. Newmarket had been visited occasionally by his father and grand-father – James I had built stables there – but Charles made it his own. He enjoyed and increasingly valued its informality, which allowed him to 'put off the King.' He built himself a house opposite the Maidens' Inn, and established a string of Arab horses which he fed personally on bread soaked in beer and fresh eggs. Then, dressed in the plainest of country clothes, he would gallop across the heath with the other jockeys, often first past the winning post to the accompaniment of drums and trumpets acclaiming him victor.

Bowls was a favourite summer game; Duke Cosmo observed Charles throwing a wood. Ninepins was also popular, as was real tennis. Football was played in the villages, and no season or event of the agricultural year was allowed to pass without some celebration, usually marked by mumming plays, hobby horses, fiddles and bagpipes. For winter evenings, dominoes was popular; the gentlemen preferred backgammon or cards, particularly cribbage. Among the aristocracy, the Elizabethan tradition for making music in the home was revived, in part by Charles's own love of music; from France, he had brought with him a whole range of new and improved instruments, including the dulcimer and viol.

It would be a mistake, perhaps, to imagine a predominantly rural England working quietly in blissful contentment; in 1665, for instance, one third of all households were exempt from the Hearth Tax (two shillings for every hearth) on grounds of poverty. The workers, or their leaders, occasionally spoke vigorously, even vociferously, about their liberties. But about their many local duties, all of which were rigidly enforced, they were silent. In the village there was no abstract right to live, nor right to work; merely obligations. To do one's duties as an unpaid local official; to mend the roads and clear out the ditches. 'The poor are provided for', wrote one satisfied local official from an obviously well-behaved village. 'The stocks and whipping post are in good repair; hues and cries duly pursued; highways and bridges in repair; warrants executed; watch and ward duly kept, and all things belonging to my office are in good order to the best of my knowledge.'

Anyone who had a 'competent estate, a good reputation, and a tolerable education', could be required to serve as a local justice. He had to license ale-houses, enforce the poor laws, inflict fines on those who infringed the weights and measures regulations, and admonish labourers who violated the Statute of Apprentices. He punished those who erected cottages on the waste without permission; he could even inflict banishment. Two justices in Hertfordshire did just that in 1664 when they ordered three Quakers to be transported to Barbados. The local justice was also expected to prosecute for Sabbath-breaking and non-observance of Lent. He imprisoned vagabonds and trespassers. He fixed the price of goods sold at market. As a link between the county and parish, he alone was responsible for the appointment of minor officials (also unpaid) such as churchwardens, who kept the parish accounts, and constables, who kept the peace.

Considering the devastation caused by the Civil Wars, the countryside had either not suffered as much as is usually supposed, or else recovered remarkably quickly. Wages were not disproportionately low; an artisan could earn as much as twenty shillings a week. A pound of best beef, mutton or veal, cost only three pence; cheese about two pence a pound. Taxes, particularly after the frequent exactions made during the Civil War, were low. Direct taxation was negligible, except during the Dutch wars. Provided the harvest was good, trade prosperous and the landlord merciful, the artisan had enough. Books were beyond the average man's pocket. Dugdale's 'St Paul's', a small folio unbound and in sheets, cost fourteen shillings and six pence. Clothes, which indicated status and position in society, could bring a man near to ruin unless he was careful. Breeches and doublet might cost £8, while another £3 would be needed for lace cravat and ruffles. Then there was the sword, *de rigeur*, another £2. The hat and silver hat-band, another £2. Shoes at four shillings a pair. Silk stockings and gloves, say £1. Finally, a good periwig, another £2. In all, a fashionable suit with trimmings might cost £20; five months' wages for the artisan. For Charles's coronation, the Duke of Buckingham spent £3,000.

'Fewness of people is the real poverty', noted Sir William Petty in 1662. England could support twice its population, 'were they rightly employed.' After the disruption of the Civil War, an increasing number of labourers had drifted from the villages to the comparative economic freedom and opportunity in the cities. This sudden mass of casual urban labour prevented wages rising, and low wages would eventually cause unrest. Nonetheless, the various shocks which the economy suffered immediately after Charles's restoration – the disbandment of 50,000 soldiers, the land settlement or lack of it, war with the Dutch – were less severe than they might have been primarily because of a parallel (albeit slow) expansion in trade and industry. Those who remained in the countryside began to profit from a renewal of interest in small industry. Nowhere was this more startling than in the 300,000 acres of fenland marsh being drained in Norfolk and Suffolk. Charles's father had granted the Earl of Bedford a patent for drainage, but the Civil War had delayed progress. In 1663, its furtherance was entrusted to a new corporation authorized to act as commissioners for sewage, making whatever local levies were thought necessary. When Evelyn visited King's Lynn in 1670, he was amazed to see engines and mills draining away the mud. He claimed there were weeds which, benefiting from the fertile reclaimed land, grew 'as high as a man on horseback.' 'The great improvement made of lands since our inhuman civil wars', as an agricultural expert Houghton noted, 'when our gentry, who before hardly knew what it was to think . . . fell to such an industry and caused such an improvement, as England never knew before.'

Suggestions were made for horticultural improvements 'by which means parks have been disparked, commons enclosed, woods turned into arable.' Bishops consulted together how to make the most of what lands had been left

56

them. Crops tried experimentally during the Protectorate were now systematically exploited. Stock-breeding increased, with the result that markets were better supplied than at any time within living memory. Pepys told his parents in 1663 that it was 'not good husbandry for such a family as yours to keep either hogs, poultry, sheep, cows . . . there being meat of all sorts, milk, butter, cheese, eggs, fowl and everything else to be had cheaper . . . at the market.' Charles made a determined effort to renew the prestige of wool by banning imports, believing (in part justifiably) that English wool offered the greatest variety of weaving. The government also passed an Act insisting that the dead were buried in woollen shrouds; later it was made compulsory for coach linings to be made from wool. It was said that, by the export of cloth, England might continue to pay for her imports.

Elsewhere, the tin mines of Cornwall were at full stretch; so were the lead mines of the Mendips. Licences, under the nominal control of the Mines Royal, supervised copper mines in Keswick and in Staffordshire; brass foundries were established in Nottinghamshire. Even the tobacco industry flourished. Charles was alone among the Stuarts in approving the weed. His grandfather, James I, had issued a 'Counterblast' demonstrating that taking tobacco was an ignoble habit reducing man to a chimney and making him prone to melancholia. Plantations established in Gloucestershire and Herefordshire, however, had had no difficulty in growing the crop in abundance. Although the methods of curing were haphazard, by 1664 smoking was an accepted social habit. Coal, 'a very offensive fuel', had not replaced wood as the chief source of fuel, but was being widely used; a prosperous coal trade exporting to Portugal and the Mediterranean existed. Likewise the manufacture of glass, not only for the gilt coaches of the rich, but for the cottages of the labourers; there were few houses in Restoration England that did not boast their new window panes. Thanks to Charles and his European education, England now acquired numerous luxuries. The French influence brought the plum, the pear, the peach, the nectarine and the melon. From Holland came the tulip, the carnation, and the lily of the valley.

Charles recognized that this revival of trade and industry would be of little effect without efficient transport systems. An Act of 1662 empowered local surveyors, in whose hands upkeep of the roads had been for over a century, to levy six pence in the pound to widen all roads to a minimum of eight yards. The following year the first Turnpike Act was passed, establishing toll gates in Hertfordshire, Cambridgeshire and Huntingdonshire. Many highways remained impassable, however, and public transport was avoided where possible and hated where not. 'What addition is it to a man's health or business', wrote one disgruntled stage coach passenger, 'to ride all day with strangers, often times sick, ancient diseased persons, or young children crying, to whose humours they are obliged to be subject, and many times are poisoned with their nasty scents and crippled by the crowds of boxes and bundles? Is it for a man's health to travel with tired jades, to be laid fast in the foul ways and forced to wade up to the knees in mire, and afterwards sit in the cold till teams of horses can be sent to pull the coach out?' Nor was such transport cheap. The journey from London to Exeter took about four days and cost forty shillings (£22 in today's money); in winter it cost five shillings extra, but with no guarantee of arrival time. These much publicized 'flying coaches' always added to their printed bills that they could only complete the journey 'if God permit.' Mail was carried at two pence (about 8p) per sheet per eighty miles.

At the beginning of Charles's reign, river transport was equally poor; most goods were transported by pack horse. Coal, iron, wool and crates of clay for the potteries, all travelled in this manner. Signposts were almost unknown; Pepys, riding from Huntingdon to Biggleswade (a journey of some twenty miles), had to employ two guides 'that led us through the very long and dangerous waters – because of the ditches on each side – of the road.' A good result of this lack of communication was the preservation of local characteristics. A man from Cornwall, for instance, was incomprehensible to a man from London.

*   *   *

The State which Charles inherited, therefore, was rich and vigorous in many ways. It was not, however, an instrument of social service, nor an establishment for the political education of the masses. At best (or worst), it could be a military force which provided a guarantee for law and order. The changes which occurred as a result of Charles's restoration should not lead one to the conclusion that England in the early 1660s was a different country from that of the Commonwealth. Continuity was an important ingredient of the restoration settlement. Much of the legislation of 1660 was a completion of that already agreed upon by the Long Parliament of 1641, and only two of the statutes passed by the Long Parliament were repealed. By comparison, fulfilling the new promises made in the Declaration of Breda was proving less straightforward. The nervous approach of the Government toward the land question, for instance, arose because the sale and resale of lands during the Interregnum had created a situation so complex that, had Charles not decided to recompense only those whose property had been forcibly confiscated, the entire legal framework might have collapsed. There was no wholesale displacement among the more aristocratic landed gentry. Although many new titled families appeared during the reign, very few of these replaced existing landed families, and very few of those disappeared because they had had to dispose of their estates.

And while it is true that it was the countryside which had suffered most from the chaos of civil war – the broken fences, the looting soldiers, the disintegration of law enforcement, the butchered cattle, the disruption of those intangible bonds which hold communities together – the quintessential gentleman of the early 1660s remained, as he had been before Cromwell, and before Charles I, one who

> . . . lives in his own grounds,
> And within his own bounds;
> Has room for his hawks and his hounds;
> Can feast his own tenants with fowls and with fishes;
> And from his own store with good store of dishes,
> And not with damned wine but with good English ale
> O'er their faithful hearts can prevail.
> And nothing to others does owe,
> But from his own house hears his own oxen low.

Chapter Three

Imperial whores

To ensure a Protestant Stuart succession, Charles needed a wife. Unfortunately, none of his family had discovered marital bliss. His brother's marriage to Anne Hyde was less than successful; James was cynically unfaithful and she had become sick with worry. Minette was to marry Louis XIV's brother, the Duke of Orléans, a homosexual, homicidal maniac, who liked wearing high-heeled shoes, perfume and rouged cheeks. Then there was the Queen Mother, whose volatile treatment of Charles's father had caused much unhappiness. Nonetheless, Charles was persuaded to consider the possibilities; there had been his 'affair' with Jane Lane; the fat Mademoiselle de Montpensier; the Duchess of Châtillon; Henrietta, the younger daughter of the Dowager Princess of Orange; Lucy Walter and the girl from Jersey by whom he had children. 'Odd's fish', he told Clarendon, 'they are *all* foggy.'

But now Charles was King. The financial needs of his Government were great, and the prospect of a considerable dowry and whatever useful political alliances could be gained through marriage, were uppermost in the advice of his ministers. The Spanish presented Charles with 'a whole litany of marriages', offering to endow almost any Saxon, Danish or Dutch princess into whose bed Charles might officially wish to romp. With Spain and France Charles was on reasonable terms; with Brandenburg and Denmark he held ineffective although long standing treaties. Friendship with Holland was deteriorating, however, so a Dutch maiden was a possibility.

With Portugal, diplomatic relations were more complicated. Engaged since 1640 in a conflict against Spain for independence, Portugal had become a pawn in France's struggles against Spain for European domination. Portugal had maintained her old alliance with England by preserving the friendship of the exiled Stuarts. She needed manpower to fight the Spanish, and was ready to pay for such assistance. The trade in bullion brought from her overseas possessions, with some of those possessions themselves, might be transferred to whomever was ready to help. There was an available Portuguese princess, Catherine of Braganza. In return for permission to enlist English troops for her defence, Portugal now offered a dowry of over half a million in cash, as well as Tangier, the island of Bombay and free trade with Brazil and the East Indies. The opportunity seemed too good to miss.

Clarendon tried to dissuade Charles from this particular match, urging him to give more thought to a Protestant wife, but a marriage treaty was signed on 23 June, 1661. England agreed to guarantee the defence of the Portuguese East Indies, and supply 10,000 auxiliaries for the battles against Spain. Charles considered he had made a good bargain, quite apart from Catherine's magnificent dowry. Under the guise of a diplomatic alliance, he had secured control over the remnants of a world-wide colonial enterprise no longer capable of being sustained by the Portuguese. The marriage contract brought England its first sugar and mahogany, and gave English merchants openings in the Mediterranean and Far East.

Charles had not met the lady. 'I have often been put in mind by my friends', he had told the assembled Commons, 'that it was high time to marry, and I have thought so myself ever since I came into England. If I should never marry till I should make such a choice against which there could be no foresight of any inconvenience, you would live to see me an old bachelor, which I think you do not desire to do.' The Commons, aware of Charles's reputation, had laughed. 'I can now tell you', the King had continued, 'not only that I am resolved to marry, but whom I resolve to marry, if God please . . . And trust me, with a full consideration of the good of my subjects as of myself, it is with the daughter of Portugal.'

Others were not quite so excited. One Captain Cooke, 'a man of great conversation and repute', reported that Lisbon was a poor and dirty place, its palace windows without glass, the royal family accustomed to dine off fruit with only the occasional bird, and the Portuguese King a rude and simple fellow. Nonetheless, the following May, Catherine arrived at Portsmouth – sick. Charles was not there. He was with his mistress, Barbara Palmer. When he arrived in Portsmouth, five days later, he was horrified. 'They have brought me a bat', he said.

Charles and Catherine were married the following Wednesday, 21 May, 1662, first secretly and according to the rites of Rome, for Catherine's sake and at her request, and later publicly by the Bishop of London. To the bride's mother, Charles wrote: 'being now freed from the dread of the sea and enjoying in this springtime the company of my dearest wife, I am the happiest man in the world. I cannot sufficiently either look at her or talk to her.' To Clarendon he wrote: 'her face is not so exact as to be called a beauty, though her eyes are excellent good, and not anything in her face that in the least can shock one. On the contrary, she has much agreeableness in her looks altogether as ever I saw.' A small, frail woman of twenty-three, the new Queen made a habit of dressing her hair in tight corkscrews which projected from her ears. Her top front teeth stuck out, distorting her upper lip. Charles told Clarendon that he 'must be the worst man living (which I hope I am not) if I be not a good husband. I will contain myself', he declared, 'within the strict bounds of virtue and conscience.'

'An Historical Poem' put the matter more clearly:

> Twelve years complete he suffered in exile
> And kept his father's asses all the while.
> At length by wonderful impulse of Fate
> The people call him home to help the State,
> And what is more they send him money too,
> And clothe him all from head to foot anew;
> Nor did he such small favours then disdain,
> But in his thirtieth year began to reign.
> In a slashed doublet then he came to shore,
> And dubbed poor Palmer's wife his Royal whore.

*　　*　　*

Clarendon, when later he wrote his autobiography from the comparative safety of exile, could not bring himself to utter her name. 'There was a Lady of youth and beauty', he wrote, 'with whom the King had lived in great and notorious familiarity from the time of his coming into England, and who, at the time of the Queen's coming or a little before, had been delivered of a son whom the King owned ... When the Queen came to Hampton Court, she brought with her a formed resolution that she would never suffer the Lady to be so much as spoken of in her presence.' How much Queen Catherine knew about Barbara Palmer before her arrival in England, one can only guess, but it cannot have taken her long to find out. At their first meeting, the Queen's nose bled and she fell in a faint. 'She [the Queen] has publicly defied me', Charles said irritably to Lady Barbara. 'I am the governor', he added. It was not a view shared by many.

Barbara had been first seduced, she claimed, by the Earl of Chesterfield. Rather, she had seduced him. With a friend, Anne Hamilton, she had written to the Earl: 'my friend and I are just now abed together contriving how to have your company this afternoon. If you deserve this favour, you will come and seek us at Ludgate Hill about three o'clock at Butler's shop, where we will expect you. But lest we should give you too much satisfaction at once, we will say no more. Expect the rest when you see ...' and then they had signed their names. So began, at the age of fifteen, the career of the 'lewdest as well as the fairest of all King Charles's concubines.'

Born in 1640, her father, the second Viscount Grandison, had been killed in the Civil War. Her mother had then married the cousin of her first husband, Charles Villiers, second Earl of Anglesey. Barbara was thus the cousin of

CATHARINA VXOR CAROLI II REGIS
MAGNÆ BRITANIÆ ETC.

Catherine of Braganza, in a miniature by Samuel Cooper. "The Queen . . . is low and slender, and of a solid, grave countenance, quick wit and a great housewife." Halifax wrote of Charles: "he sat down out of form with the Queen, but he supped below the stairs."

George Villiers, second Duke of Buckingham and Charles's boyhood friend. Her beauty was soon noticed. When she came to London 'she appeared in a very plain country dress. But this was soon altered into the gaiety and mode of the Town, which added a new lustre to that blooming beauty of which she had as great a share as any of her sex; she became the object of divers young gentlemen's affections.'

Chesterfield was not the most worthy of young gentlemen, although he gave Barbara a taste of high living. Continually in and out of gaol, he was thought 'exceedingly wild.' Another young gentleman was Roger Palmer, a law student of the Inner Temple. Why she married him remains a mystery, but she did on 14 April 1659, although the marriage did nothing to dampen Barbara's liaison with Chesterfield. In fact, quite the reverse. Chesterfield was deeply involved in various plots to restore the Crown and needed a reliable messenger to Charles in exile. It was said he chose Barbara. Whether true or not, within a year she was secure as the King's mistress.

Her prestige increased with the advent of her first child by Charles, Anne, called Palmer until Charles agreed to the name of Fitzroy being given to his children by Barbara. On the Saturday before his Coronation, Charles took Barbara to the Cockpit Theatre within Whitehall Palace where he showed 'a great deal of familiarity.' She continued to prance around the Town, boasting of the 'lewdness and beggary of the Court' and got pregnant again, presumably by Charles. She then persuaded Charles to make Roger Palmer an Earl, thereby establishing her own social respectability. After all, the market price at the Restoration for a baronetcy was only £500. So why not an earldom? Charles agreed. But, as if to emphasize who was being ennobled, he ordered the title to be restricted to children 'gotten on Barbara Palmer, his now wife.' The warrant was issued for the earldom of Castlemaine and barony of Limerick. The matter did not end there. Barbara insisted on cash. Although Clarendon stopped some of the grants subsequently made her by Charles, Barbara began to acquire considerable sums of money from the King's privy purse, as well as bribes from those who sought to buy her influence.

But now the Royal marriage was imminent. Catherine had arrived at Portsmouth and Barbara, about to give birth to her second child, announced that she intended to lie in at Hampton Court Palace where the King and Queen were to begin their married life. Charles protested and went to Barbara's house to pacify the lady. Catherine, unaware of these excitements, waited patiently at Portsmouth. Barbara celebrated the Royal wedding day by laundering her underclothes in public, and setting them out to dry in the Palace grounds. Still not content, Barbara secured the extraordinary promise that she would be appointed a personal attendant to the Queen as a Lady of the Bedchamber. She also insisted on the dismissal of a gang of dirty monks and lady courtiers whom Catherine had brought with her from Portugal. 'Yesterday', reported Chesterfield, 'these [monks] complained that they cannot stir abroad without seeing in every corner great beastly English pricks battering against every wall, and for this and for some other reasons they are speedily to be sent back to their own country.' Few were in any doubt what were those 'other reasons.' Lady Castlemaine had had her child – a boy – and she called him Charles. The King

Barbara Castlemaine with her first child, Anne Fitzroy (born 1661), in a miniature by Dixon. Born Barbara Villiers in the autumn of 1641, daughter of the 2nd Viscount Grandison and grand-daughter of Sir Edward Villiers, half brother of the 1st Duke of Buckingham. In April 1659, she married Roger Palmer, but her liaison with Charles began soon after. Palmer was made Earl of Castlemaine in 1661, and Barbara created Duchess of Cleveland (inter-alia) in her own right in 1670. She married a second time, in 1705, Major General Robert Fielding in 1705 and died in Chiswick four years later. Among her lovers were William Wycherley, John Churchill (the future Duke of Marlborough), Lord Chesterfield and Jacob Hall, a rope dancer. She had five children by Charles and founded – if that is the appropriate term – the noble houses of Sussex, Cleveland, Grafton, Lichfield, and Northumberland. She was known as the 'royal whore'. Charles, in a more sensible moment, called her a ''damned jade, meddling with things (she) had nothing to do with.''

hurried to visit them, omitting to tell the Queen.

Catherine, now established in London, became distressed by the requests for Barbara's presence in her Bedchamber. 'The King's insistence upon that particular', she said, 'can proceed from no other ground but his hatred of my person. He wishes to expose me to the contempt of the world. And the world will think me deserving of such an affront if I submit to it. Before I do that I will put myself on board any little vessel and so be transported to Lisbon.' 'You have not the disposal of your own person', Clarendon reminded her icily. 'You cannot go out of the house where you are without the King's leave.'

In vain Charles pleaded his good intentions. He swore he had not touched Lady Castlemaine since Catherine's arrival at Portsmouth. Catherine did not believe him. In retaliation, Charles threatened that he would further honour Lady Castlemaine were there not a change of heart 'in certain quarters.' After all, he had 'undone this lady and ruined her reputation, which was fair and untainted till her friendship with me, and I am obliged in conscience and honour to repair her to the utmost of my power. And therefore I shall expect a conformity from my wife herein which shall be the only hard thing I shall ever require of her which she herself may make very easy. For my Lady Castlemaine will behave herself with all possible duty and humility unto her, which if she fails to do in the least degree she shall never see my face again.'

Clarendon was disgusted at Charles's behaviour, although he responded with customary loyalty. He may well have been fat, pained by gout, pompous in phrase and ludicrous in his patronizing manner. But at fifty-one he remained, as ever, the King's man. 'I cannot believe', he told Catherine gently, 'that you are utterly ignorant as to expect the King your husband, in the full strength and vigour of his youth, of so innocent a constitution, as to be reserved for you whom he had never seen, and to have had no acquaintance or familiarity with the other sex.' Catherine was crushed. She asked Clarendon to request of the King his pardon for 'any passion or peevishness I may have been guilty of, and assure him of all future obedience and duty.' Charles then wrote to his Chancellor saying that he had resolved to appoint Lady Castlemaine to his wife's Bedchamber. 'And whosoever I find to be Lady Castlemaine's enemy in this matter', he went on, 'I do promise upon my word to be his enemy as long as I live.'

The King sent for Catherine. He sent for Barbara. Lady Castlemaine kissed the Queen's hand. 'I cannot say there was no discomposure', reported an onlooker. Charles's behaviour toward Catherine remained cold, and when he sat down at dinner in the great hall at Hampton he often ignored her, preferring the conversation of his mistress. Catherine decided she had no alternative but to concede absolutely. 'On a sudden [she] let herself fall first to conversation and then to familiarity, and even in the same instant to a confidence with the Lady.' Alas, it was too late. Catherine had misunderstood her function in Charles's life. By her emotional possessiveness, she had ended any potential influence over Charles. 'Henceforth', observed Rochester, 'the King kept her for breeding.' All of her children were born dead.

Barbara Castlemaine was not without rivals, however. There was Mistress Winifred Wells, one of Catherine's Maids of Honour, 'a big, splendidly handsome creature' marred only by a 'certain air of indecision which gave her the physiognomy of a dreamy sheep.' 'As her father had faithfully served Charles I' (she came from a Royalist family), 'she thought it would ill become his daughter to decline to be served by Charles II.'

There was Jane Middleton, also pursued by the Duke of York. She too was less than perfect.

> Middleton, where'er she goes,
> Confirms the scandal of her toes.

She carried 'about her body a continued sour base smell that is very offensive, especially if she be a little hot.' Charles moved on to fresher pastures – to Lady Chesterfield, for instance, an 'exquisite player of the guitar', a habit Charles had brought from the Continent. There was Frances Stuart, La Belle Stuart, reported to have the finest legs in the world. It was widely believed (or hoped) that she could be stripped naked, accidentally as it were, by comparing her body unfavourably with those of other women. After all, she frequently lifted her skirts to prove that her legs could not be bettered, so why not the rest of her clothes? Charles thought the game 'a fine ruse.' (La Stuart's profile was to be used as the model for Britannia on English coinage.)

All the Royal portraitists were kept busy making copies of semi-nude pictures of these mistresses, and even Pepys acquired what was, in effect, one of the first pin-ups in wide circulation. Charles evidently enjoyed the knowledge that portraits of his ladies in various degrees of undress were to be found in the best homes of England, although such was their proliferation that wrong identification sometimes resulted. The Lely picture of a nude Nell Gwyn, for example, is more probably of the Duchess of Portsmouth, and one of the Lely portraits of Charles looks uncannily like other pictures of Barbara. That most of Charles's women were similar in physique, heavy-lidded, langourous and fleshy, has merely added to the confusion.

Absurd though they seem, Charles's women were essential to his vision of himself as the warrior king, a proof of his continuing virility. From 1660 onward, he was never as young as he liked to be thought; he was not the reincarnation of Henry VIII, even if in weaker moments he hoped he was. He needed the manifold services of his women, although he rarely treated them seriously. At his first New Year's Eve Ball as King, Charles insisted on calling the first country dance of the evening 'Cuckolds All A-row'. Later, Pepys records, 'a child was dropped by one of the ladies in dancing, but nobody knew who, it being taken up by someone in a handkerchief. The next morning all the Ladies of Honour appeared early at Court for their vindication, so that nobody could tell whose this mischance should be. But it seems that Mistress Wells fell sick that afternoon, and hath disappeared ever since, so that it was concluded that it was her.' It was also concluded that the child was the King's, especially when it became known that Charles had had the foetus dissected in his closet. In his opinion, Charles said, the child had been a month and three hours old. Since it had also been a boy, the person who had suffered most by this abortion was himself.

Despite these diversions, Charles remained attached to Lady Castlemaine. He paid off her gambling, now almost £100,000 a year. He gave her official lodgings in the Palace, rooms immediately above his own, connected by private stair, where she gave birth to a second son whom she called Henry. Catherine fell ill and announced to the world she was dying. Charles rushed to her bedside, saying 'live for me, if you love me.'

Castlemaine now used this bawdry to gather about her a clique led by Henry Bennet, later elevated as Earl of Arlington. Bennet cultivated the air of a grandee and sported a black scar on the bridge of his nose (it was often thought to be a black patch). Otherwise, according to Buckingham, he was undistinguished.

> Two goggle eyes, so clear, tho' very dead
> That one may see thro' them right thro' his head.

Also in the gang was Antony Ashley Cooper, Chancellor of the Exchequer, later promoted Baron Ashley. From the north came the Earl of Lauderdale, a giant red-headed Scotsman with an inflamed face and violent speech. In attendance was Barbara's thirty-four year old cousin, Buckingham, now thought of as a 'lecherous chemist, fiddler, statesman and buffoon', who, according to Dryden:

> Laugh'd himself from Court, then sought relief
> By forming parties, but could ne'er be chief.

Last was Sir Charles Berkeley, later Earl of Falmouth, and by repute the King's pimp. With the exception of Berkeley (who was replaced by Clifford), Barbara's circle had the same membership as the King's 'cabal' of 1667.

Her first overt political act was to advocate the appointment of Bennet as

The Earl of Arlington, from the studio of Lely. Born Henry Bennet in 1618 at Saxham in ▷ Suffolk, the son of a lawyer, he was educated at Westminster School and Christ Church, Oxford. Created Lord Arlington in 1665, after ten years of "useful" service to Charles; he managed the mistresses. He failed, however, to warn Charles of the Dutch invasion, allowed himself and his wife to be bribed by Louis XIV, almost destroyed the marriage prospects of Charles's niece Mary by alienating William of Orange with his arrogant, overweening formality, and was eventually booted out of government for supporting Shaftesbury. He died six months after Charles, declaring at the last moment his lifelong devotion to Catholicism. The black mark on his nose is usually thought to be a scar suffered as a result of a Civil War wound; in fact, it was a strip of black plaster constantly renewed to emphasise a cut received in a duel.

69

ambassador to France. Clarendon resented the appointment, with promptings from Louis who growled that Bennet 'knew no more of the constitution and laws of England than he did of China.' Partly to annoy Clarendon, but also to please his mistress, Charles made Bennet Secretary of State and Paymaster General. As it turned out, this suited Barbara even more, and Clarendon began to suspect that Barbara's chief ambition was to dispose of the Chancellor himself; after all, it was she who had persuaded Bristol to attack Clarendon in the Lords. When Bristol had been eventually committed to the Tower, Charles, knowing of his involvement with Barbara Castlemaine, had warned him of his arrest, and Bristol escaped to France where he remained for four years. It was not Lady Castlemaine's most successful foray into politics. But for Charles it was an omen.

Nonetheless, he forgave her. Shortly after the birth of her son Henry, the two were together again at Oxford, complete with all their family. Charles disliked being away from his children. He would often ask Lady Castlemaine's nurses to bring out his offspring so that he could dance with them in his arms. Soon Barbara had given birth to a fourth child, Charlotte, although the arrival of yet another 'royal charlie', whom Charles freely acknowledged as his own, was too much for some courtiers. Three of them surrounded Lady Castlemaine late one night the following week while she was walking across St James's Park, accompanied by her maid and a page. They shouted she was a whore and a good deal else and told her that Jane Shore, the mistress of Edward IV, had finished up on a dung-hill alone and despised.

Despised Lady Castlemaine may have been, but alone she was not; before long she was pregnant, 'slipping her filly', again. When the court moved to Oxford, the King and Queen stayed at the Dean's lodgings at Christ Church, while Barbara, complete with Charles's sons Charles and Henry, was accommodated opposite Merton College in the house of Antony Wood, the university historian. Barbara gave birth to her fifth child in December 1665. A notice written in Latin and English was pinned by an unknown hand to her door; it read:

Hanc Caesare pressam a fluctu defendit onus

or

The reason why she is not duck'd?
Because by Caesar she is fucked.

A thousand pounds was offered for information leading to the culprit; alas, none was found.

Angered, Barbara began securing rewards for services so generously given to the Monarch. 'Her principal business', wrote Clarendon, 'was to get an estate for herself and her children.' First she 'procured round sums of money out of the Privy Purse.' Then other grants were made, inconspicuously, to her uncles, the Earl of Suffolk and Viscount Grandison, who passed on the proceeds to her. She bought, on credit to the King, a £850 ring from the City jeweller, John Le Roy, and ordered two diamond rings costing £1,100 and £900 for which Charles had to pay out of Customs receipts. She was reported to have lost £25,000 gambling in one night, and her critics said of her and Charles that they 'sit at cards and dispose of the revenue of the Kingdom.'

Catherine at last gave birth to a son, premature and dead. Charles was not present. But there was now medical evidence that Catherine could conceive, although Clarendon relates how certain of the women around the King, including Barbara, persuaded Charles it had been a false conception. 'He suffered himself now to be so totally convinced by these ladies', wrote Clarendon, 'that he did as positively believe that she [the Queen] never had, never could be, with child.'

Catherine celebrated, however, by giving a birthday ball, and Charles ordered the Court to turn out in a new black and white uniform of calf-length vest with white underskirt, 'the legs ruffled with black ribbon like a pigeon's leg.' Barbara was present, though not very active; she was thought to be pregnant again. The star of the show was Frances Stuart – 'a glorious sight . . . in black and white lace and her head and shoulders dressed with diamonds . . . with the King in his rich vest of some rich silk and silver trimming.' Barbara was furious and stormed out, leaving Charles in the arms of Frances. 'It was come to pass', noted Evelyn, 'that she [La Belle Stuart] could no longer continue at Court without prostituting herself to the King.'

Charles soon asserted his rights, although the evening when the deed was done did not proceed as he had intended. 'It was near midnight', remembered the Count of Grammont. 'The King encountered his mistress's women who respectfully put themselves in his way, informing him in a whisper that Miss Stuart had been very poorly since he left but had now gone to bed and, thank God for it, was getting some sleep. "That remains to be seen", he observed, thrusting aside a maid who obstructed his passage. And indeed he did find the Stuart in bed, but she was not sleeping: and also the Duke of Richmond, who sat at her bed's head and seemed, according to the evidence, even less asleep. The stupefaction on one side, the rage evinced upon the other, were such, as in a similar surprisal, may easily be imagined.' The Duke bowed deeply and retired. Frances rushed to the Queen for help, although what Catherine was supposed to have done is not clear.

Charles was profoundly hurt, or at least as hurt as he thought fitting in the circumstances. Later and reluctantly he agreed that his 'former mistress' should be allowed to marry the Duke of Richmond; both were then banished from Court. Minette urged Charles to be more tolerant, but the King replied: 'I do assure you that I am very much troubled that I cannot in everything give you the satisfaction I could wish, especially in the business of the Duchess of Richmond, wherein you may think me ill-natured. But if you consider how

72

hard a thing 'tis to swallow an injury done by a person I had so much l . . . [here the word is scratched out; was Charles going to write 'loved'?] . . . a person I had so much tenderness for, you will in some degree excuse the resentment I use towards her. Therefore, I hope you will pardon me if I cannot so soon forget an injury which went so near my heart.' It was the nearest Charles came to writing a straightforward love letter. He wrote nothing so direct to Barbara.

*   *   *

Barbara, meanwhile, was planning revenge against her enemies at Court. Besides Clarendon, there was the Earl of Southampton; as Lord Treasurer, he meddled in Barbara's money. At his death in 1667, she seized the opportunity of his 'absence' to grab her first fixed pension, a ninety-nine year allowance of £1,000 a year taken from the profits of the Post Office and granted to her nominees. As to Clarendon, she ensured he took the blame for the government's mistakes. To spite Charles, she leased out her affections elsewhere. A courtier named Henry Jermyn was honoured. Then there was a running foot-man. She even seduced a Miss Hobart, one of her Maids of Honour, who 'blushed at everything but never did anything to raise a blush herself.' Indeed not, for Miss Hobart later achieved the unique distinction of having had both King and Mistress. All of which irritated Charles, especially when Barbara became pregnant again and not by him. 'God damn me, but you shall own it', Barbara shouted at Charles. 'I will have it christened in the chapel at Whitehall and owned as yours, as other Kings have done. Either that or I will bring it into Whitehall Gallery and dash its brains out before your face.' 'I did not get this child', replied Charles, bewildered. 'Whoever did get it', said Barbara, 'you shall own it.'

Pepys noted later that 'the King is mad at her entertaining Jermyn, and she is mad at Jermyn's going to marry from her.' (Jermyn had now married one Mary Falmouth.) 'So they are all mad, and thus the nation is governed.' The Court believed, and frequently repeated, that at the reconciliation between Charles and Barbara, 'she made him ask her forgiveness upon his knees, and promise to offend her no more so.'

◁ Frances Stuart, in a portrait by Lely: "The prettiest girl in the world", according to Minette. Charles was crazy about her; he wrote

"While alone to myself I repeat all her charms,
She I love may be locked in another man's arms,
She may laugh at my cares and so false she may be
To say all the kind things she before said to me:
O then, 'tis O then, that I think there's no hell
Like loving too well."

Frances Stuart became Duchess of Richmond in March 1667, and thereafter Lady of the Bedchamber to the Queen. Alas, she caught smallpox and died soon after.

'How imperious this woman is', Pepys wrote, 'and hectors the King to whatever she will.' Clarendon always believed that his eventual dismissal had come about through 'the Lady and her party'; almost his last act was to stop another annual grant of £2,000 payable to one of Barbara's nominees. 'The woman will sell everything shortly', he said. Pepys sympathized. 'This business of my Lord Chancellor's was certainly designed in my Lady Castlemaine's chamber', he remarked. Even the new Archbishop of Canterbury, Gilbert Sheldon, who later endowed the Sheldonian Theatre in Oxford, protested against Lady Castlemaine's increased meddling. 'Sir', he told Charles, 'I wish you would put away this woman that you keep.' But, as Barbara was quick to point out, the Archbishop was not the most reliable of authorities on moral behaviour. Sheldon was 'as very a wencher as can be', she told him; at that very moment, he was quarreling with the poet Sir Charles Sedley, accused of seducing one of Sedley's girlfriends. The nation, said Pepys, continued to observe how its Sovereign was 'only governed by lust, and women, and rogues about him.'

Burnet did not agree. Affection for the Monarch was strong, he maintained. Charles had told him 'he could not think God would make a man miserable for taking a little pleasure out of the way.' The King knew that many felt increasing dismay at Barbara's interfering, although he realized it was not Barbara herself that was objected to, nor even her politicking. It was her cost, thought disproportionate to her services and to the economic difficulties of the Crown. If anything, Barbara was more popular than the Queen, to whose position Charles throughout remained stubbornly loyal if distant. He was told that the Queen's death would solve a problem or two, but he asserted he could no more divorce her than poison her. His bastard children also presented no real embarrassment, except again for their increasing cost. Acknowledgement of Charles's bastards relied initially on their mother's claim of the King's paternity, until the grant of a noble title made the arrangement more formal. As Sir John Clayton wrote to Sir Robert Paston: 'England in a few years may be so happy as to see a House of Peers truly noble when they are all extracted out of Royal blood.' Charles was to create six dukedoms and one earldom for his illegitimate sons. Four of his daughters became countesses. Henry Palmer (later Henry Fitzroy) who, during his infancy, had been speculatively assigned to the Earl of Falmouth, was later created Earl of Euston and Duke of Grafton. Charles acknowledged him as the most accomplished and best loved of all his children, including the Duke of Monmouth.

*   *   *

Barbara's bossiness pushed Charles into looking elsewhere for home comforts. He was lucky, in several ways.

Hard by Pall Mall lives a wench call'd Nell.

> King Charles the Second he kept her.
> She hath got a trick to handle his prick,
> But never lays hands on his Sceptre.

Eleanor Gwyn was to be one of the few women ever to capture Charles's affections. She was small, slender and had big breasts. The heart-shaped face, hazel eyes and chestnut brown hair were a striking contrast to the well travelled lust of Castlemaine. Her father had died in an Oxford prison: her mother floated away drunk in a ditch in Westminster and drowned. Ironically, Nell was a protégé of Lady Castlemaine. Under Barbara's sponsorship, she rose to become the leading comedienne in the King's own theatrical troupe. She was mistress to the actor, Charles Hart, a great-nephew of Shakespeare; later, she had Sir Charles Sedley. When she eventually had the King, she dubbed him her Charles the Third.

Nell was born in a London alley on 2 February 1650. Her mother kept a brothel in the Covent Garden district of London where, according to Pepys, Nell was brought up 'to fill strong waters [brandy] to the guests.' In 1664, thanks to her elder sister Rose, she became an orange girl in the King's Theatre. She performed every night, taking time off only to seduce Dryden and make a brief excursion to Epsom where she stayed one summer as mistress of Lord Buckhurst, afterwards the sixth Earl of Dorset. 'Pretty, witty, Nell' was so much in demand as a speaker of lusty prologues and sexually titillating epilogues, it was said she had every playwright in the land dangling upon her finger.

Her last appearance was as Almahide in Dryden's two-part heroic play *The Conquest of Granada*. By now she had other conquests to attend. The production had already been postponed for several months whilst she was confined, giving birth to a child (some said it was her eighth), a son. Its father was Charles. In gratitude, he was to set her up in a fine house in Pall Mall.

She remained illiterate and with difficulty scrawled an awkward 'E.G.' at the bottom of her letters, written for her by others. 'A true child of the London streets', she never pretended to be more than she was, nor interfere in matters outside the particular sphere ascribed her by Charles. Unlike her rivals, she was to make no ministers, appoint no bishops, and for the complex issues of international politics she had no concern. For Charles, she became a licensed court jester presiding over his stag parties. Her generosity, invariable good temper, wit and infectious giggle, appealed to a King hedged in by too many advisers.

Above all, Charles admired her loyalty. She never forgot old friends and, according to her own testament, remained faithful to her royal lover from the beginning of their intimacy until his death. Charles, of course, was openly unfaithful to her, but only, he protested, with other members of his paid harem. There was Jane Roberts, a clergyman's daughter; Moll Davis, who was frequently to display her £700 ring and boast of the house in Suffolk Street, both provided by Charles. Even Catherine, normally tolerant of the King's 'pretty little fools', stalked out of the Palace Theatre when Moll came on to dance.

*　　*　　*

Barbara, meanwhile, got jealous. She launched herself on none other than Charles Hart, and 'by this means' (according to Pepys) 'she is even with the King's love for Mistress Davis.' An actor was a person of a *low* social order, and any depths to which Charles could sink, she could also. One afternoon she had Jacob Hall, a rope-dancer performing in a booth at Bartholomew Fair. She forced a footman to share a bath with her, an odd reference to this unusual phenomenon.

Charles was finally provoked. He promised Barbara anything she desired. She desired that her mother's uncle, one Dr Henry Glenham, 'a drunken, swearing rascal and a scandal', be consecrated Bishop of St Asaph. He was. She desired that her ex-lover, Dr Thomas Wood, the Dean of Lichfield and Coventry, be promoted Bishop of the same diocese. He was. She desired to meet with Bishop Braybrooke. Charles, not realizing that the good bishop had died in 1404 and been buried in the old St Paul's Cathedral, granted the request. It transpired that the Bishop's mummified body, 'all tough and dry like a spongified leather', had fallen out of its tomb. Barbara, accompanied by a gentleman and two gentlewomen, told the puzzled keeper that she wished to be alone with the Bishop. For what purpose was never discovered, although the antiquary Henry Coleraine remarked that 'though some ladies of late have got Bishopricks for others, yet I have not heard of any but this that got one for herself.' Evelyn was shocked. When he came to this episode in his diary, he left a space. Many wondered how Charles could spare time for the problems of government, so devouring were his ladies.

The crisis was to explode after Easter 1668 when the London apprentices, in a moment of drunken moral fervour, looted a number of brothels. Pepys heard one of them shout 'why do we not go and pull down the great one in Whitehall?' Soon after, a mock petition from the harassed prostitutes of London was widely distributed. Entitled *The Poor Whores' Petition*, it was addressed to 'the most splendid, illustrious, serene and eminent Lady of Pleasure, the Countess of Castlemaine . . . That your Petitioners having been for a long time connived at and countenanced in the practice of our venereal pleasure (a trade wherein Your Ladyship hath great experience, and for diligence therein have arrived to high and eminent advancement for these late years). But now we, through the rage and malice of a Company of London apprentices and other malicious and very bad persons . . . have sustained the loss of our habitations, trades and employments.'

76

The petition appealed for protection to the nation's 'chief whore', Lady Castlemaine, in return for a tax agreed to by all prostitutes. It was signed by 'Us, Madam Cresswell and Damaris Page.' Madam Cresswell, a notorious brothel-keeper, was later (in 1681) 'convicted after above thirty years practice of bawdry.' Madam Page, the 'seaman's friend', also had her brothels sacked. The Duke of York was distressed. He had lost a tenant, he said, who paid him £15 a year for her wine licence. Charles was speechless. *The Poor Whores' Petition* was evidence of venal opposition to him and his rule. Hitherto, he had allowed almost no published personal criticism. Even after the disasters of the Dutch war, he tolerated criticism only as long as it was indirect. Something would have to be done. Barbara must be pensioned off, permanently.

Barbara was 'horribly vexed.' The *Petition*, she declared, was a 'libel not very witty but devilish severe against her and the King; and I wonder how it durst be printed and spread abroad, which shows that the times are loose, and come to a great disregard for the King or Court or Government.' The times were to get looser. Within a week, another broadsheet was circulating entitled *The Gracious Answer of the most illustrious Lady of Pleasure, the Countess of Castlem . . . to the Poor Whores' Petition – given at our Closet in King Street, Westminster.* 'If women have not children by their own husbands', it went on, 'they are bound (to prevent their damnation) to try by using the means with other men.' The Countess then describes why she has recently left the Church of England for the Church of Rome, a conversion which shocked many and confirmed the worst suspicions of the rest. The Church of Rome, she was made to say, is a place where 'venereal pleasures, accompanied with looseness, debauchery and profaneness, are not such heinous crimes and crying sins, but rather they do mortify the flesh.'

The joke had gone far enough. Charles tried to put a stop to it. Within days of the publication of *The Gracious Answer*, he borrowed £11,500 from his City banker, goldsmith Alderman Bakewell, with which he acquired Berkshire House for Barbara. If she was to continue within his sight, he said, she must exist independently of him. 'She is now busying herself', the French ambassador added cynically, 'getting her gift valued and having the house furnished.'

As if to make his intentions clear, Charles publicly flirted with one Lady Harvey, the wife of his ambassador to the Levant and by repute a lesbian. He was again 'mighty hot upon the Duchess of Richmond.' According to an eyewitness, 'he [Charles] did on a sudden take a pair of oars or sculler, and all alone, or but one with him, go to Somerset House [the home of Frances Stuart, the Duchess] and there, the garden door not being open, himself clambered over the wall to make a visit to her . . . which is a horrid shame.' The King also pursued Mistress Gwyn: 'saw pretty Nelly', wrote Pepys . . . 'she seemed a mighty pretty creature.' And mighty devious. Learning that Charles was to visit Moll Davis, she asked Mistress Moll to her lodgings and there mixed an overdose of jalop into her pudding. Moll passed out and was not seen for several days.

* * *

Barbara was a tougher proposition. In January 1667, she acquired a further £4,700 a year in pensions granted once more out of the Post Office profits. Cash appeared from another, less expected quarter. Charles was anxious to secure a lasting alliance with Louis XIV to consolidate his colonial and trading ambitions against the Dutch. Louis, for different reasons, also wanted the alliance. He instructed Colbert, his ambassador at the time in London, to court Madame Castlemaine – with expensive presents, if necessary – and persuade her to persuade the King of the wisdom of this alliance. 'I have read with great pleasure', Louis added drily, 'the curious details you have despatched about the intrigues of the English Court and the highly involved imbroglios of the principal ladies there.'

Barbara was not slow to recognize the potential. Colbert was soon replying: 'I have given away everything I brought from France not excepting my wife's skirts . . . As for Lady Castlemaine, if we lavish handsome gifts on her, King Charles will understand that we believe she rules him in spite of denials. We ought to dispense no more than ribbons, dressing gowns and other little fineries.'

The reply was blunt. 'The King [Louis] highly appreciates the confidence you have cultivated with Lady Castlemaine . . . His Majesty sets great store on the counsel of this lady, and since you add that she seemed to you very well disposed to [our] alliance . . . His Majesty wishes you to cultivate this good beginning with her.' Barbara made sure that she took credit for the alliance which was eventually concluded, and Charles, 'in consideration of her noble descent, her father's death in the service of the Crown, and by reason of her own personal virtues', created her Duchess of Cleveland, Countess of Southampton and Baroness Nonsuch of Nonsuch Park in Surrey. She promptly sold Berkshire House, pocketed the proceeds and built a new red-brick residence, Cleveland House, in St James's. She also took a lover to show Charles just how independent she felt she was. John Ellis, 'the epitome of lewdness', was a student at Christ Church.

> What push'd poor Ellis on th'imperial whore?
> 'Twas but to be where Charles had been before.

Thereafter, Charles and Barbara were to drift apart, their usefulness to each other at an end. At the signing of the treaty – in fact organized by Charles and his sister, Minette – Minette had brought with her as one of her Maids of Honour a fat Breton called Louise de Kéroualle. When brother and sister came to discuss what farewell presents they should give each other, Charles said: 'I will take Louise.' Which he did. Barbara proceeded to have William Wycherly, and his infatuation provoked his finest play, *The Country Wife*. Later, she galloped on to John Churchill, in whom she met her match. He demanded money from her as fast as she could supply it. Pathetically, she also had Sir Edward Hungerford, a drunken and ageing knight who also desired 'to be where Charles had been before.' The Duchess announced that her price was £10,000. Arrangements were made. Then, in a darkened room, she said she would give out he was incapable unless a further fee was paid. Pope wrote:

> Who of ten thousand gull'd her knight,
> Then ask'd ten thousand for another night;
> The gallant too, to whom she paid it down,
> Liv'd to refuse that mistress half-a-crown.

She was to dabble one last time in affairs of State. She had a double affair with Ralph Montagu – an ambitious courtier and ambassador to France now conspiring to impeach the new and formidable Lord Treasurer, the Earl of Danby – and one Alexis, Marquis de Châtillon, First Gentleman of the Bedchamber to Louis XIV. Danby, on behalf of Charles, was negotiating a peace between France and Holland, Spain and the Holy Roman Empire. In return for a neutralizing settlement, Louis was to pay Charles £500,000 a year for three years until Charles could risk explaining to Parliament this otherwise inexplicable manoeuvre.

Montagu discovered and became jealous of Barbara's liaison with the Marquis; whereupon, according to Barbara, he seized Charles's daughter Anne and seduced her. Montagu was dismissed and turned for help to the French ambassador in London. He could, he said, bring about the fall of Danby – no friend to the French. His price would be £25,000 down, and a pension of £3,000 a year for life. He then had himself elected to Parliament (giving him immunity from arrest) and produced in the House of Commons Danby's letter which had ordered him to request the £500,000 from Louis XIV. Parliament was shocked at Charles's apparent duplicity. Danby was impeached and sent to the Tower for an indefinite period. Charles had to dissolve Parliament, it was said, because of Montagu's jealousy of Barbara and Barbara's access to the King. This was, to put it mildly, a simplification; nonetheless, Charles told Barbara: 'I care not who you love.'

Barbara managed to squeeze a final £25,000 out of Charles, but the principal Commissioner of the Treasury, the Earl of Essex, stopped the payment. If the King wished the £25,000 to be paid, Essex told Charles, then somebody else should do it for he would rather surrender his office than pay it. Charles took him at his word and dismissed him. 'The Duchess was ever his friend and kept him in', noted John Verney. But as Charles lay dying, she was fondling her newest lover, Cardonell Goodman, an indifferent actor known as 'Scum'.

Eventually, she developed dropsy 'which swelled her gradually to a monstrous hulk', married a bigamist after the death of her husband, and died in 1709, forgotten. Her epitaph was vicious, but appropriate. It read:

> Let Ancients boast no more
> Their Lewd Imperial Whore.

It was to be a grim end for one whom Pepys had acclaimed 'in a higher command over the King ... not as a mistress, for she scorns him, but as a tyrant, to command him.' Burnet thought differently. 'He [Charles] has a very ill opinion of men *and* women', he wrote, 'and is infinitely distrustful. He thinks the world is governed wholly by interest.' Barbara and his other mistresses gave him plenty of evidence for that.

Chapter Four
Dreadful prospects

If England at the Restoration was not what Charles had expected, London must have been a greater shock. Within a square mile it housed over 400,000 people who lived, ate, slept, shopped, took their pleasures, worshipped, were born, wed, died and buried in a city where overcrowding was accepted as the norm. Its local administration, consisting of 126 parishes – most not more than three acres – was inadequate. Its seven gates, all of whose names survive – Aldgate, Bishopsgate, Moorgate, Cripplegate, Aldersgate, Newgate and Ludgate – were obstructive to traffic, and its only bridge blocked with gates at both ends and by overhanging houses built either side of its narrow width. Carts which trundled across it got jammed between the houses, bringing masonry and wood crashing down on to the already rickety structure.

Public transport was unknown. Private hackney coaches cost a shilling a mile or eighteen pence an hour, although these new-fangled devices were thought dangerous as the streets were roughly paved (if at all), drains like the Fleet Ditch left unrailed, and street lighting did not exist. Soap boilers, lime burners, brewers, dyers, tanners and suchlike, contributed to the 'coughing, snuffing . . . barking and spitting' which was commonplace. Hangings turned yellow and flowers died. Disease was rampant, pure water unknown. Apart from the more traditional (and fatal) ailments such as tuberculosis and small-pox, which annually carried off thousands, the Bills of Mortality lists such delights as 'headmouldshot, horseshoehead, and water in the head.'

Most of the capital was sited on the northern bank of the Thames. Peckham and Vauxhall to the south were rural resorts. But then so was Islington to the north (five miles from the Tower of London), and was particularly distinguished for its cowsheds. What is now Trafalgar Square was the furthest extent of the suburbs; Kensington was a separate village. So too was Westminster which, although the administrative centre of England, was not part of London, the two being separated by fields. In contrast to London's noise and bustle, moreover, Westminster was essentially rural. In July 1671 a bullock ran berserk in Palace Yard, tossing half a dozen people and causing

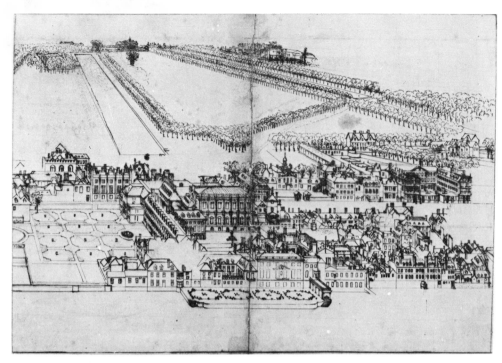

Whitehall Palace; a pen drawing by Leonard Knyff. Henry VIII had originally conceived it, confiscating 180 acres from assorted monasteries from Charing Cross in the north, to what is now Buckingham Palace in the west. Like so many other things, Henry never finished it; his daughter Elizabeth inherited a ramshackle, labyrinthine maze covering a mere 23 acres. It was not a 'private' palace; the main London to Westminster road went through the middle (now called "Whitehall"). Charles II tidied it up as much as he could – tennis courts and a cockpit were replaced by an exercise ground, now Horse Guards Parade; the King used it as the centre of his administration since it was conveniently situated between Parliament and the City. It housed a picture gallery, a banqueting hall, the Council Room, the King's Closet, a bowling green, Scotland Yard, offices for all the principal Ministers of State, the Chapel Royal and, over-looking the river, the Royal Bedchamber. Much of it was burned down in two extensive fires in the 1690s.

such alarm that lawyers and judges in Westminster Hall thought the Fifth Monarchists were again up in arms. To the east, beyond the city walls, were the Liberties, shanty towns which housed the poor. What was true and disgusting of the City, was more so in the Liberties – where the working people lived.

Charles made several attempts to improve London. Indeed, one of his first Acts had been to insist that all householders on or near a street be required to show a candle in their window 'from such time as it shall grow dark, until nine of the clock in the evening, upon pain to forfeit the sum of one shilling for every default.' An Act appointing commissioners of refuse had been passed in 1662 authorizing the raising of a levy to pay for new vaults, sewers and drains. The same Act had prohibited the disposal of ashes or other rubbish in the fronts of houses, and ordered each inhabitant to store his waste until such times as a collector arrived to take it away. The enforcement of these provisions was haphazard, not least because Charles found himself restricted by the City's inherited autonomy. London was, in effect, a kingdom within a kingdom, governed by a Lord Mayor whose power was absolute. The Mayor was nominally the chief coroner of London, chief butler to the King and chief magistrate of the City, with power to make his own ordinances and by-laws. His moral authority was increased, paradoxically, by the City's lack of representation in Parliament, only three miles away. It returned four members, whereas Cornwall (by comparison, almost depopulated) returned forty. The Lord Mayor had the excuse thereby to govern as he wished, within the bounds of his authority; when anarchy threatened in early 1665, Charles found himself almost powerless to act.

*   *   *

In the winter of 1664 a blazing star had been observed in the northern skies. It had made a 'rushing, mighty noise, fierce and terrible, though at a distance, and but just perceivable.' Within a month, London had been flooded with books and pamphlets foretelling the worst. One was entitled: *Come out of her, my People, lest you be Partaker of his Plagues.* Another wrote: 'These terrors and apprehensions of the people led them into a thousand weak, foolish and wicked things.' Men claiming to be itinerant priests shouted obscenities and dire warnings: 'Yet forty days, and London shall be destroyed.' Some said they could see a flaming sword coming out of a cloud with its point hanging directly over the city. Others saw hearses and coffins, and there heaps of dead bodies lying unburied. Those who could not see were reviled as profane. It was a time of God's anger and dreadful judgements were approaching. 'Despisers' would wander and perish.

Before long, the reality was as horrifying as had been imagined. A tradesman in East Smithfield, for instance, discovered his pregnant wife had the plague. When she began her labour he could get neither a midwife to assist her in child-birth, nor a nurse to tend her sickness; both his servants had fled when they discovered the woman was infected. He ran from house to house 'like one distracted', but the best he could find was a watchman who promised to send a nurse in the morning. 'The poor man, with his heart broke, went back, assisted his wife what he could, acted the part of the midwife, brought the child dead into the world, and his wife in about an hour died in his arms where he held her dead body fast till the morning.' The watchman arrived bringing with him the nurse. They found the man still sitting with his dead wife in his arms. 'So overwhelmed with grief was he, that he himself died a few hours after without any sign of the infection upon him, but merely sank under the weight of his grief.'

In May 1665, forty-three deaths from bubonic plague were reported. By June, the number had increased to 600. In July, the deaths were counted by the thousand. In September, over 30,000 perished in London alone. No one knew where to turn for help. Remedies were desperate. Every street corner promised the latest cure. 'Infallible preventive pills against the plague', read one. 'Never failing preservatives against the infection', read another. 'Sovereign cordials against the corruption of the air.' 'Anti-pestilential pills.' 'Incomparable drink against the plague, never found out before.' 'The Royal antidote against all kinds of infection.' London became a hypochondriac's paradise.

Panic was inevitable. Without waiting to see how widespread the outbreak, 'the richer sort of people, especially the nobility and gentry from the west part of the city, thronged out of town with their families and servants in an unusual manner.' 'I find all the town going out of town', wrote Pepys, 'the coaches and carriages being all full of people going into the country.' In Whitehall, 'the court was full of wagons', 'with goods, women, servants and children; coaches filled with people of the better sort, and horsemen attending them, and all hurrying away; besides innumerable numbers of men on horseback, some alone, others with servants, all loaded with baggage and fitted out for travelling.'

The plague could not have struck at a worse time, as Charles realized. The City was full of those who had 'flocked to London to settle in business, or to depend upon and attend the Court for rewards of services, preferments, and the like.' It was estimated that, in 1665, London had nearly 100,000 extra inhabitants.

Charles tried to stop the exodus, ordering that a pass must be obtained from the Lord Mayor's office before anyone could leave the city. The Mansion House was beleaguered. It was then rumoured that Charles intended to place turnpikes and barriers on all roads out of London to prevent people travelling and thus risk spreading the disease. Within hours, it seemed, 'there was hardly a horse to be bought or hired in the whole city.' By mid-July, 10,000 houses had been deserted. Over 200,000 people had fled. Others shut themselves in, and 'kept their houses like garrisons besieged.'

Charles issued instructions to all constables and churchwardens that they were to stay at their posts and set an example. But petty crime flourished. Hired nurses, whose job was to tend the sick, often starved, smothered, or 'by other wicked means' hastened their patients' ends. Watchmen broke into houses they were supposed to be guarding, murdered the inhabitants, and stole whatever valuables they could find. Relief, especially for the poor, was scarce. Charles ordered a thousand pounds a week to be distributed in London. Collections were to be held among the nobility and gentry of England for immediate dispatch to the Lord Mayor of London. But, as Charles remarked to the French ambassador, although the plague was chiefly among the poor, 'the poor [were] the most venturous and fearless of it, and went about employment with a sort of brutal courage.' 'Employment has ceased', wrote an eye-witness; 'the labour, and by that the bread, of the poor were cut off.' Those in domestic service 'were turned off, and left friendless and helpless, without employment and without habitation, and this was really a dismal article.'

Worst hit of all were the merchants. Their ships could go nowhere because no one would unload their cargoes. 'No port of France, or Holland, or Spain, or Italy, will admit our ships and correspond with us', wrote one. Boats were turned away from Leghorn in Italy and from Portugal. One vessel, having unloaded its cargo of cloth and cotton 'by stealth', had its shipment burned upon discovery. Those who had smuggled the goods ashore were shot.

In England, the calamity was equally pathetic. Beyond London, many who were 'grown stupid or melancholy by their miseries', wandered about the countryside hiding 'in secret, uncouth places, almost anywhere, to creep into a bush or hedge and die.' Local inhabitants, out of pity, left food for them at a safe distance. But the victims were often too weak to reach the food and died in the attempt. 'And then with long poles and hooks at the end of them, the bodies [were dragged] into these pits, and then throw the earth in from as far as they could cast it, taking notice how the wind blew . . . that the scent of the bodies might not blow from them.' 'And thus great numbers went out of this world, who were never known, or any account of them taken.'

The apparent indolence and promiscuity of the Court was, of course, said to have brought this 'terrible judgment upon the whole nation', and when Charles moved the Court to Oxford, relations with the University became strained. 'The greater sort of the courtiers were high', Antony Wood wrote, 'proud, insolent, and looked upon scholars no more than pedants or pedagogical persons . . . Though they were neat and gay in their apparel, yet were they very nasty and beastly, leaving at their departure their excrements in every corner, in chimneys, studies, coalhouses, cellars. Rough, rude, whore-mongers; vain, empty, careless.'

It became clear, however, that if it had not been for Charles's tenacity, the chaos would have been worse. His measures were strict if tardy, although it is an indication of their effectiveness that some even questioned Charles's intentions, suspecting he was using the present difficulties as a camouflage for the establishment of absolute rule. First, he legislated against the excesses of which the Court was accused. 'All the plays and interludes which, after the manner of the French Court, had been set up, and began to increase among us, were forbid to act.' Gaming-tables, public dancing rooms and music-houses 'which multiplied and began to debauch the manners of the people' were also closed. Jack-puddings, puppet-shows and rope-dancers, all forms of street entertainment 'which bewitched the common people', were stopped. Alas, some regulations were not put into effect until the following year.

Next, Charles attempted to isolate the disease. Examiners were appointed to every parish in London. Their job was to report any sick person to the constable who then authorized that person's house to be shut up. Each infected house was given two watchmen, one for day and one for night, who were 'to

86

have a special care that no person go in or out of such infected houses upon pain of severe punishment.' Each house was to be 'marked with a red cross of a foot long in the middle of the door . . . and with these usual printed words: "Lord, have mercy upon us!" ' Hackney coaches were forbidden, 'till their coaches be well aired.' The burial of the dead was to be 'at most convenient hours, always either before sun-rising or after sun-setting, with the privity of the churchwardens or constable and not otherwise.' Graves 'shall be at least six foot deep.'

In addition, each householder was 'to cause the street to be daily prepared [kept clean] before his door, and so to keep it clean swept all the week long.' The 'sweeping and filth of houses' must be 'daily carried away by the rakers.' Special care was to be taken that 'no stinking fish, or unwholesome flesh, or musty corn, or other corrupt fruits of what sortsoever, be suffered to be sold about the city.' No hogs, dogs, cats, tame pigeons or ponies were to be kept within any part of London. Any stray dog was to be killed and special 'dog killers' were appointed. As a result, 40,000 dogs were destroyed and five times as many cats. Pigs were not allowed to wander about the streets. Taverns, ale- and coffee-houses were to be closed at nine o'clock in the evening. No wandering beggars were to be allowed into London 'in any fashion or manner whatsoever, upon the penalty provided by the law, to be duly and severely executed upon them.' And to make sure that these instructions and a hundred others like them were carried out efficiently, Charles ordered that aldermen, deputies and common councilmen meet 'weekly, once, twice, thrice or oftener (as the cause shall require) . . . to consult how the said orders may be duly put in execution.' Today, these measures seem primitive. For Stuart England, they were revolutionary. The idea of sweeping the street in front of your house and then having the rubbish removed that same day by a refuse collector, was almost beyond imagination.

Charles also asked the College of Physicians to send prescriptions for cures, which it did. Nathaniel Hodges recommended the use of oily substances 'to cover over the stomach with a plaister, to guard it against corrosive effluvia.' Hodges believed that both health and disease could be attributed to the 'nitrous spirit' which exhaled from the bowels of the earth. Diffused through the air by the heat of the sun, this 'nitrous spirit' preserved all plant and animal life except when it was corrupted by natural causes such as excess moisture or heat.

◁ London scenes during the Great Plague, 1665; from a contemporary broadsheet by John Dunstall. The total number of deaths, according to the bills of mortality, was 68,596 from an estimated population in London of 460,000. This is almost certainly an underestimate. Plague was a common occurrence throughout Europe, although London had been unusually free of it in the first half of the seventeenth century; an epidemic in Vienna in 1679 caused at least 76,000 deaths. The first symptom was shivering, followed by a rapid rise in temperature, vomitting, headache, intolerance to light, backache, apathy, inflamed eyes, swollen tongue, diarrhoea, buboes in the armpit or groin, haemorrhage of the skin, a tearing pain and death. The process usually took about three days.

Thereafter it degenerated into a 'pestilential miasma.' The need for personal and public cleanliness did not occur to him.

A tour of the west country had been arranged for the summer of 1665, but Charles delayed his departure several times until he was sure that his orders to combat the disease were being effected. Against advice he had visited the dying, among them the Puritan Admiral Lawson. Beyond what he had already done, he now felt there was little his presence could accomplish. He was told his life was more valuable than any pointless sacrifice, so he proceeded to Portsmouth as planned and thence to the Isle of Wight. Nonetheless, he insisted on being kept fully informed, and travelled regularly to Hampton (against advice) for Council Meetings. At Salisbury, he promised what help he could – the Plague had spread there – and at Oxford in October met with the remnants of Parliament to review the situation. It was desperate.

'October 16th. Walked to the Tower. But Lord! How empty the streets are, and melancholy', reported Pepys, 'so many poor sick people in the streets, full of sores . . . They tell me that in Westminster, there is never a physician and but one apothecary left, all being dead.' Evelyn was moved likewise. 'Went through the whole city', he wrote, 'when having occasion to alight in several places about business of money, I was environed with multitudes of poor pestiferous creatures, begging alms. The shops universally shut up; a dreadful prospect.' Others were more allegorical. Thomas Vincent's sermon, 'God's Terrible Voice in the City', expressed the religious hysteria which wracked the common people. 'Now Death rides triumphantly on his pale horse through our streets', he boomed, 'and breaks into every house almost where inhabitants are to be found. Now people fall as thick as leaves in autumn, where they are shaken by a mighty wind.' 'The whole British nation wept', wrote another. Many ran straight into church, but most parish churches were deserted, their priests having died or fled. 'The people made no scruples of desiring such Dissenters as had been a few years before deprived of their livings by virtue of the Act of Parliament called the Act of Uniformity, to preach in the churches. Nor did the church ministers in that case make any difficulty of accepting their assistance. So that many of those whom they called silenced ministers had their mouths opened on this occasion and preached publicly to the people.' Had the Plague continued for another year, it was believed, many religious differences might have been reconciled.

Charles declared himself amazed by his countrymen's lack of resolution. After all, there had been few years in the seventeenth century that had escaped the plague; its visitation was more or less annual and more or less anticipated. Many had forecast an epidemic for the 1660s. Spotted fever had already attacked England in 1658, and pleurisy and pneumonia been prevalent in 1664. The excessively hot weather in the summer of 1665 had not augured well. Nonetheless, few had expected the magnitude of the disaster. In London, one in seven died. Norwich, Southampton, Portsmouth, Sunderland and

Newcastle were ravaged. Oxford, with Charles in residence, remained immune. Those who like Antony Wood professed themselves shocked by the sinfulness of Charles's courtiers were not sure whom to blame for their salvation.

Charles determined that never again would the plague be as destructive. Each city was to provide a place remote from its boundaries where a pest-house could be erected. No household goods coming from a place reportedly infected were to be received in any city, village or hamlet; no unwholesome food was to be exposed for sale; and no more ale-houses licensed than necessary. Collections were to be made for the relief of the poor in infected places. Rubbish was to be removed regularly from ditches, and drains to a place outside the city; the burial of the diseased in already over-crowded church-yards was forbidden.

The idea of Public Health was also stimulated by the statistical observations of Captain John Graunt, a Fellow of the Royal Society. The *Natural and political observations on The Bills of Mortality* asserted that a statistical knowledge of the causes of death was essential in determining the prevalence, fatality and, therefore, cure of disease. Graunt concluded that only seven per cent of Londoners lived till they were seventy; that from 100 births, 36 died before the age of six and only one lived to seventy-six; that only one in a thousand died of gout, and that gouty people were often the longest lived; and, most significantly, that after 1665 the plague was no longer the most common disease. It was rickets.

* * *

London was slow to revive. The Court did not come back until after Christmas. One man, wishing to defumigate his house, put too much gun-powder into the mixture and blew the roof off. 'Of all the common hackney prostitutes of... Hatton Garden and other places... all the impudent, drunken, drabbing bayles and fellows, and many others of the Rouge Route', noted one Boghurst, 'there are but few missing.' 'Pray God continue the Plague's decrease, for that keep the Court away from the place of business', wrote Pepys. 'And so all goes to wrack as to public matters.' 'Henceforth may those in authority act more cautiously', pleaded Dr Hodges, 'and from our misfortune posterity take warning.' Posterity hardly had time to catch its breath, however, before disaster struck again.

Warnings of fire, like warnings of the Plague, had been frequent; every Quaker meeting house, for instance, had resounded for the last decade to prophets of hell-fire – the Quakers were renowned for their accurate prophecies – although their maniacal tone had often mitigated their effectiveness. 'London, go on still in thy presumptuous wickedness', one pamphlet had read in 1658. 'Put the evil day far from thee, and repent not! Do so London. But if the fire make not ashes of the City and bones also, conclude me a liar for ever. Oh London! London! Sinful as Sodom and Gomorrah! The decree is gone out; Repent or burn!'

The Fire of London in 1666, however, started less than cataclysmically. A baker called Farynor who lived in Pudding Lane later testified that he was woken up shortly before two o'clock on Sunday morning, 2 September, by a servant experiencing a choking sensation. Farynor decided that his oven was on fire and quickly emptied the house. He forgot a maidservant who slept on and was suffocated. An onlooker reported that it took over an hour for Farynor's house to burn out, during which all the neighbouring houses were evacuated. Chamberlayne was later to attribute the rapid spread of the fire to the drunkenness of the baker and sloth of his neighbours, 'all filled with drink and all in a dead sleep.' There is little evidence to support this – indeed, the Lord Mayor himself soon arrived on the scene to see what, if anything, was required. London had seen a hundred such fires before and no one seemed alarmed. These were merely a few flames which, as the Lord Mayor put it, 'a woman might piss out.'

But the wind changed and swept a few sparks into neighbouring Thames Street. Here, in its cellars and warehouses, were the stores of tallow, oil, spirits and hemp, brought by coasters to the port of London. On the open wharves hay, timber and coal lay heaped. In no time at all, the area was ablaze. St Magnus the Martyr was gutted in minutes and London Bridge itself attacked.

Pepys, who lived less than a quarter of a mile from Pudding Lane, had no sense of alarm when he arose to a bright and cloudless Sunday morning. Not until his maid brought rumours that some three hundred houses had already been destroyed did he feel obliged to investigate. He walked unhurriedly to the Tower 'and there got up upon one of the high places, Sir J. Robinson's little son going up with me.' It must have been like many another Sunday outing.

But the sight which greeted them at their 'high place' staggered even Pepys. 'I did see the houses at that end of the bridge all on fire, and an infinite great fire on this and the other side the end of the bridge.' Alarmed, he ran down Whitehall to inform the Court, pausing only to visit the waterside for a closer view of the damage. Arriving breathless at the Palace, 'people came about me, and I did give them an account dismayed them all.' Charles remained calm, and ordered Pepys to return and instruct the Lord Mayor to pull down whatever houses were in the path of the fire and thus stay its progress.

Dr Taswell, afterwards Rector of Newington but at the time a boy at Westminster School, provides a first-hand account of what happened next. 'As I was standing upon the steps which lead up to the pulpit in Westminster Abbey', he recalled, 'I perceived some people below me running to and fro in a seeming disquietude and consternation. Immediately almost, a report reached my ears that London was in a conflagration. Without any ceremony, I took leave of the preacher, and . . . myself saw great flames carried up into the air at least three furlongs; these at last pitching upon and uniting themselves to various dry substances, set on fire houses very remote from each other in point of situation. The ignorant and deluded mob . . . vented forth their rage against the Roman Catholics and Frenchmen, imagining these incendiaries (as they thought) had thrown red-hot balls into the houses. A blacksmith in my presence, meeting an innocent Frenchman walking along the street, felled him instantly to the ground with an iron bar . . .'

Four thousand Frenchmen and Papists were in arms, it was reported. Taswell remembered that 'every person, both in the City and the suburbs, having procured some sort of weapon or other, instantly almost collected themselves together to oppose this chimerical army.' Surgeon Thomas Middleton confirmed the worst fears; 'I saw the fire break out from the inside of Laurence Poulteney steeple, where there was no fire near it. These, and such observations, begat in me a persuasion that the Fire was maintained by design.'

Charles ordered in the Guards. Officers were posted 'watching at every quarter for outlandish men', 'because of the general fears and jealousies and rumours that fire balls were thrown into the houses by several of them, to help on and provoke the too furious flames.' Pepys came across the Lord Mayor in Canning Street 'like a man spent, with a handkerchief about his neck.' To the King's message of exhortation he cried, 'Lord! What can I do? I have been pulling down houses; but the fire overtakes us faster than we can do it.' Charles gave instructions that the Earl of Craven should assist the Lord Mayor and his magistrates in whatever ways were deemed necessary, and that was that. After all, it was a Sunday. The ordinary machinery of government did not function on a Sunday. With his brother James, Charles came down from Whitehall in the Royal barge to see the extent of the damage. From the river there seemed to be nothing unusually spectacular. Apart from giving more instructions about pulling down further houses which needed clearing, the King was told that the existing arrangements were adequate.

In fact, they were pitiful. There was, for instance, no efficient fire-fighting equipment. Leathern buckets, ladders, axes and iron fire-hooks were supposed to be kept in each city church, but their provision had been neglected. There were also some curious devices called fire squirts. Each was a hollow cylinder about two feet in length, with side handles and a suction piston at one end. Their maximum capacity was less than a gallon. Together with some half-dozen portable cisterns, they represented the entire fire-fighting appliances of the City of London. And what use could such appliances be against such a 'dreadful fire' which, 'by the permission of Heaven and Hell, broke loose upon this Protestant city from the malicious hearts of barbarous Papists?'

At nightfall, wrote Pepys, 'we saw the fire as only one entire arch of fire from this to the other side of the bridge, and in a bow up the hill for an arch of above a mile long: it made me weep to see it. The Churches, houses, and all on fire, and flaming at once, and a horrid noise the flames made, and the crackling of houses at their ruin. All over the Thames', he continued later, 'with one's face in the wind, you were almost burned with a shower of fire-drops . . . As it grew darker, [the fire] appeared more and more . . . a most horrid, malicious, bloody flame.' Charles watched the flames from his window at the Palace of Whitehall: the fire was still far away.

By Monday morning, it was a different story. Charles awoke to be told that the fire now extended half a mile. He summoned the Privy Council and appointed his brother to take command of the City. Reports of the confusion came in rapidly. The Lord Mayor had failed to pull down sufficient houses to prevent the fire spreading. Evelyn blamed the merchants, 'tenacious and avaricious men' who 'would not permit, because their houses must have been the first.' Charles set up five fire posts, each to be provided with bread, cheese and beer to the value of five pounds. A reward of one shilling was to be given to 'any man who was diligent.' The parish constables were each ordered to provide fire-fighting troops of one hundred men. The militia were called up from Middlesex, Kent, Surrey and Hertfordshire, the seamen summoned from Deptford and Woolwich and told to blow up whatever was thought necessary.

Charles again set off from Whitehall by barge; roads were to be torn up and long trunks of elms hollowed out to carry water from the river. 'The flames', reported an eyewitness, 'march along both sides of the way, with such a roaring noise as was never heard in the city of London.' Charles was everywhere. Not content with having delegated responsibility to his brother, he appeared on the scene to command rescue operations himself. The *London Gazette* – admittedly officially sympathetic – describes how Charles was 'never dispairing or slacking his personal care, wrought so well that day.' The King and James were 'out of their care to stop and prevent the fire, frequently exposing their persons with very small attendants, in all parts of the town, sometimes even to be intermixed with those who laboured in the business.' Charles 'was frequent in consulting all ways of relieving those distressed persons . . . notwithstanding His Majesty's own indefatigable and personal pains to apply all possible remedies to prevent it [the fire], calling upon and helping the people with their guards.'

Already the toll of buildings destroyed was considerable. The Watermen's Hall was gone, and All Hallows-the-More church so shattered by the intense heat that part of its roofless shell later fell down in a gust of wind. The Boar's Head in Eastcheap vanished; the Post Office, with its secret apparatus devised by Charles for tampering with, copying and forging letters, destroyed. The Fire reached Guildhall itself, and opposite, the Royal Exchange. 'Here, if anywhere,' wrote the Rev. Samuel Rolle, 'might a man see the glory of the world in a moment.' But not today. The Royal Exchange, reported Vincent, 'is now invaded with much violence.' 'The yellow smoke of London', wrote another, 'ascendeth up to heaven, like the smoke of a great furnace; a smoke so

Pen and ink drawing by Jan Wyck showing the damage inflicted on old St. Paul's by the Fire. In fact, gunpowder was eventually used to demolish the remains of the central tower; Wren even used a battering ram, manned by thirty labourers, to knock down the walls. The foundation stone for the new Cathedral was not laid until 21 June, 1675; seven hundred and fifty three cartloads of rubbish were carried away, however, before reconstruction could begin. The new Cathedral eventually cost £738,845.5s.2½d, approximately £8½ millions in today's money. It was completed in 1710, and had taken thirty-six years to build. "This Phoenix is arisen," wrote Evelyn. Wren was to be buried in his own cathedral with his famous epitaph *Si monumentum requiris, circumspice*. If you seek a monument, look about you. There were those who thought such an epitaph should have been applied to Charles himself.

great as it darkened the sun at noon-day. If at any times the sun peeped forth, it looked red like blood.' Evelyn reckoned the column of smoke fifty miles in length; it was said it could be seen as far away as Berwick-upon-Tweed on the Scottish border.

'Any money is given for help', wrote one bewildered citizen, 'five, ten, twenty and thirty pounds for a cart, to bear forth into the fields some choice things . . . and some of the countrymen had the conscience to accept of the highest price which the citizens did them offer in their extremity.' 'The riches of London and the substance of the inhabitants thereof', wrote Waterhous, 'were as well devoured by suburban thieves and by the countrymen's extortion for their carts and conveyances as by the Fire; all of which had their respective share in laying a load upon London's broken back.'

Charles rode into the City on horseback with an escort of Guards, carrying one hundred gold guineas in a pouch slung from his shoulder, which he gave personally to the workmen as rewards. Frequently he dismounted and grabbed the nearest spade and bucket. He was bespattered with mud and dirt, his lace costume dripping with sweat, his face blackened; with James, he manhandled 'the water in buckets when they stood up to the ankles in water, and playing the engines for many hours together . . . which, people seeing, fell to work with effort, having so good fellow labourers.' ' 'Tis fit your Lordship should know', a correspondent told Lord Conway, 'that all that is left, both of City and suburbs, is acknowledged, under God, to be wholly due to the King and the Duke of York who, when the citizens had abandoned all further care of the place, and were intent chiefly upon the preservation of their goods, undertook the work themselves. And with incredible magnanimity rode up and down, giving orders for blowing up of houses with gunpowder to make void spaces for the fire to die in, and standing still to see those orders executed, exposing their persons not only to the multitude, but to the very flames themselves . . . sometimes labouring with their own hands to give example to others.'

As dawn came on Tuesday, Cheapside was ablaze and St Paul's itself threatened. Its spire had collapsed as long ago as 1561; Cromwell had stabled his horses inside, and the cathedral now housed a blacksmith's forge as well as numerous traders who erected their stalls between the pillars. Nonetheless, the old cathedral was still considered the emotional and spiritual heart of the City; indeed, the booksellers of Paternoster Row kept their valuables in St Faith's – the crypt of St Paul's – because they believed the cathedral could never be destroyed. Charles ordered the Exchequer be removed to Nonsuch in Surrey; the Queen Mother made arrangements to leave for Hampton; James struggled to persuade the justices of neighbouring counties to send help; Merchant Taylor's Hall burnt; Gog and Magog shrivelled with the rest; the flames, in Dryden's phrase, were 'wading through the streets.' They 'rushed like a torrent down Ludgate Hill', and 'with rage and greediness . . . marched up Fleet Street.' And then, at eight o'clock on Tuesday evening, flames broke out on the Cathedral roof. The timber blazed so fiercely that Taswell was able to read from a pocket edition of Terence by its light. The roof 'melted and runs down as if it had been snow before the sun . . . Now great flakes of stone scale and peel off strangely from the side of the walls.' 'The very stones are crumbled and broken into slivers and slatts', observed another. 'Near the east wall', Taswell relates, 'a human body presented itself to me, parched up, as it were, with the flames; whole as to skin, eager as to flesh, yellow as to colour. This was an old decrepit woman who [had] fled here for safety, imagining the flames would not have reached her there. Her clothes were burnt, and every limb reduced to a coal.'

The fire burnt itself out on the fifth day; there was almost nothing left to destroy. 'I can say but this', wrote a member of Lincoln's Inn, 'that you may see from one end of the City almost to the other. You can compare London (were it not for the rubbish) to nothing more than an open field.' Charles ordered an immediate survey of the destruction. Within the City, 373 acres had been devastated; only 75 had been relatively undamaged. Eighty-seven parish churches had been destroyed, 4,000 streets and 13,200 houses. An area about a mile in length and half a mile wide had been completely laid waste.

No one agreed how many had died. The *London Gazette* said none. The Bills of Mortality claimed six. Evelyn, walking among the ruins, noticed 'the stench that came from some poor creatures' bodies.' The total number of such bodies will never be known, but the physical desolation was shattering. 'In five or six miles traversing about it', recorded Evelyn, 'I did not see one load of timber unconsumed, nor many stones but what were calcined white as snow. The people, who now walked about the ruins, appeared like men in some dismal desert . . . the ground and air, smoke and fiery vapour, continued so intense that my hair was almost singed, and my feet unsufferably surbated . . . I then went towards Islington and Highgate, where one might have seen two hundred thousand people of all ranks and degrees dispersed, and laying along by their heaps of what they could save from the fire deploring their loss.'

Charles despatched tents from the army, ordered that wooden shelters be erected, and set up food distribution centres in Bishopsgate, Tower Hill and Smithfield. 'We have taken care', said his Proclamation, 'to secure the said markets in safety, and prevent all disturbances by the refusal of payment for goods or otherwise.' He rode out to Moorfields to address the homeless, and assured them that the destruction was not the result of any Papist plot. Many of those detained on suspicion he had examined personally. The citizens had nothing to fear. Their King would, by the Grace of God, live and die with them, 'taking a particular care of them all.' Privately, he began to acknowledge that a scapegoat would have to be found. Among the Frenchmen apprehended was twenty-six year old Robert Hubert, who had admitted he had lit a fire-ball on the end of a long pole and pushed it through a window of a house in Pudding Lane. Farynor, although convinced that his house had been maliciously fired, denied there was such a window. Hubert declared that his only reward had been a pistole, with the promise of five more should he successfully accomplish his task, whatever that was. He was asked to identify the place where he had started the fire – by now this would have been almost impossible. But, by some extraordinary chance, Hubert led his captors to the exact spot. The Lord Chief Justice told Charles that Hubert's story was so muddled not a word of it was believable. Clarendon agreed. 'Neither the judges nor any present at the trial did believe him guilty', Clarendon wrote later, 'but he was a poor distracted wretch, weary of his life and chose to part with it in this way.' Hubert was found guilty and hanged at Tyburn.

Unfortunately, one scapegoat was not enough for an angry populace. 'The plot was not only for London', it was believed, 'but for the destruction of the principal cities and towns in England.' Frenchmen, Dutchmen and Catholics were arbitrarily arrested and imprisoned by local magistrates. 'Since the Fire', wrote a merchant, 'both seamen and landsmen are rampant and outrageous for revenge upon the enemy.' The question remained; who exactly *was* the enemy? 'The generation of Fanatic vipers' for instance, Presbyterians who, since the fire, 'look a little starched, and will have it the judgment of the Fire of London is for the sins of others not so holy as themselves?' The Duke of York was a Papist. Perhaps he was to blame. Some even blamed Charles; after all, he too was a Papist – at heart.

Sir Richard Browne then produced for a committee of the Commons, set up by Charles to investigate the origins of the Fire, 'some desperate daggers, fit for massacres', two hundred of which he said had been found among the rubble. A host of gossipmongers testified they had heard so and so say that so and so had heard that London would be destroyed between May and October. 'It was a hard matter to forbear smiling at their evidence', remembered Clarendon. Nonetheless, the committee's report was presented to Parliament the following January. It consisted of a selection of the evidence, but offered no conclusions. The Council remained unconvinced. 'Not withstanding that many examinations have been taken', it decided, 'yet nothing hath yet been found to argue it to have been other than the hand of God upon us, a great wind and the season so very dry.' Even so, the City's Monument to the Fire eventually carried an inscription proclaiming that the fire was 'begun and carried on by the treachery and malice of the Popish faction.'

For Charles, the most important task was reconstruction. The Monument, erected to commemorate the Fire, declares boldly: 'London rises again, whether with greater speed or greater magnificence is doubtful, three short years complete that which was considered the work of an age.' Oldmixon's *History of London* makes a similar boast. 'To the amazement of all Europe', it writes, 'London was, in four years' time, rebuilt with so much beauty and magnificence that they who saw it in both states, before and after the Fire, could not reflect on it without wondering where the wealth could be found to bear so vast a loss.' Other evidence suggests that it was well over a decade before many of the more substantial buildings were rebuilt. By 1670 the church-wardens of St Bartholomew Exchange still could not list the names of their parish householders. Yet no effort had been spared to draw up plans for a new model city. Only six days after the Fire was out, Christopher Wren – Deputy Surveyor of His Majesty's Works – submitted a plan to Charles. Evelyn also drew up a plan but was piqued by the speed with which Wren had delivered. 'Dr Wren got a start on me', he complained, 'but both of us did coincide so frequently that His Majesty was not displeased.'

The final destruction had been so vast that it was suggested the capital be temporarily removed elsewhere and York was recommended. Sprat recalls it was the intention of all good men to construct 'a new city . . . on the most advantageous seat of all Europe for trade and command', and although the

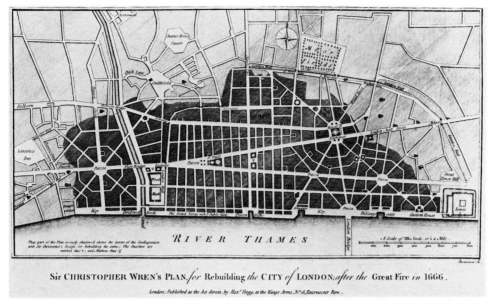

Sir CHRISTOPHER WREN's PLAN, for Rebuilding the CITY of LONDON; after the Great Fire in 1666.

London; Published as the Act directs, by Alex.ʳ Hogg, at the Kings Arms, N.º 16, Paternoster Row.

Sir Christopher Wren's plan for Rebuilding the City of London after the Great Fire of 1666. The darkly shaded area shows the "extent of the conflagration." For the 52 churches to be rebuilt, Wren was to be paid £100 a year; for St. Paul's Cathedral he received £200 a year. The embankments of the Thames were to be raised three feet to prevent flooding, and a riverside walkway, forty feet wide, constructed to show off New London. The approach road to Ludgate was to be ninety feet wide, thus allowing a proper view of the triumphal arch to be erected in commemoration of Charles. The Fleet ditch, or sewer, was to be transformed into a canal after the Dutch example. Wren was in Oxford during the Fire, but presented the King and Council with his plan only six days after the Fire had died down. But, as Sir Nathaniel Hobart, Master in Chancery, shrewdly observed: "The rebuilding of the City will not be so difficult as the satisfying of all interests." Wren's ground plan was never realised, not one jot of it.

City informed Charles they had 'no common stock, nor revenue, nor any capacity to raise within itself anything considerable towards so vast an expense', this reluctance was not shared by the people of London. 'The citizens, instead of complaining', reported Henry Oldenburg, 'discourse almost of nothing but of a survey for rebuilding the City with bricks and large streets.' Charles said he wanted to make London 'appear to the world as purged with fire (in how lamentable a manner so ever) to a wonderful beauty and comeliness, than consumed by it.' A proclamation was issued prohibiting the reconstruction of houses until and unless they conformed with the general building regulations contained in the proclamation. 'Noisesome trades' were to be removed to a special quarter of the City, lanes and alleys tolerated only where necessary.

England too wanted a resplendent capital city. Lyme Regis forwarded £100 for its restoration; Marlborough in Wiltshire sent £50. The Countess of Devonshire contributed £40, and all church collections made on 10 October were sent to the fund. In total, however, these charitable donations were insufficient to cope with the estimated £7,370,000 needed for rebuilding, in spite of a contribution from Cousin Louis, and no allowance was made for compensating those whose entire livelihoods had vanished, literally overnight. One resident wrote: 'Some reckon roundly, and say London is ruined, England is ruined.'

Wren's plans for London were spectacular. In place of Ludgate was to be a triumphal arch in honour of Charles, the founder of New London. The road leading from there to the City was to be ninety feet wide, with Finsbury Circus a huge piazza. A quay with a public walkway some forty feet broad was to be constructed along the northern bank of the Thames, with the Royal Exchange appearing like a Roman Forum set in a garden. Around were to be the other main offices of State – the Excise, the Post Office, the Mint and a new Insurance Office. Fleet Ditch was to become an elegant canal. Charles was overjoyed and the plan accepted in principle by the Council on 18 October 1666.

Unfortunately, Wren's plan, although encouraged by Charles, was never realized except for the elegant churches. It was 'unhappily defeated by Faction'; any attempt to develop Wren's scheme, it was thought, would have involved the City in ruinous delays and the consequent loss of trade. Wren's title of 'Principal Architect for rebuilding the Whole City', hides the fact that his plan was not approved by Parliament. Charles made repeated attempts to block the piecemeal, entrepreneurial building schemes which threatened to reduce London to the same mess as it had been before. He insisted, for instance, that many of the trading halls be erected alongside the river, not only for convenience and safety but to improve the river frontage; he discouraged plans for new open markets and urged that sufficient covered market spaces be provided within the City; at meetings of the Privy Council he demanded to see all that the speculators proposed. He fought for a better City, but in the end, he failed.

To add to the troubles, the winter of 1666 was exceedingly cold. At New Year, the Thames was packed with ice. Rents had quadrupled since the devastation and the price of coal rocketed. 'The major part of the houses built upon the ruins of London', wrote one irate citizen, 'are let to alehouse keepers and victuallers, to entertain workmen employed about the City.' Many of the new houses proved so expensive to build that ordinary citizens could no longer afford them. Wren noted later that 'the great numbers of the rebuilt houses of London . . . are uninhabited.' Only Charles, it seems, was prepared to take a wider view. He drove through Parliament an Act 'for the better paving and cleansing of streets and sewers in and about the City of London.' He appointed a Commissioner for sewers whose responsibility was to lay out and maintain all sewers and drains, and to charge their cost on all householders in proportion to the benefits derived. He proposed the establishment of a regular body for fighting fires, although the resulting Act merely provided for a larger store of buckets, ladders and squirts. Meanwhile, the ruined churches became hideouts for thieves and beggars, and their churchyards used by City housewives to hang out dirty washing. And, as a Dutch visitor remarked, 'it will be a long time before the people of London forget their wild rage against foreigners.'

1666 was, as Dryden described it, Annus Mirabilis. The nation's self-esteem had been severely dented, and with the Customs House destroyed, it was even more difficult to collect the Excise. In Scotland, there was insurrection. France captured Antigua, an island which the English no longer had troops or supplies to defend. Whether interpreted as the vengeance of God, or merely the work of the French, the Plague and the Fire convinced the citizens of London these were troubled times. Suspicions against the French and, consequently, all Papists, festered. Another, more dangerous feeling revived. Men began to 'reflect upon Oliver, what brave things he did, and made all the neighbour princes fear him.'

*   *   *

And then, in June 1667, fifty-one men-of-war, three frigates, six armed yachts, four fire-ships and a hundred galliotts of the Dutch fleet, sailed into the King's Channel, one of the main approaches to the Thames, and began burning and looting. A force of artillery over-ran Canvey Island, killing sheep for provisions, while the Kent militia was called out to defend Sheerness Fort being attacked by the Dutch. The Dutch flag was hoisted over the fort and the English flag burnt for all to see as the artillery seized quantities of sawn timber, masts, spars, iron, brass, barrels of gunpowder, resin and tar. The Dutch, it seemed, were invading England.

Panic struck the Thames estuary. Men were told to take command of boats only to discover that these boats no longer existed. Repeated attempts were made to heave a chain, previously laid across the river for protection against such an invasion, into position, but such was its weight that it kept sinking into the mud. 'I found scarce twelve of eight hundred men which were then in the King's pay, in His Majesty's yards', wrote Albemarle (Monck). 'And these so distracted with fear, that I could have little or no service from them. I had heard of thirty boats, which were provided by the directions of His Royal Highness; but they were all, except five or six, taken away, where I know not.'

The Dutch then plundered the Isle of Sheppey, destroying the embankments of the Thames to allow flooding. They snapped the secret chain by sailing straight through it, captured the frigate *Unity*, whose crew deserted as the first shot was fired, and sank the other 'guard ship', *Charles V*. 'The river was full of moving craft and burned wreckage', reported one, 'the roar of guns was almost continuous; the shrieks of the wounded could be heard even above the noise of battle, the clangour of trumpets, the roll of drums, and the cheers of the Dutch as success after success was won; and above all hung a pall of smoke, illumined only, as night closed in, by the gleam of flames on all sides and the flashes of guns and muskets.'

Next to be seized was the flagship, *Royal Charles*, 'with a boat of nine men who found not a man on board her.' The whole business was absurd. The Dutch had only to open fire and the English fled. Albemarle ordered that the *Royal Oak*, *Royal James* and *Royal London* be scuppered to prevent the Dutch towing them away. Guns were taken out of the men-of-war and placed along the banks of the Medway to fire at the Dutch as they passed up river. At least, that was the intention, but, as Albemarle noted later in his report, 'I stayed all night on the place by the men. And having no money to pay them, all I could do or say was little enough for their encouragement.'

The Dutch fire-ships then set the remainder of the Fleet ablaze. 'The destruction of these ... stately and glorious ships of ours', remembered Edward Gregory, Clerk of the Check at Chatham, 'was the most dismal spectacle my eyes ever beheld. And it certainly made the heart of every true Englishman bleed.' The racket was deafening. Only one man, 'who stood and burnt in one of our ships at Chatham', deserved praise. Captain Archibald Douglas, who had strenuously defended the *Royal Oak*, earned immortality through the pen of Marvell:

> And on the flaming planks he rests his head,
> As one who hugs himself in a warm bed.
> The ship burns down and with his relics sinks,
> And the sad stream beneath his ashes drinks.

Albemarle ordered all the surviving ships to be sunk where they lay at anchor. Sixteen men-of-war were cut loose; some drifted away and grounded on the mud flats. The Dutch decided to risk their luck no further and sailed away, taking the *Royal Charles* in tow and firing their cannon as they went in celebration.

The Dutch 'invasion' had a long and complex history. England had been intermittently at war with Holland for almost fifty years; only the English Civil War, the problems of Commonwealth rule, and the euphoria following Charles's restoration had interrupted a continuing and mutual hostility between the countries. A brief but bitter two-year struggle during Oliver Cromwell's time in 1652 had ended in stalemate. Sir William Monson, an English vice-admiral during the reign of Charles I, had written that 'our eyes and tears make it clearly appear that they [the Dutch] and their cunning courses are the immediate causes of the poverty that daily assails our glorious kingdom.' Holland, another writer had concluded, was 'the great bog of Europe.' As for its inhabitants, they were 'generally boorish ... with-out doubt very ancient, for they were bred before manners were in fashion. You may sooner convert a Jew than make an ordinary Dutchman yield to arguments that cross him. They are the pismires of the world.' 'A Dutch man is a lusty, fat, two-legged cheese-worm; a creature that is addicted to eating butter, drinking fat drink and sliding, that all the world knows him for a slippery fellow. An Hollander is not an High-lander, but a low-lander; for he loves to be down in the dirt, and Boar-like to wallow therein.' Another pamphlet, issued frequently during the early years of Charles's reign, was entitled *A Dutchman's Pedigree or A Relation showing how they were first bred and descended from a horse-turd, which was enclosed in a Butter-Box.* 'Out of which dung', concluded the writer, 'within nine days space sprung forth men, women and children. The offspring whereof are yet alive to this day and now commonly known by the name of Dutchmen.'

The reason for this jealousy was twofold. First, it seemed that wherever England was struggling to develop her trading empire, the Dutch had got there first. Gothenburg in Sweden was planned and laid out by Dutch engineers; in Norway, then part of the Danish Kingdom, the copper mines belonged 'in part to the estates and treasurer of the King of Denmark, while the rest was owned by two merchants of Amsterdam.' And, of course, the Hollanders built boats; the word 'yacht' is Dutch. One balladeer noted pessimistically:

> The Dutchman hath a thirsty soul,
> Our cellars are subject to his call . . .
> To the new world in the moon away let us go,
> For if the Dutch Colony get thither first,
> 'Tis a thousand to one but they'll drain that too.

Dutchmen also made the first authenticated discovery of Australia. Willem Janszoon, sailing south from New Guinea, reached the west coast of Queensland and christened it 'New Holland'. Heavily laden Dutch fleets rounded the Cape of Good Hope to India several times a year; on the West African coast, the Dutch prospered; they had a settlement on the Hudson in the middle of the English colonies. In the rich spice islands, which the Dutch East India Company wished to keep as its exclusive preserve, the Dutch had seized the island of Amboyna from the Portuguese. Later, the English also set up a trading post on the island, and before long the Dutch were accusing the English of conspiring with the natives against them. The suspect Englishmen were tortured, confessions extracted and nine of them executed. In England, the affair was known as the Massacre of Amboyna.

Since the beginning of Charles's reign, moreover, the Dutchman seemed to be taking over England. He had shown the Englishman how to reclaim his fenlands; Dutch methods of crop rotation, as well as 'the long-legged, short-horned Cow of the Dutch breed', had been adopted wholesale. The Friesian cow, still the best breed for milking, had arrived as did a vast porcelain industry. A German visitor to Bristol in the late eighteenth century observed 'small wooden houses . . . These are called Dutch houses, having been imported ready made and having formed at one time an important article of

Illustrations from 'The Dutch Boar dissected; or a description of HOGG-LAND: a contemporary broadsheet'. "A Dutchman is a lusty, fat, two-legged cheese-worm; a creature that is so addicted to eating butter, drinking fat drink and sliding . . .

Their quagmire isle
('twould make one smile),
In form lies like a custard:
A land of bogs
To breed up hogs
Good pork with English Mustard".

Yet Charles's nephew became ruler of the States-General (Holland) and eventually King of England.

traffic between this country and Holland.' The Dutch had infiltrated English manufacture; a shortage of skilled workers in the cloth finishing processes had compelled English merchants to have their materials dyed and made ready for market – in Holland. Screws and lapped dovetail joints, a method of furniture construction invented by Dutch craftsmen, was replacing the Birmingham nail. The Dutch cabriole leg, later to be featured in the work of Chippendale and Sheraton, began its popularity at this time. Even gardening fell under Dutch influence; high, thick, clipped yew hedges and box trees fashioned into

102

fantastic shapes – heraldic beasts, ships and religious tableaux – were the epitome of Restoration elegance. They were Dutch in inspiration.

In science, the Dutch again excelled, while in the arts they were without equal. Rembrandt, van Mieris, Jan Steen, all came from Leyden; Cuyp from Dordrecht; van Goyen and Paul Potter from The Hague. The influence of Dutch architecture was no less profound; the style known as Georgian Vernacular, usually thought of as typically English, is Dutch in origin. The sash windows, the combination of broad surfaces of brick with stone quoins, were Dutch ideas. And when London had burned down in 1666, the old insanitary and inflammable plaster-and-lath houses were being replaced by dwellings made of brick. And who, according to Wren, were masters of brick building? The Dutch.

Jealousy of the Dutch had a deeper cause than envy of commercial or artistic success, however. There was the growing awareness in England of a political rival on the continent of Europe whose style embodied much that England and Englishmen coveted. 'Scarce any subject occurs more frequent in the discourses of ingenious men', wrote William Aglionby, 'than that of the marvellous progress of this little state.'

The United Provinces of the Netherlands had come together in January 1579 to protect their territory and religion against the absolutism of Philip II of Spain to whom, by treaty, they belonged. In effect, these provinces were a federation of sovereign republics each of whom had its own 'States' or assembly elected from the burgher aristocracy of the towns and the landed nobility. Representatives were sent to a central assembly called the 'States-General' which administered trade and supervised military and foreign policy. Eighty years of bloody military struggle had ensued, before Spain finally acknowledged their secession. Then, taking advantage of the political chaos crippling much of Europe, the United Provinces (or Holland) had grown strong and Dutch influence had prospered.

The Dutch state was international in a way that England wished to be but was not. When he came to sell off Calais, for instance, Charles admitted that, despite proclaimed ambitions to the contrary and notwithstanding his own peripatetic youth, England with Scotland was an offshore island. Holland, on the other hand, was the intellectual centre of Europe. In the 'city of Amsterdam, whose enjoyment of this freedom has made it great, and admired by the whole world; in this flourishing state, the city without a peer, men of every race and sect live in the greatest harmony . . .' The university towns were cosmopolitan to an extent unthinkable in Stuart England; in Leyden, one third of the students were English. The Republic enticed the most original 'scientists' of the age, among them Descartes, Spinoza and Locke. Was there, asked Descartes, a truth which did not admit of doubt? Yes, only one. The function of the mind itself proved the mind exists. For the rest, only the self-evident truths of mathematics offer any degree of philosophical consolation.

103

Spinoza deflected this empirical method toward a consideration of the State. If honesty is to be valued above servility, and sovereigns are to govern without being subject to mob rule, then it is necessary to allow 'freedom of judgement' and 'so to govern men that they can express different and conflicting opinions without ceasing to live in harmony.'

No seventeenth century society provided so thoroughly for its poor, and hospitals and schools were founded and maintained on a scale that made England's occasional Royal or merchant endowment look pitiful. Holland was also the first society in Europe that could reasonably be described as a meritocracy. A communistic spirit prevailed: de Witt, the Dutch Chief Minister at the beginning of Charles's reign, eschewed all forms of luxury. He preferred to walk about his business rather than take a carriage. When the office of Licenser to the Press was later forced upon Charles, the presses of

PLATE I

Top Left , Bottom

Charles as a young man, probably aged about 14, in a miniature by David des Granges. Beautiful, knowing, wise, yet already cunning. "Odd's fish, I am an ugly fellow" can never have been as true as Charles apparently believed, and said. Unlike President John F. Kennedy, whom Charles the King much resembles, Charles the man was rarely concerned with personal vanity. Nonetheless, both men knew the value of public show; the paraphernalia of a Royal procession was essential for the promulgation of authority.

Top Right

Miniature of Charles, by an unidentified artist. "His face is rather grave than severe, which is very much softened whensoever he speaks. His complexion is somewhat dark, but much enlightened by his eyes... he is the most knowing of Princes." Perhaps Charles also remembered the old Scottish saying, taught him by the Covenanters: "When one is inclined to kiss his neighbour's wife, it is proper to shut all doors and windows."

PLATE II

Top

Van Dyck's painting of Charles, James and Mary, who became Princess of Orange.

> "Fair was the dawn; and but e'en now the skies
> Showed like to cream, inspired with trawberries:
> But on a sudden, all was changed and gone
> That smiled in that first sweet complexion."

Bottom

A view of Plymouth Sound by G. van Edema. Edward Hyde, the Earl of Clarendon, had said: "for all that I have yet seen, give me old England." In 1675, two hundred ribbon-loom weavers of London rioted for better wages; there were weavers' riots in Colchester in 1676 and in Trowbridge in 1677; there were dockyard strikes in 1665, 1666 and 1667. The Restoration Land Settlement "made the enemies of the constitution masters, in effect, of the booty of three nations"; the Army, including garrison troops, never exceeded 7,000 men. Education, on the other hand, would divert "those whom nature or fortune had determined to the plough..."

PLATE I

PLATE II

PLATE III

PLATE IV

Leyden and Utrecht printed for the opposition, and boats sailing from London to Rotterdam carried English books and newspapers to Europe.

Worst of all was that Dutch banking families such as the van Neck brothers were financing English private business and government on a considerable scale. Joshua van Neck became a baronet; his son, who personally underwrote a government loan of over a million pounds, joined the peerage as Lord Huntingfield. The Bank of England was originally floated with Dutch capital; the London Stock Exchange was a copy of the Amsterdam Bourse. Even the 'excise', the convenient form of indirect tax that was to be in part Charles's financial salvation, was copied from Holland, the word itself being a corruption of the Dutch 'accijns'. 'By God', wrote Pepys, 'I think the Devil shits Dutchmen.'

Charles had always had mixed feelings about the Dutch. It was to Holland he had gone for support soon after the beginning of his exile. At first, he had been well treated; after all, his sister Mary was married to the Stadholder (ruler of the 'States-General') William II of Orange, and Charles doted on his sister. But a stipulation of the 1654 Treaty of Westminster concluded between the Dutch and Cromwell had been that Charles should be denied refuge in The Hague. Six years of wandering throughout Europe had given Charles cause to remember his sudden dismissal. And when, in March 1660, he crossed into Holland en route for England, on this occasion to be welcomed as a conquering hero, he did not forget. The Dutch treated him with utmost

PLATE III

Portrait of the young Louis XIV by Pierre Mignard. Of the French court, a contemporary wrote: "It was possible to tell the women from the men only when it was time to go to bed."

PLATE IV

Top

Anthony Ashley Cooper, 1621–83, the first Earl of Shaftesbury. Educated at Exeter College, Oxford and Lincoln's Inn. For all his malevolence, one of the most astute politicians of his time. Orphaned at ten, a royal ward, he was returned (under age) to both the Short and Long Parliaments of 1640. Fought against Charles I, an ally of Cromwell, a correspondent of Monck. Charles II appointed him to the Privy Council in 1661 ... Or was he, as Dryden reckoned:

"In friendship false, implacable in hate,
Resolved to ruin or to rule to State?"

Bottom

Eleanor Gwyn (or is it the Duchess of Portsmouth?) from the factory of Lely. One of Miss Gwyn's many lovers wrote of her (or was it Jane Roberts?); "It was hard to find one with limbs more brawny, conscience more supple, or principles more loose; all these, extreme qualifications for a lady of pleasure." In the popular imagination, as in the portraits, Charles's ladies were more or less interchangeable.

Syndics of the Cloth Makers of Amsterdam (1662) by Rembrandt. Andrew Marvell thought Holland "the indigested vomit of the sea . . .

> Among the blind, the one-eyed blinkard reigns,
> So rules among the drowned, he that drains".

"The Interest of Holland", by a wealthy Leyden clothier, Pieter de la Court, gives a different view. "Toleration and freedom of religion is not only exceedingly beneficial for our country in general, but particularly for the reformed religion, which may and ought to depend on its own evidence and veracity". Charles had a copy of this pamphlet.

deference and feasted him sumptuously, but he was not impressed. He acknowledged that, since commercial and maritime rivalry dominated Anglo-Dutch relationships, a peaceful accommodation would be necessary if conflict was to be avoided; within months of Charles's Restoration, a delegation from Holland was received in London. Although two years of hard bargaining followed, the resulting treaty solved little. From his ambassador in The Hague, Charles learned that the Dutch had also concluded a treaty of mutual commercial and military aid with England's other trading rival, France. Charles was not surprised; despite his admiration for and envy of the many Dutch achievements, he remained sceptical of the Hollanders.

Recognizing the strength of popular anti-Dutch feeling, Charles quietly encouraged English trade in defiance of the Dutch. Already, in December 1660, soon after his first meeting with the Dutch ambassadors, Charles had granted a charter to a company called 'The Royal Adventurers into Africa'. Members of the Royal family, including brother James and cousin Rupert, as well as favourites at Court such as Monck, were shareholders. Charles himself promised to subscribe £6,000, though the money was never paid. The company wished to develop trade with the east coast of Africa; its immediate purpose was to annoy the Dutch who had a monopoly there. Robert Holmes, a Civil War veteran and close friend of Charles, was sent by the King to capture and loot whatever Dutch possessions he could find along the coast of Gambia, a duty which Holmes carried out with brutality. Captain Richard Nicolls was sent by Charles to achieve similar results in the Dutch colony of New Netherlands on the east coast of America. Nicolls's expedition was given a certain legality when Charles granted James, as Duke of York, lands in America which included the area of Dutch settlement – 'by chance', Charles said. Nicolls forced the Dutch to surrender New Amsterdam, capital of New Netherlands, renaming it New York in honour of James. Charles could play 'the Dutch game', as he called it, as well as any other. 'What we want', grumbled Monck, 'is more of the trade the Dutch now have.'

Charles urged English businessmen to study the Dutch example, and coaxed life into a range of new minor skills such as printing, textile-dyeing, paper making, sugar refining, glass blowing and linen bleaching, all to combat the Dutch. Ship-building, Charles demanded, should be restored to its former English pre-eminence. The 'new draperies' of East Anglia and the serge industry of Devon were pressed into action against the textile industries of Leyden. The Dutch traded methodically, Charles said. They taught accounting and book-keeping. They encouraged banks and legal methods of settling disputes and debts. Businessmen played an important part in the councils of the nation, believing that national prosperity was best served by the collective endeavours of the merchant class. Dominance at sea was essential, and learned treatises were written to show that control over what were described as 'The British Seas' had existed since the time of King Alfred. English kings had always maintained that foreign vessels should lower their sails when ordered to do so by an admiral or lieutenant of the Royal Navy, although in Charles's reign the practice had become traditional with no justification in law. That the Dutch refused to lower their sails, however, was a clear example of perfidy. Had not James I issued a proclamation in 1609 declaring all the fisheries along the English coasts to be Royal preserves? And had not the Dutch ignored this proclamation? Had they forgotten how often English soldiers had assisted their struggles for independence against the French and Spanish?

> The Dutchman at first
> When at the worst
> The English did relieve them
> They now for thanks,
> Have played base pranks
> With Englishmen to grieve them.

Whatever the strength of popular feeling, and however ambivalent his own attitude, Charles was in a difficult position. While he received with sympathy petitions sent to the Commons by City merchants complaining of Dutch obstructions to their trade, for which they were now claiming compensation, Charles feared the financial strain that open war would bring. The City was insistent; the Dutch, they said, had proclaimed themselves 'Lords of the Southern Seas' and behaved with unspeakable arrogance. The Commons asked Charles to 'make some speedy and effective measure to redress the wrongs, dishonours and indignities done to His Majesty by the subjects of the United Provinces.' Charles was reluctant; like the Dutch rulers, he knew that prosperity came through peace. Clarendon agreed: 'The war is not so necessary', he wrote, 'as they [the merchants] had thought it to be.' In an attempt to mollify the Dutch, Charles had sent a trusted friend, Sir George Downing, as ambassador to The Hague. Not everyone shared the King's confidence; 'Downing', said Pepys, 'is a perfidious rogue.' In fact, Charles's hopes had come to naught. The Dutch hated Downing; de Witt had regarded him as an agent provocateur and a major cause of the worsening Anglo-Dutch relations. In December 1664, the Dutch had ordered twenty-four new men-of-war as reinforcements for their Fleet. In England, despite Charles, the Commons had voted two and a half million pounds to be spent on preparations for hostilities. 'Never was anything so unanimously applauded', one pamphleteer had written, 'by all men of all persuasion and interests as a Dutch war.' As it happened, the money had been granted just in time; war was declared in January 1665.

*　*　*

The Dutch had been well prepared. Their ships were 'very great, and well mann'd and gunn'd, full of great animositie and earnestness to fight.' The Dutch authorities fed their seamen well, paid them regularly and looked after their dependants. The lack of comparable employment for the poor on land made it unnecessary for the Dutch, unlike the English, to press men into naval service; many foreigners, including Englishmen, volunteered for service in the Dutch navy. It comprised a force of some 100 vessels, mounting 4,800 guns, with crews totalling 21,000 men. By comparison, the English fleet was, as Pepys noted, 'but a scarecrow to the world. God knows! the King is not able to set out five ships at this present without great difficulty, we neither have money, credit, nor stores.'

In 1660, the naval debt had stood at £1,284,452, of which arrears in pay amounted to £500,000. Pepys, an employee of the Navy, recorded in his diary: 'did business, though not much, at the office, because of the horrible crowd and lamentable moan of the poor seamen that lie starving in the streets for lack of money.' Charles had concerned himself with naval matters soon after his

Restoration; as Burnet observed of Charles, 'he understood navigation well; above all, he knew the architecture of ships so perfectly that in that respect he was exactly rather more than became a Prince.' Charles had begun by reorganizing Naval administration which, although extensive, had over-reached itself during Cromwell's European ambitions; the debts would soon be paid off, Charles thought, and the English Navy strong again. He revived the office of Lord High Admiral, designating his brother James, and restored the old Navy Board; among those he appointed, known as the 'Principal Officers of His Majesty's Navy', was Pepys, now Clerk of the Acts and Secretary to the Board, with responsibility for keeping official records. (Pepys knew nothing of naval administration and little of sea and ships when appointed. He had obtained the job through his cousin, the Earl of Sandwich.) In addition, three commissioners were elected. These were Lord Berkeley, Sir William Penn and Peter Pett, the last being resident commissioner at Chatham Dockyard, the most important naval base in England and only a few miles from London. Its river, the Medway, was narrow and eminently suitable for the launching and repairing of His Majesty's ships, which His Majesty visited frequently. Chatham was also near the wooded area of Kent and Sussex, thus minimizing the transportation of those huge tree trunks needed for ship-building. Any war with the Dutch, it was argued, would emphasize Chatham's strategic advantages. It was well placed to defend London, and sufficiently near the North Sea to strike quickly at any Dutch patrol. Pett, with his warden-ship of Chatham, was a key man in the protection of England.

Charles was well pleased with his man. In 1661, he had asked Pett to build a new Royal yacht, which Charles later sailed down the Thames with much display and pleasure, declaring it was a very fine boat indeed. With the gratification of his Royal master, whose love of sailing was equalled only by his love of horse-racing and ladies, Pett must have felt secure at Chatham, just as Charles must have felt secure with Pett.

All was not as it seemed. John Hollond, having spent many years in previous naval administrations, presented James as Lord High Admiral with a discourse entitled *The Navy Ript and Ransackt: or a Brief Discovery of some few (of the many) Rents and Leaks of the Navy.* In it, Hollond listed the evils arising from the non-payment of wages; unpaid creditors had gone bankrupt and been thrown into prison, thereby causing suffering to their families; the embezzlement of stores such as timber and rope, often taken by the dockyard-men in lieu of wages; the unreliable supply of victuals, only half of which ever reached their proper destination.

Pett also began to insist that he could not obtain what was needed to do his job properly. He estimated he would require a thousand more dockyardmen to effect the programme of repairing and fitting out ships now being ordered by Parliament and Charles. Writing to Pepys, he complained that, of the oars delivered recently to the yard, 'not one of eight is worth anything.' The pressed men sent to Chatham to crew the ships were no better, 'pitiful creatures who are fit for nothing but to fill the ships full of vermin.' They were 'in no way fit for service, being made up of all sorts of country trades, and such a ragged crew as never was seen.'

It is extraordinary, therefore, that the first major engagement between the Dutch and the English on 3 June 1665, in Southwold Bay off Lowestoft, had resulted in a Dutch defeat; 'a greater victory never known in the world', commented Pepys. The Dutch commander, Van Obdam, had been blown up with his flagship, and the rest of the Dutch fleet retreated in disarray. Jan Evertsen, Obdam's second-in-command, had been thrown into a canal upon his return and a commission of inquiry set up at The Hague to investigate the defeat. A number of officers were found guilty of neglecting their duty and of cowardice. Some were shot, others publicly degraded. But, within two months, the Dutch fleet had been ready to do battle again under Admiral de Ruyter, newly returned from the West Indies.

Meanwhile, the Earl of Sandwich, now one of James's lieutenant-admirals, had decided to teach the Dutch a lesson by capturing their merchant fleets from the Mediterranean and Indies. Their cargoes, he thought, would be of immense value, both financial and political. Charles had favoured the idea but, unfortunately, both fleets had escaped and taken refuge in the harbour of Bergen. The King of Denmark and Norway, himself at odds with the Dutch, promised, in consideration of half the booty, to remain inactive while the English looted the treasure now sheltering in his harbour. Unfortunately again, the local Danish commander was not informed of the King's promise, and, when the English fleet attacked, he opened fire and drove them off. Charles was furious; Parliament declared war on the Danes who, as a result, joined forces with the Dutch.

Louis XIV, mindful of his earlier treaties to aid the Dutch in the event of war, had sent cousin Charles an 'ambassador extraordinaire' to avert the crisis. The Plague had kept the King's entourage constantly on the move, from Whitehall to Hampton Court, from Salisbury to Oxford, with the French emissaries now in tow to whom Charles maintained that, since the Dutch had been the aggressors, there was no obstacle to a new Anglo-French alliance. By the end of the summer, Louis's patience had been exhausted. He had informed the peripatetic monarch that unless Charles accepted French terms of mediation, Louis would have no choice but to declare war himself. Bluff had been answered with counter-bluff. Charles signed a treaty with France's enemy, Spain, although, as Spain was unlikely to be of military assistance to England, the document had been little more than a temporary commercial arrangement. The bluff had failed. In January 1666, France had declared war on England. 'The subject is too vexatious to discourse upon any more', noted one politician. 'I am glad this farce is at an end.'

The confused policy which had guided the war thus far, was in part a result of the mutual suspicions between King and Parliament. The Commons had accused Charles of being lazy and spendthrift; he had accused them of interfering. Certainly, Charles's finances were in chaos, and his war ministry, such as it was, in organizational disarray. Numbers of Cavaliers, having received no compensation for their losses during the Civil War (as had been promised), felt their loyalty had not been appreciated. When the call had come from Charles for unity and action, many had been unwilling to give either, in spite of a common hatred for the Dutch. It was not surprising, consequently, that the 'Four Days Battle' off Ostend had resulted in one of the bloodiest defeats ever suffered by an English fleet. Evelyn had visited the broken Navy at Sheerness two days later. 'Here I beheld that sad spectacle, namely more than half that gallant bulwark of the Kingdom miserably shattered, hardly a vessel intire, but appearing rather so many wracks and hulls, so cruelly had the Dutch mangled us.' Incredibly, under Charles's leadership and insistence, the English had struck back without delay. Charles himself had visited the dockyards, ordering the men to go back and fight. One expedition under Sir Robert Holmes had sailed into the Vlie Channel, set fire to 150 merchantmen, and during a skirmish on the island of Terschelling, destroyed many houses and stores. When the Fire of London began four weeks later, the Dutch regarded it as divine retribution for this English plundering.

Conditions in the English Navy had not improved, however, and Pepys had noted sadly: 'Want of money in the Navy puts everything out of order; men grow mutinous.' Pett recorded the 'sad conditions' at Chatham caused by 'the multitude of sick and wounded sent from the fleet' who were 'obliged to sell their rags to keep themselves from starving.' Violence against naval conscription was frequent; a mob of forty seamen armed with pistols and swords had attacked buildings in Dartford, where impressed men had been incarcerated by a local constable, and released them. Pett found it impossible to persuade the shipwrights to continue at work because of money owed them, so Pepys and the Navy Board had insisted on a meeting with the government. They confronted Charles in Whitehall and laid 'open the ill state of the navy; by the greatness of the debt; greatness of the work to do against next year; the time and materials it would take and our incapacity through a total want of money.' Pepys had said that £50,000 was immediately necessary. Charles had offered to advance £5,000. 'There was', said Pepys later, 'a long silence on all hands.' Charles wanted peace. He had already begun negotiating with Holland through the Holy Roman Emperor's ambassador Lisola, while continuing other negotiations with Louis XIV. The Earl of St Albans, in charge of negotiations with France, told Charles that, in return for certain favours, Louis would be willing to pressure the Dutch into accepting peace. Accordingly, Charles had thought it unnecessary to equip a large battle fleet for 1667. Instead, one or two lesser squadrons based around the coasts would be sufficient to protect the English (and interfere with the Dutch) merchant shipping. It had proved a fatal decision.

'The Estates preparation for war goes on with might and main', Samuel Tucker had reported in February, 1667, to Arlington from Rotterdam, 'and no time is neglected in equipping the ships, no not so much as Sundays . . . Some will have it best to make peace with the sword in hand.' The Dutch were actually contemplating an invasion of southern England, he said. Their intention was to reinforce a rebellion against Charles which a certain Samuel Raven had assured them would spontaneously arise, if sufficiently provoked.

In May, English envoys had arrived at Breda to secure peace. While the English were haggling over procedure, de Witt, realizing that a victorious Dutch fleet might be the 'best plenipotentiary for peace', decided upon a raid into the mouths of the Thames and the Medway, where he knew by intelligence that most of the English men-of-war were laid up. With the dockyard installations destroyed and the bulk of the English fleet crippled, he argued, the Dutch would be in a stronger position to negotiate.

Preparations for the attack had been carried on in secrecy, and, as both the Thames and the Medway were complex rivers to navigate, bribes were offered to English refugees for assistance. One, Thomas Dolman, was put in charge of 4,000 troops and told to secure such land bases as were necessary to prevent the Dutch being trapped up river. Another, Robert Holland, who had served as a captain in the English navy during the Commonwealth, was appointed commander of the fire ships attending the main Dutch fleet. To divert attention from any conglomeration of vessels in the Dutch ports, de Witt dispatched a squadron under van Ghent to the Firth of Forth to cause as much damage as possible, while, on 27 May, the main Dutch fleet under de Ruyter set sail for the Medway. The English men-of-war were to be captured or burnt 'in order to humiliate the English to the utmost.' De Witt wrote to his brother Cornelius on 10 June saying the negotiations at Breda were making little headway; he hoped, therefore, de Ruyter would administer such a rap as was 'necessary to curb the English arrogance.'

In fact, Charles had been warned of the Dutch preparations, although not of their extent. Dr Mews, one of the English peace delegation at Breda, had written to Secretary of State Williamson from The Hague that 'all the gang of rebels here with the addition of some malcontents out of England and Scotland have met in The Hague . . . certain it is they have great business in hand; and I presume will very shortly attempt to execute it.' Charles had not been alarmed; the Dutch would remain inactive, he presumed, since Louis was even then over-running the adjacent Spanish Netherlands. Louis's presence alone would keep the Dutch forces occupied. Arlington dismissed the Dutch preparations as mere 'bravado', believing that the Dutch could not afford a war. As a pre-caution, however, he wrote to each of the Lords Lieutenant of the maritime counties on the East and South-East coasts; 'his Majesty commands me particularly', he said, 'to mind you that, in all places where you shall be obliged to make head or appear to the enemy, you make the greatest show you can in numbers.'

The advice had been ignored, and the sudden appearance of the Dutch fleet in the Medway, not to mention the spectacle of what seemed to be the entire English fleet burning at anchor, sent terror throughout England. The alarm was so great, recorded Evelyn, 'as put both Country and City into a panic, fear and consternation, such as I hope I shall never see more: for everybody were flying, none knew why or whither.' Hundreds beseiged the bankers to withdraw their money, only to be informed that twenty days notice was required. 'Never were people so dejected', Pepys continued, 'as they are in the City all over at this day; and do talk most loudly, every treason, as, that we are bought and sold, that we are betrayed by the Papists and others about the King . . . They look upon us as lost, and remove their families and rich goods in the City.' 'There is hardly anybody at Court', he added, 'but do look as if he cried . . . The truth is I do fear so much that the whole Kingdom is undone, that I do this night resolve to study with my father and wife what to do with the little that I have in money by me.' Pepys concludes; 'I made my will also this day.'

The Dutch now blockaded the Thames, causing a sharp rise in the price of all seaborne goods. A letter to Sir Brampton Gurdon, a City merchant, noted that 'our bulwarks are gone, the glory of the nation . . . We are at this time far more distracted than at the Fire . . . the Fire was but a flea biting to this.' And James Bentham, writing in late June to Williamson, said: 'the beacons are on fire, and some say that Harwich, Colchester and Dover are burned, and the King gone out of town or out of the world. There is much whispering of bad persons, and the King and Council are blamed that the ships were left without defence.' John Rushworth observed that the people's rage was such that they were 'ready to tear their hair off their heads.' He added: 'we are betrayed, let it light where it will.'

First, Clarendon was blamed. He had never been in favour of war against the Dutch, and had obviously failed to prepare England's defences. Trees were cut down in front of his house, his windows broken, and a gibbet set up outside his gate. Others blamed Pett. Some blamed Charles. Pepys heard that 'the night the Dutch burned our ships, the King did sup with Lady Castlemaine, and they were all mad in the hunting of a poor moth.'

Attempts to minimize the disaster were ignored; the official *London Gazette* even stated that the Dutch 'can have but little reason to brag of their success, and less encouragement to make any farther attempts on these parts.' Lord Castlemaine (Barbara's husband) noted contemptuously: 'I confess I was troubled when I heard a ship fell into their hands which His Highness the Duke of York once made use of . . . but I was soon again satisfied, when I call'd it to mind . . . that this Vessel [the *Royal Charles*] could not choose but have an ill end, seeing it had Cromwell for its founder.' Charles sent begging letters to the clergy and the legal profession, claiming that only 'the speedy raising of a considerable army' could save the day and the Kingdom. To the East India Company, he wrote: 'we have thought fit to apply to you for a present loan of twenty thousand pounds for the use of our Navy.' Pett was arrested and sent to the Tower, while Charles set up a general inquiry into the state of the Navy. James and Albemarle were to hear all complaints about pay or conditions of service.

Charles gave instructions to his ambassadors at Breda to conclude a treaty with the Dutch on whatever terms were available. It was agreed, accordingly, that England would accept modifications to its Navigation Act which allowed the Dutch greater trading privileges. The English also agreed to abandon the required salute at sea, except in the 'English' channel. England was to retain New York and New Jersey, while she surrendered most of her settlements in West Africa. In the East Indies, the Dutch remained intact.

For some, the bitter fighting hardly seemed to have been worth the trouble. But the Dutch were jubilant. De Ruyter was given a gold cup, and medals were struck to commemorate the Medway victory. One of these, showing the English ships burning in the river, referred to England as a *'mala bestia'*, a brute beast. The Dutch later called in many of these unfortunate medals by way of apology, but in England the memory lingered.

The Dutch diplomatic triumph, however, was brief. Louis XIV, pursuing his ambitions in the Spanish Netherlands, ignored his treaty with Holland and proceeded to isolate the Dutch on land and at sea. Charles was soon writing of 'having [my] dominion of those seas asserted', and once again declared war against the Dutch, this time allied with Louis. De Witt was to be arrested, tortured and then banished, or such was the official intention. But the mob caught him and his brother, tied them back to back, carried them to a nearby gibbet, suspended them by the feet, disembowelled them and cut out their hearts. They were to be succeeded by Charles's nephew, William.

In England, the Treaty of Breda was greeted with long faces. Pepys recorded that 'nobody [is] speaking of the peace with any content or pleasure; but are silent in it, as of a thing they are ashamed of.' Charles attempted to raise twelve new regiments, each of a thousand men, for the defence of England against any future Dutch invasion. But, as memories of Cromwell's standing army were still fresh, the measure was blocked by those who feared that Charles might use this opportunity to establish a military dictatorship. In vain he asked 'what one thing he had done since his coming to England, to persuade any sober person that he did intend to govern by a standing army.' Elsewhere, 'a quaker came naked through the Hall [Westminster Hall], only very civilly tied about the loins to avoid a scandal, and with a chafing dish of fire and brimstone burning upon his head . . . crying "Repent! Repent!" ' . . . The Kingdom never in so troubled a condition in this world as now; nobody pleased with the peace, and yet nobody daring to wish for the continuation of the war, it being plain that nothing do nor can thrive under us.'

Parliament reassembled on 10 October 1667, and appointed a committee to inquire into 'the miscarriage of affairs in the late war.' For once Charles and Parliament were agreed. 'Commissioner Pett of all men living', said Pepys, 'did make the weakest defence of himself.' Albemarle blamed Pett, the Privy Council blamed Pett, and Andrew Marvell, MP for Hull, also blamed Pett:

> After this loss, to relish discontent,
> Someone must be accus'd by Punishment.
> All our miscarriages on Pett must fall;
> His name alone seems fit to answer all.
> Whose Counsel first did this mad War beget?
> Who all commands sold thro' the Navy? Pett.

Pett was dismissed as Commissioner for the Navy and died four years later, forgotten. The river was not clear to navigation for another three. The dockyardmen continued to complain about their squalid conditions. Charles felt that the country had its just desserts for not providing adequate monies for its defence. Bitterly he reckoned he had done his best, diverting the proceeds of customs, excise, hearth money, the sale of prizes and of Dunkirk, to the prosecution of the war against the Dutch. He also came to believe he had been badly served by his ambassadors and intelligence service. He had been ill-informed about the appalling conditions in the Navy, although probably he had himself to blame for that. He had been misled by the Earl of St Albans who had relied on Louis to mediate with the Dutch.

Clarendon later considered that the Dutch had missed a great chance and were mistaken to have withdrawn as early as they did. Charles agreed. Although his behaviour during the sudden crisis had been less than exemplary, it needed all his cunning and authority to steady the country's nerve. The Plague had been an act of God; at least, that is what men believed. Just so the Fire, obviously started by the French, although on behalf of God. But the destruction of the Fleet was manifestly someone's fault. Someone, other than a minor official such as Pett, would have to pay for it. Arlington wrote to Ormonde that if 'he [Pett] deserve hanging, as most think he does, and have it, much of the stain will be wip'd off of the Government which lies heavily upon it.' Charles knew this was unlikely; if he was to preserve the monarchy, let alone his own life, he would need to be more ruthless in government than hitherto.

Chapter Five
The liberty of conscience

As the first of the regicides had been executed at Tyburn, in November 1660, less than five miles away another group of revolutionaries had gathered at Gresham's College in London. Their proposals had belied their intent; they called themselves The Invisible College.

The conspirators numbered fifty-five. And on 28 November 1660, following a rousing call to arms by their quondam leader, Christopher Wren, they had each agreed to pay a subscription of one shilling per week to further their ambitions at an institution for 'psycho-mathematical learning'. Two years later, Charles had allied himself with their cause and, on 15 July 1662, they had received from him a mace and been incorporated as "The Royal Society for the Improvement of Natural Knowledge by Experiment".

Within a decade, committees had been established to investigate pharmacy, agriculture, antiques, chronology, history, mathematics, ship-building, travel, mechanics, grammar, chemistry, navigation, architecture, hydraulics, the weather, statistics, longevity, geography and monsters. The Society's members personified a fresh approach to the problems which confronted a post-Restoration world still confused by events of the previous twenty years. Together, they represented a vigorous age of scientific discovery, and their work marks the beginning of modern Britain, inquiring and purposeful, not after territory or gold as often in previous times, but after knowledge itself; such men as Newton, Boyle, Petty, North, Sandwich, Hooke and Goddard, with Locke, Dryden and Pepys to chronicle their work. And, of course, Wren.

How much this group owed to Charles is not clear. He granted Royal Patronage to many enterprises, only a few worthwhile. The French ambassador, however, believed that although Charles was unreliable in most things, he never failed to spend two or three hours a day at scientific experiments with his chemist Dr Williams. The King was frequently discovered meddling in his private laboratory when affairs of State were at their most chaotic. As to the Society itself, Charles attended its meetings, urged the admission of a London haberdasher whom he knew, sent to ask why some

116

Frontispiece to Sprat's History of the Royal Society.

plants contracted when touched, and made the Society gifts of cash and gadgets he himself had been given by visiting foreign dignitaries. Certainly his presence loomed in their proceedings, and the sudden burst of activity in the Society's investigations after incorporation must be in part a result of Charles's encouragement.

Charles's fascination for things mechanical was well known. Evelyn recalls how, during the worst days of the Plague, he visited Durdans in Surrey and was amazed to discover Hooke and Petty at work devising new rigging for Charles's ships and toy chariots for Charles's children. The Society itself approved a 'new fashion gun' (that Charles had recommended to their attention) 'which could shoot off often, one after another, without trouble or danger, very pretty'; calculating machines; machines for weighing air; pneumatic engines; a device for producing wind by falling water – such were the inventions which Charles's sponsorship produced. The official Journal of the Society, called the *Philosophical Transactions*, enumerated 'undertakings, studies and labours of the ingenious in many considerable parts of the world.' A treatise on the revolutionary optic glasses being made in Rome; a new method of curing disease by the transfusion of blood; a dissertation on mulberry wine-making in Devon; diagrams of an hygroscope which measured humidity, and of a baroscope that could estimate for the first time the smallest variations in air pressure.

With such an array of subject matter, it is no wonder men felt dwarfed by the immensities of knowledge that suddenly appeared before them. Even Roger North, an architect, barrister, writer, yachtsman, musician and scientist who devised theories concerning the refraction and speed of light, found himself sufficiently dazzled to note later: 'the very remembrance of these things is a delight, and while I write methinks I play. All other employments that filled my time go on account of work and business: these were all pleasure.' And Immanuel Kant, the German philosopher writing a hundred years later, looked back to the reign of Charles as one when 'a new light flashed upon all students of nature.' 'The study of nature', he goes on, 'entered on the secure methods of a science, having for many centuries done nothing but grope in the dark.'

Dryden for one had little doubt as to Charles's role in this outburst; the poet must 'freely and without flattery ascribe it to the Court; and in particular to the King, whose example gives a law to it.' Dryden also suggests a reason. 'His [Charles's] own misfortunes and the nation's afforded him an opportunity which is rarely allowed to sovereign princes, I mean of travelling and being conversant with the most polished courts of Europe; and thereby cultivating a spirit which was formed by nature to receive the impressions of a gallant and generous education. At his return, he found a nation lost as much in barbarism as in rebellion; and as the excellency of his nature forgave the one, so the excellency of his manners reformed the other . . .'

Medieval scientific investigation had usually been preoccupied with theories which governed nature, as if in accordance with some predestined order, rather than with any particular evidence which confronted or confirmed them. Consequently, the medieval scientist had rarely experimented systematically. Descartes, however, in his *Discourse on Method*, had doubted everything except his own existence, and from thence proceeded to deduce the existence of God and of the whole material universe. 'These long chains of reasonings which geometrics are accustomed to using to teach their most difficult demonstrations, had given me cause to imagine that everything which can be encompassed by man's knowledge is linked in the same way; and provided only that one abstains from accepting any for true which is not true . . . there can be nothing so distant that one does not reach it eventually, or so hidden that one cannot discover it.' Such an atmosphere had permeated the intellectual circles of Europe with which Charles, through his enforced exile, had become familiar. And such views were in contrast to the God-fearing Puritanism of England.

Methodology, and a parallel demand for new instrumentation with which to test this methodology, was the key. By the mid-seventeenth century, scientists in Europe were so keen to exchange information, that societies were being founded to promote this co-operation. In 1657, the Academica del Cimento (Academy of Experiments) had been established in Florence. In 1666, Louis XIV (on the advice of Colbert, elder brother of Louis's ambassador in London) established a regular French Academy which included Descartes and Pascal. The State appointed the Academicians and paid their salaries. The Royal Society in England had had similar beginnings. Since 1640, small groups had gathered in Oxford and London to compare scientific notes. Members included Dr Bathurst, later President of Trinity College, and Dr Willis who presided over an experimental club which convened at an apothecary's shop, later Tillyard's, in The High. When these groups had been incorporated and amalgamated by Charles in 1662, the resulting prestige had ensured that membership expanded rapidly, and it was soon necessary to choose among the candidates for admission. Together, these men radically changed the nature of scientific investigation practised hitherto in England; not the *idea* of scientific enquiry, that is, but its careful documentation. Previously, scholars had usually worked alone. They had scorned empiricism, published their results in Latin and clung to what was generally accepted as authority. Now, encouraged by Charles's own example, the scholar invaded the workshop or the laboratory or wherever his scientific curiosity took him. He communicated his results in English, and was openly criticized by his fellow members who reckoned they were at the threshold of knowledge and not its last days. Under the secretaryship of Henry Oldenburg, their findings, whether collective or individual, were published for all to read alongside the most stimulating discoveries from wherever such information could be gleaned. Nothing was unknowable that could be known, it was argued; and nothing was unpublished that could be found.

When the Invisible College had first gathered during the Civil War, Wren remembered later, their intention was '. . . the satisfaction of breathing a freer air and conversing in quiet, without being engaged in the passions and madness of that dismal age . . . By this means, there was a race of young men

119

Sir Christopher Wren, by Kneller. Born 20 October, 1632, at East Knoyle, Wiltshire, son of the Rev. Christopher Wren, then the local rector but later Dean of Windsor. Educated at Westminster School, and at Wadham College, Oxford. At 29, he became Professor of Astronomy and was described as "a miracle, nay, even something superhuman." President of the Royal Society (1681–3). His gift for devising models to demonstrate his scientific theories brought him to Charles's attention; the King asked him to repair old St. Paul's. In 1663, Wren's uncle Matthew, Bishop of Ely, suggested he design a new chapel for Pembroke College; in 1664 Archbishop Sheldon commissioned a theatre to house academic ceremonies at Oxford University. Small in stature, neat, Wren aroused little personal antagonism until, aged 85, he was removed as Surveyor-General, being accused of the mismanagement of accounts. "I am dismissed," he wrote, "having worn out (by God's mercy) a long life in the Royal service, and having made some figure in the world." MP for Plympton (1685–7) and Weymouth (1701–2); Wren died on 23 February, 1723.

provided against the next age, whose minds, receiving from them their first impressions of sober and generous knowledge, were invincibly armed against all the enchantments of enthusiasm . . . Nor indeed could it be otherwise, for such spiritual frenzies which did then bear rule, can never stand long before a clear and deep skill in nature.' Under Charles's guidance, they did not.

*　　*　　*

Who were this 'race of young men'? Wren was not yet thirty when Charles had come to the throne. Already an acknowledged expert in optics, meteorology, physiology and the laws of motion, he was appointed early in 1661 Professor of Astronomy at Oxford in succession to his teacher, Dr Seth Ward. His association with the Royal Society, however, brought him into contact with Charles whom he presented with a series of drawings, made through a microscope, of insects. Later, Wren made a large-scale model of the moon for Charles, and the King, much impressed, invited Wren to take charge of the fortifications of Tangier, part of Queen Catherine's dowry. Wren excused himself on grounds of health, although, ironic as it now seems, this was his first architectural commission.

Charles's interest in architecture sprang primarily from personal need. A predilection for yachting, and the lack of a Palace from which he could easily indulge this sport, persuaded him of the need for a new building at Greenwich. In the event, only the western wing, known as King Charles's block, was completed, its single two-storey unit being designed by John Webb, a pupil of Inigo Jones. But when London was almost destroyed by fire, personal need became public necessity. 'The stones of Paul's flew like granades', Evelyn had reported. 'London was, but is no more.' Eighty churches had been gutted or seriously damaged, and the greater part of St Paul's Cathedral left in ruins. Charles appointed a commission, which included Wren, to supervise the reconstruction. Science could also be used in service of the State; of the three-man commission, one was an astronomer, the other two mathematicians. Their proposals, had they been accepted, would have created a different London. But, as we have seen, the citizens of London forestalled their magnificent plans by rebuilding piecemeal even while the commission was in session. In despair, Wren went back to Oxford and to astronomy, although his fascination for architecture continued. In 1669, Charles finally persuaded him to accept the post of Chief Architect to the Crown.

If Wren seemed a miracle of youth, Isaac Newton was even younger; eighteen, when Charles was crowned. While Wren was exercising himself over the rebuilding of St Paul's, Newton was investigating the laws of motion. The ideas which eventually produced his theory of gravitation occurred to Newton, according to tradition, as he watched an apple falling from a tree in his orchard. From his observations, he determined the movements of the whole solar system and calculated a host of associated lesser phenomena; the tides, for example, were understandable in terms of the inertia of water in relation to the gravitational pull of either the sun or the moon. But Newton's influence was to be more fundamental than the discovery of laws of motion: his *Principia*, written during the last ten years of Charles's reign, dominated science for the following two hundred. It showed how mathematics could explain the phenomena of the heavens and the earth; and it answered the most puzzling question that had troubled man from the beginning – what was it that kept the planets moving about the sun in apparent order?

The answer led Newton to another idea, at first sight contradictory to the spirit of the age. Scientific knowledge, at least in its empiric form, he argued, is incomplete. It is not a substitute for metaphysics, nor does the one preclude the other. The law of gravity is not the *cause* of gravitational pull, merely its law, the formula by which observable phenomena relating to gravity can be measured. Complete knowledge of the universe, Newton believed, would show it to be not the mere mechanism that Descartes supposed, not a thing set going and left to amuse itself, but a unit coherently and continually directed by some unseen, intelligent force. The world is thus both geometrical and theological. Religion and science are not antagonistic, but explicable in terms of one another. The purpose of scientific enquiry, therefore, is to square the new thinking with a divine plan.

Like Wren, Newton benefited from Charles's patronage; in 1665, fear of the Plague had shut Cambridge University. Newton, then at Trinity College, went home to Woolsthorpe in Lincolnshire. There, encouraged by friends at the Royal Society and by Charles, he unearthed during the following eighteen months the discoveries upon which his subsequent work was based. As Pope said later:

> Nature and Nature's laws lay hid in night.
> God said, Let Newton be! And all was light.

Newton alone would guarantee Charles's reign a place in the history of science. But Newton was only one of many. Robert Boyle, for example, seventh son of the first Earl of Cork, was thirty-three at Charles's restoration. Within a year he had produced a work of considerable long-term effect, *The Sceptical Chymist*, published in 1661. Hitherto, chemistry had been based on the four elements of Aristotle – fire, earth, air and water. Boyle demonstrated by way of a dialogue between Themistius (representing Aristotle) and Carneades (representing himself) that such elements did not provide a comprehensive description of matter.

Like Newton, Boyle was convinced that science was not a substitute for religion. Observation of natural phenomena, he claimed, was an incitement to divine aspirations. 'They who would deter men from the scrutiny of nature', he

Sir Isaac Newton; an engraving by J. Honbraker. Born Christmas Day, 1642, in Woolsthorpe, Lincolnshire. Educated at King's School, Grantham, and Trinity College, Cambridge. Lucasian Professor of Mathematics at Cambridge University (1669–1701), president of the Royal Society (1703–27), Master of the Mint (1669–1727). Aloof and friendless, Newton suffered much personal criticism ... "shoes down at the heels, stockings untied, surplice on, and his head scarcely combed". Nonetheless, his own dictum was the spirit of the age; "the best and safest method of philosophising", he wrote, "seems to be first to enquire diligently into the properties of things, and then to proceed more slowly to hypotheses for the explanation of them." To this end, Newton wrote over two million words on theology, alchemy, the elixir of life, gravitation, mathematics, optics and the apocalypse.

noted, 'tend to deprive God of much of the glory due to him.' Boyle investigated the expansive force of freezing water; he discovered the role of air in the propagation of sound; he enquired into specific gravities, crystals, electricity, colour, hydraulics and, like Newton, the properties of light when refracted.

Medicine and surgery also made notable and parallel advances during Charles's reign. Thomas Sydenham, for instance, had obtained his licentiate from the College of Physicians in 1663. His approach to medicine was simple, but revolutionary. He was the first doctor to insist upon the accurate, clinical observation of disease, accompanied in its diagnosis by as many drawings and diagrams as possible. He recorded in detail (for the first time) the virulence of the Plague; he disapproved of bleeding as a universal panacea, and condoned its use only as a last resort; he analyzed measles, at least so as to distinguish it from smallpox, and noted the tendency of such diseases to lead to pneumonia.

Edmund Halley, who, with Hooke, designed and constructed the Greenwich Observatory, proposed to catalogue the southern stars. With Charles's help, he sailed to St Helena and there listed over 300 stars, including a new constellation, *Robur Carolinum*, named in honour of Charles. Later he calculated the orbit of a comet, observed in 1682, which now bears his name; his correct prediction of its return (1758) was an early application of Newton's laws of motion. Halley also originated the methodology by which geographical and physical features of the earth are reproduced, and devised the first meteorological survey.

*   *   *

Charles was also acutely interested in the writings and teachings of two major philosophers of his time, Hobbes and Locke. Although Hobbes's major work *Leviathan* was published before Charles's reign (in 1651), and Locke's chief essays *On Toleration* and *Concerning Human Understanding* were not in print until shortly after Charles's death, both thinkers influenced and were influenced by Charles. Hobbes had taught Charles mathematics when in exile, and later received a Royal pension. Clarendon wrote *A Brief View and Survey of the Dangerous and Pernicious Errors to Church and State in Mr. Hobbes' Leviathan*; but as long as Mr Hobbes enjoyed Charles's favour, he was safe. Charles relished his company – 'here comes the bear to be baited', he would say – and hung his portrait in the Royal Chamber; Hobbes dedicated his *Problema Physica* to the King.

Hobbes argued that the unlimited authority of a sovereign's power is the guarantee of peace in the State. The sovereign *is* the State, since all acts and opinions have their sanction in him. Although formulated during the Civil War and first published during the Commonwealth, this notion found its fullest vindication in Charles's reign. Charles had been restored without conditions; he had been given, by Parliament, absolute control over the armed forces; he had been empowered by statute to remodel corporations at will, and his judges frequently considered themselves mouthpieces of the Royal wish; he was even protected from seditious talk by a special Treason Act. In practice, however, he rarely used these absolute powers, preferring to trade their existence for other more subtle statecraft. But the Test Act of 1673 and the Act of 1678, for instance, imposed a State religion with secular penalties. The idea advocated by Hobbes that peace was best secured by strong government, and that such government was achieved by a concentration rather than a division of power, appealed to Charles. Was it not true that *any* government entailed coercion? The question was not of its extent, therefore, but of its justification.

In the propagation of such contentious views, Charles's protection was essential, as Hobbes well knew. A condition of this protection became that, after 1668, no further works were to be published which might antagonize popular feelings, although, with Charles's help, all Hobbes's works were published in Amsterdam. Unauthorized editions of them filtered back to England, and no other Englishman of the day gained such high repute abroad. Distinguished visitors to England often made a point of paying their respects to the old man.

John Locke was even more a product of Charles's society. Two years younger than Charles, he had learned medicine at Oxford, and in 1666 attended Ashley Cooper, then Chancellor of the Exchequer. Ashley Cooper had been impressed and Locke joined his household in the Strand a year later, operating on the Chancellor in 1668 and supervising the birth of his son shortly after. Patronage by Ashley Cooper brought Locke into contact with Charles, and Charles approved Locke's appointment as secretary to the Council of Trade and Plantations of which Ashley Cooper, now the Earl of Shaftesbury, was President. As secretary, Locke helped devise the constitution of Carolina in the Americas – a model for the later American constitution – and the first draft is in his handwriting.

Science, Locke argued, had stressed the need for rational, logical and precise explanation. Why should not politics and its study assume a similar course? After all, the word 'philosophy' – and both Locke and Hobbes thought of themselves as philosophers – was used in Charles's reign to mean what is now called science. Locke wanted a more empirical, scientific approach to the problems of government; he believed that the origins of the body politic were found in common consent, with every man under an obligation to follow the wishes of the majority. To preserve property, which was the main object of the State, a known and established law with judges to implement it and a power to guarantee it, must be acknowledged. This power, 'sacred and unalterable in the hands where the community have once placed it', must rest with a Prince or Sovereign. Only when that Sovereign betrays the trust placed in him, did the subject have the right to rebel. Thomas Jefferson and his co-authors of the American constitution were to acknowledge the influence of Locke, and Voltaire frequently was to cite Locke as his model.

*　　*　　*

The years following Charles's Restoration, in other words, were a ferment of intellectual excitement; at every turn, one senses an inquiring society. Statistics, thought William Petty, were indispensable 'in order to get good, certain and easy government.' With John Graunt, he had produced in 1662 *Observations upon the Bills of Mortality*, a work which was the first thorough statistical survey since Domesday Book. Pepys began his official classification of ships as part of a growing desire to adopt the new 'scientific approach' in administrative problems relating to military and naval matters. (Pepys had earlier recorded in his diary that, to further his advancement, he arose at four in the morning to learn the multiplication tables.) Evelyn was an expert on engraving, trade, numismatics, gardening and the problems of London smoke. Thomas Burnet, Master of the Charterhouse, one of many writers who popularized scientific theories about the origins of the universe, wrote his *Sacred Theory of the Earth* and dedicated it to a grateful monarch. John Wilkins, a founder of the Royal Society, speculated in *The Discovery of a World in the Moone* that the planets might be inhabited. The sense of wonder which permeates Milton's *Paradise Lost* (published in 1667) and *Paradise Regained* (1671) was commonplace:

> Before their eyes in sudden view appear
> The secrets of the Hoary Deep – a dark
> Illimitable Ocean, without bound,
> Without dimension, where length, breadth and heighth
> And time and place are lost.

John Aubrey, another Fellow of the Royal Society, gives the clue to what united them all. 'When I was a child and so before the civil wars', he wrote, 'the fashion was for old women and maids to tell fabulous stories, night-times, of spirits and of walking of ghosts, etc . . . When the wars came, and with them liberty of conscience and liberty of inquisition, the phantoms vanish. Now, children fear no such things.'

Such curiosity about the world and all that it entailed had a darker side. The Licensing Acts (the first of which had been passed in 1662) stipulated that all books concerned with science had to be authorized by the Archbishop of Canterbury, the Bishop of London or the Vice-Chancellor of either Oxford or Cambridge. The only newspapers to appear between 1660 and 1679 were official government sheets. The editor of one declared his motto to be: 'a public mercury should never have my vote. It makes the multitude too familiar with the actions and counsels of their superiors.' Sir Leoline Jenkins, then Secretary of State, had few doubts about the dangers of knowledge. 'Printing', he said, is 'a sort of appeal to the people.'

Coffee houses, one of the few public meeting places for men of science, were to be suppressed in 1675 because they were 'the greatest resort of idle and disaffected persons.' And in 1683 the University of Oxford officially condemned and burnt many of the treatises on political theory discussed above, including the works of Hobbes and Milton. Such books, the university was to affirm, 'are filled to deprave good manners, corrupt the minds of unwary men, stir up seditions and tumults, overthrow states and kingdoms, and lead to rebellion, murder of princes and atheism itself.' Aubrey was worried lest his *Lives* fell into the wrong hands and he be charged with 'scandalum magnatum', libel upon his superiors.

As for popular education, the Restoration was a calamity. The Act of Uniformity in 1662 had subjected all schoolteachers to episcopal licence and imposed oaths of non-resistance. All but one of the schools founded in Wales during the Interregnum, for instance, were closed. Grammar schools, thought to have caused the Civil War because they had educated too many people above their station, were officially disapproved. Equality of educational opportunity was discouraged because it diverted 'those whom nature or fortune had determined to the plough or the oar or other handicrafts from their proper design.' Mr Wase, in his *Considerations Concerning Free Schools*, published in 1678, was to write that 'the multiplying of these foundations is represented as dangerous to the government.'

It would be naive, accordingly, to overestimate any immediate effects of the apparently liberal and scientific views which were popular in the early part of Charles's reign. But it would also be a mistake to underestimate the sense of bustle which characterized that society. Even Sir John Reresby, a High Tory Anglican, noted later that, as a result of Charles's reign, 'most men were now convinced that liberty of conscience was a thing of advantage to the nation.' No attempt was ever made by Charles to curtail the activities of the Royal Society or of any of its members. As long as it received the King's blessing, however tacit that blessing might sometimes be (Charles always sent venison for their annual dinner), it was secure. While the King busied himself in his Palace Garden at Whitehall, either tending the herbs he grew for his laboratory, or mixing cordials, or endeavouring to fix mercury, then the scientific curiosity which such mild eccentricities symbolized could flourish. When Charles's personal chemist devised the notorious 'King's Drops' to cure the sick, Charles preferred to put them into drink because the resulting mixture encouraged the drinker to reveal his secrets. The King particularly liked administering this potion to recalcitrant ministers.

It may be that Charles's passion was no more than that of a rich dilettante. Whether he understood the work being initiated by Newton or Locke may be doubted. But what remains surprising is the large number of scientists and thinkers who, at one time or another, found themselves graced with a Royal patronage apparently limitless in its interests. A painting by Thomas Danckerts shows Charles in front of Ham House being presented by the Royal Gardener with the first pineapple grown in England. The look of cynical amusement, disbelief and yet obvious pleasure at the gift is clear. As Dryden concluded: 'whatever his [Charles's] favourites of State might be, yet those of his affection were men of wit.' Dryden summarized the gratitude felt by those who owed some measure of advancement to the King:

> His conversation, wits and parts,
> His knowledge in the noblest useful arts,
> Were such dead authors could not give,
> But habitudes of those who live . . .
> His apprehension quick, his judgment true;
> That the most learn'd, with shame, confess
> His knowledge more, his reading only less.

Chapter Six

Tunnage and poundage

Charles appeared to lavish cash and property on his mistresses, his friends and his horses. His scientific hobbies, which he pursued too often and too well for general approval, also absorbed more money than anyone had anticipated; and the most spectacular Royal pageantry that England had seen in sixty years proved very costly. Yet, as Charles told the Commons in 1663: 'let me and you think never so well of ourselves, if all the world knows or believes that we are poor . . . if our friends think we can do them no good, or our enemies believe we can do them no harm, our condition is far from being prosperous . . . If you do not give me some present supply of money to enable me to struggle with those difficulties I am pressed with, I shall have a very melancholy summer.' The question remains, therefore, how Charles managed to pay for all his indulgences.

In 1660, the actual cash in the Exchequer had amounted to £11. 2s. 10d. Charles had been informed that the national debt exceeded £3M, a trifle by today's standards but daunting enough for a penniless King. In addition, there were the public and private debts of his father, his own multifarious borrowings during the years abroad, as well as massive arrears of pay owing from the Commonwealth and Protectorate administrations. The Convention Parliament had declared itself not unwilling to help, but, like its successors, failed to do so. All it was initially prepared to settle were the debts of the Army and Navy, each about £750,000. A Poll Tax had been authorized, which, it was estimated, would raise £210,000, plus a levy of assessments at the rate of £70,000 per month for eleven months. In total, the two taxes would raise just under £1M. With this, Charles would have to pay off eighteen regiments of foot, thirteen regiments of horse and fifty-nine garrisons. In fact, the tax only raised two-thirds of what was needed; Charles was expected to find the balance. The settlement had also made no provision for extraordinary expenditure; so when the Commons had more or less insisted that Charles went to war with the Dutch, one of the better informed members, Sir Thomas Lee, suggested that Charles defray the cost of such a war out of his own income.

The annual cost of a peace-time administration had been estimated in 1660 to be £1,200,000. Had Parliament agreed to advance this amount to the Crown, it would have been a generous allowance; after all, it was twice what Charles's father had been given. But it was also less than half of what Cromwell had actually spent. Out of this sum, Charles was expected to pay for everything concerned with the administration, as well as all his personal expenditure. He had been persuaded to forgo some of the more traditional sources of Royal revenue, such as the Court of Wards, provided an equivalent income could be found from elsewhere. So a committee of the Commons had offered a further £400,000 per annum to be raised from the Customs (a tax on imports), plus another £250,000 from Excise (a tax on home-produced goods). Crown Lands, it was estimated, would yield an annual return of £100,000 and the Post Office £21,000. Together with various other bits and pieces, the Crown might reasonably expect to receive about £865,000 per year. But what about the remaining £335,000? Charles had asked the committee to look again.

In doing so, the committee members had begun to discover that their estimates were hopelessly inaccurate. Excise, for example, would yield but £250,000, and then only 'if better collected'. A tax on salt had been proposed, and rejected. A tax on paper and parchment was discussed. So was the issuing of wine licences. Reluctantly, these had been agreed upon, although the revenue they had provided was pitifully small. Charles, it seems, was to be left permanently short of £300,000 per annum.

At Court, the financial situation seemed forlorn. Clarendon calculated that, between Michaelmas 1661 and Michaelmas 1662, Charles's expenditure had amounted to £1,588,234, while his income was less than half that. Charles had begged Parliament for more support. He had already told them that, such was his poverty, he had not 'been able to give my brothers one shilling since I came into England, nor to keep any table in my house but what I eat at myself. That which troubles me most', he added cynically, 'is to see so many of you come to me at Whitehall, and to think you must go somewhere else to seek your dinner.'

Parliament had eventually acknowledged it had been parsimonious. It voted an extra tax of two shillings on every hearth which, it hoped, would realize the

Documents from the Public Records Department, showing handwritten ledgers from the ▷ customs office of the port of London in 1661. "The thing which is nearest the heart of the nation is trade and all that belongs to it," Charles wrote to his sister, Minette, on 14 September, 1668. The legal rate of interest was fixed at 6 per cent; the English merchant tonnage doubled between 1660 and 1668; exports and imports increased by 50 per cent between 1660 and 1685; the East India Company doubled, and the African Company quadrupled, its nominal stock; by 1685, customs and excise yielded as much in revenue as the total parliamentary allowance given to Charles in 1660. Short term advantages, however, had long term disadvantages. The Navigation Act's indirect shipping subsidy, for instance, diverted capital from industrial development at home. Nonetheless, it was reckoned that trade increased the national wealth by at least £2 million per annum, almost certainly an underestimate.

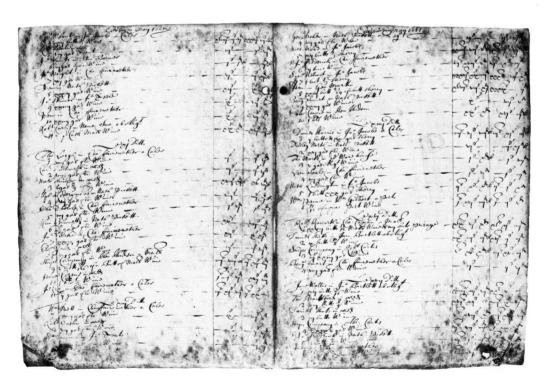

deficit. In fact, in its first full year of collection, the tax had only yielded £80,000. Anyway, it was argued, there were other sources of income for the Crown. Charles still received annual rents from the Duchy of Cornwall, for instance, which totalled £15,000 per annum. (They cost £5,000 per annum to collect.) He could also tax the carrying of water to and from Westminster. There were the monies he had inherited from such as the Company of Frame-Work Knitters and from the Company of Tobacco Pipe Makers. Both paid him an annual corporation fee, of £3 each.

Charles had been forced to sell off Crown property to make ends meet, and by 1678 he had disposed of lands worth £1,300,000. By 1685, there were almost none left. He had also been obliged to sell to the French Cromwell's stronghold of foreign policy, Dunkirk, for 5 million livres, about £400,000. Though the garrison had been a strategic idiocy, the country's pride had been dishonoured by the sale. Clarendon was blamed, although Charles himself had not escaped disfavour. The hearth tax was violently attacked as an invasion of the Englishman's right to privacy, and its existence used by the Parliamentary opposition to provoke endless trouble toward the end of Charles's reign.

*   *   *

Economy had proved useless. In the first year of Charles's administration, the income from tax had amounted to only £700,000, and Charles had been compelled to borrow money from City merchants at high rates of interest to continue the administration at all. In 1663, he had given orders that the Navy be halved, his household reduced and his family put to board wages. But to little effect. By the time the wars with the Dutch had begun, Charles's financial affairs were so chaotic that the City refused to lend him any further cash, even at what was then considered an enormous rate, ten per cent interest. In January 1666, with France and Denmark declaring war on England, to support the Dutch, Charles had pleaded there was no further money to continue the war. After the Four Days Battle, with the English fleet broken and in disarray, with much of London wasted by the Plague or destroyed by the Fire, many thought the world as they knew it was coming to an end; by October 1666 the Commons had been forced to concede that Charles needed money. He had been given £1,800,000 in addition to the £2½M already voted for the war. In all, the Commons had protested, Charles had now been given the equivalent of four and a half years' ordinary revenue to spend on the war alone. 'I do not pretend to be without infirmities', he had told them angrily, 'but I have never broken my word with you; and if I do not flatter myself, the nation never had less cause to complain of grievances, or the least injustice or oppression, than it hath had in these seven years it hath pleased God to restore me to you. I would be used accordingly.' He insisted that if the war was to continue it should be financed

132

properly. Already, he pointed out, he had been forced to borrow against anticipated revenue in order to pay off *last* year's fleet. So how, in these circumstances, could they expect him to make adequate preparations for the coming campaign against *three* foreign enemies?

Charles's problems were not helped by the confused manner in which the State collected its taxes. 'When anyone fails in business', Ashley Cooper noted, 'or a gentleman wants to part with an old servant, interest is made to get them into the Customs as if into a hospital.' Those employed to collect the taxes were paid less than £50 a year. They could be dismissed without reason, and were usually recruited from those unfit for other employment. Collecting taxes could also be dangerous. At several Quarter Sessions in 1660, men were sent to prison for assaulting excise officers. The system of collection, moreover, invited corruption. Between the granting of a tax by Parliament and its receipt, there was always a considerable delay. Thus, the practice of using 'farmers' had developed. The farmer was a private speculator (or one of a syndicate) who would advance the government cash in return for the right to levy taxes in a particular area. Inevitably, anyone who was able to advance the government large sums of cash in lieu of uncollected taxes, stood to prosper. In Ireland, for example, Lord Ranelagh accumulated a fortune from his obviously profitable farm of the Irish revenue. Petty had estimated (in 1662) that because of false declarations, the cost of collecting, and general corruption, the government received only half of what had been paid.

The Commons suspected bungling on a large scale, and had made some attempt to control the disorder, although they believed that the culprit was Charles rather than the system itself. In the Supply Act of 1665, the Commons had insisted that a register be kept in the Exchequer of the receipts from taxes voted and money spent. The following year they had further ordered that £380,000 of the money allocated was to be used specifically for the payment of seamen's wages. Finally, ignoring the functions of Chancellor and auditor of the Exchequer, they had brought in a bill to appoint a permanent authority responsible for the administration of public accounts. Charles, who suffered from the misappropriation of public funds as much as anyone, had blocked the move and offered to appoint his own commission. But disasters in the war against the Dutch had annihilated all hopes of compromise, and Charles had been compelled to accept a statutory commission with power to subpoena any royal servant (i.e. member of the government) and cross-examine that servant under oath. The purpose was that 'this whole Kingdom may be satisfied and truly informed whether all the same monies and provisions have been faithfully issued out'; in other words, to control how Charles spent his money.

The farming of taxes was abandoned, and a new branch of the civil service established. Not surprisingly, it expanded rapidly. Whereas there had been only ten customs and excise officers at Exeter in 1646, by 1685 there were seventy-one; in all, there were 763 in service in 1672. Other recommendations were even less well received. The idea of a national bank having a coinage of its own called bank money and lending cash on the security of real estate, had been advocated during the Commonwealth. Bankers, thought Clarendon, 'were a tribe that had risen and grown up in Cromwell's time, and never were heard of before the late troubles.' But since Charles was now prevented from any form of non-Parliamentary taxation, he frequently had to borrow against anticipated revenue. So banking was coming to be accepted as a necessary, although unfortunate, adjunct of Royal finance. In an attempt to balance his books, Southampton, Charles's Treasurer, had supplemented one source from another; in response to the suspicions of misappropriation which such financial juggling had inevitably aroused, Southampton now undertook, at the Commons' insistence, to make payment 'in course' as registered. In 1667, for example, £584,978 had been assigned for the particular purpose of building thirty ships of war.

None of these attempts to regularize Charles's expenditure or to control tax collection more strictly, however, began to solve the real problem. It was admitted that Charles could not live independently. Monies would have to be granted him. But these were never enough, as Charles regularly reminded Parliament. Yet he was expected to conduct a vigorous foreign policy, pay off debts, rebuild the Navy, and finance the pageantry of royalty which public relations demanded. It was impossible. The intention, obviously, was to make Charles financially dependent on Parliament.

The immediate effect, however, had been to undermine foreign policy. When he had begged money in 1665 to finance the war against the Dutch, Charles had been told he would only get the money provided he declared war within three months and 'not make a sudden peace and get all that money for private occasions.' To an extent, the Commons were justified in their suspicion that monies they had granted previously for use in the war, had mysteriously disappeared. When Charles again begged Parliament for money in 1669, he told them '[I] do affirm to you that no part of those monies that you gave to me for that war have been diverted to other uses, but on the contrary; besides all those supplies, a very great sum hath been raised out of my standing revenue and credit and a very great debt contract, and all for the war.' Parliament did not believe him. Instead they refused to finance him adequately because (they said) he was lazy, inefficient and careless in the administration of government.

The constant threat of war also caused prices to rise sharply. Coal sold for thirty pounds a chaldron, five times the norm. 'The true English valour we talk of', Pepys wrote, 'is almost worn out.' Creditors of every kind, from seamen to contractors, besieged the Admiralty. The government was threatened with bankruptcy. The Navy was £1M in debt. Sailors rioted in the Strand. Charles, characteristically undaunted, rode into their midst telling them he would personally guarantee their pay. Rioting such as this led only to the gallows, he said; recognizing his courage in facing them, the sailors dispersed. Charles's own poverty, however, was such that he even had to give up supplying paper for the Council table. Peace, or at least a peace treaty, was the only hope. Although it would be expensive, it would be cheaper than war. Charles asked Parliament for a further £300,000 to build more ships and give strength to any treaty.

A lack of ready cash had also pushed Charles into unwise short-term bargains, such as those derived from his Portuguese marriage. Anxious to revenge himself on the Dutch who had destroyed his fleet first at sea and then in the Medway, Charles persuaded himself of the advantages of a secret treaty with France against the Dutch which would, as he told his sister Minette, 'join profit with honour'. Fortunately, Louis XIV wanted a treaty as much as Charles, but for more political reasons. For promising to declare himself Catholic and thus aligning himself with the French cause, Charles would receive from Louis a £200,000 down payment, plus £800,000 per annum (£400,000 being paid in advance) for as long as the war against the Dutch continued. The Lords, meanwhile, promised Charles a further wine tax which would yield an estimated £300,000 a year. But Charles had long since learned to distrust such promises, and pressed on with his secret negotiations. These were to be concluded and a treaty signed at Dover, in May 1670.

Charles was proven right to ignore Parliament's apparent generosity. When it reassembled in October, the Commons were informed by Sir Orlando Bridgeman that the King was now £1,300,000 in debt and needed a further £800,000 to pay off the Navy. Proposals for an entertainment tax – those who went to the Playhouse should pay a one shilling tax for the privilege of sitting in a box, and sixpence for sitting in the pit – were laughed aside. Charles's friends complained that such a levy would be a tax on the King's pleasures, to which Sir John Coventry enquired whether the King's pleasure did not in fact lie among the men or women who acted? An extra tax proposed on the import of sugar and tobacco was similarly defeated. The Commons simply did not seem able or willing to face reality. The following January the Council was told that, since the Restoration, necessary expenditure had exceeded actual income by £400,000 per annum. And provision had still not been made to pay off pre-Restoration debts.

Charles was becoming exasperated with Parliament's obduracy. On the advice of Clifford (now Lord Treasurer), in January 1672 he 'stopped the Exchequer' and declared the government bankrupt. Being hopelessly in debt to the bankers, Charles merely suspended their claims on him. It was angrily believed that this would force the banks to suspend their credit to more ordinary customers, but this did not happen. In fact, a commercial panic seems to have been averted by the personal intervention of Charles. He wrote to all the bankers assuring them that their debts would be met eventually and in full. In return, he requested them to honour likewise their own obligations.

The Council now felt able to authorize a further £750,000 (to re-equip the fleet) out of monies that had been set aside to repay the bankers. Meanwhile, Louis invaded Holland. Parliament was shocked, but Charles told them he was now 'forced to a most important, necessary and expensive war', although of course he did not tell them why. Worse, which he also did not tell them, the promised French money was nearly as slow in coming as Parliament's own grants. Colbert (the ambassador) noted that the King once more 'finds himself . . . without money and without credit, his revenues, which consist chiefly of import and export duties, diminishing very much during the war, and his expenses increasing every day by the purchase of arms.'

Charles had no choice but to ask again for supplies. Parliament agreed, reluctantly, provided that Charles assent to a Test Bill, by which anyone who refused the oaths of allegiance and supremacy and the sacrament according to the rites of the Church of England was to be denied public office. Charles had already told the Commons: 'I will deal plainly with you. I am resolved to stick by my Declaration [of Breda]', a Declaration which had guaranteed 'liberty to tender consciences'.

The Test Bill was aimed specifically at Roman Catholics; it was blackmail, as Charles well knew. To agree to such a bill would also be contrary to his secret treaty with Louis. Charles was caught. Louis was persuaded by his ambassador in London to offer Charles a last minute bribe of £500,000, but it was too late. The rain was pouring through the roof of the Royal Mews and in urgent need of repair. The Commons wanted peace with the Dutch. Both cost money. The fact that the Dutch were offering, among other things, an indemnity of £200,000, made peace that much more acceptable. 'Let the Money Bill come first', Charles urged Parliament. Parliament would not hear of it. The Test Bill was rushed through both Houses, and Louis betrayed. But Charles got his money.

* * *

For the first ten years of his reign, therefore, Charles seemed permanently in debt and his administration limited by a continuous lack of ready cash. And yet, by the end of his reign, only fifteen years on, Charles had paid off all his debts, as well as all the debts inherited from his father. He managed to support a host of mistresses and their offspring, inaugurate a prodigious number of building works including the new St Paul's Cathedral, indulge his scientific curiosity and his sporting activities to the full, as well as leave the monarchy richer than it had been before and, in terms of the private resources it could command, richer than it would be again. How did this come about?

Charles had long since realized that 'the thing which is nearest the heart of this nation is trade and all that belongs to it.' As a result, under Charles's insistence, the tonnage of English merchant shipping doubled during his reign; ship building became one of the three or four largest employers of wage labour. The average number of English ships passing through the Baltic Sound in 1670, for instance, was over twice what it had been in 1660. In 1640, goods from the various English colonies imported and then re-exported had amounted to no more than five or six per cent of the total trade. By 1685, English ships engaged in trade with America and India alone had multiplied eight times. Exports and imports rose during Charles's reign by nearly fifty per cent, and although retail prices fell (because of greater production), the revenue to the Crown from this general increase leapt to £6M per year. The Hudson's Bay Company tripled its capital between 1670 and 1688; the African Company quadrupled its nominal stock. 'He is a bad merchant', it was said in 1674, 'that cannot make six times as much money by trade as he can by land.' Evelyn invested £250 in stock of the East India Company in 1660; by 1680, he found it was worth three times as much.

Charles supervised this expansion in three ways. As to his personal finances, in return for a voluntary surrender of all feudal tenures and purveyances – the cause of much trouble between his father and Parliament – Charles persuaded a surprised but grateful Parliament to grant certain customs and excise levies to him and his successors in perpetuity. Among these were the taxes on beer, cider, mead, crude spirits, coffee, chocolate, sherbet, tea and tobacco. Parliament also gave Charles an additional tax for life on other goods yet to be decided but eventually to include wine and cloth. At first it might seem that the surrender of feudal tenures was damaging to the Crown; the loss of purveyance, for example, cost Charles £100,000 per annum in household expenses. And although land and the military service pertaining to that land were now little more than feudal anachronisms, the Court of Wards had had as its purpose not merely the enforcement of military service but the possibility of extracting money from, and therefore personal control over, a large proportion of the landed classes. But the tax on wine and cloth, for instance, was yielding £600,000 by 1675. Likewise the tax on beer, cider, ale and coffee; in 1663 this yielded a mere £300,000. By 1674 it had grown to £700,000. By 1682, Charles's personal income from these levies alone exceeded his annual parliamentary grant. In these circumstances, it was perhaps necessary for him to plead poverty lest Parliament decided to revoke its previous grants to the Crown.

Second, Charles shaped much of his foreign policy to the preservation of this trade, beginning early on with an overtly protectionist measure, the Navigation Act of 1660. Its declared object had been 'the increase of shipping', but its implications were greater. As Josiah Child said later: 'this kingdom being an island, the defence of which has always been our shipping and seamen, it seems to me absolutely necessary that profit and power ought jointly to be considered. And if so, I think none can deny but the Act of Navigation has and does occasion the building and employing of three times the number of ships and seamen that otherwise we should or would do.' The

Venetian ambassador took a more ominous view. Charles was now 'in a position to give the law to foreign princes, this being the true way to enlarge dominions throughout the world, the most easy for conquests and the least costly for appropriating the property of others.'

Charles had inherited a dismal trading empire. The Merchant Adventurers were in debt, the Levant Company unable to compete with the French. Public interest in trade was slight. Charles, on the other hand, upheld the belief that commerce was an affair of state because 'it conduces more to a universal monarchy than either arms or territory'; to Charles, it was also conducive to balancing the books. A flood of trade legislation filled the Statute books; herring fishing was encouraged, the packing of butter subjected to definite rules, measures of corn and salt were standardized. Most important of all, the Council of Trade recognized that 'the balance of trade (by which it is understood the proportion that the commodities have in value to the commodities imported) is the main course of exportation and importation of bullion.' In other words, if England's wealth was to be measured in terms of bullion reserves, trade must show a favourable balance in order to increase these reserves. We remain haunted by that same belief today.

The first Navigation Act had affirmed that no African, Asian or American goods could be imported into English or Irish ports except in ships belonging to Englishmen, and manned by crews of at least seventy-five per cent Englishmen. No goods could be exported from any English colony except in English (or Irish) owned ships. Foreign merchants were thereby excluded from English colonial trade, and from the coastal trade of England or Ireland. There was a host of lesser regulations – the import duty on Dutch fish was doubled, and various articles such as sugar, tobacco, raw cotton, ginger and indigo, all produced in the English colonies, were only to be shipped to England or English possessions. Charles was also active confirming the privileges of existing trading enterprises, as well as supporting the establishment of new ones. A Royal Fishery Company was set up to exploit the abundance of herring around the English coast. The Hudson's Bay Company was founded to capitalize on the furs and skins of northern Canada. Charles's brother James and cousin Rupert began the Royal African Company in 1663 to trade English manufactured goods for gold and ivory, and maintain the supply of negro slaves for the expanding plantations in the American colonies.

Not all the companies were successful. The Royal African Company itself suffered because many negroes died en route and there were constant disputes about the price of survivors. £17 per head was thought a generous offer for a slave weakened and diseased by the voyage. The Fishery Company was similarly unfortunate. Its fleet was ill-equipped for the task it had been set, and no one was prepared to pay for its renewal. It was suggested that the necessary capital be raised by lottery, but one lottery in 1664 raised just £818, of which £500 had already been spent in its collection. It only needed the diversion of a war to end this particular experiment, and by 1667 the Royal Fishery Company had ceased trading.

But these were exceptions. In general, trade flourished. To Portugal, England sent coal, cloth, corn, fish, lead and tin, all of which were paid for in bullion, sugar, mahogany, fruit or wine. Barley, oats and wheat were exported to Holland; sprats to Rotterdam; cloth to Turkey. A measure of the increased wealth of England can be seen in the abundance of luxury goods which filled the ports. Green tortoise-shell from Jamaica, singing birds from Rotterdam, periwigs from Rostock, 'marmerlade' boxes from Bilbao; from France, cucumbers, preserved ginger, hair-powder, looking-glasses and toothbrushes. Evading the Customs Duty on such goods was highly developed. A ship with 'fine and high-customed goods' would unload at sea into a collier which then smuggled the contraband in under its coal. Silks and spices were brought in under apples or onions; likewise Flemish soap, iron from Stockholm, brandy from Bordeaux, resin from Norway, canvas from Brittany, wine from Cadiz, carpets from Smyrna – there appeared no limit to the rich variety of goods which Charles's encouragement of trade brought to England.

Charles's reign, therefore, marks a turning point in England's economic history. The resulting prosperity gave a boost to other industries, ship-building not the least among them, and there was a steady transition to a new type of economy. The colonies offered a protected market for English goods, as well as a cheap source of raw materials which stimulated home production. And the trading companies, such as the East India, acquired such wealth and possessions during this period that the foundations were laid for future military conquests and strength. The power that England was able to muster during the wars of Marlborough thirty years later has its origins in the trade and foreign policies of Charles. As he told the French ambassador with pride: 'England enjoyed a profound tranquillity and enriched herself, while all the neighbouring states were drained or ruined by the war; . . . the English would one day thank him [Charles] for having kept them by prudence in so happy a state and so advantageous for their commerce.'

Not since the days of the Elizabethan pirates had such a spirit of adventure prevailed. Liverpool, Plymouth and Bristol prospered. For sixty years men had been absorbed by problems at home; now, freed from civil war, freed from worrying over much about politics or religion, inspired by a witty, easygoing, earthy King, Englishmen worked 'to increase the limits of their dwelling.' Trade joined 'the countries themselves and the inheritance of them to these His Majesty's dominions, laying a just foundation for making them an affair of State, and of far greater care, weight and import to the Crown than others.' In this way, men believed, 'the Empire of England is rendered more august, formidable and considerable abroad.'

Third, Charles was to be fortunate in the appointment as Lord Treasurer, in succession to Clifford, of Sir Thomas Osborne, created in June 1674 Earl of

Danby. Danby had already had an extraordinary career; having fought in the Civil War on the Royalist side, he succeeded to his father's baronetcy in 1647, and worked in Cromwell's Civil Service; subsequently, he was created Viscount Osborne of Dunblane (in the Scottish Peerage), Viscount Latimer, and made a member of the English Privy Council. As Earl of Danby and Charles's Treasurer, he was to be dismissed, committed to the Tower and there left untried for five years. Eventually released, he played a part in the conspiracy which brought about the Revolution of 1688, became Chief Minister of the Crown to William III and gratefully created Marquis of Carmarthen. Again impeached and again dismissed, he was promoted Duke of Leeds and lived on into the reign of Queen Anne.

In 1673, Danby ruthlessly rationalized the Royal finances. He announced that the Fleet would be reduced and all salaries and pensions stopped until the backpay of seamen's wages had been settled. He struck another bargain with the French King, by which Louis would gain England's political support and Charles, in return for dissolving an anti-French Parliament, would gain an annual subsidy of £100,000. Such an amount was obviously small compared with the total needs of the English crown, but Danby took the view that every little helped. Charles prorogued Parliament, but that, as Louis immediately pointed out, was not dissolution. Danby then secured another offer from Louis of two million livres (£166,000) provided Charles adjourn Parliament until the following April. Pretending to be confused by currency rates of exchange, Charles managed to extort an extra £50,000 out of the unfortunate French ambassador Courtin. When the latter complained, Charles shouted at him: 'For God's sake, do not speak to me of this affair. Go to the Treasurer and do as you and he shall understand the matter; as to myself, I am driven to despair whenever it is mentioned to me!' Charles and Danby had fooled the French King, extracting money from Louis while offering little in return.

More importantly, Danby was concerned with the philosophy of tax itself. With Charles repeatedly forced to raise large sums of cash in a hurry, no existing method of taxation could ever realize the sums required at the appropriate speed. What was needed was a new system of raising monies, rather than a further examination of how and on whom Charles spent his income.

Previously, tax was thought to fall on the vices of the people, including their consumption of foreign and, therefore, unneeded commodities. The rule was that 'taxes ought first rather to be laid upon luxury than necessity; and secondly, rather on things of foreign than domestic growth.' In an age of expanding trade and industry, however, such ideas were restrictive. Indirect taxation should be an incentive to expansion, not a deterrent. It was also believed that a man's total expenditure was a reliable test of his ability. As Petty noted: 'Every man ought to contribute according to what he taketh to himself and actually enjoyeth.' But to tax only according to consumption made no allowance for the man who earned much and spent little. It also penalized the poor at the expense of the rich; the tax on beer, for example, was unfair since the poor man drank twice as much beer as the rich man. 'Though the rich man spends more in excisable things than the poor man doth', another writer, John Carey, observed, 'yet it is not his all; whereas the other's poverty gives him leave to lay up nothing, but it is as much as he can do to provide necessaries for his family out of all which he pays his proportion.'

What was wanted, Danby argued, was a tax in proportion to every man's income. Such an 'income tax' would allay 'the true and proper grievance of taxes.' It could be obtained by imposing taxes on the actual or assumed income received from property of all kinds. Meanwhile, and in addition, a poll tax (or better still, a poll tax plus an excise levy on certain luxury goods) could be directed primarily at the rich.

Political intrigue was to remove Danby before his ideas could be fully effected. Charles felt his loss keenly. Temple wrote in his Memoirs: 'nothing he [Charles] said to me moved me more than when he told me he had none left with whom he could so much speak to them in confidence since my Lord Treasurer's being gone.' Charles even caught a fever. His life was despaired of, although a sea voyage from Woolwich to Portsmouth was the more likely cause than Danby's absence. But from henceforward, Charles's urgent requests for money grew less. 'The Government begins to thrive marvellous well', observed one envious City merchant, 'for it eats and drinks and sleeps as heartily as I have known it.'

In truth, the prosperity began to touch most levels of society, and speculating one's capital became an accepted, although not acceptable, pastime. The Tontine, named after its inventor, an Italian, Tonti, was a lottery in which a group of individuals each contributed £20 to a general fund, the total being lent to the State until only one of the group remained alive. The State then repaid the investment, sometimes with interest, to the survivor. 'What is the hazard of losing twenty pounds', declared the prospectus of one such scheme, 'in comparison to the great advantage that may be obtained by survivorship?'

*   *   *

Charles managed his finances and those of the government with a mixture of skill, blackmail and good luck, characteristics which might be thought central to his other policies, and by 1680 the English Treasury was being recommended to foreign investors as a safe deposit. The King himself managed to slip the parliamentary yoke by encouraging trade and exploiting the customs revenue therefrom. Under Danby, various developments emerged from the exigencies of government which proved useful precedents for later fiscal reforms. The idea of a national debt; the possibility of lending money on the security of a proportion of the national revenues; the appropriation of a tax to a specific object and the subsequent payment 'in course'; the concept of a national bank whereby repayments of money borrowed become more reliable, thereby encouraging investment. Lastly the idea of paper money. The Exchequer bills guaranteeing the repayment of money were, after all, were negotiable bits of paper.

As to the view that Charles's financial management was ineffably corrupt: Pepys had been told long ago by his master Sandwich that 'it was not the salary of any place that did make a man rich, but the opportunity of getting money when he is in place'; and when Pepys had taken over the office of treasurer to the commissioners for Tangier, his immediate predecessor Povey had assigned him three-sevenths of the 'rewards and considerations' that went with the office. Payments were frequently made to important secretaries of government offices in lieu of fees; such perquisites were thought a legitimate, even essential, part of a public servant's salary. A bill of 1667 which would have imposed an oath on all holders of parliamentary office forbidding them to receive such payments was rejected. So was a bill of 1678 designed to stop the Lord Treasurer, or his Commissioners, or the Lord Lieutenant of Ireland, from taking undue advantage of their places. Such bills were vetoed not through self-interest, but because offices of State were regarded as a freehold capable of lease or of resale, and forfeitable only through neglect or abuse. The system may have been haphazard, but it was not venal.

The Commons also rejected a bill which would have prevented Members from holding any other office during the sitting of a Parliament. Such a measure, it was suggested, would change the constitution from a monarchy to a commonwealth, in that service to the Crown would become incompatible with service to Parliament. The contrast with today is striking, although this should not cloud one's appreciation of how and why the system functioned. 'Rewards and considerations' had one notable side-effect. They opened the highest offices to the middle and lower classes. Since the holding of high office no longer depended upon the wealth necessary to sustain that high office, lesser men felt able to compete for recognition. Pepys, for instance, was the son of a working tailor.

The commercial class grew rapidly in Charles's reign, as they became increasingly conscious of the prerogatives attached to wealth and civic status. And since the government lacked adequate sources of credit, it was often forced to turn to those who could afford to finance, say, a fleet and its provisions out of their own money. Many were Nonconformists; William Penn the younger, Sir Robert Viner (later Lord Mayor and Charles's banker), and Sir Josiah Child, a governor of the East India Company whose personal fortune was reckoned to be £250,000. They became an estate of the realm. Regarded as socially inferior by the Tory ruling class, these entrepreneurs joined the opposition and thus provided substantial backing for the new Country or Whig Party. Charles, on the other hand, was delighted to accept their frequent offers of hospitality, reckoning he could divert if not suppress their political ambitions.

reckoning he could divert if not suppress their political ambitions.

Many confusions remained, however; the normal expenses of a peace-time administration were still mixed up with the extraordinary expenses of war; the mad methods of book keeping which have defied satisfactory analysis ever since; the inability to decide what the King was accountable for and what not – his hereditary income, such as could be estimated, was thought beyond accountability; the understandable although destructive financial attitude of the Commons toward Charles's government – in 1673, Sir William Coventry wrote to one Mr Thynne: 'if ever Parliament sit again, whoever shall have sat at condemning any man for life or limb will, I believe, be questioned, this point and matter of money being the only guard the people have against an army they so much dread.'

Nor were all the results of the Navigation Act and its subsidiaries beneficial. Although Adam Smith was later to note in this *Wealth of Nations* that these Acts were 'perhaps the wisest of all the commercial regulations of England' – they brought the widespread colonies into a trading scheme one of whose purposes was to feed the mother country – at the time opinion was divided. Roger Coke contended that the system injured English trade; Dutch prosperity, he argued, had increased because of it. Josiah Child agreed. Because of the high interest rates on trading loans demanded by English merchants, 'the Dutch low interest has miserably lessened us in all trades of the world not secured to us by laws, or by some natural advantage.' In the plantations there were too few authorised ships to cope with the increased trade, and, as a result, quantities of Barbados sugar and Virginian tobacco were left to rot at the docks. Evasion of the law often seemed not only necessary but essential.

The equality boasted of by political and economic theorists was a long way from reality. England's poor made the aristocracy rich, and money, then as now, entailed power and freedom.

Chapter Seven
Weathering the storm

After the disaster in the Medway, it was clear to Charles that he would need to exercise a much stricter control over his government. Clarendon, his principal adviser, had grown old, however, and more than a little tiresome. He was in poor health and Council meetings were often held in his house with the Chancellor propped up in bed. Charles later told Ormonde 'the truth is his [Clarendon's] behaviour and humour was grown so insupportable to myself and to all the world else, that I could not longer endure it; and it was impossible for me to live with it and do those things with the Parliament that must be done or the Government will be lost.' Clarendon would have to take the blame for the Dutch fiasco, the Fire, the Plague and anything else that came to mind. Among his crimes were 'sniping in public employments', raising 'monuments of his greatness, while the kingdom groaned under his oppressions', insolence to the King in that he had declared Charles to be Popishly affected, mismanagement of the wars against the Dutch, denigrating Parliament, recommending a standing army, hindering the operation of the Act of Uniformity, and 'upon all occasions discouraging the poor and suffering Royalists.' In August 1667 Clarendon was dismissed; Osmund Airy wrote that Charles 'abandoned the wise old man to whom he owed his throne.'

Secretly, Charles told Clarendon to leave the country for France, never to return. Although removed by Charles as a necessary political sacrifice in the interests of stable government, had it not been for Charles, Clarendon might not have escaped with his life. Threatened with impeachment, Clarendon agreed to go, in November 1667; Charles promised that his honours and estate would remain untouched; the safety of the realm demanded new counsellors and a new policy, Charles explained, and Clarendon's public dismissal (although not his private deal) would signify that the Crown acknowledged the need to make amends with Parliament. In a country still unaccustomed to the bloodless transference of power, the replacement of Clarendon caused littlé fuss. Arlington told Ormonde: 'I cannot but be of the opinion that . . . public affairs will be bettered by this change', and Charles consolidated this new 'good will' by telling Parliament that from now on they must feel free to call to public account whom they pleased. Privately, the King knew he had lost one of his most trustworthy companions.

This reconciliation between King and Parliament came not a moment too soon. Charles's foreign policy, such as it was, seemed threatened by his cousin's warlike attitude on the Continent. Four months before Clarendon's impeachment, Louis XIV had launched another violent attack upon the Spanish Netherlands, and then announced the terms on which he would end the war and conclude peace. But the French generals had found the campaign a walkover, literally, and were urging Louis on to further conquests. Louis said he still preferred diplomacy where possible, and had sent a new ambassador to London, a French Protestant called the Marquis of Ruvigny. Like his predecessors, Ruvigny was to acquaint himself fully with economic and political conditions in England. Such information was for the 'service and . . . glory' of Louis; a supply of English convicts would be welcome, incidentally, as they made excellent galley slaves.

From the point of view of Versailles, England was an island which needed educating into her predestined place in a French Europe with Louis as its natural leader. Louis was rich, respectable, fanatically hard-working and ambitious. Although he had never travelled through Europe except as head of a conquering army, his knowledge of European affairs gleaned from his horde of spies, agents and informers, was formidable. He was convinced that English friendship could be bought, or at least subsidized. After all, was not Charles permanently in debt?

This co-operation had long been threatened, however, by the Anglo-Dutch confrontations which had diverted Louis's grand European designs. Charles, with Clarendon, had tried to assure Louis that it was the Dutch who were the aggressors. In any case, he had told the flotilla of French ambassadors sent to bribe the English, it was not Charles who had sought war with Holland but Parliament. For a small consideration, of course, he might cajole or even dismiss Parliament; but if Louis felt bound to fulfil his Dutch obligations, then it would be curious indeed to see the Grand Monarch allied to the Dutch Republicans.

While England had been scrapping with Holland, therefore, France and England had also been nominally 'in conflict'. Hostilities had been confined to the diplomatic front – Charles had tried to double-bluff Louis by initialling a commercial treaty with Spain; Louis had instructed the French ambassador in Madrid to tell the Spanish Government that, if the treaty with England were formalized, the French King would consider himself absolved of *his* treaties with Spain. Louis had then signed an agreement with Portugal, England's sole remaining ally, to the effect that Portugal's existing treaties with Spain and England were 'to be reviewed'. Stockholm and Vienna, meanwhile, had been encouraged by Louis to decline offers of an alliance with England, and

Frederick III of Denmark had been persuaded to declare war on England, although for no particular reason. 'His [Louis's] heart is constantly ablaze with two consuming subjects', the Venetian ambassador in London noted. 'One is jealousy of his own greatness . . . the other is the desire to surpass, with acts of true magnificence, the finest examples that present themselves for his emulation.'

Charles had been unimpressed. In April 1667, he had sent Louis a written promise – 'on the word of a King' – that he would not ally himself to an enemy of France for a year, during which time he would attempt to restore Anglo-French relations. The promise meant little to Louis; without waiting for the Anglo-Dutch wars to end, he surprised Europe with the publication of his *Traité des Droits de la reine* . . . In it, he presented himself as the defender of an abstract justice which entailed bestowing on all known territories the ultimate benefits of French civilization. This policy, the text concluded, had been agreed upon 'by the unanimous consent of all the famous universities.' Charles had remained unimpressed. His written promise had already indicated to Louis that, despite the probable hostility of Parliament to any French/Catholic alliance, Charles knew emotionally and politically where his best friends lay. Was not Charles's mother Louis's aunt? And was not his favourite sister, Minette, the French King's sister-in-law? Perhaps it would be to Charles's advantage if he now appeared to value these family bonds.

Expedience, Charles had told Parliament in October 1667, favoured an alliance. What was needed, as Sir William Temple had frequently said, was an European league which might curb the encroaching power of France. Privately, however, Charles began to see any new continental commitment in terms of his financial advantage. After all, a Franco–Dutch alliance might, without any compensation to England, carve up the Spanish Netherlands and its new American Empire. 'France will have us or Holland always with them', Charles noted later. 'And if we take them [the overseas territories] not, Holland will have them.' To aid him in this view, Charles now appointed a group of men who had little in common other than their previous opposition to Clarendon who had departed, paradoxically, to France. By coincidence, none of Charles's new henchmen was a devout member of the Anglican Church; one was a Roman Catholic, one a crypto-Catholic, one a lapsed Presbyterian and the other two by inclination, if not affirmation, Dissenters. By coincidence also, they shared a lust for power and its attendant opportunism; Charles always valued the unscrupulous in others because it enabled them to betray each other should the need arise. In fact, this junta was just one of what became hereafter a series of modulating groups who enjoyed a small measure of Royal confidence, and who were thus useful as protection for Charles against Parliament. They could take the blame. Being mutually distrustful and jealous, they could be manipulated by Charles in a manner which had eluded him with Clarendon. 'When rogues fall out', he observed, 'the master is like

Thomas, Lord Clifford of Chudleigh; a contemporary engraving. Born 1 August, 1630, near Exeter, distantly related to the Earl of Cumberland. Educated at Exeter College, Oxford, and the Middle Temple. Aggressively energetic, even violent, pro-French, pro-Catholic, an ally of James, ennobled in February 1672, politically naive, and a friend of Arlington. (Clifford and Arlington signed the original Secret Treaty of Dover.) "He was a valiant, uncorrupt gentleman," declared Evelyn, "ambitious, not covetous; generous, passionate, a most constant, sincere friend." After the Test Act of 1673, Clifford declared for Catholicism, retired to his home at Ugbrooke beyond Exeter, received a general pardon from Charles, buried the Secret Treaty in his garden, and then, according to Evelyn, killed himself.

then to know the truth.' The uniqueness of this particular group hinges on the further coincidence that their initials spelled out their status, the Cabal.

The idea of a cabal or ruling clique was not new. The word derives from the Hebrew 'qabbalah', meaning tradition, or those invested with the authority necessary to uphold that tradition. Such a group was not in any sense a cabinet. Since three of this particular lot were West Countrymen, they hardly ever met or made collective decisions. Their loose association had other purposes, which they were the last to understand, and only then after it was too late.

Chief among them was Henry Bennet, Lord Arlington, the protégé of Barbara Castlemaine. He had 'the pedantick carriage of a true penman' and possessed the one quality important to Charles; he had no loyalties other than to the King. Arlington's agent during the Dutch wars had been Thomas Clifford, later, in 1672, Lord Clifford. He believed that Charles should rule as a Tudor despot; though he professed to be a free-thinking Catholic, he preferred to live according to his horoscope. A privy counsellor and commissioner to the Treasury, a reckless, arrogant and jealous man, his usefulness lay in his self-proclaimed role as trouble-shooter. Guaranteed to shout his mouth off at almost any opportunity, Clifford provoked his diplomatic adversaries into indiscretions. He eventually poisoned himself, or so it is widely believed.

The Duke of Buckingham was best known as a wit, adulterer and bully. Patron of Dryden and author of a vicious (although supposedly satirical) attack on his childhood companion and friend Charles, his vindictive ridicule flattened hypocrisies and punctured ambitions. Rich, a braggart for whom the notion of treason was meaningless, in every way he epitomized Charles's new breed of ministers – faithful only to the King, loyal above factional interest. At least, that is what they all said. Next was the Earl of Lauderdale; with his 'high Scotch' pronunciation, he was more or less incomprehensible. Coarse and blustering, his 'Saracen fiery face' added to his bizarre appearance. Last was Anthony Ashley Cooper, now Lord Ashley, later Earl of Shaftesbury. Weak in health and shifty in purpose, he is sometimes portrayed as a sincere and diligent worker for the Royal cause. Cromwell had instinctively distrusted him in the not unreasonable belief that anyone who reckoned two names inadequate would stop at nothing. Ashley said he believed in Parliament and in the desirability of religious toleration; Charles, devoted to promoting the idea and image of monarchy, admired Ashley's love of advertisement and self-publicity. A cripple, driven by the simple need to prove himself, Ashley with his ambition for political power eventually overreached himself; but he was a clever man who mercilessly exploited for his own purposes the weaknesses of others. As such, he was an obvious recruit for Charles.

Roger North provides a glimpse of the Cabal's workings. He describes the functions of Will Chiffinch, page to His Majesty's bedchamber and confidant to Charles's ministers. 'Chiffinch was a most impetuous drinker', wrote North, 'and, in that capacity, an admirable spy. For he let none part with him sober, if it were possible to get them drunk. And his great artiface was pushing idolatrous healths of his good master. Nor, to make sure work, would he scruple to

George Villiers, 2nd Duke of Buckingham (c. 1675), in a portrait by Lely. According to Dryden, Buckingham was

> "A man so various that he seemed to be
> Not one, but all mankind's epitome."

Born 30 January, 1628, at Wallingford House, Westminster; the elder surviving son of the 1st Duke, the military leader during the reigns of James I and Charles I, assassinated in August 1628. One of the richest men in England, the 2nd Duke enjoyed a boisterous life; he punched a fellow member of the House of Lords during a debate, was constantly in and out of favour with Charles (he had accompanied the King in exile), married the daughter of Cromwell's henchman, Fairfax, supported the Whigs but would not vote for the exclusion of James, hated Danby, took bribes, openly insulted Charles, was sent to the Tower, and died broken by the King's steel will in 1687. Nonetheless, he was buried in Westminster Abbey, not far from his life-long friend and supporter, King Charles II.

JOHN DUKE OF LAUDERDALE
BY S. COOPER

John Maitland, 2nd Earl and 1st Duke of Lauderdale, in a miniature by Samuel Cooper. The effective ruler of Scotland for most of Charles's reign. Born in East Lothian on 24 May, 1616. A Presbyterian and zealous Covenanter, he had been on good terms with the English Parliamentarians. But he was also highly educated, knew the Classics and Hebrew, and supported the monarchy. He fought with Charles at Worcester 1651, was captured and imprisoned for the next nine years. He was released when Monck entered London, and joined Charles at Breda. His rule north of the border was brutal; he formed the "Highland Host" which turned Scotland into a police state. His atrocities have never been forgotten, or forgiven. After a rising of Galloway peasants in 1666, of a hundred prisoners, ten were hanged from one gibbet in Edinburgh, the rest before their own front doors. Some had their feet crushed by contracting iron boots. The Archbishop of St. Andrews was pistolled, slashed across the face, had his left hand cut off and his skull crushed by the horses of the great Duke of Lauderdale, who thought the mewing of a cat preferable to good music and had a tongue so large that he sprayed his listeners with spittle.

150

put his master's salutiferous drops . . . into the glasses. And, being a Hercules, well-breathed at the sport himself, he commonly had the better, and discovered men's characters which the King could never have obtained by any other means.'

Louis, meanwhile, sent emissaries to explain away his recent declarations of war on England; little more than scraps of parchment, he said. Louis now offered Charles mutual support against any rebellious subjects, the temptation of a joint expedition to the Spanish West Indies, and hinted that should Charles contemplate retaliatory action against the Dutch at some future date, the French King might be of some assistance. Charles told Louis that in his heart he favoured a French alliance; but Parliament was against it, and England had neither the resources nor inclination to continue hostilities against anyone. In secret, Charles told Arlington to draw up a treaty with Holland and Sweden against France, an alliance whose purpose would be to secure peace between France and Spain, although Spain was not to be consulted. The treaty was to indicate that, as a last resort, peace would be 'forced' on France and Spain; such was 'the indecency of the word', Charles wrote later, 'I would willingly have left it out.'

This Triple Alliance was signed in January 1668. 'God be thanked it is done', wrote Arlington, 'and that both the world abroad and at home understand it to be both honourable and safe for His Majesty, and foretell we shall find the Parliament much better complexioned for it.' Charles and his ministers, it seemed, had secured a notable diplomatic triumph, and the spectacle of an English King heading a Protestant alliance against the two dominant Catholic European powers cheered many hearts.

In private, however, Charles assured Ruvigny (although he forgot to tell Arlington) that the Alliance made no difference to his relations with Louis. In a letter, Charles reminded Louis that he, Charles, had always favoured a French alliance, at the right price. He had never considered his request for a French subsidy, plus a share of the French conquests in the Spanish Netherlands (including a channel port), plus various other commercial privileges, to be an unreasonable price for neutrality. Arlington, Charles said, had wanted the French to commit themselves to an all-out war of revenge against the Dutch, but this would have been too disruptive. Charles always preferred peace to war. And anyway, he had been rebuffed by Louis. Charles had been left with no alternative (he explained to Louis) other than to sign an alliance with Holland and Sweden. 'I believe you will be a little surprised at the treaty I have concluded with the States', Charles wrote to his sister Minette. '. . . Finding my propositions to France received so cold an answer, which in effect was as good as a refusal, I thought that I had no other way to secure myself.'

Louis said he cared nothing for the Alliance or its threats. It confirmed what Louis had already asserted, namely that it was he with his grand design who sought the peaceful unification of Europe. It was the Dutch and the Spaniards who, assisted by numerous off-shore islands, were the belligerents.

Louis was being steadily and skilfully outmanoeuvred, however. Against the Dutch, Charles was pursuing a policy of limited war, both military and economic, from which England had emerged thus far with modest successes, at the expense of the Dutch, around the world. He had no European ambitions like Louis; he wished to threaten neither France nor Spain, except in so far as they endangered England's trading interests. He hoped primarily to strengthen the power of England and unify its people, as well as to consolidate his constitutional monarchy, politically in alliance with Parliament although financially independent of it. To assist this financial independence, Charles was happy to extract money from Louis, although he knew that in return Louis would expect Charles's support. So he concluded peace with the Dutch, for decades the bellicose neighbours of France; Louis would either have to appear the aggressor against Holland (and its new-found ally England), or else bribe Charles and his ministers for their compliance.

Charles enjoyed his role as broker. He was delighted that the King of France, in whose country Charles had been an impoverished exile only ten years before, now acknowledged that English friendship had to be bought. Louis was a Catholic, Charles's brother had declared himself a Catholic, and Louis wanted England to be Catholic. But Parliament and the country hated the Catholics, Charles told him. Louis suspected that Charles would swear to anything if he thought it politically or financially advantageous to do so, and Charles led him on in that belief. Nominally, Charles was for religious toleration; legally, he was for the Anglican Church. Probably he was for Catholicism. He might be persuaded to announce publicly his conversion to Roman Catholicism, although the price for such a declaration, Charles warned Louis, would be high.

Louis sent Colbert (the younger) as special ambassador to persuade Charles that Holland was their main enemy. Charles told Arlington, who had a Dutch wife, to busy himself organizing an extensive anti-French league, consisting of Holland, Switzerland, Brandenburg, Luxembourg, and Saxony. Buckingham, who despised Arlington, told Colbert that Arlington could be bribed. Clifford hinted to Colbert that the Dutch might go to war if they suspected they were being betrayed, and gave the impression that both Charles and his brother 'favoured' an alliance with Louis. Not only had Charles acquiesced in James's conversion, knowing the political danger of such acquiescence, but, according to James, had announced at the same time his own intended conversion with tears in his eyes. Charles had even begun to ask advice, it was said, 'about the ways and methods fittest to be taken for the selling of the Catholic religion in his kingdoms, and to consider of the time most proper to declare himself.' James knew nothing of any secret dealings between Charles and his French cousin, and it is possible that Charles truly

Charles on horseback, with Louis XIV in hot pursuit trying to buy Charles's support; a contemporary Dutch cartoon. Louis offered, or was persuaded to offer, money – to Charles, Charles's mistresses, Charles's ministers and even Charles's children, in 1660, 1662, 1664, 1665, 1666, 1667, 1668, 1669, 1670, 1671, 1673, 1674, 1676, 1677, 1679, 1680, 1681, 1682, 1683 and 1684. No-one knows how much money was eventually paid over; Charles didn't say, and Louis never admitted it. In total, however, it was probably in excess of £3 million, for which Charles gave almost nothing in return.

wished to become a Catholic but feared to do so unless he had the support, albeit unspoken, of Louis. His wife, his brother, his brother's wife, his favourite sister, his favourite mistress, all were Catholics and not without influence. But Charles also knew well that parliamentary opposition to his father had been inspired as much as anything by the doleful Roman Catholic atmosphere at Court. Even if he covetted the benefits of absolute power now being grasped so assiduously by his cousin, he rejected them as impractical. The £140,000 which Charles eventually extracted from Louis was insignificant compared with the total needs of the Stuart administration, yet Charles could not resist the excitement of financial blackmail. He decided to investigate, therefore, the possibilities of an agreement with Louis in contradiction to his existing agreement with Holland and Sweden. After all, it would be a personal arrangement between cousins, accomplished in spite of, and if necessary against, the wishes of Parliament. In brief, an exercise of the Royal prerogative.

153

It became difficult, if not impossible, to know exactly who was deceiving whom when Louis now revealed, through Arlington, that de Witt had also approached Louis with suggestions for a secret treaty between Holland and France to partition the Spanish Empire. Arlington was affronted and thus easily persuaded by Charles into the idea of a French arrangement, although at Charles's instruction he continued to discuss with the Dutch outstanding details from the Triple Alliance, now two years old. Buckingham was kept negotiating a commercial treaty with France, while Colbert urged Charles to wait until after a successful military campaign against the Dutch before publicly declaring his conversion. With 20,000 ex-Cromwellian soldiers garrisoned in or near London, he argued, such a declaration might be suicide. A victorious warrior King, on the other hand, might find his subjects more willing to accept change as fundamental as this. Charles said he was convinced, though as passionate as ever for Catholicism. In fact, neither the English ambassador in Paris, nor the French ambassador in London, knew anything of Charles's secret negotiations with Louis.

Colbert was shown the draft treaty of an agreement between Charles and Louis on 18 December 1669. Charles demanded £200,000 in return for his declaration of Catholicism, and the promise of more cash and/or military aid in the event of a rebellion in England. In addition, a further £600,000 was to be the price for Charles's help against the Dutch, with Ostend, Minorca and the Spanish American possessions as booty. Charles's demands were, according to Louis, 'a thunderclap which took his breath away.' Charles twisted the screw further by allowing the Commons to vote an additional levy on the import of wine and vinegar which, inevitably, fell most heavily on imports from France. He also enlisted the aid of Minette, Louis's sister-in-law, and it was she who engineered the compromise which both sides agreed to sign at Dover under cover of a State visit by his sister, as Duchess of Orléans, to England.

Charles had not seen Minette for nine years, and planned extensive celebrations to welcome her, including concerts, plays and dances. She was the only surviving relative for whom he had the remotest affection, witty, like her brother, though shy. According to the Bishop of Valence, Minette 'had a clear, strong intellect. She was full of good sense and gifted with fine perception . . . Her whole conversation was filled with a sweetness which made her unlike all other Royal personages . . . The grace of her soul seemed to animate her whole being, down to the tips of her feet, and made her dance better than any woman I ever saw.' She had a big nose and round blue-black eyes, which coloured a wicked smile. Married to a pervert, she too had become adept in the world of political intrigue. In this, she was an admirable foil to Charles, and their mutual trust doubtless grew from their common distrust of all politicians.

'For the perpetual union and friendship between the two kings and their states', the treaty began, 'articles so secret and advantageous to both monarchs have been agreed upon that a treaty of similar importance can hardly be found in any period of history.' It was a proud boast; an even prouder boast followed. 'The lord king of Great Britain, being convinced of the truth of the Catholic religion, and resolved to declare it, and reconcile himself with the Church of Rome as soon as the welfare of his kingdom will permit.' Louis promised 6,000 foot soldiers, plus a subsidy, should Charles ever need help to support this declaration. He also promised not to commence hostilities against Spain, thus allowing Charles to claim he had honoured a major principle of the Triple Alliance. The two Kings further agreed to declare war on Holland 'to reduce the power of a nation which has so often rendered itself odious by extreme ingratitude to its founders and the creators of its republic', for which agreement Charles was to be paid £250,000. The exact timing of the war was left to Louis, although Charles insisted it was delayed until after his religious affirmation.

Minette was certain she had scored a triumph by uniting her brother and brother-in-law. There were fireworks in celebration, although few realized what was actually being celebrated. The Queen and the Duchess of York came to Dover; lavish presents were exchanged, and Minette returned to France. Eight days later she was dead. Her dying words were of Charles: 'I have loved him better than life itself.' She was only 26.

Charles and Louis were stunned by the news of Minette's death, with Louis now doubly resolved to carry out his part of the treaty whose achievement had, in its final stages, owed much to her. But Charles now wanted to negotiate a second treaty (again to be 'secret'), identical to the first except that it would omit references to Charles's proposed Catholic declaration. Only Arlington and Clifford had known of the first treaty, so Charles was anxious to involve Buckingham and Lauderdale in the second. Buckingham was sent to Louis who spoke passionately and at length of the French desire to combine with the English against the Dutch. Louis would insist, he told the Duke flatteringly, that Buckingham command the English expeditionary troops.

Louis's primary interest was to dismember the Spanish Empire; toward the Dutch he felt merely irritation. For Charles, Buckingham argued, the Dutch were the main problem. The essential aim continued to be one of maritime, and thus trading, supremacy, which the two Anglo-Dutch wars had left unresolved. As it turned out, the later annihilation of the Dutch gave a phenomenal boost to England's trading empire, and enabled Chatham and Marlborough to challenge the power of the Bourbons at the beginning of the next century. That the initial advantage had been gained at French expense, both in cash subsidy and more importantly in diverting Louis from his grand designs, was a singular accomplishment for Charles.

At the time, the second secret treaty merely postponed when and how to tell Parliament, which still assumed that English foreign policy depended on the Triple Alliance. Louis began to insist that Charles declare his conversion, reminding Charles that the renegotiations had not absolved him from his earlier promises. The Pope was dying, Charles pleaded. The theologian needed to perform this great work (of Charles's conversion) had to be a chemist, since Charles still had one or two lingering doubts, minor of course, but which needed resolution. In addition, he told Louis, anti-Catholic feeling in England was on the increase. The timing of his conversion was critical; after all, Louis had promised to come to his rescue in the event of trouble. Charles had even been forced to prorogue both Houses of Parliament. These were difficult times. 'A great diminution', wrote one observer, 'is like to befall mankind next summer.'

Charles's difficulties were real enough. Apart from stopping the Exchequer, Charles had been forced to accept a petition from both Houses of Parliament against the growth of Popery. In need of cash to re-equip the Navy for the forthcoming (although as yet secret) war, he had been obliged to appease Parliament by issuing a proclamation requiring all Jesuits and Roman priests to leave England before May 1671. Diverting Parliament from its increasingly anti-Catholic, anti-French attitude, would be difficult.

Tensions with the Dutch, however, were exacerbated by the refusal of part of the Dutch fleet to salute the yacht *Merlin* as it was taking Lady Temple from The Hague, and a reluctant Downing was dispatched to remind the Dutch of their treaty obligations in saluting English ships. It was a minor incident, but it provided Charles with an excuse to withdraw, albeit temporarily, from his obligations to the Triple Alliance. And when, in the channel, Admiral Holmes was ordered to attack a much larger fleet accompanying a Dutch merchant convoy and was lucky to escape with what battered remnants he did, the way was open to sign yet another treaty which this time openly committed England to an alliance with France. Out of apparent deference to his new French ally, but more importantly to distract Louis from his demands for Charles's 'conversion', Charles was able in 1672 to issue a Second Declaration of Indulgence (the first, favouring the Puritans, had been published by Charles in 1662 in an attempt to fulfil his promises at Breda, but after a Bill to give the Declaration legal sanction was defeated in the Lords, it had been withdrawn). The new Declaration suspended all penal laws against non-conformists and recusants, and guaranteed Catholics freedom from molestation provided they worshipped at home. Charles no doubt reckoned that a short, sharp and decisive action against the Dutch, in partnership with his cousin Louis, would enhance his prestige at home as well as confuse those who thought his Second Declaration of Indulgence a further manifestation of 'deep Popish designs'. Holland would not be able to resist the combined naval and military strength of Europe's two most powerful nations. Should the outcome prove successful, England, and in particular England's merchants, had much to gain. Not only would their great trading rivals be annihilated but, when the King of Spain eventually died, there would be material benefits in plenty from England's share of the Spanish Empire.

Charles's own position seemed strong. His recent successes – the re-establishment of religious toleration, the monies acquired to re-equip the fleet – had been gained not with the consent of Parliament, which he had prorogued, but through exercise of the Royal prerogative. By replacing Clarendon with a gang of able although self-seeking career men, Charles hoped he had secured his administration against parliamentary interference. Coincidental with the declaration of war, Charles signified his pleasure with these men by creating Arlington an earl, Lauderdale a duke, Clifford a baron and Ashley the Earl of Shaftesbury. Only Buckingham, already a duke, apparently went unrewarded. North of the border, 'never was a King so absolute as in poor old Scotland', wrote one contemporary; Ireland was dominated by the autocratic Earl of Essex; as to Parliament, as long as the war was short, Charles had no further need of them or their money. He hoped that the Declaration of Indulgence would unite his subjects behind him. Its purpose, as Arlington admitted, had been 'that we might keep all quiet at home while we are busiest abroad.' In victory, Charles believed, all would be forgiven.

It was not to be. His brother James was confirmed as Lord High Admiral, with the French admiral, d'Estrées, nominally under his command. At their first encounter with the Dutch fleet, 29 May 1672, d'Estrées failed to obey orders; the result was a shambles. By 10 a.m. the Royal flagship had been shot out of the water, with 200 of its crew killed. James transferred to the *St Michael*, but that too was badly holed and made to port, with James forced to transfer again. The *Royal James*, captained by Pepys's cousin, the Earl of Sandwich, by now one of England's most experienced seamen, was blown to bits. In all, the English casualties were estimated at 2,500. Like most naval conflicts at the time, the Battle of Southwold was claimed as a victory by both sides. But its undeniable result was that the English failed to gain control of the North Sea, thus making any proposed landing on the Dutch coast hazardous.

The second encounter was similarly farcical. James was ordered to intercept the Dutch East India Fleet and destroy it. In the pursuit he got lost, and half his fleet was wrecked in a storm. The Dutch arrived safely in Holland, and Charles called off any naval engagements until further notice.

Louis, meanwhile, had invaded Holland by land and compelled the Dutch to sue for peace. But the terms offered by Louis were, as we have seen, so humiliating that the Dutch people overthrew the republican government of the brothers de Witt, and gave power to their rivals, the House of Orange. The new Stadholder, William III, calmly opened the dykes and the noblest army of Europe flopped to a muddy halt within sight of Rotterdam. Charles was horrified; William was his nephew. Realizing his uncle's embarrassment, William began to deal separately with Charles and Louis. Louis told Charles to send representatives to the French headquarters for the conclusion of a treaty with the Dutch. Knowing of their mutual suspicion, Charles sent

Buckingham and Arlington hoping thereby to avoid any firm committment. Arlington was instructed to appease Louis, and Buckingham told to dazzle the youthful William with hopes of sovereignty under English–French patronage. William was not taken in. He refused to concede any territories, let alone consider Arlington's demands such as expenses for the war, subsidy for the herring industry and certain 'readjustments' in trade. The Buckingham–Arlington expedition foundered, and they dutifully signed yet another agreement with Louis promising not to conclude a separate peace with William. William, undaunted, dispatched two secret envoys to England, intending to negotiate a separate peace with Charles. Charles hesitated, postponing the next meeting of Parliament until the following April (it was now October 1672), trusting that by then a more general peace would avoid the need to betray Louis so openly.

Charles could not let William think or know that it was almost impossible for him to continue at war. 'The King finds himself . . . without money and without credit', noted Colbert. The French subsidies were proving inadequate, the rivalries among his ministers uncontrollable. Charles had already told them that if any of their quarrels hindered his foreign policy, those responsible would pay. In November, he removed Sir Orlando Bridgeman, the Lord Keeper, because of his refusal to place the Great Seal on the Declaration of Indulgence, and replaced him with Shaftesbury who assumed the title of Lord Chancellor. Clifford was promoted Lord Treasurer, leaving Arlington disgruntled at being passed over. Buckingham, drunk and in debt, 'out with the King and everybody else', was quietly put aside.

Parliament had to be recalled to vote further supplies, and Shaftesbury, ignorant of the original Secret Treaty of Dover, drafted a speech in which he compared relations between the English and the Dutch as between the Romans and the Carthaginians. 'What is the use of his Great Council of Parliament', said a member of the Commons, Sir Thomas Lee, 'but to inform the King he has been misled and mistaken by his Privy Council.' In return for the monies which Charles needed for the fleet, Parliament wanted the Declaration of Indulgence repealed, or at least modified. 'What is the discretion for a man to be angry with his own hurt', Charles pleaded, 'and have a care not to be left without a fleet this Spring?' But the Commons were insistent. Charles had been misinformed about his powers, they said. A Test Bill was hustled through both Houses of Parliament. James panicked; should the Bill become Law, he would be forced to resign all his offices. Charles was trapped.

Clifford, unexpectedly loyal, defended Charles in the Lords, but in such a violent manner that the King (who was present) thought Clifford did more harm than good. And when Arlington told Shaftesbury of certain terms in the Secret Treaty of Dover, although not the crucial one, he too agreed that withdrawal was the wiser course. It would be expedient to admit a tactical defeat; all that remained was to do so courteously. 'The King in a short but very gracious speech', reported Sir Edward Dering, 'said he would issue a proclamation in accordance with the address the day before presented to him by the two Houses, desired that they would consider the time of the year, the necessity for setting forth the fleet very speedily, and proceed with the bill for supply. The answer exceeding pleasing to the House.' 'We are mighty busy here', noted Sir Thomas Player, adding, with more than a touch of sarcasm, 'swearing against the Pope.'

The Declaration of Indulgence was cancelled; the Test Bill became Law. A bill for the ease of Protestant dissenters was added, and Parliament adjourned. James resigned his offices in June 1673 and alienated what little support remained by marrying a bigoted and Francophile Catholic, Mary Beatrice d'Este of Modena. (His first wife, Anne Hyde, had died in 1671.) Court gossip began to speak of Monmouth, still young, glamorous and fresh from heroic military exploits in France, as a possible successor. Clifford resigned, and was replaced by Sir Thomas Osborne, later the Earl of Danby. Arlington was again passed over. Those of the Cabal who knew of the original Secret Treaty dumped all their incriminating documents on the unfortunate Clifford who buried them in his garden beyond Exeter, where they were not discovered for 250 years. Clifford then poisoned himself, but not before he had told Shaftesbury the full contents of the second secret treaty. Shaftesbury was astonished, but also hurt at having been deceived by Charles. Suspicions of a plot subordinating Whitehall to Versailles lingered on, although Charles's deviousness had ensured an unusually plentiful supply for continuance of the war, against a Protestant neighbour and in part on behalf of a Catholic enemy. He tacitly allowed the flood of anti-Dutch propaganda which appeared, thus giving tacit support to his secret Catholic ally, Louis. Dryden wrote:

> What injuries so 'er upon us fall
> Yet still, the same religion answers all;
> Religion wheedled you to civil war,
> Drew English blood, and Dutchmen's now would spare;
> Be gull'd no longer; for you'll find it true
> They have no more religion, faith, than you.

In other words, in spite of the minor upheaval caused by the Test Act, matters were as before. With Parliament adjourned, Charles reckoned that even the Test Act could be modified or removed, given time. Only part of the Cabal had been sacrificed; anyway, Charles had always regarded it as expendable.

There remained the business of war. A peace conference between England, Holland and France convened in April 1673 at the neutral city of Cologne, failed to produce any conclusions. William called for a supreme effort in defence of the fatherland, and in this spirit the Dutch fleet once more engaged superior Anglo–French forces off Texel in August 1673. Again the French Admiral d'Estrées failed. First he got separated from the main fleet; then he got

159

lost in the rain and fog. 'It was all fire and flame', remembered one eyewitness. Both admirals had to transfer their flag three times. As Prince Rupert, the English Admiral, recorded later, 'it was the plainest and greatest opportunity ever lost at sea.' The French Admiral's behaviour astonished Rupert; 'it wanted neither signal nor instruction', he wrote later, 'to tell him (the French Admiral) what he should then have done; the case was so plain to every man's eye in the whole fleet.' One Captain reported that although he had been given strict orders not to speak against the French, he could scarcely get half a dozen men to cheer their ships. The Army, gathered for the proposed invasion of Holland, was said to be full of Papists, hired for the overthrow of English liberties. Charles had inspected the troops at Blackheath and later at Yarmouth, but no one could tell whether he ever intended they should fight.

Rising prices and press gangs increased English opposition to the war, while on the Continent William secured alliances with Spain and the German Emperor against France. Louis found himself diplomatically surrounded. From being the agent of divine justice commissioned to punish an upstart, the French King had finished up hated by his major ally and confronted with a lengthy conflict. Charles was told that his Queen was 'in consumption' and could only live a few months. He had already been talked into considering a divorce and re-marriage for diplomatic purposes. There would be at least one condition, Charles said, in the selection of any future wife; he would not rely on portraits.

Charles's policy, or lack of it, had become hopelessly confused. It is possible that until now Charles's desire to see religious toleration had been balanced with his obvious and personal need to see England prosperous. This desire had allowed him to follow a devious, although consistent, line. He would encourage Louis's grand designs, but only in so far as they directly benefited England, either in cash or in reducing the trading monopolies of England's rivals. At the same time, he would refuse to push hostilities against the Dutch too far, since it was they rather than the Catholic French who were England's natural religious allies. He would make whatever promises were necessary as to his own religious commitments, as long as such promises were reasonably discreet. Should these promises be discovered, he could easily claim to have been deceived in the interests of his country. As a precaution, he would allow these delicate machinations to be initiated by his ministers, specially hired for their ingratiating servitude, so that should anything go wrong, Charles could protest he had been betrayed.

This strangely tortuous policy had begun to fall apart. James, by his precipitous re-marriage, had declared too boldly for one side, and Charles was confronted with a Parliament (reconvened in October 1673) demanding that James's marriage be annulled. Charles talked of 'gaining time'; James replied that they were 'losing time'. In vain Charles tried to reassure Parliament about his religious intentions. 'I shall be ready to give you fresh instances', he told them, 'of my zeal for preserving the established religion and laws, as often as any occasion shall require.' But it was too late. 'Pray God direct his Majesty', wrote one Member, Sir Christopher Musgrave, 'for . . . things never looked with a more dreadful aspect. If the session continue, I believe particular persons will be brought upon the stage.'

There was little Charles could do to stop the blood-letting. Lauderdale was attacked for somehow having misappropriated £400,000, 'of which the Duchesses of Cleveland and Portsmouth had the greatest share.' Arlington told the French ambassador it was impossible in this atmosphere to continue the war. Buckingham wanted Charles to 'accept' the good terms offered by Holland and abandon the French alliance. The newly arrived Osborne was also strongly anti-French. 'The King calls a cabinet council', reported the Venetian ambassador, 'for the purpose of not listening to it, and the Ministers hold forth in it so as not to be understood.' In November, all London flocked to a great Pope burning. An additional attraction was the effigy of a 'typical Frenchman', which could be shot at by the crowd. The Queen believed she would be assassinated. The Commons demanded a debate on their four great grievances, the growth of Popery, the standing army (which they themselves were financing), the French league and the 'evil counsellors'. Lauderdale was impeached. No wonder that John Wynne could write a month later: 'a party in the House would drive the King upon precipices and introduce a Commonwealth once more'. Parliament was again adjourned.

Colbert did all he could to preserve the French alliance and promote the war against the Dutch. Charles, unscrupulous to the last, demanded £1,400,000 as the price for this friendship. Bribes were pressed on Ministers and Members of Parliament, while Charles was urged by Buckingham to publish an edited version of the Secret Treaty to demonstrate that partnership with France already existed. Charles again summoned Parliament, again playing for time. 'No proposals of peace have yet been offered,' he told them, and suggested disclosing his 'proposed' treaty to a select committee of both Houses. Finally, with a cynicism extreme even by his standards, fumbling with his notes and coughing apologetically, he added: 'and I assure you there is no other treaty with France, either before or since, not already printed which shall not be made known.' The lie was a calculated risk, but it paid off. By 191 to 139 votes, the Commons thanked Charles for his address, and then set about his Ministers.

Lauderdale was removed by unanimous vote, accused of raising in Scotland 20,000 foot and 2,000 horse for the pernicious design of menacing the English constitution. The fact that he had raised these troops for the specific purpose of helping Charles in the event of rebellion was now deemed irrelevant. Buckingham was next. His crimes were unspeakable, almost literally. He too had raised troops in Yorkshire. He had called Charles an arrant knave. He had sought to be all things to all men, 'the debauchees by drinking with them, the sober by grave and serious discourses, the pious by receiving the sacrament.'

161

He had hobnobbed with the King of France. He had broken the Triple Alliance by his machinations with the French. Buckingham blamed Clifford, now dead, and Arlington, now in disfavour. He was, he told the Commons, a tragic victim of circumstance who could hunt with a pack of hounds, but not with a pair of lobsters. Which particular lobsters he had in mind was not clear. Next, Arlington was 'run down'. He was the 'great conduit pipe' through which all things unpopular had passed. It was reported abroad that he was a Papist at heart. He was accused of embezzling the treasures of the Kingdom for his own purposes, of advising the King to enter upon a war the country could not possibly afford, of obtaining commissions for Papists, of harbouring a priest in his household, and of being 'popishly affected'. He too was impeached. It was, in all, a 'bloody week of impeachments and accusations' – against everyone, that is, except Charles. The Cabal was gone. It had outlived its purpose.

Charles now attempted to make peace with the Commons. A master of flattery when the occasion demanded, he submitted to both Houses a letter from the Dutch in which terms of peace that might be acceptable to Parliament were outlined. 'If you shall find the terms such as may be embraced', Charles told the Commons, 'your advice will have great weight with me.' He stressed how much he desired their 'advice and assistance'. After two days of debate, both Houses agreed 'to advise' the King to make a 'speedy peace'. In this new spirit of co-operation, Charles declared himself willing to listen to other grievances. A standing army, other than the Militia, said Colonel Birch, 'though of but sixteen hundred, is able to make the Kingdom jealous.' Charles agreed. A Bill to ensure the proper election of Members to Parliament was discussed; Charles thought it very sensible, as he did a Habeas Corpus Bill. A Bill to prevent the illegal extraction of money also received Royal approval, as did a Prisoner's Transportation Bill. Finally, in February 1674, the Commons passed a Bill sent from the Lords guaranteeing that James's children would be brought up Protestants.

The Dutch, meanwhile, had entrusted their interests to the Spanish ambassador. Their terms of peace were simple; Holland agreed to honour the flag of British ships in British waters, and to pay an indemnity of £200,000. Trading disputes in the East Indies were referred to arbitration, and a new commercial treaty was to be negotiated. In the event, Charles emerged with advantage. He had gained much while losing nothing, except perhaps a little pride, whereas William of Orange had lost part of his territory and Louis his Grand Design. France and Holland had not settled their differences, and henceforward were to be progressively weakened by a prolonged struggle, again to Charles's advantage. Charles could reasonably announce to the Commons, therefore, that he had, with difficulty obtained a 'speedy, honourable and (he hoped) lasting peace.'

Colbert returned to France, disgusted and dumbfounded by Charles's duplicity. 'If Aristotle . . . were to come again to this world, he could not find words to explain the manner of this government', wrote Colbert's successor to Louis. 'It has a monarchical appearance, as there is a King, but it is very far from being a monarchy.' To the French, Charles's methods of government were unfathomable; to many others, he was just too clever. Having obtained a tolerable conclusion to the war and allowed the Commons the privilege of feeling free to discuss their grievances, Charles again adjourned them. Members were offended, but not surprised. They went home 'reproaching one another that they had sat so long upon eggs and hatched nothing.' With Parliament gone, Charles was able to ignore their 'advice' about Lauderdale, who continued to rule in Scotland. Arlington managed to survive for a few months, until Charles removed him to the less conspicuous post of Lord Chamberlain. Buckingham lost his temper once too often. Charles was saddened by his departure. Government would be dull without him. In gratitude, Charles agreed to a pension for Buckingham's mistress, the Countess of Shrewsbury, on which proceeds she retired to a nunnery in France.

Across the seas, New York was recovered after its capture by the Dutch. The Hudson's Bay Company steadily encroached on French trade, the territories of Carolina and Pennsylvania added to Charles's possessions. The Dutch were left to fight for their independence, Louis was left with his dream of European hegemony fading. England, at peace and neutral, could only profit from the confusion. 'The King is intent on enjoying life', reported the Venetian representative in England. The lessons learned throughout the eight years of crisis since the departure of Clarendon had been prodigious. Catholicism, or the threat of its imposition, involved dangerous politics; Shaftesbury was still active, and now organizing a Country Party to oppose Charles's new ministers, whoever they might be. But as one counsellor wrote to Charles: 'we are not altogether in despair, that the old honest party will weather the storm.' Indeed it would, as long as Charles remained in control.

Chapter Eight

Supple hams and no brains

Louis XIV now determined to win over Charles. In the autumn of 1670, he had arranged for a distant cousin of both his and Charles's, Louise-Renée de Penancöet de Kéroualle, to visit England and thereby see 'what may grow out of this situation, and of the terms on which she and the King have come to stand mutually.' Louis was well aware that Charles had already met Mademoiselle de Kéroualle during Minette's visit to Dover, when, aged nineteen, she had been maid of honour to Charles's sister; also, that when Minette had urged Charles to choose a jewel from her casket as a parting gift, the King had asked for Louise. 'She is the only jewel I covet', he was supposed to have said. When Minette had died, Charles had once more begged for Louise's services, claiming, according to some, that this would be a last link with his beloved sister. Buckingham, hoping to regain some of Charles's lost affection, had travelled secretly to France asking Louis to release the young lady from her French royal duties. Everyone knew, he argued, how malleable Charles could be in the hands of a woman.

Charles had been so delighted at Louise's arrival that he gave her lodgings in Whitehall Palace, and visited her every morning at nine. For a while, she had resisted his advances. 'Do not repulse temptations too strongly', the Seigneur de Saint-Evremond had advised her. 'Perhaps you are vain enough to be pleased only with yourself, but you will soon get tired of pleasing and loving yourself.' Dryden also had no illusions as to what was intended. In *The Fair Stranger*, penned to Louise, he wrote:

> Your smiles have more of conq'ring charm,
> Than all your native country's arms . . .
> You make us captive by your stay;
> Yet kill us if you go away.

'I am going to Arlington's place at Euston', Colbert had written to Louvois, the French War Minister, 'and as the King's inclination for Mademoiselle de Kéroualle, who is to go there with me, is rising, I foresee that he will often run across from Newmarket to see her.' 'We hope she will so behave', he had added, 'that the attachment will be durable and exclude every other.' The ruse had worked. Louise had been persuaded to wander about 'for the most part in her undress (without stays and in negligees) *all day*', observed a shocked Evelyn, adding 'that there was fondness and toying with that young wanton.' Worse, it was rumoured that Charles and Louise had taken part in a mock marriage ceremony with Arlington, Colbert and Lady Sunderland standing around making obscene jokes while Charles finally bedded Louise. A few months later, Madame de Sévigné gossiped in a letter to her daughter: 'La Querouaille, whose fortune had been predicted before she left this kingdom, has fully verified it. The King of England was passionately fond of her . . . in short, she is now about eight months gone with child. Poor Castlemaine is turned off; such is the fate of mistresses in that Kingdom.' Saint-Evremond noted more pointedly that the silk ribbon which girded the waist of Mademoiselle Kéroualle had now united France and England.

Parliament had not been slow to realize what was happening. Louise 'was quite out of definition of an ordinary mistress . . . her Chamber was the true Cabinet Council.' Before long, she had extracted her dues from Charles; as soon as their son had been born and named Charles Lennox, she had petitioned Charles to grant her English nationality and so 'benefit by the gifts and honours which King Charles wanted to lavish on her.' Among these were the leases in Ireland he had apparently promised her, in Dublin, Donegal, Fermanagh and elsewhere, as well as a pension of £10,000 per annum. Then there was her title. Charles had dutifully promoted her Duchess of Portsmouth, Countess of Fareham, and Baroness Petersfield. She had also wanted the titles relating to Alresford and Alton, which were refused, so had insisted that her son was ennobled; Charles Lennox was created Duke of Richmond, Baron Settrington and Earl of March. Even that had been insufficient. What was to be done about her penniless sister, Henrietta, she asked? Charles had been persuaded to grant a pension of £600 per annum and marry her off to Philip Herbert, Earl of Pembroke. Girolamo Alberti, a Venetian diplomat passing through London, reported that English public opinion cherished 'the suspicion that, by her means, the ministers of the most Christian nation [France] can insinuate and persuade the King here [in England] to do all that they wish.'

Louis had been delighted by this, his only, success with Charles, and in November 1673 had given Louise the ducal lands of d'Aubigny, later making her the Duchess. In England, however, Louise had begun to inspire fury and jealousy. One night she discovered a note pinned to her bedroom door.

> Within this place a bed's appointed
> For a French bitch and God's annointed.

Shaftesbury had wanted to indict her before a Grand Jury as a national nuisance; and Rochester, in a ditty entitled *The Royal Buss*, began:

> Portsmouth, the incestuous Punk
> Made our most gracious sov'reign drunk.
> And drunk she made him give that Buss
> That all the kingdom's bound to curse,
> And so red hot with wine and whore,
> He kicked the Commons out of door!

Anne, Charles's niece and the future Queen, later described Louise as 'the greatest jade that ever was', adding that she 'goes to St Martin's morning *and* afternoon, because there are not enough people to see her at Whitehall Chapel.' Lady Sunderland wrote that the Duchess 'is so damned a jade . . . she will certainly sell us whenever she can for five hundred pounds.' Rochester agreed; as for Charles,

> Restless he rolls about from whore to whore
> A merry monarch, scandalous and poor;
> To Carwell the most dear of all his dears,
> The best relief of his declining years,
> Oft he bewails his fortune, and her fate:
> To love so well, and be beloved so late.
> For though in her he settles well his tarse,
> Yet his dull, graceless ballocks hang an arse.

Nonetheless, Louis's plan, had brought results. In February 1675, Ralph Bridoake, an especially close friend of Louise, had become Bishop of Chester, and it was thought that Judge Jeffreys owed his rapid advancement to her. Not only had she recommended the young lawyer to Charles, but had taken the King regularly to his house where Jeffreys's lavish hospitality had quickly ingratiated him. 'See by what I have done by my Lord Sunderland', she flounced later, 'whom the King never had a good opinion of till I recommended him. I have made Lord Halifax an Earl, upon his application to me. The King was pleased to make the Earl of Essex a commissioner to the Treasury . . . ever since I gave myself up to him.' 'Nobody shall come to Court or to any preferment', she concluded, 'but those who will be my creatures. The King of England hath promised to support me, and I am allied to most of the sovereign princes abroad.' She was even to boast that she could make Monmouth the 'greatest man in the Kingdom'. As one pamphleteer succinctly put it:

> Monmouth's tamer, Jeff's advance,
> Foe to England, spy to France.

Why had Charles allowed himself to become ensnared by this avaricious betsy? The war, the endless secret treaties, the greed of his ministers, the

166

Louise-Renée de Penancoët de Kéroualle, Duchess of Portsmouth, in a portrait by Pierre Mignard. Born 1649, near Brest in Brittany. The least popular of all Charles's mistresses, she secured an annual "pension" of £10,000. Her apartment in Whitehall had "ten times the richness and glory beyond the Queen's." She survived – her lover, Charles, her son (the Duke of Richmond), her fellow mistresses (among them Barbara Castlemaine and Nell Gwyn), and eventually, aged 70, met Voltaire who said she had "a face still noble and pleasing, that the years have never withered." She founded a hospital for nuns and died, aged 85, a true Catholic, in Paris. "Dearest Fubbs," wrote Charles. "What contentment can there be," asked Evelyn of Louise, "in riches and splendour of this world, purchased with vice and dishonour!" "Nelly, you are grown rich, I believe," said Louise to Mistress Gwyn, "by your dress; why, woman, you are fine enough to be a queen." "You are entirely right, Madam," Nell Gwyn replied, "and I am whore enough to be a duchess."

bumptiousness of Parliament and the hypocrisies of its factions, had confirmed Charles's distrust for politics. Louise, on the other hand, for all her absurdities, provided Charles with a comfortable domesticity he had not known since he was twelve. That she carried herself with an assured grandness, demanded his respect; that she was intelligent and sympathetic, allowed Charles to grumble away about his deteriorating relations with Parliament and what he felt was the increasing mood of religious bigotry in the country. Almost alone among Charles's mistresses, she appeared to have some comprehension of what he was attempting politically, while remaining a comfort at night to her beseiged lover. Charles was obviously aware of her usefulness to Louis. But then, Louis was the least of his problems.

*   *   *

Much though he might have wished it, Charles could not govern without Parliament indefinitely. He needed their money and, therefore, needed a treasurer who could manage Parliament. To this end, as we have seen, he appointed Sir Thomas Osborne, created Earl of Danby in 1675. According to Burnet, Danby 'gave the King great ease by assuring him all things would go according to his mind in the next session of Parliament.' Danby's policy had a double purpose; to persuade Parliament that Charles was a good Anglican after all, and to create through the skilful deployment of patronage a group within Parliament loyal to Charles.

Danby was not the first, nor the last, to bribe the Commons. But he understood before others the need for an organized Parliamentary party which could help win the day for the Crown. Buckingham had already become French paymaster for what Ruvigny, the French ambassador, called 'this filthy traffic' of bribery, while Shaftesbury with Arlington now began to form alliances inside the Commons, hostile to Danby. As Danby had less cash at his disposal than his rivals, in spite of a resurgence in trade brought about by England's present neutrality, he advised Charles that they had two alternatives; either Charles must 'fall into the humours of the people' and accept control by Parliament, or they must reorganize the Royal finances so as to provide the resources necessary for managing Parliament. Whatever else, Charles would have to convince the world he was true to the Church of England.

Thomas Osborne, 1st Earl of Danby, Marquis of Carmarthen, 1st Duke of Leeds, etc., in a ▷ portrait from the studio of Lely. Born 20 February, 1632, at Kiveton, Yorkshire. His third daughter married one of Charles's illegitimate children, the Earl of Plymouth. Burnet said that Danby was "the most hated minister that had ever been about the King." A zealous Protestant, a fanatical organiser, corrupt, grand, greedy, arrogant, sinister, untrustworthy, brilliant, strict, Danby was for Charles the perfect servant. The Commons impeached him, and he was sent to the Tower for almost six years. But he lived on to serve James II, William and Mary, and Queen Anne. He knew about the Stuarts, and his support of Charles and the House of Orange was of immense consequence for the political development of Great Britain.

Although such a declaration was anathema to Charles, he agreed, for a time, to accept Danby's advice. A conference of bishops informed Charles that the existing laws against Roman Catholics were sufficient, provided they were enforced more rigorously. Notwithstanding James's Catholic predilections, an order in Council was passed suppressing all Catholic worship, except in the chapels of the Queen and of foreign ambassadors, exiling all Catholic priests from England and banning all Catholic laymen from Court. A conventicle Act was to be enforced against Puritans, and a brass statue of Charles's father erected at Charing Cross to remind all passers-by, including Charles, that Charles I had died for the Anglican faith. When Parliament reassembled on 13 April, 1675, Charles announced: 'The principal end of my calling you now is to know what you think may yet be wanting to the securing of religion and property, and to give myself the satisfaction of having used the uttermost of my endeavours to procure and settle a right and lasting understanding between us.'

Danby, who considered the orders against the Catholics and Dissenters sops to Parliament, had meanwhile been offered Spanish money to secure mediation with France; consequently, he was ready with his bribes. But the Commons were not ready for Danby, and threatened to impeach him, claiming he had 'violated the ancient course of the Exchequer.' What's more, they demanded the withdrawal of all English forces still in the service of the French King, 'that the French may no farther be encouraged to ruin us and the rest of our neighbours.' When the votes were cast, however, the motion polled an equal number for and against, whereupon scenes not unfamiliar since, although apparently shocking then, ensued. The counting was disputed, honourable members spat at their opponents, periwigs were torn off and thrown about, swords flashed and the mace itself hurled to the floor and trampled on. Eventually, the mace was wrenched free and brandished by the Speaker to restore order.

Charles retaliated by introducing, through Danby, a Bill whereby all Members of Parliament would be required to take an oath affirming that it was unlawful 'on any pretence whatsoever to take up arms against the King.' Further, such Members must forswear 'any alteration in the government of Church or State as it is by law established.' Shaftesbury argued in the Lords that such a Bill would be an invasion of the privileges he and his fellow peers had acquired by birth, conveniently forgetting that this was hardly so in his case since he was (by birth) a mere Dorset baronet.

Charles himself followed the proceedings until midnight. And when another question of privilege, the case of Shirley *v.* Fagg, arose, normal parliamentary business ceased altogether. Fagg was a member of the Commons being sued by Shirley. The Lords had ordered that Fagg appear before them to answer Shirley's petition. The Commons, not unnaturally, resented being thought answerable to the other House, especially when the Lords accused the

Commons of 'transcendant misbehaviour, breach of privilege, Magna Carta, subversion of government, and other high, provoking and diminishing expressions.' Charles thought the indiscipline had gone on long enough, and summoned members of both Commons and Lords to appear before him in the Banqueting House. He accused 'ill-men' of trying to fix a dissolution, and thus a general election, from which he realized the opposition expected to gain against Danby and himself. The 'ill-men' refused to listen. Exasperated, Charles told them: 'I must confess the ill designs of our enemies have been too prevalent against those good ones I had proposed in behalf of my people. And those unhappy differences between my two Houses', he concluded, 'are grown to such a height that I find no possible means of putting an end to them, but by a prorogation.' Whereupon Charles went straight back to Windsor, and to Louise.

It was only a temporary respite. Danby urgently tried to rally support, and his secretaries wrote personal letters to more than a hundred members of the Commons, calling upon 'old friends of the loyal party.' Don Pedro Ronquillo of Spain was installed in Westminster, and told to spare no expense in procuring a Parliamentary settlement favourable to Spain. The Dutch busied themselves persuading English public opinion against the French, in the hopes of driving Charles into a war to their advantage. Louis, whose annual campaign against William III of Orange had been less than successful, informed Charles that if he dissolved Parliament and thus avoided any anti-French alliance, Louis would grant him an annual subsidy of £100,000. And Shaftesbury fomented what anti-Papist feelings he could by spreading rumours about Irish cut-throats and standing armies.

When Parliament reassembled, Charles, in his opening speech, began apologetically. Yes, he had not been 'altogether so good a husband' as he might have been. Yes, he had been extravagant in his private life, although 'far from such extravagancy in my own expense as some would have the world believe.' All he wanted was a little money to pay old debts and build new ships. 'Time will serve to make many excellent laws, and to give you the honour to be the repairer of all our breaches.' It was not to be. Parliament seemed determined to prove its authority over the Crown. By a narrow margin, 172 to 165, the Commons refused to make provision for the debts, voted less than was needed for the proposed warships, and appropriated the whole of Charles's existing Customs revenue (a principal source of his income) to the Navy. In addition, the Commons wanted all his monies to be administered in future not by the Crown or its officers, but by the chamber of London, a demand which, in effect, involved the establishment of an alternative government. Fortunately, the motion was defeated.

In the Lords, Shaftesbury revived the Shirley *v.* Fagg issue, and brought in a Bill for the dissolution of Parliament. Only a titanic effort by Danby had this particular move defeated, by a mere two votes. The squabbling was again

Hortense Mancini, Duchess of Mazarin. Said to be a millionairess, a lesbian (with among others, Charles's daughter Anne), and a swordswoman of no mean achievement. The youngest niece of Cardinal Mazarin, married to an Italian gentleman in Rome, a dark lady with jet-black curly hair, she was given by Charles an annual "pension" of £4,000 and, in 1677, "raised above all the other ladies behind the throne." She ran off with a Prince from Morocco, but lived in Kensington Square where she died on 2 July, 1699.

getting beyond control. An attempt to discuss the bribing of Members was greeted with derision, as was a quip from an aged Member, Sir John Birkenhead: 'I am afraid of a dissolution', he remarked, 'because as God is my witness, I am afraid the next will be worse.' Much laughter. 'A standing Parliament is as grievous as a standing army', observed another Member, Sir Harbottle Grimstone. More laughter. Charles took the hint. He prorogued Parliament for an unexpected period of fifteen months. 'Parliaments are to be feared', concluded the French ambassador later, 'and it is like a miracle to see the King resist them without arms so long.'

Still Charles tried reconciliation. At a private supper party, Shaftesbury urged Charles to try another Parliament, but the King suggested that Shaftesbury might be better employed in Dorset. Charles also tried to patch up relations with Louis, who was now protesting that he saw no reason to pay his promised subsidy since Parliament had not been dissolved. Charles argued that such a dissolution might lead to an even stronger anti-French lobby in any newly elected Parliament. Louis paid, although only in quarterly instalments. In return, Charles agreed to yet another clandestine treaty (which he wrote out in his own hand), renewing not only his previous secret treaties with Louis, but accepting that the common enemy was Holland with which neither King would treat except together. Danby refused to sign; eventually Lauderdale signed as witness, although he too had reservations.

Another emissary arrived from Louis in the shape of Hortense Mazarin. Dressed as a male cavalier, she had landed during a storm at Tor Bay and made straight for London protected by a miniature Negro slave and Madame de Sévigné's advice that England had 'neither faith, nor law, nor priest.' Although invited to England by Arlington in the desire that she would replace the noisy Louise in Charles's affections, Hortense, the favourite niece of Cardinal Mazarin, was twenty-nine, had black curly hair, and spoke several languages fluently. Before long, Courtin, the current French ambassador, was reporting satisfactorily that Charles 'appears to have been attracted by her beauty, and though the affair has so far been conducted with some secrecy, it is likely that this growing passion will take the first place in the heart of that prince.' Louise sickened, grew thin, gave birth prematurely, and wept.

Unfortunately, Hortense soon made off with a prince of Morocco, thereby abandoning her annual pension of almost £4,000 bestowed by Charles, and Courtin reported the return of Louise. 'Her skin has grown so fair and fresh that I cannot imagine how Charles, palled as he is with beauty, will be long in her company without becoming once more her slave.' Arlington, who had backed Hortense, fell even further into disfavour. But Danby, who had been careful to maintain relations with Louise (he had arranged for her to be paid £55,000 during this period), survived. He urged Charles to conclude a maritime treaty with France, fearing that, unless there was some public agreement between the two monarchs, Louis might be tempted to blackmail Charles with the various secret treaties. Meanwhile, the latest Franco-Dutch negotiations were at stalemate, and William let it be known that he wished to come to England for advice and support. Danby told Charles to refuse permission until after a peace had been agreed, but Charles now began to see himself again as the one man who could resolve these interminable European conflicts. Charles could only fulfil this role, Danby suggested, with the tacit approval of Parliament; and so, reluctantly, Charles agreed to make preparations for another bout with the Commons.

Louis immediately sent Courtin almost £20,000 for 'service in Parliament', that is for subsidizing opposition to Danby if the latter showed anti-French tendencies. The Dutch, Spanish and Imperial ambassadors began to organize lavish dinner parties, with suitable entertainment, for those Members who might prove co-operative. Shaftesbury immersed himself in the new Green Ribbon Club, a propagandist organization against 'that Court party'; Lord Holles wanted a cabal consisting of himself, the Duke of York and the French ambassador in opposition to Shaftesbury; and Danby, who was mobilizing proxy votes in the House of Lords, talked of joining Lauderdale and heading a Protestant, predominantly anti-French, alliance. The Privy Council, meanwhile, committed one alderman Jenks for making an inflammatory, and, as it turned out, prophetic, speech calling for a new Parliament to prevent the further spread of French influence. He had been 'put upon the exploit by a great man turned citizen', Jenks claimed enigmatically. 'I never saw the people in such fears as they are in', noted one observer. 'They keep guards in all places as in time of war.'

The fifteenth session of the Cavalier Parliament met on 15 February 1677, and proved even more futile than the previous two. For some weeks the Opposition had showered London with pamphlets arguing that, under a forgotten law of Edward III, a Parliament which had not sat for a year was *ipso facto* dissolved. In vain Charles reminded the Houses that he had called them together 'that [they] might have the opportunity to repair the misfortunes of the last session, and to recover and restore the right use of parliaments.' 'Let all men judge who is for arbitrary government', Charles went on, 'they that foment such differences as tend to dissolve all parliaments, or I that would preserve this and all parliaments from being made useless by such dissensions.' The warning was not heeded. Still enraged by Shaftesbury's apparent questioning of their right to exist at all, the Commons, or at least those Members still loyal to Charles, ordered whoever was responsible for the Edward III pamphlets to apologize on their knees for showing contempt of the King and the House. Shaftesbury was unrepentant, so Charles sent him to the Tower where he insisted on having his own cook lest attempts be made to poison him. 'You see, my Lords, what he thinks of me', Charles told Parliament. A chastened House voted Charles the money he needed for the fleet. And, as news of fresh Dutch defeats came in, the Commons petitioned

Charles to enter the war – against France.

That Charles was 'in no condition to declare war', according to Sir Joseph Williamson, was of little consequence. That the petition was the work of 'but three or four rascals . . . that would engage him [Charles] in a war and then leave him in the lurch', was equally irrelevant. The Commons wanted war. Repeatedly they had told Charles to 'enter into a league, offensive and defensive, with the States-General', although, of course, they had proved unwilling to give Charles the money to do so. 'You see how I suffer', Charles told Courtin. 'I put myself in trouble with my subjects for love of the French King. I am resolved to keep my promises to him, but I beg him to help me a little and make peace before winter.' Again, Charles adjourned Parliament. Danby noted in a memorandum that 'while differences continue, prerogative must suffer, unless he [Charles] can live without Parliament.'

This idea had become increasingly attractive. Nonetheless, as Charles told Sir John Reresby in confidence, 'I know it is said I intend the subversion of religion; that I intend to govern by an army and arbitrary power, to lay aside Parliaments and raise money by other ways. But every man – nay, those that say it most – knows it is false.' 'There is no subject that lives under me whose safety and well-doing I desire less than mine own, and should be as sorry to invade his liberty and property as that another should invade mine. Those members that pretend this great zeal for the public good are of two kinds', Charles concluded, 'either such as would subvert the government and bring it to a Commonwealth again, or such as seem to join with that party and talk loud against the Court, hoping to have their mouths stopped by places or preferments.'

Charles was momentarily diverted by the arrival in London of William Bentinck, one of William of Orange's more trusted aides, sent to discuss a possible marriage between William and his cousin, the Duke of York's elder daughter, Mary. Arlington had suggested much the same deal three years earlier, but Charles had been nervous of such an open affront to Louis. When Charles now agreed that his nephew could visit some months later, he acknowledged that, despite his continuing dialogue with Louis, the anti-French camp in England was gaining ground. Courtin reported sadly: 'they are ready to sell their shirts off their backs, to keep the Netherlands being seized upon us.' Lady Chaworth wrote to her brother: 'The Prince of Orange they now say shall come this winter in order concluding a match with him and Lady Mary by the King's great inclination to it, though the Duke likes it not.' Charles's reaction to his brother's reluctance was blunt; 'God's fish', he said, 'he *must* consent.'

Perhaps Charles hoped that, by allowing this marriage, he could persuade his nephew William to accept the best terms that he, Charles, could wring out of cousin Louis, thereby appearing to be the 'redeemer of all Christendom from a universal calamity.' Perhaps he hoped to make the Dutch feel grateful, so they would grant him lucrative trading concessions. Either way, he continued to demand a subsidy from Louis, continued to urge that William make peace with Louis, continued to keep Parliament at bay – they 'would never be quiet or easy to him while the war lasted abroad', he said to Sir William Temple – and continued to watch dismayed while Louis and William fought it out in Flanders, marching and countermarching and achieving nothing.

Charles went off sailing, unwilling or unable to pursue these matters further. He sailed along the south coast from Brighton to Plymouth where he encountered such blustery weather that the local people thought him drowned. But his three ships arrived safely at six one morning, whereupon he inspected the fortifications, received the local gentry, and spent the evening shooting at Port Eliot near Saltash. Then, he journeyed by land to the village of Newmarket for the annual September horse meeting. En route, he called on Barillon, the latest French ambassador, to assure him that, whatever might befall between Charles and William, he would not forget his promises to Louis.

William, meanwhile, had landed at Harwich and was also making his way to Newmarket, 'like a hasty lover', as Temple hopefully observed. He had already caused offence by ignoring a lavish reception prepared for him by the Mayor and Corporation of Ipswich. But at Newmarket he was greeted by both his uncles, and taken to the races. James hated William instantly, describing him to Barillon as 'a self-opinionated young man, who had been badly brought up.' William refused to talk politics until he had met the Princess Mary, so Charles again went off to the races and that was that. 'The State and horse politics resemble one another', Coventry noted; 'those appear most confident that know the least.' Eventually William got his way, and the Court packed its bags a few days earlier than planned, leaving Newmarket for Whitehall where William finally met Mary. William promptly declared himself 'well pleased with her person and all those signs of such a humour as had been described to him upon former enquiries', and asked for her hand. Mary burst into tears upon sight of her grim, prematurely aged and large-nosed cousin.

Charles would not be rushed, however. He wanted to discuss other matters first, he said, whereupon William, never the most tactful of men, threatened to go home. 'It shall never be charged against me', he told Temple, 'that I sold my honour for a wife.' Reluctantly Charles conceded, hoping that if William felt he was getting his own way, he might be more ready to talk politics. 'I will trust him', Charles told Temple who had become the intermediary. 'And he shall have his wife, and you shall go immediately and tell my brother so, and that it is a thing I am resolved upon.' Barillon was furious. And disgusted. 'To think that the eldest daughter of the Crown should sleep in Protestant arms', he reported.

The wedding two weeks later did not proceed as planned. The jewels William had intended to give his bride arrived late; fear of smallpox kept the

Queen, James's wife, Mary's sister Anne, as well as the Archbishop of Canterbury, absent. Mary cried, William looked stern. When he uttered the words 'with all my worldly goods I thee endow', and placed a symbolic handful of silver coins on Mary's Bible, Charles gave her a nudge and told her to 'gather it up and put it in her pocket for it was all clear gain.' Nor was the wedding night an overwhelming success. 'It was said that William went to bed in woollen drawers', one gossip related. 'When Charles suggested he take them off, [William] replied that since he and his wife would have to live together for a long time, she would have to get used to his habits.' A few nights later, however, William was discovered trying to break into the bedroom of one of Mary's maids-of-honour. In France, Louis was beside himself with rage. To James he wrote: 'You have given your daughter to my mortal enemy'; even when his temper had cooled, Louis was still to be heard muttering 'two beggars are well matched.'

Charles and William at last settled down to some hard bargaining, and not a moment too soon; Louis had ordered all subsidies to cease, and rumours of a Papist insurrection were everywhere. 'Heard that the city was alarmed that the Papists plotted a massacre', one Essex parson recorded. 'Was the marriage a pillow to lull us asleep?' But William went back to Holland having agreed to very little except to work for peace rather than war. 'A most costly Pope' was burned in the streets of London, 'his belly filled full with live cats who squawked most hideously as soon as they felt the fire.' So Charles sent Lord Feversham, a French Hugenot in English employ, to Louis with the outlines of an agreement which he believed would probably meet with William's approval.

Louis was in no mood for reconciliation; if anything, his successes in *this* year's summer campaign against the Dutch had inflamed his ambition. Ignoring Feversham, he now prepared for a new onslaught against Flanders. Charles saw his opportunity. Against his will, he told everyone, he was being forced into another war, this time against France. Parliament would have to be summoned, troops mobilized. To emphasize he meant business, Charles dispatched envoys to allied governments with plans for *his* campaign, but by 15 January 1678, the date on which Parliament was to be called, Louis was again offering money. Parliament was again, temporarily, postponed. Charles told Louis he would be delighted to take the French money, but only if Louis agreed to a treaty with Holland. Louis refused, so Parliament was summoned and Charles appealed to both Houses for a united Kingdom to save Europe. He had only made 'such alliances with Holland as are for the preservation of Flanders', he told them. What with a rebellion in Virginia, Princess Mary's dowry, the defence of Algiers and worsening relations with France, he had desperate need of a 'plentiful supply'. His most fervent wish had always been to secure an honourable peace in Christendom. This had been denied him. Consequently, 'it shall not be my fault if that be not obtained by force which cannot be otherwise.'

For years the Opposition had demanded a war against France, and here was Charles agreeing to such a war in return, of course, for a 'plentiful supply', the very opposite of that which the Opposition wanted to give him. As a result, the Commons found themselves granting Charles £1,000,000 for the waging of war against France, while at the same time stopping the import of French goods which, through the loss of Customs revenue, deprived Charles of almost the same amount. 'And thus they [the Opposition] go on', Southwell remarked to Ormonde, 'contending and disputing every particular step that is made, having a greater number of able and conscientious speakers, though they are outdone in votes.'

Louis, meanwhile, was again marching across Europe; Charles told Reresby that unless something was settled soon, the French King would have finished his business. Charles sent 800 troops to Ostend, while trying to organize some form of quadruple alliance – between Holland, Spain, the German Empire and England – against France. Secretly, he also instructed Danby to make peace overtures with Louis, again, adding that he would probably only need £500,000 a year for the next three years. Inevitably, Louis rejected Charles's proposals; Charles must have known he would. He was near the end of his tether, a condition not improved by the discovery that William was now actively trading with Louis.

After a short adjournment, Parliament reassembled to consider the state of the nation; their behaviour left Charles in no doubt about that. Sir John Ernly remarked that every tub must stand on its own bottom. Lord Russell preferred to talk about the right saddle being put on the right horse. 'An house is on fire', he concluded mysteriously. 'Will you not quench it?' Louis XIV was a glass bottle, said Colonel Birch, which might easily be broken with an English crab-tree cudgel. Members had been so heavily bribed, and by so many different sources, that many were now unclear as to what their position was supposed to be on any given subject. The Commons decided that a treaty with William would be contrary to the safety of the Kingdom. 'I am willing', added the senile Sir Philip Warwick, 'like Balaam's ass, to crush my master's foot when an angel stands in the way.'

Charles blamed himself for their behaviour; by trying to please all, he had pleased none. He offered to disband part of his army but recognized that, while Louis and others were reducing the English Parliament to a state of near impotence, the French King was proceeding, relatively undisturbed, with his European conquests. William, Charles argued, should accept the latest proposals for peace being offered by the French at Nymegen; and Louis, in return for Charles's neutrality, should promise a single payment of £500,000. 'The continual noise of horse, foot, dragoons, cuirassies, guidons, aides-de-camp, and a hundred such words repeated ten thousand times a day in Whitehall Gallery', wrote Henry Savile, 'have frightened away even the thoughts of the least indulgence to a man's pleasure.' Louis let it be known he would refuse to conclude any peace with Holland until his ally, Sweden, was restored to all its continental possessions lost during the wars. William, feeling betrayed, refused to sign anything. Charles, in despair, was forced to halt the disbandment of the army and send troops once more to Flanders. Parliament, disappointed at having been denied its war with France, did not know what to think. Danby considered the possibility of bolstering the Royal authority and his own power with a standing army – anything, that is, to get rid of this troublesome Parliament.

Eventually, at the end of July 1678, amid a general and understandable feeling of exhaustion, Louis agreed to a treaty with the Dutch which was duly signed at Nymegen. But the compromise was less than happy. Louis had cause to be displeased with Charles, stopped his subsidy and instructed his ambassador to do 'everything possible to make trouble for the King of England.' Charles had cause to be displeased with Louis; the promised subsidy, having dangled just outside Charles's grasp for so long, now seemed gone for ever. Charles offered to reduce his demand, and sent Sunderland to Paris with a promise of English troops and the offer of an available Princess (Anne) for any potential Swedish marriage alliance. William had cause to be displeased with Charles; he had promised much and delivered nothing. William had 'shed bitter tears over the peace', reported the Duke of Luxembourg, and Mary, having displayed true aristocratic resource and fallen in love, had had her first miscarriage. Parliament had cause to be displeased with Charles; on two occasions, they suspected, he had ignored them and concluded treaties with France. Charles replied that Parliament had sought to rob him of his prerogatives in foreign policy, much as it had tried to do in finance. But Parliament retorted that Charles had rejected two of the three Anglo-Dutch treaties promoted by Parliament, while clinging to his alliances with Louis. Worse, he had somehow prevented Parliament from going to war with France.

This surfeit of displeasure weakened Charles's authority in England. Political acrobatics were seen to be no substitute for good government. A host of discontented ministers now united as the 'country opposition' and vowed hostility to Charles. Chief among these was the ominous figure of Shaftesbury, the 'pygmy', as Dryden called him in a less than charitable reference to an accident in Shaftesbury's youth which had left him disfigured and in pain. What motivated the Earl is difficult to discern. His physical disability had left a bitter resentment against the careless finery of the Court. From being a passionate supporter of Charles, he had become increasingly stung by the sarcastic mockery of Charles's cronies against his country origins, his reckless pursuit of power, his love of intrigue apparently for its own sake and his opposition to the majesty of the Crown. That he seemed to have neither religious beliefs nor political principles made him an easy target for abuse.

179

Some maintained that his fulminations were mere tub-thumping, with little more significance than a delight in anarchy. But others now saw in him the one man resourceful and skilful enough to rally opposition against a standing army, a French subsidy and the rule of Catholicism, an alliance in which there would be no place for Parliament.

Shaftesbury realized that Charles did not wish to establish a standing army. The Crown could not afford it. A French subsidy was probable, but hardly significant in its amount. As for Catholicism, Shaftesbury was too intelligent for its threat to be taken seriously. But the widespread belief in a 'conspiracy' gave him an opportunity for revenge on all who had ridiculed him. First, it was known that, as early as 1662, Charles had proposed to the Vatican a scheme for the gradual conversion of the Anglican Church to Rome. The Vatican had turned down Charles's suggestion on the grounds that it could not sustain a lengthy battle against a hostile English Parliament. Second, Charles seemed permanently enamoured of France. By birth and up-bringing he was already half French. After the defeat of the Dutch, the ideal of Government, of society and of literature appeared to be French. Military glory and diplomatic success, in Europe and overseas, looked now to belong exclusively to France. Every petty ruler of Europe worshipped the idea of monarchy which Louis personified, both in his symbol – the rising sun – and in his motto: *Nec Pluribus Impar*. Third, the ferocity of anti-French, anti-Catholic feeling had pushed Charles further and further toward an absolutist government, if only to rid himself of a tiresome problem for which he could see no other solution. From this impending absolutism, Shaftesbury, through Parliament, now wished to save the country.

Charles had never underestimated the power of Parliament, if only to make trouble; after all, it had proved quite effective against his father. Clarendon's ideal of a loyal Parliament and gracious King working together in happy partnership had long since collapsed. The relationship between the Crown and Parliament was in continuous debate, thereby preparing the ground for that form of constitutional monarchy which developed peacefully in England over the next hundred years and which has survived to the present day. The initial problem had been that neither King nor Parliament was willing to concede that the one could legislate while the other administered; each resented the power apparently held by the other. Charles had slowly come to realize that his part of the bargain, even though protected by Law, had to be supported by treaties entailing either the promise of troops or the guarantee of cash from foreign powers such as Catholic France. Such treaties, however, could only be used in England as a final threat to secure monarchical power. For Charles that power was absolute, as real to him as it had been to Henry VIII. The difference was that initially Charles had lacked the money to make that power effective. Paradoxically, as Charles increased his personal control, the institution of monarchy declined. Parliament and its privileges believed they had little to fear from the Crown; thus, when Charles found his authority challenged, he felt he had no choice but to suspend Parliament, during which, of course, tensions built up for the next confrontation. Thugs were hired to beat up recalcitrant Members, although it was admitted that such measures had only short-term advantages. When Sir John Coventry had his nose split for daring to speak against the King's pleasures, the offenders had been promptly banished for life and the splitting of noses made a capital offence without benefit of clergy. One of the few weapons left to Charles had been bribery.

But bribery had only become important because of an essential development in the nature of Parliament itself. In the Tudor Parliaments, sessions were short and infrequent. Members travelled to London and stayed briefly, to vote or refuse money, offer criticism of the Crown's policy in so far as they understood it, or transact a little business on behalf of their locality. Then, they had gone home. The Long Parliament from 1640 to 1660 had changed all that. Nominally in continuous session, it had given the middle-class, local land-owners a taste for administration. The Cavalier Parliament, from 1660 to 1678, with its nineteen discontinuous sessions, forced Members for the first time to maintain two homes, one in their constituency and one in London. As today, this involved financial sacrifice, especially as in the 1670s Members were unpaid. Remunerations which did not conflict with the demands of conscience were, therefore, welcome.

Shaftesbury, more than anyone, including Louis, took advantage of this naive corruption. His plan was simple. As long as the present Parliament, by now known appropriately as the Pensionary Parliament, continued to exist, his opposition would be unlikely to achieve the majority necessary to bring down Danby and the government. He must force a dissolution, therefore, and organize the constituencies in preparation for new elections. His Country Party would become the embodiment of opposition to the French Catholic absolutism entailed by Charles's 'Court Party'.

The origins of this two-party, parliamentary democracy, are mirrored in the nicknames which the two parties adopted. The Court Party was thought of as 'Loyalist', 'Yorkist', or 'Tantivy', which implied scurrying to Rome. 'Tory' sounded even better since it was Irish slang for robber and outlaw, and reminded the faithful of the Duke of York's known affection for the Irish, who were mad. 'A tory is a monster with an English face, a French heart and an Irish conscience', noted one pamphleteer, 'a creature of a large forehead, prodigious mouth, supple hams and no brains. They are a sort of wild boars, that would root out the constitution [and] blow up the two bulwarks of our freedom, Parliaments and Juries.' In fact, for the first ten years of Charles's reign, the 'Court Party' had been stronger than at any time during the previous sixty. With its massive royalist majority, the Cavalier Parliament encompassed men loyal to the Crown from all quarters of political society, town and country, nobility and gentry. Thus, its power was widely based, and would have been linked inextricably to the monarchy had not Charles displayed such a predilection, however understandable, for those who had served him well during exile. By favouring the old guard in the appointment of his first ministers, Charles had failed to capitalize on the sympathy offered him at his Restoration; the abuse with which the growing autocracy of his Party was greeted reflected in no small measure the disappointment of those who had felt themselves passed over or unrewarded in the early years of his reign. 'The King's conscientious good friends are (as they have always been) little regarded', noted one Member, Sir Robert Wiseman, 'both in themselves and in the principles they own . . . undoubtedly, if such men and their principles were at this day regarded, all would speedily do well.'

The Country Party, on the other hand, thought its description too modest since it implied social ostracism, even disability. 'Petitioner' sounded more respectable as it suggested petitioning the King to meet Parliament, although such a description did not suit the Court Party. 'Fanatic' was thought more appropriate. And since 'tory' was Irish slang, how about 'whig', which was Scottish slang and meant outlaw or Covenanter? Since the Country Party made a habit of petitioning the King, the Court Party would abhor the practice. Petitioners and Abhorrers. 'Snivelling saints' was how Judge Jeffreys described these Whigs. As many were Dissenters, 'conscientious, prick-eared vermin' was thought too good; 'his principles are like chaos . . . his language is "Overturn, Overturn". His prayer is a rhapsody of holy hickops, sanctified barkings, illuminated goggles, sighs, sobs, yexes, gasps and groans.'

In the summer of 1678, the prospects for this Country Party looked uncertain. Charles had armed forces in Scotland and England, and Danby was keeping a steel grip on the administration. Shaftesbury's only hope was to expose what everybody suspected, but nobody had yet been able to prove, namely that the Government was involved in a vast conspiracy to sell out England either to Catholicism or France or both. Fortunately, Shaftesbury did not know about the original secret treaty of Dover, although he had his suspicions; nor that Charles was still taking money from the French ambassador as part of the price for his continued neutrality; nor that when Parliament had been screaming 'no popery' at the end of April 1678, the English Jesuits had quietly held their provincial congregation less than a mile away in the rooms of the heir to the throne at St James's Palace. But, as Charles realized, it was only a matter of time.

How far Charles supported Danby in this gathering conflict is puzzling. Danby had given a public toast at a loyalist banquet, for instance – 'confusion of all that were not for a war with France' – which was quite at odds with the spirit of Charles's secret negotiations with Louis. In spite of Charles's known affections for France, Danby saw Charles as the Protestant champion of Europe. The marriage of William and Mary, with its implicit benefits for

England, was a notable coup in this context. But the policy had its perils. Danby's parliamentary success had been achieved in part by patriotic appeals to Crown *and* country. The Non-Resisting Bill, by which all but Anglicans and Cavaliers of the purest stock were to be excluded from the legislature, had been intended to strengthen the quality and reliability of this nationalist party. But its result had been to increase the determination of those 'Whigs' who saw themselves being forced out of political life for ever. Had the Bill become law, the 'Tories' might have established the very absolutism against which many of them had fought only thirty years previously.

Charles certainly paid lip service to Danby's policies. He had rewarded Danby with the Garter in April 1677, and given him permission to marry his third daughter Bridget to one of the King's illegitimate sons, Charles Fitzcharles, Earl of Plymouth. Yet Danby's apparent desire to precipitate a confrontation against France was contrary to Charles's inclinations. Danby's value lay in his reorganization of the demoralized Court Party to challenge the growing strength of the Opposition. He survived five complicated years in which Charles had seemed less than consistent in his declared intentions, although infinitely careful to manoeuvre his chief minister into positions of vulnerability should any of their policies collapse. True, Danby had refused to sign Charles's most recent pact with Louis. But what was in a signature?

Charles had gone off to Windsor when news came that peace had been concluded between Louis and William at Nymegen. A touch of ague was spoiling Charles's summer. Pepys, who came down to visit the King once a week, noted that Charles was happiest when hunting and fishing. The more Charles visited Windsor, the better he liked it. During the Civil War, the castle had been occupied by squatters and its fabric made 'ragged and ruinous'. By 1678, however, Windsor had been much restored. According to Evelyn, the feasts of St George were notorious for their high spirits; the 'banqueting stuff was flung about the room profusely', he remembered, 'the cheer . . . extraordinary, each new knight having forty dishes to his mess, piled five or six high.'

Charles preferred to spend his time watching a special water fountain which he had installed in the gardens, measuring the rate of its flow with his watch. He swam in the river. He planted trees. He played tennis and bowls. He studied his exotic birds in their gilded cages; his favourite, 'Cockatoo', he kept in the dining room. In the evenings he liked to watch an entertainment in St George's Hall or play basset with the Queen. When he went to the lavatory, which he did every night at Windsor before he went to bed, he liked to be accompanied by two attendants, one to hold the candle, the other to hold the paper. Apparently he enjoyed their company. He was then tucked up in bed by the Gentlemen and Grooms of the Bedchamber, who complained to him about their troubled nights. 'Several circumstances made the lodging uneasy', grumbled Lord Bruce, 'the great grate being filled with Scotch coal that burnt all night, a dozen dogs that came to our beds, and several pendulums that struck at the half, quarter and the hour, and all not going alike; it was a continual chiming.'

London and its problems seemed far away. At Windsor, Charles could lead the life he relished and worship the God of his choosing. He did not know, of course, that less than ten miles away lived one Robert Ferguson. 'What strategems and devices, what ways and means', Ferguson was writing, 'will not disaffected persons find out to blacken a government they have a mind to overthrow.'

Chapter Nine
Bible mad

A desire to overthrow the government preoccupied many men throughout Charles's reign. The Civil War had not quenched the thirst for revolution, although its horrors provided Charles with a useful threat when political debate became unruly. This obsession was often inspired by religion, whether Catholic, Protestant, Quaker or a dozen other forms of Dissent, as numerous pamphlets affirmed. One entitled *Babel and Bethel: or, the Pope in his Colours*, for instance, was typical of the many anti-Catholic broadsheets which were circulated. With frequent references to Charles, it was subtitled 'The Church of England's supplication to his Majesty, our gracious Sovereign, the true Defender of the Faith, to protect her [the Church] from all the Machinations of Rome and its bloody Emissaries'. It began in appropriately bloodthirsty style:

> Rome's scarlet whore doth here in Triumph Ride,
> And spurns off Sovereign Crowns in Height of Pride.
> Poor Christians and brave Cities too she Burns
> And Stabs and Poisons daily serve her Turns.

'Why should we not fear that their malice' (i.e. that of the Catholics) 'though not their power, is as great now as heretofore?' an anonymous writer inquired. 'And why may we not expect, if opportunity should offer itself to them to see as many villanies transacted as in times past, for all their pretended loyalty to the King?' As we have seen, Charles's flirtations with France had made Louis seem almost as frightening as Philip of Spain and his Armada a century earlier. Louis's aggressiveness against Protestantism both in France and Holland had revived many hatreds and dubbed him 'the declared champion of Popery and the hereditary, natural, inveterate enemy of our King and nation.' James's much trumpeted conversion to Catholicism had not helped. That the King's brother was ignorant of his adopted Church, and that he angered the Pope as much as he did the Archbishop of Canterbury, did not lessen the fear of a Catholic heir-apparent with its attendant threats of persecution and flame.

BABEL and BETHEL: or, The POPE in his Colours.

WITH

The Church of *ENGLAND's* Supplication to his Majesty, our gracious Soveraign, the true Defender of the Faith; To protect her from all the Machinations of *Rome*, and its bloody Emissaries.

"Babel and Bethel: or The Pope in his Colours", a contemporary anti-Catholic tryptych of 1679. On the left is the Pope: London is in flames; Wakeman is giving Charles poison, while Godfrey lies dead; Protestants burn at the stake. On the right sits Charles, as the Church of England's protector; traitors and such like get their just reward. Catholics, said Chief Justice Scroggs, have "ways of conversion . . . by the powerful and irresistable arguments of a dagger." In fact, Catholic laymen numbered no more than 260,000, from a total population of around 5 million; there were only 230 secular priests in England and about 250 regulars, including 120 Jesuits and 80 Benedictines. There were just 21 Catholic peers, and of these only 10 were eligible to vote.

"In vain Rome plots, while Charles the sceptre sways;
May steel and gibbet end all traitors' days."

Charles apparently died a Catholic; so did his brother James; his Queen; his mother; his treasurer, Lord Clifford, his friend, Buckingham, his cousin, Louis, and his mistress, Louise. On 25 October, 1970, Pope Paul VI canonized forty English Martyrs including six executed by Charles or his government as traitors.

The Catholics were not alone, however, in suffering verbal assaults. 'The two plagues of the nation', wrote one commentator, 'rose up from the bottomless pit, and are the priests and the lawyers.' Protestantism was lampooned because it was associated with the Dutch who 'acted . . . hellishly like devils. Do not wonder at their barbarous and inhuman cruelties, since from Hell they came and thither without doubt they must return again.' The Scots Presbyterians provided their own epitaph. One eyewitness, writing of a typical Sunday morning's sermon, noted that 'a mournful spirit is very agreeable to the Gospel. That the mourning which the Lord requires is an inward, serious, bitter mourning. That those who do thus mourn aright are blessed.' The diarist adds: 'this was a tolerable good day to me', in spite of there being 'a very filthy rain.' All of which would hardly recommend itself to the Stuart Court.

Charles faced a multiplicity of faiths, each anxious to discredit the others. In 1676, Danby had attempted a census of religions in England. For the province

186

of Canterbury, a total population of at least 3,000,000, the number of adult non-conformists was estimated at 93,000; the province of York was assumed to contain one-sixth of this total. In all, there were less than 150,000 Dissenters in England and Wales. They included the Muggletonians who believed in cursing and swearing, the Ranters who burned Bibles, the Adamites who spurned clothing, the Brownists who were a congregational sect, the Familists who rejected all but love, the Anabaptists who abhorred infant baptism, the Antinomians who differentiated between the sins of the wicked and the sins of the Children of Light, the Sabbatarians who kept the Sabbath with Jewish fanaticism, the Fifth Monarchists who awaited the Resurrection of a thousand years, quite apart from Baptists, Independents, Presbyterians, Quakers and Puritans. Although it would be wrong to exaggerate their numerical significance, the collective influence of these Dissenters was real enough and their various manifestations seemingly infinite. 'It is a sad thing to consider', wrote one observer, 'what a world of heresies are crept into this nation; every man thinks himself as competent a judge as the very apostles themselves. If the power of interpreting Scriptures be in every man's brain, what need have we of a Church?'

To the pragmatic Stuart mind, this religious confusion was farcical. As Sir Thomas Meres told the House of Commons, 'we changed religion pretty well in Henry VIII's time, and Edward VI; and in Queen Mary's time all the clergy turned Popish except an hundred and sixty. About forty years ago the Church of England was at its height, and then we had changes in the late time of rebellion, and now we have a Church of England again if we can keep it. We are a mutable people . . .' 'There is nothing that can prevail more to persuade a man to be an atheist', added Samuel Butler, 'as to see such unreasonable beasts pretend to religion.'

Charles's own convictions were a puzzle to his contemporaries. As King, he was nominally Head of the Church of England and Defender of the Faith, although Halifax thought Charles 'had not enough religion to have convictions.' Charles seemed to have no religion, concluded Burnet, Bishop of Salisbury. 'Both at prayers and sacrament, he, as it were, took care to satisfy people that he was in no sort concerned in that about which he was employed.' Charles was known to think that Presbyterianism was no religion for a gentleman; but, on the other hand, he had employed no fewer than ten Presbyterian chaplains in 1660. At his Restoration, the King had offered Bishoprics to three leading Presbyterians, and summoned the meeting at Worcester House, Clarendon's residence, to discuss Presbyterian grievances. Yet, as Halifax had noted, 'when he [Charles] came to England, he was as certainly a Roman Catholic as that he was a man of pleasure.' Charles himself wrote to the Catholic Sir Robert Moray that 'Our Saviour would certainly leave some body or power to whom the Church might have recourse for solution of difficulties, and he very well knew where that power must be lodged.'

In public, Charles remained conspicuously loyal to the Church of England, ignoring the promises made to the Scottish Covenanters during his years of exile. He used the Anglican Book of Common Prayer, and was a regular communicant throughout his reign. He had prevented his mother from forcibly converting his younger brother Henry to Catholicism by instructing Ormonde to snatch the intended victim at the dead of night in a cloak and dagger operation that had become a *cause célèbre* throughout Europe. He had also insisted that James's daughters, Mary and Anne, were brought up as Protestants. Advised by Lord Mordaunt that 'nothing can secure the Crown that destroys the Mitre', Charles had gone to morning service in the Chapel Royal the very first Sunday he had returned to London. Bishop Wren, who only recently had been released from twenty years' imprisonment in the Tower for preaching against the Puritans, had delivered the sermon.

The truth is that, toward all religions, Charles maintained a distance. 'My Lord, My Lord', cried one preacher to the sleeping Lauderdale, 'you snore so loud you will wake the King.' 'Beyond sea', Charles said, 'it seemed as if people worshipped God in earnest – but here, in jest.' He was contemptuous of the English clergy, regardless of sect. 'They will do nothing and have me do everything – and most of them do worse than if they did nothing.' Of a non-conformist parson to whom he had given a benefice, Charles said that he was 'a very silly fellow', adding that 'his nonsense suits their nonsense, for he has brought them all to Church.' The disease of sermons about which he wrote to his sister, expressed a scarcely veiled disregard for the established Church, an attitude which found much sympathy among his people. One Londoner, watching a herd of Bishops arriving at Westminster Abbey in their robes, exclaimed. 'Lord! How people did, most of them, look upon them as strange creatures, and few with any kind of love or respect!' Whether religion was any more to Charles than virginity had been to Elizabeth, was a topic of much dispute. Elizabeth had used her virginity as a trump card in foreign policy; was Charles, in his dealings with Catholic Europe, working the same trick with religion? Were his Catholic inclinations any more than a passing fancy to help secure alliances abroad and peace at home? No one knew. When d'Aubigny, a Roman Catholic peer, had urged Charles to declare himself more positively in favour of Roman Catholicism prior to his Restoration, Charles had replied that d'Aubigny was 'very much mistaken in the temper of England as to its indifference to religion', adding, enigmatically, 'of which I may reasonably be thought to understand somewhat.'

Charles had always understood that a religious settlement, acceptable to most if not all of the main factions, was essential for peaceful government. In 1660, the Anglicans had been straining for revenge after twenty years of deprivation. The Papists, hated by everyone, had looked for support to a King who, with Catholic mother, brothers and sister, they had good reason to believe would support their cause. And the Presbyterians and Dissenters had

Mr. Rose, the Royal gardener, presenting Charles outside Ham House with the first pineapple grown in England. In a painting by Thomas Danckerts. What does Charles's expression reveal? Disbelief? Disdain? Or disgruntlement at this buffoon with his silly fruit? Perhaps dyspepsia.

intended that the power they had come to enjoy under Cromwell's protection would continue. After all, Charles's father had promised at the Treaty of Newport to accept Presbyterianism as the national religion of England with toleration for sectaries, and Charles had already declared himself in favour of 'a liberty to tender consciences' at Breda. It was argued that Charles had agreed to such a naive declaration of religious tolerance out of deference to General Monck and his Presbyterian followers who had feared that, upon Restoration, Charles would be forced to declare exclusively in favour of Anglicanism and thus against Presbyterianism. Monck had known, however, that Charles had no liking for those who had bullied him in Scotland.

At the Restoration, Charles's moral authority had been much stronger than that of his immediate predecessors. The Civil War had brought the Church of England and Crown close together, with Charles I's death now assuming mythic proportions. Charles's first expressed aim had been to find 'an accommodation' between the Presbyterians and Anglicans; the debate as to what this 'accommodation' should entail and how it was to be effected, had continued throughout the summer of 1660. The preliminary meeting at Worcester House between the bishops and leading Presbyterians had resulted in a declaration, drafted by Clarendon and published by Charles, which offered various compromises. No one was to be denied the Lord's supper simply because he refused to kneel; the clergy would no longer be compelled to wear the surplice; and a national synod was to be convened to review the whole paraphernalia of Church ceremonies as well as the obsolete language of certain sections in the Book of Common Prayer. The Presbyterians said the declaration gave them too little; the Anglicans maintained that it conceded too much, although a full-scale conference at Syon College was promised to continue and widen the discussions.

What Charles thought of these wrangling divines is not known, though he must have realized that any religious settlement which accepted, or appeared to accept, the hierarchical claims of Anglicanism, would inevitably fail in its passage through a House of Lords still dominated by Presbyterians. On the other hand, he argued, ecclesiastical affairs still lodged within the Royal prerogative. Since he was Supreme Governor of the Church, religious matters were no concern of Parliament. The meeting at Worcester House had been a practical attempt to reconcile the Presbyterians, who constituted a substantial number of both Houses of Parliament, with the Church of England, which constituted the majority of the population.

When the Cavalier Parliament had replaced the Convention Parliament the following May, however, the balance had tipped the other way. With Parliament full of Anglican loyalists and Royalists, a compromise which included major concessions toward the Presbyterians would be doomed. A third religious conference at Savoy House had lasted for ten weeks. The Puritans had begun to seem unnecessarily pedantic, insisting on the use of 'Lord's Day' instead of 'Sunday', and 'Minister' instead of 'Priest'. Charles said that a restoration of the episcopacy was essential for the continuance of accepted constitutional order. The fundamentals of religion were obvious, and their earthly manifestations merely shaped by convenience and the dictates of the modern state. With the bishops now firmly re-established in the Lords, it had mattered little what any Puritans or Presbyterians might want. When the clergy met in November to revise the Prayer Book and outline a new liturgy, over 600 changes had been proposed. These emphasized the priestly character of the ministry, the diminishing effect of Baptism and the authority of the Thirty-nine Articles. The package was a blow to Presbyterian hopes, in spite of a preface which had declared coldly that 'it hath been the wisdom of the Church of England to keep the mean between the two extremes of too much stiffness in refusing, and of too much easiness in admitting, any variation from it.'

Charles had reluctantly accepted Convocation's recommendations, and the revised liturgy was approved by Parliament in April 1662. It only remained for the Anglicans to legalize their triumph by demanding the establishment of a State Church whose monopoly would be safeguarded by penal legislation. The Bill of Uniformity which followed had seemed to Charles the abandonment of any peaceful religious settlement. It imposed the revised Prayer Book, ordered all clergy to sign a declaration denying the Solemn League and Covenant, and made the acceptance of the Thirty-nine Articles obligatory. Any man possessing a benefice and not in holy orders by episcopal ordination before St Bartholomew's Day (24 August 1662), was to be disabled and deprived. Even vestrymen were now compelled to swear a non-resistance oath, and an oath 'to conform to the liturgy of the Church of England as it is now by law established.' Over a thousand clergy were expelled from the Church of England before the summer was out, to the infinite satisfaction of the bishops who duly celebrated their victory.

Again, it is not certain how Charles had viewed this legislation enacted in his name. Clarendon, presumably on Charles's instructions, had opposed the harsher penalties embodied in the Bill, although he admitted later his own feelings were that once the Bill had been passed it should be enforced. Clarendon also admitted, however, that Charles had continued to pester him for expedients to mitigate the penalties even after the Bill had become law. And on 26 December 1662, as we have seen, apparently acting on his own initiative while Clarendon was ill, Charles had published a Christmas greeting in which he asserted that, despite the Act of Uniformity, his Indulgence to tender consciences promised at Breda would be carried out. To this end he proposed to introduce a new Bill in Parliament; meanwhile, out of his mercy, he wished to dispense with the execution of all penal laws against 'such as shall live peaceably, modestly and without scandal.' The prisons were opened and those Quakers, Anabaptists and Recusants who had been arrested, were released. The Speaker of the Commons had promptly informed Charles he was acting beyond his prerogative, and Charles's proposed Bill had been thrown out.

Despite numerous attempts, therefore, compromise among the squabbling factions had proved impossible. Charles's personal inclinations, however, had become clearer. At Worcester House he had wanted to reduce the old power of the bishops, and encourage individual clergymen to exert some authority within their own domain. When that suggestion had foundered, he had tried again at the Savoy although realizing that both conferences were probably no more than holding actions against the vaunting ambitions of the Anglicans. When the second conference had collapsed and some form of anti-Presbyterian, anti-Dissenter, legislation had become inevitable, Charles had tried to modify the harsher aspects of that legislation. And when that had failed, he had reaffirmed his promise of Indulgence made at Breda. Nor had he been unmindful of promises made to those Catholic loyalists who had helped him after the murder of his father. He let it be known that he never regarded a union between the Roman and Anglican Churches as impossible, provided

191

that the Papacy accepted the hierarchical independence of the Church in England, an idea now voiced by Archbishops of Canterbury more than 300 years later as if it were revolutionary. Charles had undoubtedly been shocked by Parliament's high-handed treatment of the religious settlement, and thereafter had treated religion as a political pawn, keeping his own views to himself. The only visible Church *he* knew, he observed once, was Harrow Church, because it was on a hill.

The triumph of Anglicanism, meanwhile, had continued unchecked. The Act of Uniformity had been followed by other, more vengeful measures. In 1664, Parliament had rushed through the Conventicle Act making illegal all assemblies of five or more persons under pretence of any religion other than Church of England. After a third conviction, offenders were to be transported to one of the new plantations in Virginia or New England. Should they return, execution awaited them. Informers were encouraged to break open houses of non-conformists. The Quakers had suffered worst. Many were arrested; in Bristol, not a single adult Quaker had remained free. In Scotland, a similar Act had prescribed torture with racks, thumbscrews and the iron boot against obstreperous Presbyterians. De Laune, in his *Plea for the Non-Conformists*, claimed that nearly 8,000 had died in prison. In 1663, the Five Mile Act had prohibited non-conformists from taking part in local government, while all preachers and teachers who refused the statutory oaths were forbidden to come within five miles of a corporate town, with the Militia authorized to disperse suspected meetings.

Charles had ignored the laws whenever and wherever he could. In January 1663, he had ordered the release of all Conventiclers in Newgate Prison, provided they were not seditious. In the summer of that year, he had attended a Dissenter meeting in Bath; indeed, at Lewes such meetings were reported to be more frequent than in Cromwell's time, and at towns where large numbers of Dissenters lived such as Taunton, Norwich and Dover there had been no startling record of persecution. Offences against the Acts seem to have been more condoned than punished. Benjamin Whichcote spoke for many when he wrote: 'man has as much right to use his own understanding in judging of truth, as he has the right to use his own eyes.' 'Those who differ upon reason', he added, 'may come together by reason.'

Charles had struggled to make such a viewpoint more widely accepted. No doubt his Declarations of Indulgence (1662 and 1672) were in part attempts to win the political support of those shut out from the State Church; no doubt family considerations had made him seem more concerned with the welfare of dispossessed Catholics than with Protestant Dissenters. But, unlike Cromwell, Charles had no army to enforce his will; he had been powerless to prevent non-conformists from suffering heavily in the early years of his reign. They had been excluded from political life, municipal administration and the universities, and were liable to heavy fines and long terms of imprisonment.

Bunyan, a Dissenter, had written *The Pilgrim's Progress* during twelve years in Bedford Gaol.

Charles realized that this harshness arose partly from the identification of dissent with sedition. The hysteria still generated by the confusions of the previous twenty years needed a scapegoat. Rumours of plot and counter-plot had abounded during the early 1660s, and always the villains were Dissenters. Later it was the Catholics; during the Fire it had been the French; at other times it was the Dutch. More recently it has been the Jews.

But the Restoration settlement (or lack of it) had also acknowledged that the Church of England did not control a monopoly or even a majority of the Protestant faithful. Theological discussion, and not just at the universities, had become more open than at any time since the Reformation. Should faith be kept with heretics? Were good works necessary for salvation? Many Presbyterians, ostracized after the Restoration, had gone over to Anglicanism, not to the established, State-oriented, lapsed-Catholic variety, but to a new low Church party. Of these, the Independents, for example, rejected altogether the institutional conception of the Church, dissociated it from the State, and thought each congregation a separate entity. They took the Bible as the Word, in principle and in detail, and thus became the progenitors of Wesleyanism and Congregationalism. Their most notable leader was George Fox, whose followers called themselves Children of the Light, or Quakers. Popularly believed to be lunatics who smeared excrement on the doors of rich men's houses and paraded naked through the streets shouting that the Lord God would besmear the people as he had been besmeared, they had been regularly persecuted; the Quaker Act of 1662 had caused 15,000, estimated to be nearly half their total number, to suffer assorted legal punishments. Fox had appealed directly to Charles, promising him that the Quaker's abiding principle was to 'seek peace and ensure it'; another Quaker, Robert Barclay, had been more specific. International politics, he had told Charles, were subject to a morality inspired by Christian values, as applicable when dealing with other nation states as when dealing with one's own. In an extra-ordinarily modern passage, Barclay had written that men go to war 'upon every slender pretext ... they sheath their swords in one another's bowels; ruin, waste and destroy whole countries, expose to the greatest misery many thousand families, make thousands of widows and ten thousand of orphans ... merely to satisfy the lust and ambition of great men – they being often times ignorant of the ground of the quarrel, and not having the least occasion of evil or prejudice against those their fellow Christians whom they thus kill.'

Another prominent Quaker, Margaret Fell, saw Charles at least once a week for almost two months pleading the case of fellow Quakers in prison. Her record of these visits is revealing of Charles's whole religious outlook. 'The man', she wrote, 'is moderate and I do believe hath an intent in his mind and a desire to do for [us] if he knew how, and not to endanger his own safety. He is dark and ignorant of God, and so everything fears him.' Charles agreed to bring the prisoners' case before the Council, or else speak to the judges before they went out on circuit.

Despite their persecution, the Quakers, or Friends as they became known, had become an influential voice of English dissent. Many had found fulfilment in the new colonies, although in Puritan Boston they had their ears cut off or were hanged. At home, prevented from holding public office, they had concentrated their intelligence and energy on commerce and industry. Their belief in fixed prices, their frugality and reputation for integrity, for instance, had led many small businessmen to entrust money to the Quakers for safe keeping; it was no accident that many of the early banks were owned by Quakers.

Little of this philosophical debate and dissent percolated to the village, where the local parson still depended on the tithe, levied on corn, timber and pigs, together with various fees and offerings. If the parishioner possessed ten lambs, one went to the parson; an annual income of forty pounds would be reckoned fortunate, while a Cambridge don who was also a priest rarely earned more than ten pounds a year. At this level it was unlikely that the Church of England would attract men of ambition or intellectual fervour.

Yet religion remained the first discipline in all education. The Bible was universally read, even if differently interpreted, its language providing an essential link between the educated and working classes. The parish, with its parson, was a symbol of things permanent in a shifting social scene, an essential unit of local administration. There were more than 10,000 in the England of Charles's reign, most having not more than 500 inhabitants. Their affairs were regulated by four unpaid officials, the constable, the surveyor of highways, the overseer of the poor and the churchwarden, assisted by a parish clerk (an office usually held for life) plus a sexton and bell ringer. The churchwarden's accounts reveal the range of their activities; money spent on beer for the bell ringers, or 'when the organ came home'. 'Given to a woman to remove out of the parish, 1s.' 'Spent to remove her, 6d.' They had also to report, to their local Consistory Court, if any parishioners had been unlawfully married, if any schoolmasters, physicians, surgeons or midwives had practised without licence, and if anyone was under suspicion of immorality. Such courts had come under the jurisdiction of the archiepiscopal courts, above which was a Court of Delegates. Originally established by Henry VIII, this had consisted of a tribunal of clergy and laity to which appeal might be brought from any of the lower courts. The relative jurisdiction of the clerical and lay courts became obscured during Charles's reign, although it was generally agreed that between them these Church Courts had authority, albeit increasingly ineffective, over all cases loosely described as matrimonial, moral offences, and the probate of intestate wills. They were not concerned with bringing dissenters

194

back into the fold. Thus 'the common people', observed one foreign visitor, 'enjoy a liberty which is incredible, every man following that religion and those rites which most suit his fancy.' 'Madam, wise men are of but one religion', Shaftesbury told a lady inquirer. 'Which one was that?' she replied. 'Madam', said Shaftesbury, 'wise men never tell.'

In the towns, parish administration was weaker. Those who, in 1662, had abandoned their livings rather than submit to episcopacy, found a ready audience among the prosperous middle class. Baxter, in Great Russell Street, attracted huge crowds every Sunday. 'I preached to a pretty full congregation at the house of Jeffrey Beck', recorded another unlicensed preacher, Oliver Heywood. 'The Lord made it a refreshing night to many souls, though our adversaries watched and gnashed their teeth when they saw so many coming together.'

In short, as Charles's reign progressed, it became apparent that, such was the variety of religions, the principles of moral conduct must depend upon other disciplines. Such principles were, as Ralph Cudworth pointed out to Charles, like similar intellectual truths; discoverable by 'an inward and active energy of the Mind itself.' Consequently, superstition declined, and witchcraft, without fuss and certainly without portents, became less and less a nightmarish preoccupation. When a country juryman declared 'this Judge hath no religion, for he doth not believe in witches', he was ignored. With an abundance of religious sects from which to choose, the English intellectual accepted that a new age of rationalism was dawning. The sentence of excommunication was seen for what it was, a meaningless threat. As Man had ceased to expect miracles from God, now he had fewer reasons to believe in signs from the Devil. For this change, there were two primary causes – the existence and tenacity of the Dissenters, and, to a lesser extent, Charles himself.

The desirability of religious toleration had never been in doubt for Charles, if only for reasons of expediency. 'It is a very dangerous thing to encourage several sects of religion in the same kingdom', Samuel Parker noted. 'Every one of them would wage war against another, each of them to the Church established by Law. It was found by the experience of all ages that differences in religion always ended in blows . . . The Christian world had seldom been engaged in civil war which was not raised under a pretence of religion.' The essential consideration, therefore, was how best to preserve the peace and 'provide . . . such a settlement of religion as would prevent any disorder in the state upon these pretences.' Charles's letters to the Anglican archbishops immediately after the Act of Uniformity had underlined this practical concern. 'None are in their sermons to bound the authority of sovereigns', he had written, 'or determine the differences between them and the people, nor to argue the deep points of election, reprobation, free will, etc.' Charles had been able to promote this idea of toleration, moreover, because of Parliament's inability to enforce the oath stipulated in the Act, and when he issued his

Declaration of Indulgence in 1672, he had pointed to the failure of the 'many and frequent ways of coercion that we have used for reducing all erring and dissenting persons, and for composing the unhappy differences in religion.' It had become 'evident', he maintained, 'by the sad experience of twelve years, that there [was] very little fruit of all those forcible courses.'

Again and again it was Charles who argued against coercion. 'Constantine himself hardly spent so much of his own time in private and public conferences to that purpose', observed Clarendon later. The King assured a group of Lincolnshire Quakers who had presented a loyal address that it 'was not his mind that any of his subjects who lived peaceably should suffer any trouble upon account of their judgments or opinions in matters of religion.' 'I am confident', wrote an historian of the Royal Society, 'there can never be shown so great a number of contemporaries in so narrow a space of the world, that loved truth so zealously, sought it so constantly and upon whose labours mankind might so freely rely.' It was unlikely that a King who subscribed so openly to such views would take an opposite stand in religion. In fact, Charles became sickened by the Church of England's arrogance and intolerance, not just against Catholicism, which affected him personally, but against all forms of dissent. He determined to flatten the pretence of those who had imposed a distasteful religious settlement upon him, and dealt the Church of England a series of crushing blows from which, in a sense, it has never recovered to the present day.

Whereas immediately before Charles's reign, the bishops had comprised nearly one-third of the Lords, by the end they numbered less than one-eighth. With the exception of Archbishop Sheldon, no priest ever held high office under Charles. The dominance of Bishops in government was destroyed. The medieval tradition whereby the Church existed as a separate estate also ceased to exist. An Act of 1661, which had nominally restored ecclesiastical jurisdiction, demanded that such jurisdiction should only be permitted provided nothing therein 'construed to extend . . . to abridge or diminish the King's Majesty's supremacy in ecclesiastical matters.' The independent authority of Church Courts, so long a bastion of many so-called ecclesiastical freedoms, was abolished. Likewise Convocation. Forbidden to levy taxation, its *raison d'être* vanished. Likewise the High Commission, which was not restored. Eventually Parliament was to abolish 'all punishment by death in pursuance of any ecclesiastical censures', and otherwise severely to limit the authority of Church Courts.

Robbed of its traditional powers, the Church found it was no longer able even to collect rents. In 1666, the Archdeacon of Durham had reported a 'general complaint of ministers and churchwardens that they cannot get any sesses [assessments] for reparation of churches.' Bishop Burnet abandoned his Consistorial Court because it was useless, which indeed it was. 'Church-wardens' presentments [of offenders] are but laughed at', one eyewitness reported from Lancashire. And in spite of almost all the land leases belonging to Bishops and Deans having fallen in during the Interregnum, the money gained from the resale of these leases never found its way into the pockets of those who needed it most, the lower clergy ,who were, by 1678, worst off than at any time during the previous century. When John Echard had published his *Grounds and Occasions for the Contempt of the Clergy* in 1670, he had given poverty as one of the main causes. The mood was perceptibly shifting against the traditional power bases of the established clergy, with Charles encouraging individual manifestations of this shift whenever and wherever he could. 'If our Church should be an enemy to commerce, intelligence, discovery, navigation, or any sort of mechanics', one observer had written in 1667, 'how could it be fit for the present genius of this nation?' The writer, although a Bishop, was also historian of the Royal Society, whose patron was Charles.

In brief, the social and economic programme of Archbishop Laud, designed to secure forever the Church's power in the State, was forgotten. Although one of the immediate causes for the Puritan 'revolution', Laud's plans were only a culmination of the steadily increasing temporal power of the Church of England since the Reformation. In 1660, the Bishops had been restored, although they had done nothing to help restore Charles. They had expected a measure of Laud's ambitions to be realized, but they were to be disappointed. The ejection of so many ministers and schoolmasters who declared themselves dissenters, does not obscure the fact that it was the Anglicans who, in the long term, were the losers.

In 1678, however, astrologers were prophesying 'frenzies, inflammations, and new infirmities proceeding from cholerick humours', as well as 'troubles from great men and nobles'; in August, the Devil himself was said to be presiding at a general convocation of witches. The first six months of that year had witnessed three eclipses of the sun and two of the moon, a curious if slightly unbelievable number, and a blazing comet seen in April still had no satisfactory explanation. England, it seemed, was about to be punished for its sins. Memories of Scotland flooded back. As Newcastle had warned Charles then: 'if any [of your subjects] be Bible mad, over much burnt with fiery zeal, they may think it a service to God to destroy you, and say the spirit moved them.' Events were to prove for Charles that many of his countrymen were indeed Bible mad.

Chapter Ten
Horrid plots

One sunny morning in August 1678, as he was taking his daily stroll through St James's Park, Charles was stopped by one Christopher Kirkby, a bearded chemist employed in the Royal laboratory. Kirkby told the King he had discovered an hitherto secret conspiracy against Charles's life, the plot being the devilish work of certain Jesuits. Kirkby, already known to Charles as an anti-papist fanatic, was told to speak to Charles's secretary, William Chiffinch. Chiffinch refused to see Kirkby, so Kirkby again waylaid Charles and blurted out that he could bring evidence to support his discovery. Charles reluctantly agreed to 'consider' this evidence which soon appeared in the form of Dr Israel Tonge, a Church of England rector whom, it was later disclosed, spent most of his time dabbling in alchemy; 'cynical and hirsute, shiftless in the world' was how Antony Wood remembered him. Tonge gave the King an indictment of forty-three articles which spelled out in general terms 'the hellish plot.' The City was to be fired, Catholics would rise in Ireland, England would be conquered by French and Irish forces, and every Protestant who refused to recant hacked up. A Catholic administration was to be installed under the Duke of York, with the whole operation financed by Jesuits under a direct commission from the Pope. As for Charles, he was to be shot, stabbed, poisoned, or all three.

The story was neither original nor convincing, and the rector and his articles were referred to Danby. Danby realized that the alleged conspiracy might provide the excuse he lacked to cajole the next Parliament into voting extra money for Charles's foreign policy, and the French ambassador became certain that the plot was an invention by Danby to justify the maintenance of a standing army. But Charles was determined not to involve himself in what he suspected were the ravings of Tonge's mind, and refused permission for Danby to take action.

Tonge was not to be passed over. He could reliably report, he now told Danby, that Papist assassins had already attempted the murder of Charles: miraculously, their pistols had failed to go off. A *second* attempt had been made at Windsor: again, miraculously, the assassins' horses had gone lame. Even now there were treasonable letters passing hither and thither, some to the Duke of York's own confessor, Father Bedingfield. Danby travelled to Windsor to inform Charles, only to find that Charles was aware of the letters and thought them forgeries. They were barely literate, Charles told Danby, with Bedingfield's name consistently mis-spelt. But Tonge was persistent; he could now reveal that the author of the forty-three articles was none other than Titus Oates. Charles remained unimpressed; he had never heard of Titus Oates. Danby suggested that Oates be summoned before a committee of the Privy Council. Should the whole affair prove a fabrication, he argued, nothing would have been lost; at least the King could then return to his racing at Newmarket with a quieter mind. Reluctantly, Charles agreed.

Before attending the Council meeting, Oates took what he reckoned the precaution of swearing the truth of his articles and statements – which by another miracle, almost as miraculous as Charles's continued safety, had now grown to eighty-three – before a respected London magistrate, Sir Edmund Godfrey. Thus, when Oates finally appeared before the Council on 28 September, members were impressed by his apparent desire to be truthful; 'if he [Oates] be a liar', noted Henry Coventry later, 'he is the greatest and adroitest I ever saw.' Sir Robert Southwell, Clerk of the Council, agreed. Writing to Ormonde, he observed that 'their lordships were strangely perplexed, and generally fell into the belief that there was something substantial in this matter.'

The Council sat till midnight, intrigued by Oates's story. The Archbishops of Dublin and Tuam were to plunge Ireland into blood; four Irish thugs were to butcher Charles in his bed at Windsor, 3,000 cut-throats were to slice up the gentry of London; and no less a person than Sir George Wakeman, the Queen's physician, together with the Duchess of York's secretary, were to poison just about everyone else. How had Oates come into the possession of such unusual information, inquired Charles? Oates paused. Then, holding up his hands to heaven, he declared by God and his Holy Angels he had gone among the Jesuits solely to betray them. Charles laughed. Oates, shuffling about in his loose-fitting doctor's robes, began to intone the names of those Catholic peers who would lead this bloody plot; Arundel of Wardour, Powis, Petre, Stafford and Belasyse, who was to be Commander-in-Chief of the Papist Army. Charles laughed again. Belasyse was bedridden with gout and unlikely to lead a cripples' army, let alone the mighty force destined to overthrow the Kingdom.

Nonetheless, Oates's appearance before the Privy Council provoked the usual rumours. The Gunpowder Plot with its talk of midnight massacres and hell fire was, after all, only just beyond living memory. That Charles had twice during cross examination exposed Oates as a liar was, in the popular imagination, irrelevant. (Oates claimed to have seen Don John of Austria, one of the plotters, describing him as tall and fair; in fact, the Don was short and dark. Oates claimed that a ten thousand pound reward had been paid over in a certain Jesuit house in Paris; in fact, the house had long since been demolished.) Troops of monks were reported to have arrived from Jerusalem singing a *Te Deum* for the success of the plot, while in Scotland the Covenanters rode 'up and down the country like martial evangelists with sword and pistol, as if they came, not to prate down, but storm our religion.' Lady Shaftesbury carried a loaded pistol whenever she ventured out.

Charles did his best to calm the situation, and went as planned to Newmarket. But the discovery of certain indiscreet letters written by Edward Coleman, a Catholic convert and sometime secretary to both the Duke of York and his Duchess, brought him back to London. The letters, sent to leading French Jesuits, spoke of the glorious days ahead when James would succeed his brother and Catholicism reign supreme. Charles knew Coleman to be a meddling parasite, and none of the letters said a word about murder or insurrection. But, tragically, Coleman had been one of the conspirators named by Oates. It appeared that the truth of Oates's testimony stood confirmed, and when Coleman's correspondence had been read out in Council, Charles was told later, the Lords 'were all amazed.' Worse followed. No sooner had Charles arrived back in London than the body of Sir Edmund Godfrey, the magistrate to whom Oates had sworn his honour, was found in a ditch at the foot of Primrose Hill, his corpse skewered by a sword. It was said that he had clearly been murdered by Jesuits to stop his mouth.

Charles said that Godfrey had committed suicide, but the coroner thought otherwise. Large rewards were offered, by whom it was never discovered, for the capture of Godfrey's murderers; not surprisingly, two different informers came forward with two different stories, and three servants from the Queen's

PLATE V

Minette, "the centre of a thousand fêtes and Madame of France," in a portrait by Mignard. Charles wrote to his sister (she was fourteen years younger) more letters than to any other; about her health, her husband, her lovers and her clothes. To her he confided the utmost State secrets, and when she died he said: "my grief for her is so great, that I dare not allow myself to dwell upon it." Her enemies, however, maintained that she was silly, spoiled and selfish.

PLATE VI

Charles II as President of the Royal Society by M. Laroon (1684).

"Memorandum that, 28 November, 1660, these persons following, according to the usual custom of most of them, met together at Gresham College to hear Mr. Wren's lecture, viz: the Lord Brounckner, Mr. Boyle, Mr. Bruce, Sir Robert Moray, Sir Paul Neil, Dr. Wilkins, Dr. Goddard, Dr. Petty, Mr. Ball, Mr. Rooke, Mr. Wren, Mr. Hill. And after the lecture was ended, they did, according to the usual manner, withdraw for mutual converse. Where, amongst other matters that were discoursed of, something was offered about a design of founding a college for the promoting of Physico-Mathematical Experimental Learning . . ." It was decided that meetings should be every Wednesday at 3 p.m.; a subscription fee of one shilling per week, and an admission fee of ten shillings, were agreed. On December 12, the membership was fixed at 55 persons; Sir Robert Moray was chosen as the first President. Charles became a member in October 1661, and the charter of incorporation granted on 15 July, 1662. The title "Royal Society" was suggested by Evelyn.

PLATE V

PLATE VI

PLATE VII

PLATE VIII

own household were arrested, convicted and hanged, at Tyburn, like all villains. They were obviously innocent, as they protested to the end, and Charles knew it. He resolved to put the matter of Oates and his claims to Parliament in the hope of ending further speculation, reckoning he had little to fear from a proven perjurer, drunk, horse-thief, homosexual, the obscure son of an obscure Anabaptist rector of Hastings. As to the Coleman letters, Charles admitted that these were a cause for greater concern, but, for the moment, he preferred his horse racing. Perhaps for the only time in his reign, Charles misjudged the mood of his country.

The thousands of Jesuits which Tonge claimed were heading for London under direct orders from the Holy See were nothing compared with the invasions now threatening elsewhere. In far-away Whitby, 'forty horsemen armed were heard and seen to march through Skelton and Brotton in the dead of night.' In Wiltshire, hordes were riding north every night between twelve and two; in Yorkshire, they were heading south. In Sussex, 'a great light' was seen burning in the house of a local Papist while three ships lay nearby 'under pretence of fetching oysters, which have been seen several times to go on and off without any.' In Hampshire, 'a great knocking' was heard at night in Tichborne Church. 'Nothing remains', concluded Sir Edward Dering in a warning to the Commons, 'but to make our graves and lie down in them.'

* * *

PLATE VII

James, as Lord High Admiral, in a painting by Henri Gascar. Charles once remarked that his younger brother needed to have "his mistresses found for him by his priests, for penance." Nonetheless, Charles loved him, even when it seemed political suicide to do so. James died twenty-six years after Charles, aged sixty eight, feeble in mind and increasingly obsessed by Catholicism.

PLATE VIII

Top

William III of Orange, in a portrait by Lely. He disliked swearing, trivial conversation (or "whipped cream" as he called it), wine, and went to bed at ten o'clock. He was stunted, pallid and sober, and survived an attack of smallpox although it left him disfigured and suffering from a chronic cough. He was "the plainest man ever seen, and of no fashion at all."

Bottom

A view of the fair on the River Thames, during the Great Frost of 1683–4; an engraving from an original by Wyke (Thomas Wyck). The Thames was frozen over two miles from the sea; bull baiting, ox-roasting, plays and coach-races were staged on the ice. Coffee was 1 d a cup, butter 8d a pound, candles 4d a pound, sugar 5d a pound. By the end of Charles's reign, London had become insufferable – Charles hated it – except for the river. At night, the noise of the City was "between a sow gelder and a cow and a dog." There were no public conveniences; there was no public transport; street lighting remained inadequate. Public divertissements, whether of a State or entrepreneurial nature, were therefore essential; the bearded woman of Holborn, the tame rhinoceros, the calf with six legs, the Lord Mayor's Show, the Bartholomew Fair. Best of all, however, was the river; its gilded barges, its single, gaudy bridge, its innumerable sculls ferrying everyone from the Lord Chief Justice to the humblest citizen. London bordered the Thames for eight miles; gentlemen's villas, with lawns down to the water's edge, naval dockyards and bear gardens. Almost Charles's last thoughts were of the river.

The hammering which Charles had dealt the Church of England arose in part, as we have seen, from his increasing anger that the religious tolerance promised at Breda had not been fulfilled by Parliament, especially toward the sect with whom Charles apparently felt most sympathy, the Catholics. Yet, as Russell told the Commons in 1679: Catholicism was 'a ridiculous and nonsensical religion. A piece of wafer, broken betwixt a priest's fingers, to be our Saviour!' Marvell was not even sure that it should be described as a religion at all. Catholic priests are 'jugglers, and conjurors' with their 'exorcisms, whisperings, sprinklings, censings and fantastical rites.'

Popery was also associated with absolute monarchy, and with Louis XIV's dominance on the continent of Europe. 'Our jealousies of popery', Sir Thomas Meres told the Commons, 'or an arbitrary government, are not from a few inconsiderable papists here, but from the ill example we have from France.' 'Lay Popery flat', added Sir Henry Capel, 'and there's an end of arbitrary government and power; it is a mere chimera or notion without Popery.' The many plots and counterplots which had littered England during the past hundred years, had always somehow involved Catholicism; the Ridolfi Plot of 1571 to depose Elizabeth I, for instance, the assassination attempts associated with Babington and Mary, Queen of Scots, and not least the Gunpowder Plot itself, still commemorated by a special church service every 5 November. The sad reign of the Catholic Mary I had caused nearly 300 Protestants to burn for their beliefs; their end, recounted in detail by John Foxe in his *Acts and Monuments of these Latter Days*, was now a bestseller second only to the Bible. As a result, it was not unusual for Catholics to be attacked in the streets.

Charles's authority had long been compromised, moreover, by a continuing public uncertainty as to his own beliefs. Neither of his Stuart predecessors had been convincing in their patriotic adoption of Protestantism; James I had wanted to marry his son and heir Charles I to a Catholic Spanish princess, although he had eventually settled for Louis XIII's sister Henrietta Maria, who had then attempted to establish Catholic hegemony at the English Court. Charles was well aware of his ambivalent position, and had done what he could to alleviate the latent and often unreasonable hostility toward the Catholics. His proclamation of 1663, for instance, ordering all priests and Jesuits to leave the Kingdom, had not been enforced, although restrictions against the Catholics were harsh with rewards being offered for successful convictions against them. None was legally permitted to move over five miles from home without licence, and it remained a capital offence to harbour a priest. Catholic marriages were not valid in law, and no Catholic could practise any profession, nor hold office, nor transfer land.

For Catholics, however, the greatest enemy came from within. The frustration of being raised in a tradition of service, which service was now outlawed, was, as Halifax remarked, 'a burden to a generous mind that cannot be taken off by all the pleasures of a lazy, unmanly life'; the frustration of being

The Devills Tryvmph Over Romes Idoll.

"The Devill's Tryumph over Rome's Idoll"; an engraving of 1680. The Pope, mourned by nuns, priests and cardinals, is taken off to hell by his quondam ally, the Devil.

"Our great Prince Lucifer in triumph leads,
Him that on necks of princes often treads."

Of the four Popes resident in Rome during Charles's reign – Alexander VII (1655–67), Clement IX (1667–9), Clement X (1670–76) and Innocent XI (1676–89) – the first was indolent, the last three wholly preoccupied with the Turkish invasions of Southern Europe; Vienna was beseiged in 1683 by Kara Mustafa. Innocent XI was universally acknowledged as gentle, tolerant, humane and wise; he protested vigorously, for instance, against the persecution of the Huguenots by Louis XIV. None of these Popes ever interfered in the internal government of England.

aristocratic and Royalist, and yet 'live at the best an useless, and by others to be thought a dangerous, member of the nation where he is born.' The priest-, hood, isolated from Rome and thus lacking formal supervision, was in a state of 'chronic dereliction.' One priest was reported for having fucked his host's wife, another for having venereal disease. Some got drunk – one set up as an innkeeper with a nun as barmaid. Even Charles grumbled about certain foreign nuns 'gadding about' instead of attending to their religious duties. Lacking endowments, many priests finished up as private chaplains; altogether there were no more than 500 ministering to no more than 260,000 Catholics, out of an estimated national population of 5,000,000. In Peterborough, the Bishop counted just 66 Catholics in his entire diocese.

Under Charles, there were few attempts to keep this small number separate. They mixed freely in the communities of which they were an integral part, often serving as officers in the local militia. Rowland Eyre of Hassopp, for example, had his parents buried in Great Longstone parish church under a brass which showed them kneeling before a crucifix telling their beads. 'The poor Catholics of England are not really under such a heavy persecution as may be supposed', noted Henry Howard, later Duke of Norfolk. 'If we do but continue sober and humble, we shall not I hope have severe laws put in execution upon us, for the indiscretion of some few impertinent, over-zealous, busy coxcombs.' Only in the towns was a determined if occasional effort made to isolate the Catholics, although in London the preponderance of royal chapels and those of Catholic foreign ambassadors where Mass was celebrated openly, kept Catholicism alive. Whitehall Palace, a maze of apartments and corridors well fitted for Charles's devious ways, housed no one knew what, although it was easy enough to guess. As a group, the Catholics lacked obvious leaders; the Earl of Shrewsbury, premier earl of England and the senior Catholic aristocrat, had been killed in a duel. The Duke of Norfolk had been certified a lunatic and confined at Padua, while the Earl of Bristol (a convert) had long fallen from favour. Of the five Catholic noblemen said by Oates to be the leaders of armed insurrection, the youngest was sixty and he was senile.

It was Charles's brother James who had transformed this latent hostility into persecution. For a while, Charles had been able to pacify the fear of Popery with a series of anti-Catholic measures. 'Parliament must be gratified by executing the laws both against Popery and Nonconformity', Danby had told him in 1673, although, as the Venetian ambassador observed, the Catholics 'will not suffer for any other reason than that they are made the battleground in the disputes between the King and Parliament and the butt for both sides.' But James was 'a man for arbitrary power . . .', according to Shaftesbury, 'heady, violent and bloody, who easily believes the rashest and worst of counsels to be most sincere and hearty.' The probability that James was a Catholic had confirmed Shaftesbury's judgement, while the Queen's inability to produce an heir made James's accession increasingly probable. His marriage to a Roman Catholic had made it necessary to introduce Bills ensuring that all Royal children would be educated in the Protestant religion, and that in future all Royal marriages to Catholics would be unconstitutional without consent of Parliament. 'Is there any more than the breath of our King between that [Popery] and us?' asked one speaker at a Common Council meeting. 'If the presumptive heir of the crown be a Roman Catholic', he went on, 'what security can be given that the King shall live eight or nine months?'

Charles had been forced to exclude all Catholics from municipal office, close their schools and order all priests to leave the realm. Papists were to 'keep away' from Charles's person. Shaftesbury had amazed the Lords with stories of 16,000 Papists in London ready for a military coup. No one was safe. A French alliance would be proof positive of a plot to bring in Popery. Arlington had been frightened out of office, and Clifford, having admitted his conversion, had retreated beyond Exeter. Shaftesbury had mobilized, seeking to destroy first Danby and then James. Charles had tried to disguise such visible signs of Popery at Court as gave offence, but mutual distrust between King and Parliament had worsened. Pope burnings on 5 November had increased, and Shaftesbury had demanded a Test Act to smoke out the Catholics. Marvell had spoken against those 'secure men that are above either honour or conscience, but obliged by all the most sacred ties of malice and ambition to advance the ruin of the King and Kingdom ... under the name of good Protestants.' James's insistence on an army of almost 30,000 men had confirmed that, with Danby, he intended nothing less than the overthrow of the State.

*　　*　　*

The discovery of Coleman's letters, reported Roger North, 'made as much noise, in and about London, and indeed all over the nation, as if the very Cabinet of Hell had been laid open ... one might have denied Christ with more content than the Plot.' For Charles, the noise brought some relief. After six years of rumour, the battle was now in the open. Shaftesbury's tactics were clear; he would use the fears against Popery as a weapon to have James excluded from the succession, and thereby exact revenge against Charles. Charles realized that rumours of a plot made the Court vulnerable, since they confused the political and religious inclinations of the Crown with any genuine conspiracy. He would need to reassure the country and Parliament that the Court was neither involved in any plot, nor unduly favourable to Popery. He realized also that the Plot would unite the Whigs, otherwise disorganized and with no agreed policy other than exclusion. If Oates's story could be shown as mere invention, the Whigs by their militancy would leave themselves exposed. The demand for an Exclusion Bill would have to be delayed by whatever means, therefore, until Charles was sure he had enough support to destroy those who advocated it.

'We have a mighty work upon our hands', one of Coleman's letters began, 'no less than the conversion of three kingdoms.' In private, Charles told Sir John Reresby that he did not believe a word of the letters. In public, he accepted a unanimous resolution from Parliament that 'there has been, and still is, a damnable and hellish plot contrived and carried on by popish recusants for the assassinating and murdering the King.' A grateful House of

Oates his Degrees.   Sold by B. Palmer against Somerset house

Being advanced to ye Pillory, Debase'd to ye Carte Arse, and expected by his old freind to higher preferment. —1685

Titus Oates, his degrees. A contemporary cartoon of 1685, showing Oates's punishment three months after the death of Charles. As the Solicitor-General, Heneage Finch, said at Oates's trial when referring to the causes of the so-called Popish Plot; "there were ill men at work, that laboured to improve those fears and jealousies that had already possessed men's minds . . . (it is) a vindication of our religion (Protestantism) to punish such offenders as they deserve, the proper way to maintain the justice of the nation, and wipe off that reproach this man's perjury has brought upon it . . . This justice . . . lies under a very great reproach abroad, for this particular thing. Thirty-five more or less innocent people died as a result of Oates's perjury.

Commons assigned Oates a pension of £1,200 per annum, an armed body-guard and palatial apartments in Whitehall where he could better secure the life of his sovereign. Both Houses set up committees to investigate the Plot, but it was too late for committees. In Lincolnshire, for instance, an old stone was found with the mysterious engraving 'Oats shall save this land from destruction.' A thousand nobles were reported to have attended the funeral of Godfrey where the bishop preached upon the text 'died Abner as a fool dieth?' One enterprising tradesman invented the 'Protestant flail', another manu-factured silk armour to protect the gentry from savage papists. Surveyor Christopher Wren was instructed to search the cellars of the Houses of Parliament for any potential Guy Fawkes. 'If I should write you all the news and malicious stories that are told', James told his cousin, 'instead of a letter, you should have a volume from me.'

The Whig party, bullied by Shaftesbury, determined to end the existing House of Commons. James, now an acknowledged Catholic, must be expelled from the Council and a new Test Bill, excluding all Catholics from membership of either House of Parliament, must be implemented. Another thug, William Bedloe, who had earlier testified against the 'assassins' of Godfrey, turned up in the service of Shaftesbury and spelled out dreadful deeds which had supposedly taken place in the Queen's Palace at Somerset House. Bedloe was a known highwayman and robber, yet on him, as on Oates, a thankful nation bestowed a pension, bodyguard and State apartments.

Charles summoned both Houses and thanked them for their care of his person and his government, assuring them that he would assent to whatever Bills they thought necessary. They demanded that all should reaffirm their oaths of allegiance and supremacy; Charles agreed, but exempted many of his servants as well as those of the Queen who were Catholics. They demanded that Secretary of State Sir Joseph Williamson be sent to the Tower because he had given commissions to Catholic officers; Charles ordered his release. They demanded that the Queen herself be excluded from Court: Oates and Bedloe even accused Catherine of complicity in the plots against her husband; Charles dismissed the charges and refused the Commons' demand. As he told Burnet, 'though she [the Queen] was a weak woman and had some disagreeable humours', she was not 'capable of a wicked thing; and considering his faultiness towards her in other things, he thought it a horrid thing to abandon her.' The Commons demanded a Test Bill, including an amendment which specified James's exclusion. Danby, using all his influence, had the amendment quashed. In retaliation, the Commons voted for the disbandment of all forces raised since September 1677, thus considerably embarrassing Charles whose foreign policy, such as it was, depended at that moment on an army sent to Flanders at the request of Charles's only remaining ally, Spain. Instead, the Commons wanted a militia under its direct command. Remembering what had happened to his father, Charles refused.

Shaftesbury, meanwhile, was openly inciting revolution – a 'fairy fiend that haunted and deluded both Lords and Commons.' His coach, bedecked with green ribbons and protected by a surly gang armed with clubs and flails, rattled back and forth in London. From one of its narrow windows Shaftesbury peered, his flabby face wasted by disease, though still

> Politic as tho' one eye
> Upon the other seemed to spy.

Charles was forced to place cannon in Whitehall, and patrol the city at night with an entire regiment of foot. When James attempted to put out a fire at The Temple, in much the same manner as he had during the disasters of 1666, he was hounded from the scene with shrieks of 'Popish dog!'

Before long, Shaftesbury struck at Danby. Ralph Montagu, one-time

English ambassador in Paris, had particular cause to be resentful of Danby. As Lord Treasurer, Danby had once refused Montagu's application to buy the office of Secretary of State from Henry Coventry. Montagu had also been snubbed by Barbara Castlemaine, who had reminded Charles of her existence by sending off a spiteful little note about Montagu being 'an abominable little man.' Montagu had come over from Paris to defend himself only to be snubbed again, this time by Charles who, for no particularly good reason, had accepted Castlemaine's word. Montagu was struck off the Privy Council.

Unfortunately for Charles, Montagu, while in Paris, had seen various letters written by Danby, at Charles's apparent behest, negotiating yet another secret treaty with Louis. And Louis, reckoning Danby an enemy of France, now saw the present confusion as an opportunity for removing Danby. He bribed Montagu with £4,000 to publish Danby's letters. Encouraged by Shaftesbury, Montagu had himself elected a Member of Parliament to avoid arrest, and then dropped the incriminating evidence literally in the Speaker's lap. When the astonished Speaker had finished reading aloud what seemed at first merely the latest in a series of fantastic documents to have come his way, the House was shocked. Within minutes, articles of impeachment were drawn up against Danby accusing him of conspiracy to overthrow the constitution with the aid of a standing army and French money. 'He is popishly affected', concluded the Commons, 'and hath traitorously concealed . . . the late horrid and bloody Plot and conspiracy contrived by the Papists against His Majesty's person and Government.' Charles replied that there was not a scrap of evidence to support such a view; the Lords refused to impeach Danby without a hearing, especially as his letters had Charles's handwritten approval; and more in despair than anger, Charles prorogued Parliament, telling both Houses that he 'intended to get to the bottom of the Plot.'

It is not clear which plot Charles had in mind. Even for contemporary observers, the Plot, its origins, causes, details and understanding, were almost beyond comprehension. It 'could never arise out of the industry or evidence of one single man', wrote Sir Robert Southwell. Oates had 'the speech of the gutter, and a strident and sing-song voice, so that he seemed to wail rather than speak. His brow was low, his eyes small and sunk deep into his head. His face was flat, compressed in the middle so as to look like a dish or discus.' Educated at Westminster School, from which he had been expelled; Gonville and Caius College, Cambridge, from which he had been expelled; and St John's College, where he was described by his tutor as 'a great dunce' and been sent down without a degree, Oates had served as Chaplain to the frigate *Adventure*, from which he had been dismissed for sodomy; as tutor for the Earl of Norwich, from whose service he had been expelled; and thence, having been converted to Catholicism by a lunatic, a seminarist in a Jesuit College at St Omer, from which he had also been expelled. His evidence was, at best, unreliable. When asked to date a particular conspiracy, Oates declared indignantly: 'it is a great privilege I tell the month.' Eventually, he committed himself to August, 'between the first and the middle', finally agreeing to the 21st, and then only 'if it were a Wednesday.'

Bedloe was even more absurd. When describing the numbers involved in the Plot, he listed 10,000 from Flanders, 20–30,000 from Spain, and some 40,000 others from elsewhere, a total eight times larger than the entire English Army. Bedloe claimed that Godfrey had been smothered, whereas the medical evidence was that he had been strangled. And the £4,000 Bedloe said had been offered him by two Jesuit fathers to kill Godfrey (worth about £44,000 in 1978), did seem a little excessive. 'I cannot but lament the unhappy age we live in', noted the Marchioness of Worcester, 'when a man whose whole life hath been nothing but villainy and pageantry, and whose word would not have been taken for sixpence, shall now have it in his power to ruin any man.'

First to be engulfed was William Staley, the son of a wealthy Catholic banker in Covent Garden. Being drunk one afternoon in the Black Lion in King Street, Staley had been heard to shout in broken French: 'the King is a great heretic. I would kill him myself.' Six days later he was tried for high treason; the jury found him guilty without leaving the box, and Staley was hanged, drawn and quartered almost immediately. Charles interceded to allow the unfortunate young man's body to be handed over to his family for proper burial; but the Privy Council, enraged by this interference, ordered the body exhumed, its head impaled on London Bridge and its quarters displayed on four gates of the City.

Next was Edward Coleman, tried at Westminster Hall by a special commission presided over by Lord Chief Justice Sir William Scroggs and the young Recorder of London, Sir George Jeffreys. Oates told the Court of a Jesuit Consult in April 1678 which had planned the Royal assassination and whose schemes had been communicated to Coleman. When pressed for details of which he clearly had no knowledge, Oates claimed he had forgotten. Bedloe wanted to read from a prepared script, but Scroggs prevented him. Coleman was executed at Tyburn.

Next were the Jesuits implicated by Coleman – Grove, Ireland, Fenwick, Pickering and Whitbread. Whitbread was the Jesuit provincial. Some years earlier he had dismissed a scurrilous novice from St Omer called Father Ambrose, alias Titus Oates. 'When they have debauched men's understandings', shouted Scroggs at the defendants, 'overturned all morals, and destroyed all divinity, what shall I say of them? When their humility is such that they tread upon the heels of emperors, their charity such as to kill princes, and their vow of poverty such as to covet Kingdoms, what shall I judge of them?' The answer was obvious. 'They eat their God', concluded Scroggs, 'they kill their King and saint their murderer.' Guilt was not in doubt. 'You have done, gentlemen, like very good Christians', Scroggs told the jury, 'that is to say, very good Protestants.' The priests were sent to the Tower to await sentence.

It should perhaps be remembered that, as Dr Kenyon has pointed out, a seventeenth century treason trial was neither a search after truth nor an attempt to impart justice. At best, it witnessed the authority of the State, a reminder of the King's power; at worst, it was a warning. The prisoner was denied counsel, except on points of Law, and came to the Court with little knowledge of the case against him except in the most general terms. Treason was so fiendish a crime, so contrary to the well-being of the State, that no man could be allowed the luxury of an organized defence, let alone a copy of the indictment. Hearsay evidence and the evidence of accomplices were admitted, while the defendant was not allowed to subpoena witnesses on his behalf. Judgement was a foregone conclusion, punishment bloody and explicit. Those found guilty of high treason were hanged, 'cut down alive, your privy members be cut off, your bowels taken out and burnt in your view: your head . . . severed from your body; your body divided into four quarters, to be disposed of at the King's pleasure.' This barbarity, at odds with everything Charles believed, derived in part from the Law insisting that it was *the* chosen profession. In this, it has changed little to the present day. The Law bred its own recruits whose foul manners were taken for granted. Scroggs, a man whose 'course of life was scandalous' (according to North), 'and his discourses violent and intemperate', was thought an admirable Chief Justice.

Next was Lord Stafford, denounced by one Stephen Dugdale. Dugdale claimed that Stafford had told him of a conspiracy to bring back the Catholic religion. He, Dugdale, had been offered £500 for the assassinations of Charles and the Duke of Monmouth, which were to be engineered by one Evers. A proclamation was issued for the arrest of the said Evers. He was never found. Probably he did not exist.

Bedloe now identified a young Admiralty clerk, Samuel Atkins, as one of Godfrey's murderers. Unfortunately for Bedloe, Atkins had an alibi and was released, so Oates now produced a man called Lane to support his contention that Danby was suppressing evidence. But again the gang blundered. Lane denied knowledge of anything, and 'fell to arraigning Mr. Oates himself, as one that spoke the basest and most contemptible words of the King imaginable, as if he associated himself with none but whores, rogues, pimps and panders . . . and thence proceeded to such beastly, bawdy discourse that the Lords stopped his mouth and would hear him no further nor believe him so far.'

Next was Danby himself, finally cornered into resigning. With the trials of Coleman and others in full swing, Charles had dissolved Parliament which had sat for almost eighteen years, hoping to obtain a more amenable House of Commons at the subsequent elections. But when a House almost universally hostile to Charles and his ministers had been returned in February 1679, Charles ordered Danby to go into hiding; James, who had failed to live down his association with Coleman, was told to leave for Flanders; Stafford, with various other Catholic lords, was sent to the Tower as much for his own protection as for any punishment; while Charles attempted to head off any political confrontation by dismissing the Privy Council. But it was again too late. 'If we do not something relating to the succession', noted Russell, 'we must resolve, when we have a Prince of the Popish religion, to be papists or burn, and I will do neither.' The Commons unanimously decided 'that the Duke of York's being a papist, and the hopes of his coming such to the Crown has given the greatest countenance and encouragement to the present conspiracies and designs of the Papists.' An Exclusion Bill was introduced, although at its second reading, the government minority (128 to 207) was more than expected.

The trials, meanwhile, continued. Whitbread and Fenwick, together with three other important Jesuits arrested since the beginning of the year, Gavan, Harcourt and Turner, were arraigned. 'I have had a thousand letters taken from me', Fenwick protested. 'Not any of these letters had anything of treason in them at all. The evidence that is given comes to but this; there is but saying and swearing.' Apparently ignoring the evidence, Scroggs began his summing up: 'Gentlemen of the Jury, here hath been a very long evidence [two days], and a very confused one, and you cannot expect that it should be wholly repeated to you. For it is almost impossible for any one to remember it. Neither would I if I could, because a great deal of it is impertinent [i.e. irrelevant] and vainly to be repeated.' After fifteen minutes, the jury found all the prisoners guilty.

'Murder and the blackest of crimes here', thundered Recorder Jeffreys, 'are the best means among you to get a man to be canonised a saint hereafter . . . what can be said to such a sort of people, the foundation of whose religion is laid in blood?' The prisoners were sentenced to death, 'after which there was a great acclamation.' Later, when another jury had the temerity to find three Benedictine monks not guilty, the jurymen had to flee their homes for fear of the mob and Scroggs was accused of having been bribed. As he left London for the Oxford circuit, a dead dog was thrown into his coach.

Increasingly, however, the trials were a shock to many thinking people. Evelyn began to reckon Oates 'a vain, insolent man, puffed up with the favour of the Commons for having discovered something really true, as more especially directing the intrigues of Coleman . . . that he was trusted with these great secrets he pretended.' If Shaftesbury had not insisted that a vote for James's exclusion entailed a belief in the Plot, and vice versa, Oates and his cronies might have been swept aside. James was, in 'every way, a perfect Stuart', Shaftesbury noted. 'His interest and design are to introduce a military and arbitrary government in his brother's time.' Pope-burning processions were organized by the Green Ribbon Club, Shaftesbury's headquarters, including 'Jesuits' carrying bloody daggers, an effigy of Sir Edmund Godfrey with 'the cravat wherewith he was murdered about his neck', and the Pope 'in a lofty, glorious pageant. At his feet a cushion of state . . . and bloody daggers for murdering heretical kings and princes on them.' At Temple Bar, the Pope's effigy was solemnly burnt and free wine distributed for toasts of 'No Popery' and 'God Bless the King'. In other words, down with James.

Unlike the plots against Charles, those against James were real enough, although often initiated by meddlesome upper class ladies. The Countess of Powis, for instance, took into her employ a criminal called Dangerfield, lately of the debtors' prison at Newgate, who revealed to the Countess details of a Presbyterian coup. A search, organized by Dangerfield, at the rooms of a leading Whig, revealed suspicious papers, while further documents were discovered in a meal tub at the house of one Mrs Cellier. Dangerfield now decided that the business had become dangerous, and confessed he had fabricated the evidence. Alas, no one believed him. No one knew what to believe. Mrs Cellier appeared at King's Bench charged with treason. She protested that since Dangerfield was a convicted felon and an outlaw, his evidence was inadmissible. Dangerfield arrived to complain, but Scroggs slapped him down. 'What?' shouted Scroggs. 'Do you, with all the mischief that hell hath in you, think to brave it in a court of justice?' The good Mrs Cellier was acquitted, and triumphantly published her account of the fiasco, entitled *Malice Defeated*, for which she was fined and pilloried. It seemed a jolly end to such madness, a sign of the Plot's natural and inevitable exhaustion. Men had grown weary of complaining. For the moment, Shaftesbury's plans seemed disappointed.

There remained those Catholic lords put in the Tower some months earlier for safety, chief among whom was William Howard, Viscount Stafford, now brought to trial in November 1680. The usual distinguished witnesses were called, except Bedloe who had died in Bristol the previous August. Evelyn was revolted by the proceedings. 'Such a man's testimony', he said of Oates, 'should not be taken against the life of a dog.' One Edward Turberville swore that, in 1676, Stafford had tried to enlist him to assassinate Charles. In an atmosphere where a vote for Stafford might well have been interpreted as a vote for Popery, and where the feeling prevailed that if Stafford were dispatched the whole business of the Plot might be done for, the Lords found Stafford guilty by fifty-five votes to thirty-one. He was beheaded in late December 1680 and, as Burnet noted, 'vanished soon out of men's thoughts.'

Last was Oliver Plunket, titular Archbishop of Armagh, brought over from Dublin with a pack of witnesses whose dialect was incomprehensible, 'creatures', reported Ormonde, 'that no schoolboy would trust . . . with a design of robbing an orchard.' Charles admitted to Louis's ambassador that Plunket was probably innocent, but added that his (Charles's) enemies 'were still waiting for him to make a false step, and the moment was not propitious for a counter attack.' Plunket was executed on 1 July 1681. With his death, the Plot was thought to have been finally exorcised.

Oates was not, however, and on 10 May 1684, was suddenly arrested at the Amsterdam Coffee House on a writ of *scandalum magnatum*, accused of having slandered 'that traitor, James, Duke of York' at the Bishop of Ely's dinner table. King's Bench awarded the Duke £100,000 damages which, obviously, Oates could not pay; he was flung into prison where it was hoped he would remain for the rest of his life. In fact, he and his cronies had already fallen upon difficult times. Bedloe's allowance, once £10 per week, had been reduced to £2 a week before he died; that of Oates had ceased altogether. Israel Tonge had continued writing pamphlets, and Dugdale, having extracted vast sums for his 'expenses', had also had his weekly allowance cut to £2. Two days after Charles's death, Oates was to be brought to trial, before Jeffreys, now a Judge. Oates maintained that, previously, his evidence had been believed. Now, it transpired, Oates was not alone in suffering from a poor memory. John Maynard, a witness for Oates, said; 'I know nothing truly, nor can I remember anything of it now.' In desperation, Oates called to his defence Lord Huntingdon, who happened to be sitting in the well of the Court. 'I do believe', Huntingdon told Jeffreys, 'Mr. Oates's discovery found a good reception in the House of Lords.' Oates grinned, much relieved. 'But it was grounded upon the opinion that what he said was true, and that he was an honest man ... But since that time, it being apparent that there were so many and great contradictions, falsities and perjuries in his evidence, upon which so much innocent blood has been shed, I believe a great many persons who were concerned in the trials of those unfortunate men are heartily afflicted and sorry for their share in it.' Judge Jeffreys sniggered. Oates, he said, 'has pawned his immortal soul by so perjured a testimony ... He may very easily proffer the venturing of his vile carcase to maintain it.' Oates tried to argue that the witnesses were 'men that must have malice against me.' 'Hold your tongue', yelled Jeffreys. 'You are a shame to mankind.' 'I appeal to all heavens', Oates protested, 'whether I have justice done me.' Oates, said Jeffreys, so recently acclaimed as Saviour of the country, was 'a monstrous villain.'

The question remained what to do with him. In days gone by, perjury was punishable by death; later, this had been commuted to cutting out the offender's tongue. 'We do therefore think fit to inflict an exemplary punishment', Jeffreys concluded, 'upon this villainous perjured wretch, to terrify others for the future.' First Oates was to be paraded through the Courts of Justice in Westminster Hall with a notice proclaiming his offence; then he was to stand in the pillory for an hour. The following day the process was to be repeated at the Royal Exchange. The day after that he was to be whipped from Aldgate to Newgate, given a rest, and then whipped from Newgate to Tyburn. Thereafter he was to be imprisoned for life, except that every 24 April, 9, 10 and 11 August, and 2 September he was to stand for an hour in the pillory at each of Tyburn, Westminster Hall, Charing Cross, Temple Bar and Royal Exchange, lest anyone should forget the chaos he had caused. Oates told

Jeffreys he would be standing in the pillory for truth. Jeffreys's reply is not recorded. As Oates emerged from King's Bench, he was pelted with rotten eggs by a crowd estimated at 10,000.

He was not expected to survive the whipping, but he did, being dragged the last part of the way to Tyburn unconscious on a sled. He was luckier than Dangerfield who was given the same sentence. Thrashed en route by Robert Francis, a Tory barrister, Dangerfield's brain was pierced by a cane which killed him.

* * *

The effects of the Plot on the Catholics and their religion are difficult to chart. Nearly 300 years later, Pope Paul VI canonised forty English martyrs who included six executed as a result of Oates's evidence. Since 1660, no priests had been executed; between 1678 and 1681, forty-two priests were arrested. Of these, twenty were brought to trial and six executed. Of the Jesuits, nine were executed, twelve more died in prison, and three as a result of the privations caused by the restrictive legislation. In retrospect, the supposed militancy of the Jesuits can be seen as mostly a Protestant lie. When their vicar-general had been told of the Plot, he had declared that, if it were true, those English Jesuits involved against Charles deserved to be punished. As it was, many Catholics went into hiding. 'Sweet Jesus, grant us patience', wrote one, 'and make such novices as myself sneak into lurking holes.' Those who could, went abroad; in November 1678 the Earls of Cardigan and Berkshire left for the Spanish Netherlands. By the end of the year, thirty-four groups had left, another thirty-one leaving the following month.

As for Charles, he became 'weary of the vexation he had long been in.' 'The Plot', he told Halifax, 'must be handled as if it were so or not.' He always delayed signing the death warrants for longer than was politically wise, remarking, 'let the blood lie on them that condemn them, for God knows I sign with tears in my eyes.' Partly he acted out of the national interest; 'I must fear that this business will appear very foul and render us odious and contemptible through all Europe', reported one commentator. Partly Charles acted out of self-interest; he was ill, had not responded to treatment, and 'desired to be set at ease.' Although at first he had underestimated the Plot, he had soon realized that 'this imaginary plot is a plot upon a perpetual plot . . . to keep the nation so long in awe . . . till the faction may execute another plot of their own . . . The blow was at the Crown itself, when every man was made a Papist that would not play the knave and the fool.'

The compulsory disarming of all Catholics, upon which Parliament had insisted, revealed for Charles the absurdity of the whole affair. In a society without a police force, where the right to carry arms was essential, it was generally assumed that Catholics were armed to the teeth. In Westmorland, for instance, the bag was impressive. From Mr Stephenson, one broken sword; from widow Platt, one old gun; from Mr Peter Mowson, one little gun; from Mr Anthony Duckett, back, breast and head piece, all relics from the Civil War. Charles became determined to protect Catholics where he could. The proclamation, ordering all priests to quit the country or risk prosecution, was ignored. Not a single priest complied and none was charged or even arrested. Catholic houses in London were daubed with a red cross in preparation for massacre. None occurred. None of the Plot's victims had offered the smallest acknowledgement of guilt in word or deed, though many were offered a pardon in return for a full confession or indeed any confession at all. There was none. There had been nothing to confess.

*   *   *

Throughout the late 1670s and early 1680s, London suffered from bad unemployment; too many people with too little to do. Money was tight; many firms went bankrupt, and Charles was forced to cancel the free dinner normally offered to the Privy Council after its weekly meeting. A feeling of the government against the governed prevailed, not helped by the ignorance of the governed. The *London Gazette*, the only official newspaper, pretended that the Plot did not exist. It reported only Royal proclamations and the numerous executions. News circulated by word of mouth, with the exaggerations that such a process engenders. Rumour became fact, and, in the absence of information to the contrary, fear increased. Forty thousand French cut-throats were frequently said to be embarking at Dunkirk. Many doubted if survival was possible. As Stephen College wrote;

> Listen awhile and I will tell you a tale
> Of a new device of a Protestant Flail,
> With a thump, thump, thump a thump
> Thump a thump, thump!
> This flail it was made of the finest wood,
> Well lined with lead and notable good
> For splitting of brains and shedding of blood
> With a thump, thump, thump a thump
> Thump a thump, thump!

Shaftesbury waited his chance.

Chapter Eleven
The merry gang

It is sometimes believed that Charles's reign was little more than a continuous debauch wherein the wicked prospered; wherein bawdiness was thought a sign of manliness, and cynicism the mask of intelligence; wherein sensual pleasure was the criterion of good, and the condemnation of sensuality a predisposition for evil. Further, such philosophy appeared to enjoy Charles's approval. Aubrey records that this doctrine had 'free access to His Majesty, who was always much delighted in . . . wit and smart repartees.' Macaulay was later to describe the Restoration Court as men with 'foreheads of bronze, hearts like the nether mill-stone, and tongues set on fire of hell.'

It is also argued that, compared with the reign of Charles I or the rule of Cromwell, the twenty-five years following 1660 were a time of intellectual desolation. Where were the scientific discoveries to compare with those of William Harvey who, in 1628, had published his theory of the circulation of the blood? Under Cromwell, experimental scientists had been appointed to many university posts; there had even been a proposal to turn Christ Church in Oxford into a scientific institute. There was nothing to rival Charles I's art collection, moreover, which included paintings by Titian, Leonardo, Bellini, Rembrandt, Bernini and Mantegna. Where was the equal of Rubens or van Dyck, both of whom had lived in London? Where the Ben Jonson or even the new Inigo Jones? The Court culture of Charles I, which had produced men of such gentle sophistication as Thomas Carew and George Herbert, had been swept away by civil war. By comparison, Charles II's courtiers were little more than a 'merry gang, whose works were devised by blackguards, for blackguards.' Richard Blackmore, a physician and versifier, concluded that Restoration poets were 'engaged in a general confederacy to ruin the end of their own art, to expose religion and virtue and bring vice and corruption of manners into esteem and reputation.' As Dr Johnson was to write of them:

> Themselves they studied, as they felt they writ;
> Intrigue was plot, obscenity was wit.
> Vice always found a sympathetic friend;
> They pleas'd their age, and did not aim to mend.

This traditional and accepted view of Charles and his court does not bear detailed examination. It is as false as the view which holds that Charles was a lazy, indulgent and foolish King. He was often mistaken, sometimes unwise, and occasionally naive. But he was never less than astute, and too intelligent to be deceived for long. Quite simply, he loved life. He also admired scholarship and wit – which the age took to be a sign of scholarship – and there was scarcely a poet, architect, painter, sculptor or playwright who did not owe patronage or inspiration to the King. Charles appeared to understand the function and purpose of their various arts, and tolerated them as long as it seemed to him they fulfilled that function. All patronage is political, especially that of the Arts, and these men provided an eloquent commentary to political upheavals which might otherwise have lacked popular expression.

The function of poetry, for instance, was frequently propaganda, its effect a growing awareness among ordinary men and women of the apparent deviousness of the State, and its abundant creation the mirror of a vigorous and increasingly involved society. As Dryden, only a year younger than Charles, wrote:

> If love and honour now are higher rais'd
> 'Tis not the poet but the age is prais'd.
> Wit's not arrived to a more high degree,
> Our native language more refin'd and free.

And Lord Mulgrave, later Duke of Buckinghamshire, in his Essay on Poetry, expressed Charles's own view exactly:

> Of all those arts in which the wise excel.
> Nature's chief masterpiece is writing well;
> No writing lifts exalted man so high
> As sacred and soul-breathing Poesy.
> No kind of work requires so nice a touch,
> And, if well finished, nothing shines so much.

*   *   *

One of Charles's first Acts in 1660 had been to re-open those theatres closed since 1642, and the stage had soon become the most fashionable diversion of the nobility. London boasted two main companies, the Duke of York's and the King's. The actors in both were regularly at Court; the actresses, of course, were always there. Indeed, it was the first time that actresses had been allowed to play leading roles. Audiences and players knew each other well, a relationship encouraged by prologues, epilogues and the apron stage. Tickets were expensive, and the curtain usually rose at 3 p.m. which made attendance inconvenient for all but the wealthy. Most educated men, including Charles, tried writing plays. Quality was often sacrificed to quantity; Dryden wrote twenty-

John Dryden; a portrait by Sir Godfrey Kneller. Born 9 August, 1631, into a Puritan family at Aldwinkle, Northamptonshire. The first of fourteen children. Educated at Westminster School and Trinity College, Cambridge. In 1668, appointed historiographer royal and poet laureate. Converted to Catholicism about 1680, although he was buried (in 1700) in Chaucer's grave at Westminster Abbey. Known as Squire Dryden, his brilliant satires made him much disliked – Rochester hired thugs to beat up Dryden for damaging references to the Earl in the "Essay on Satire" – but also immensely popular; his famous attack on the Whigs, Absalom and Achitophel, went through nine editions in two years. No doubt an opportunist – his earliest work had been pro-Cromwell, but, with the advent of Charles, he was soon writing sycophantic pro-royalist odes – he became a loyal and powerful influence on the Stuart renaissance. Above all, he knew the proper value and usage of poetry;

> "For ev'n when Death dissolves our Humane Frame,
> The soul returns to Heav'n, from whence it came;
> Earth keeps the Body, Verse preserves the Fame."

218

eight plays, most having 'rotten architecture, but wonderful gargoyles', as well as volumes of poetry and folios of literary criticism. One critic inquired how any audience could be clever enough to understand the stories of these plays, and yet stupid enough to be interested by them when they did.

Most plays followed the French example; during Charles's enforced exile, the success of Corneille and Racine had made a deep impression. The use of rhymes, for instance; the heroic play in which its protagonists extol the virtues of a grand life and manners, remote from reality; the belief in wit for its own sake. Of the English tradition, Beaumont and Fletcher were much admired. 'They understood and imitated the conversation of gentlemen much better', wrote Dryden, 'whose wild debaucheries and quickness of wit in repartee no poet before them could paint as they had done.' It was a tendency which Dryden himself much regretted, since it included 'incorrect English, and a hideous mingle of false poetry, and true nonsense; or at best, a scantling of wit, which lay gasping for life, and groaning beneath a heap of rubbish.' The plays were loosely categorized into tragedies and comedies, although some tragedies were so inane as to be comical, and the comedies so pathetic as to be in effect tragic. Most plays had at least three plots, all running simultaneously. Dorimant, the hero of Dryden's *The Man of Mode*, is casting off one mistress, seducing another and courting a third. Curiously, or perhaps characteristically, Dorimant is not 'The Man' of the title. He appears in Act III, has little to do with the main plot (or at least the plot of Acts I and II), and disappears soon after.

Nonetheless, 'heroic drama' (as tragedy was frequently called) was, according to Dryden, 'the highest pattern of human life', although almost none of it survives in performance today. Loyalty, passion, and heaven-defying gallantry were the significant qualities of plays whose mythical heroes and heroines were known by such improbable names as Almanzor, Aureng-Zebe and Lyndaraxa. Conceived as heroic poems praising the virtues of the past for the improvement of the present, Dryden's tragedies demonstrated, even proved, the nobility of English kings who belonged, including presumably Charles, to the company of gods and heroes. Summarizing much early Restoration theatre, its attitudes and limitations, Dryden observed: 'Comedy presents us with the imperfections of human nature; farce entertains us with what is monstrous and chimerical. The one causes laughter in those who can judge of men and manners, by the lively representation of their folly, or corruption; the other produces the same effect in those who can judge of neither, and that only by its extravagances.' 'Poets', he concluded, 'while they imitate, instruct.'

That the plays were merely occasional fripperies, written for the moment and with no thought for tomorrow, does not detract from their refreshing honesty. If their wit now seems confusing and tedious, at the time it was effective and popular. These plays had in common a vitality and vehemence

219

symptomatic of their age; above all, like Charles himself, they united against that 'heinous and worst of women's crimes, hypocrisy.'

The poets readily used their skill to aid Charles in his struggles. Dryden's *Absalom and Achitophel*, published at Charles's request to turn public opinion against Shaftesbury during the Popish Plot, was almost certainly a contributory factor to Charles's ultimate victory. Its sarcasm was deadly; Charles had drawn up the outline himself. Buckingham, thought to be Shaftesbury's henchman, was christened Zimri . . .

> Stiff in opinions, always in the wrong
> Was everything by starts, and nothing long.

Bethel, Sheriff of London, and one of Shaftesbury's main supporters, became 'Shimei', who

> Did wisely from expensive sins refrain,
> And never broke the Sabbath, but for gain.

'Corah', Titus Oates, was nailed:

> Sunk were his eyes, his voice was harsh and loud,
> Sure signs he neither choleric was nor proud.

The most savage attack was reserved for Shaftesbury himself. In *The Medall, a satyre against sedition*, Dryden writes that Shaftesbury

> Groan'd, sigh'd, and pray'd, while godliness was gain,
> The loudest bagpipe of the squeaking train.

The poem is a riot of elegant abuse, as dazzling now in its comic invention as it seemed at the time, when it was read and absorbed by just about everyone who could read.

Not that the poets or playwrights were mindlessly sycophantic. For Carolean society in general, Dryden expressed a mixture of contempt and envy.

> When I consider Life, 'tis all a cheat;
> Yet, fool'd with hope, men favour the deceit,
> Trust on, and think tomorrow will repay;
> Tomorrow's falser than the former day.

Charles had appointed Dryden Poet Laureate in 1668, a post he held until after Charles's death.

Another favourite was Samuel Butler, author of the epic poem *Hudibras*. Charles, it was said,

> Never Eat nor drank nor Slept
> But *Hudibras* still near him kept.

When Butler's poem had first appeared, Charles had sent for the poet and

The Royal Charter, granted in 1663, to Thomas Killigrew for his theatre in Drury Lane.

'promised him great matters.' Nothing had come of the promise, although Charles gave Butler £300 and later issued an injunction against all piratical editions of his works. Modelled loosely on Spenser's *The Faerie Queene*, from which it also took its title, *Hudibras* concerns a Presbyterian knight who goes 'A-colonelling' with his squire Ralpho, an Independent, after the manner of Don Quixote and Sancho Panza. The importance of *Hudibras* is that whereas Dryden used poetry to praise or attack *people*, Butler organized it to lampoon *ideas*, particularly those of religious fanatics. Dissenters were 'indiscreet and horrid Metaphor-mongers.' Presbyterians

> Prove[d] their Doctrine Orthodox
> By Apostolic Blows and Knocks:
> Call Fire and Sword and Desolation
> A godly-thorough-Reformation.

In *The Elephant and the Moon,* he mocked the debates of the Royal Society as 'repartees between Puss and the Cat at a Caterwauling.' (Butler was not alone in this view. Shadwell in his play *The Virtuoso* described their enquiries as 'useless experiments upon Flies, Maggots, Eels in Vinegar and the Blue upon Plumbs.') With a profusion of 'low' imagery, mostly from the farmyard, Butler debunked the more pompous claims of the Society; that he could do so in witty, clattering rhymes, while plundering metaphysics, religion and politics for his subject matter, as well as receiving the direct approval of Charles, is a measure of the times. As Dryden noted, looking back to the age of Elizabeth, 'greatness was not then so easy of access, nor conversation so free, as it now is', a freedom

A second theatre was licensed in Dorset Gardens, Lincoln's Inn Fields, and called the Duke of York's.

Much of restoration theatre was tedious, and eventually Charles and his people tired of it; eventually, the two companies had to combine in 1682 because of declining business (Elizabethan London had supported six companies). Important innovations had been established, however; scenery was now used, actresses played significant roles, the actor had become a person of some public consequence. Most literary men wrote plays, Newcastle, Buckingham and Rochester proved diligent patrons, and no age which could boast Dryden (born 1631), Shadwell (born 1640), Wycherley (born 1640), Otway (born 1652) and Etherege (born 1634) can have been entirely without merit. Congreve, Vanbrugh and Farquhar, also known as Restoration dramatists, did not, in fact, start writing until after Charles's death.

John Wilmot, 2nd Earl of Rochester, in a portrait attributed to Jacob Huysmans. Born 10 April, 1647, at Ditchley, Oxfordshire, the son of a Royalist general who helped Charles escape after Worcester. Educated at Burford Grammar School and Wadham College, Oxford. Charles gave him a pension of £500 a year in 1661, and later made him gentleman of the royal bedchamber at £1000 a year. He was, as he boasted, the "prince of all devils of the Town"; frequently drunk, he abducted an heiress who had rejected him with an armed guard, caused a brawl at the Paris Opera, posed as a quack and sold patent medicines, and disguised himself as a footman to spy on the ladies at Court. He was also a courageous soldier, a true scholar, and one of the more disturbing poets of his age. His behaviour, he once said, came from a burning passion to affront Puritanism:

> "But man with smiles, embraces, Friendships, praise,
> Unhumanely his Fellow's life betrays:
> For hunger, or for love they bite or tear
> While wretched Man is still in Arms for fear:
> For fear he armes, and is of Armes afraid;
> From fear to fear successively betray'd."

He died, of venereal disease, on 26 July, 1680, and, like his great friend Charles, is buried in an unmarked grave.

taken full advantage of by John Wilmot, the second Earl of Rochester. In *The History of Insipids; a Lampoon*, Rochester's description of James was cutting:

> This is the man whose vice each satire feeds;
> And for whom no virtue intercedes.
> Destined for England's plague from infant time;
> Curs'd with a person fowler than his crime.

As for Charles, he was little more than a 'mutton eating King.' Using Sir Car Scrope's words, Charles replied:

> Rail on, poor feeble Scribbler, speak of me
> In as ill term as the world speaks of thee.
> Sit swelling in thy hole like a vex'd toad,
> And all thy pox and malice spit abroad.

Charles had a particular affection for the recalcitrant Earl, appointing him gentleman of the bedchamber and a naval commander. Imprisoned for attempting to abduct a famous heiress, Elizabeth Mallet; banished from the Court for similar escapades on at least six occasions; thought to have beaten up Dryden whom he loathed; recanting his 'profane and lewd writings' only on his death-bed into which he sank, exhausted, soon after his thirty-third birthday, Rochester was perhaps the most characteristic of all early Restoration poets; scurrilous, not without a touch of viciousness, relentless in his exposure of hypocrisy, admiring of and admired by Charles, free and open yet not quite the licentious wordsmith of repute:

> Be Judge yourself, I'll bring it to the test,
> Which is the basest creature, Man or Beast?
> Birds feed on Birds, Beasts on each other prey,
> But savage Man alone does Man betray.

Two other poets epitomized this same high-mindedness. Their formative years were over before Charles claimed his throne, but their later public success was in no small way thanks to Charles. First was Andrew Marvell, a collected edition of whose poems was not published until three years after his death, and only then at Charles's express desire. For much of Charles's reign, Marvell was a Member of Parliament. Originally elected to Richard Cromwell's Parliament of 1659 as MP for Hull, he remained in the House until his death in 1678, apart from a break of two years from 1663 to 1665 when he was sent by Charles on a mission to Russia. Mostly he wrote not for publication, but to amuse his friends. His output was small, and salvaged after his death by one Mary Palmer, who claimed to be his widow. In fact, he never married.

By reputation, Marvell was an austere Puritan who disapproved of the Restoration, as did another poet of Charles's early years, John Milton. Blind, crippled with gout, defender of the regicides, married three times, a

Frontispiece of "Paradise Lost – a poem in ten books", published in 1667 by John Milton. The picture also shows Milton's quill. This long contemplated heroic poem sold 1300 copies in the first eighteen months; Milton and his descendants eventually made £18 from its copyright. At the Restoration, Milton had hidden in a friend's house while a warrant was out for his arrest and the public hangman burned his pamphlets; Milton had been a member of the Parliamentary army and had written sonnets in praise of Cromwell and of republicanism. Arrested, his saviour was Marvell, a friend of General Monck, a friend of King Charles who offered Milton a Latin secretaryship. He would rise at four in the morning, dress in his customary black robes, and have his daughters read to him in Hebrew from the Bible before breakfast. He dictated his poetry in the morning, and made music in the afternoon; evenings were for visitors. "Certainly then," Milton had written in 1659, "the people must needs be mad or strangely infatuated, that build the chief hope of their common happiness or safety on a single person." (i.e. Charles).

THE
Pilgrim's Progress
FROM
THIS WORLD,
TO
That which is to come
Delivered under the Similitude of a
DREAM
Wherein is Difcovered,
The Manner of his fetting out,
His Dangerous JOURNEY,
AND
Safe Arrival at the Defired Countrey.

By *JOHN BUNYAN.*

The Third Edition, with Additions.

I have ufed Similitudes, *Hofea*, 12.10.

Licenfed and Entred according to Order.

LONDON,
Printed for *Nath. Ponder*, at the *Peacock*
in the *Poultrey* near *Cornhil*, 1679.

Frontispiece to the third edition of "The Pilgrim's Progress" by John Bunyan, published in 1679 (the first edition had been the previous year). Born at Elstow near Bedford in 1628, Bunyan was the son of an itinerant tinker. Although of Church of England stock, he was baptised by immersion into a Nonconformist community of which he became a deacon in 1653. At the Restoration, he was accused of holding a conventicle and sent to prison. His confinement was not as arduous as is popularly believed, however; he was allowed to visit his family and friends, and even occasionally preach at the meeting house. Released in 1672 as a result of Charles's Declaration of Indulgence, he was chosen pastor of the Bedford meeting and earned the nickname "Bishop Bunyan". Part II of "The Pilgrim's Progress" was published in 1684 and sold 100,000 copies within ten years. Bunyan died in 1688. Note that Bunyan's work was "licensed and entred according to order."

disappointed, embittered man who had lived to see his best hopes for Republicanism shattered, Milton struggled on until 1674 as a towering reminder that the Interregnum had not been a waste of either men or ideas. After the Restoration, Milton had been arrested. Charles, through the intercession of Marvell, had secured his release and offered him a Latin secretaryship, which he refused. In spite of the hatred with which most Royalists regarded Milton, Charles had guaranteed him freedom from prosecution. As a result, Milton's three greatest poems, *Paradise Lost*, for which he received £10,

226

Paradise Regained and *Samson Agonistes* had been published between 1667 and 1671. Like Dryden, Milton was convinced that poetry must teach, that its purpose was to

> . . . assert Eternal Providence,
> And justify the ways of God to men.

He rejected rhyme as being the 'invention of a barbarous age.' Yet his verse demonstrates an acute awareness of the relentless discussions as to what constituted the ideal state. It says much for Charles that he allowed a man who had approved his father's death, and who had actively campaigned against Charles's own return, to live out his days in comparative peace and therein produce some of his greatest work. A coincidence, maybe, but an illustration of the tolerance both political and literary which Charles affirmed.

This tolerance also found expression in the writings of John Bunyan. Bunyan came to Charles's attention only in the late 1670s. Being a Separatist both by inclination and birth, Bunyan had been imprisoned in January 1661 and not released until Charles pushed through his Declaration of Indulgence in 1672. During his confinement in Bedford Gaol, Bunyan had written *The Pilgrim's Progress*, although a further six years passed before it was published. Bunyan had been locked up again in 1677 for illegal preaching, but later spoke in the Congregational churches of London where he became known as a remarkable orator as well as an influential writer. Charles had first thought Bunyan 'an illiterate tinker'. But when Dr Owen, one of Charles's religious counsellors, told the King that he would 'gladly give up all [his] learning for that tinker's power of preaching', Charles's interests were aroused and he sent for a copy of Bunyan's works.

Like Charles, Bunyan despised those who denigrated spiritual values 'either by violence, cozenage, flattery, lying or by putting on a guise of religion.' In a language also full of 'low' imagery – 'all of a dung sweat', 'slithy rob-shop', 'loses his sheep for a half-pennyworth of tar' and 'make hay while the sun shines' – Bunyan's tone is elemental and defiant. His second allegory, *The Holy War*, published in 1682, carefully analysed the treatment of the godly in Charles's reign. Bunyan admits that Charles's actions were less simple than he had suspected, and more governed by the needs of political wisdom than was generally acknowledged.

*   *   *

If the writers and poets are a striking example of an increasingly literate society in which the Arts flourished, they are only a minor part of the story. The hundreds of balladeers and itinerant verse-mongers who crowd every page of these times, for instance, are so numerous that no one has ever counted them, while the diarists, dozens of them, provide a unique glimpse of this bustle.

John Evelyn, a landowner's son from Wotton in Surrey, was a founder member of the Royal Society, a Commissioner for the sick and wounded during the Second Dutch War, and in 1671 had been appointed a member of the Council of Plantations. A loyalist, devoted to his family and possessed of a high sense of public duty, he spent much time at Whitehall where Charles evidently enjoyed his company. At Charles's instigation, Evelyn served on Royal Committees to investigate the condition of London streets, old St Paul's and the Royal Mint. He published thirty books (including one which listed the best fruit for making cider), as well as keeping a regular diary from the age of eleven. What was thought to be the complete work was to be published in 1818, but the full text not discovered until 1953. It contains little about the man, although its rough freshness tells much of the age.

The diaries of John Aubrey, on the other hand, reveal in vivid and often whimsical anecdote the man and, incidentally, his 'friends', including Hobbes, Petty and Hooke. His jottings were not a diary in any chronological sense, merely the scrapbook of an ailing antiquarian recalling those whom he had met when young.

Samuel Pepys's diary is altogether more substantial, revealing both man and age. The son of a London tailor, educated and apprenticed in government service by wealthy relatives, Pepys mixed affairs of State with domestic worries, yet gave to both the same childlike enthusiasm. He was twenty-seven when Charles was crowned, having accompanied the King back from exile in Holland. But his political adventures, like those of his diary, begin with Charles's arrival. Written in shorthand (it was not transcribed until 1825), the diary runs for over a million words. Pepys is the journalists' journalist: 'As I was writing this very line', he reports, 'the bellman passed and cried "Past one of the clock and a cold and frosty windy morning".' His honesty compelled him to record his vanities: 'I found that coming in a periwig did not prove so

John Evelyn, in a portrait by Robert Walker. Born 31 October, 1620, at Wotton, Surrey. ▷ Educated at Balliol College, Oxford, where, according to his own admission, he spent most of his time "dancing and meeting people". He left Oxford without a degree, and took chambers in the Middle Temple where he continued "dancing and fooling more". An ardent Royalist, he nonetheless stayed in England during much of the Interregnum, cultivating his garden, "intelligent company" and Charles, with whom he corresponded in code. After the Restoration, he sat on innumerable Royal commissions, published "Fumifugium" (1661), an account of London smog, "Sylva" (1664), a treatise on trees and cider-making, "Numismata" (1697), a "discourse of medals", and "Acetaria" (1699), "concerning salads". He began his "Diary" in the early 1640's and continued it until his death in 1706; it was first published in 1818. Although Evelyn disapproved of what he described as the wilder excesses of Charles's court, he seems not to have worried about the strict censorship which Charles permitted – "to print or publish any news books or pamphlets of news whatsoever is illegal", Chief Justice Scroggs declared. Nor did Evelyn concern himself with the destruction of popular education, nor with Charles's apparent surrender at the end of his reign to the Tory and Anglican gentry, nor with Oxford University's ceremonial burning of the works of Hobbes and Milton. In 1698, Evelyn's home at Sayes Court was let to the Tsar Peter the Great, who amused himself by trampling all over Evelyn's delicately weeded flowerbeds.

strange to the world as I was afraid it would', he notes, 'for I thought that all the church would have presently cast their eyes upon me, but I found no such thing.' His descriptive skill recreates both the obviously spectacular events – such as the Fire, the Coronation and the debâcle in the Medway – as well as the minutiae of his private life.

Pepys was also a talented musician, skilful on various instruments and with ambitions as a composer. He loved the opera and went to the theatre every month. Church-going he found tedious, preferring the Harp and Ball tavern to Whitehall Chapel across the road. He was against gambling and swearing, although not averse from fucking his barber's under-age maid in Westminster Abbey. He never took communion, then as now the ultimate test of Church membership, but never forgot to thank God for his blessings. He was frequently drunk – 'fuddled', as he described it – and, although he said his wife did not satisfy him, was not as promiscuous as is sometimes believed; a life-long dread of venereal disease kept him more faithful than most. The death of his wife in 1669 was catastrophic; this, and failing eyesight, were sufficient for him to abandon his diary.

Above all else, Pepys provides a daily glimpse of Charles's court and government, as did the careers of many whose life and work became inexorably entwined with Charles and his ambitions. Christopher Wren, for example, was given his first opportunities by Charles. In 1665, Charles had sent him to France and Italy from where, impressed by the various building works in progress for Louis XIV, including Les Invalides for retired or injured French soldiers, Wren suggested that Charles mollify a Parliament made nervous by the presence of an armed guard by offering to build a hospital for military pensioners after the French model.

The Royal Hospital at Chelsea, quite apart from the reconstruction of fifty-two City churches, would have been enough to occupy most men. Appointed

Samuel Pepys Esq., Secretary to the Admiralty, from an original by Sir Godfrey Kneller. Born ▷ 1633, the second son of a tailor. Educated at St. Paul's School, London, and Magdalene College, Cambridge. Clerk of the acts in the Navy Office (1660), at a salary of £300 per annum; clerk of the Privy Seal (1660); member of the Corporation of the Royal Fishery (1664); elected to the Royal Society (1664); member of Parliament for Castle Rising in Norfolk (1673); secretary to the Admiralty (1676) at a salary of £2,000 per annum; sent to the Tower for six months (1679); commissioner for Tangier (1683); President of the Royal Society (1684); dismissed from all public offices by William III in 1689; retired to Clapham, where he died in 1703. Pepys's Diary commences 1 January, 1660, and ends on 31 May, 1669. Written in a shorthand devised by Thomas Shelton, it extends to 1,250,000 words and was not deciphered until John Smith's transcription of it appeared in 1825. Pepys also kept a journal of his voyage to Tangier (30 July–1 December, 1683), and wrote down Charles's own version of the Royal escape from Worcester. When Pepys first joined the Navy Office in 1660, the line of battle consisted of 30 battleships, carrying 1,730 guns; when he was eventually forced from office in 1689, the Navy possessed 59 ships with 4,492 guns, and that in spite of numerous costly encounters with the Dutch; "truly sir", said the orator of Oxford University when conferring an honorary degree, "you have encompassed Britain with wooden walls." Pepys is also the greatest diarist in the English language.

Samuel Pepys Esqr *Secretary to the* Admiralty.

From an Original by Sir. Godfrey Kneller.

His Autograph from an original Letter
in the possession of John Thane.

as Charles's Surveyor General in 1668, Wren was also expected to estimate the cost of sweeping the street outside Whitehall Palace, and enforce an Order in Council issued against the inhabitants of Soho who were 'erecting small and mean habitations without permission.' Although Inigo Jones had been appointed James I's Royal Surveyor as long ago as 1615, a post he also held under Charles I, Wren was the first English architect whose job, like that of the Poet Laureate, was specifically to serve the needs of the State, however trivial such requirements might be. To Charles he owed both patronage and the idea which invigorates his work. 'Architecture has its political uses', he wrote, 'public buildings being the ornament of a Country. It establishes a Nation, draws People and Commerce, makes the people love their native Country, which Passion is the Original of all great actions in the Commonwealth.'

*   *   *

Painting in Charles's reign was not so glorious, despite the King's acquisition of a huge collection of Leonardo da Vinci sketches. Both Charles's principal portrait painters were, and are, claimed as English. Neither was. Sir Peter Lely was Dutch, born in Westphalia; Sir Godfrey Kneller came from Lübeck in Germany. Charles insisted that they anglicize their names, Lely from Pieter van der Faes, and Kneller from Gottfried Kniller. Lely received an annual pension from Charles of £200, and was knighted in 1680; Kneller had been brought over from Germany by Charles in 1674. Both depended on Royal patronage; both painted the King, his mistresses and ministers endlessly. Kneller was even to paint the severed head of Charles's favourite illegitimate son, Monmouth.

The tradition of Royal portraiture had received its most recent stimulus from Antony van Dyck. He had set before the English school an aristocratic ideal of elegance and sophistication. Unfortunately, he had trained few pupils, although among these were William Dobson and the miniaturist Samuel Cooper whose clients included Monmouth and James. Charles had decided to import his own school, and Dutch and Flemish masters had flocked to Court attracted by the promise of Royal commissions. The finest portrait of a seventeenth century English admiral is by a Dutchman, Lely; Thomas Wyck, another émigré, became famous for his views of London; and van der Velde, for whom Charles had taken out a special licence in 1676, became the most notable painter of 'English' seascapes. But so skilfully did Lely, for instance, absorb the van Dyck tradition, that for years several of Lely's paintings were ascribed to van Dyck. His pictures have, in common with those of Kneller, a frozen charm, wooden stance and devious look. Encouraged, as well as paid for, by Charles, his work lived on; it was said later that Gainsborough died, as he had lived, speaking of the painters whom Charles had employed.

Music, on the other hand, was an integral part of the English tradition.

Charles's love of music was much talked of; he owned several guitars and practised hard. Trumpets and drums, dismissed by Pepys as 'dull, vulgar music', appear to have sounded off in Court at every possible opportunity. Whitehall Chapel boasted a 'Symphony of Vialls', and Pepys reported how it was there that he 'first perceived that the King is a little musical and kept good time with his hand all along the anthem.' Charles also wrote songs, predictably to those he loved. To Frances Stuart he sang:

> I pass all my hours in a shady old grove,
> But I love not the hours when I see not my love . . .

His interest was probably no greater than that of any other rich dilettante, but since Royal patronage bestowed social respectability, the impetus given to opera, for example, was crucial. He commissioned John Blow to write *A Masque for the Entertainment of the King*, the first dramatic work in which the entire text was set to music without dialogue or extraneous musical entertainments. He persuaded Matthew Locke, also in the Royal service, to write for the stage and appointed him Composer in Ordinary to the King in 1660 and later private organist to the Queen, keeping him occupied composing music for the 'King's sagbutts and Cornetts.' Henry Purcell succeeded Locke as composer to Charles's private string orchestra, and later became organist of Westminster Abbey and Keeper of the King's Instruments. Although his most famous stage works, including *Dido and Aeneas* which was written for a performance at a girls' school in Chelsea, were composed after Charles's death, Purcell's first work for theatre, *Theodosius*, written in 1680, was created at Charles's suggestion.

The birth of opera in England, therefore, owed Charles an immeasurable debt. Its general scheme was modelled at first on the French *comédie-ballet*. Each act of a spoken play concluded with a musical interlude. The chief actors did not sing at all, the play being performed by one company and the music by another. *Ariane*, a French 'opera' by Cambert and Grabu, was presented in translation to celebrate the marriage of James and Mary of Modena. It was 'only a bare collection of phrases', complained its translator, with 'expressions made fit for Sound and Harmony . . . both much worse than they are.' The effect was chaotic. The actors became confused and did not know whether to stand still while the musicians (also on stage) were performing, or walk about, or get off altogether. Such absurdities soon inspired parody. Thomas Duffett, thought to be the originator of English pantomime, wrote a musical version of Macbeth in which the three witches 'fly over the pit riding upon Beesomes . . . Hecate descends . . . in a Glorious Chariott adorn'd with pictures of Hell and Devils, and made of a large Wicker Basket.' Dryden wrote *Albion and Albanius* (Charles and James) in the hope of killing off 'opera' altogether, and in 1684 John Blow offered the King his *Venus and Adonis*. Charles was delighted and graciously allowed Venus to be sung by Mrs Mary Davis, his

Oculos exerc[it]

I. Closterman pinx.

R. White sculp.

Henricus Purcell.

Ætat: Suæ. 37. 95.

234

mistress, provided Cupid was performed by Mrs Davis's 12 year-old daughter (by Charles). *Venus and Adonis* was the model for Purcell's *Dido and Aeneas*, performed five years later.

* * *

Since Henry VIII, the idea of a monarch imbued with a love of the Arts and thus having responsibility toward such pursuits was neither unusual nor unexpected. The most that Royal patronage often achieved was more or less what it confers today, a dubious cultural respectability. Unlike today, however, there were few other patrons. And in a society as close knit as that of the 1660s, prosperity in the Arts without Royal approval was unimaginable.

Charles's interest, however, encouraged other patrons – 'this very critical age', Shadwell complains in the Preface to *The Sullen Lovers*, 'when every man pretends [i.e. claims] to be a judge' – and his example reflected an increasing preoccupation with learning. Henry Peacham, in his *Compleat Gentleman* re-published in 1661, had advocated education as a means to social improvement; 'imitate the best authors', he had written in 1622, 'as well in Oratory as in History... with much conference with those that can speak well.' In 1682, an 'eminent lawyer' drew up twenty maxims which he hoped would help his son improve his prospects in the world: 'Acquire some knowledge of physic', he advised, 'as well as divinity and law, so that your conversation may be more agreeable, though your knowledge may be only superficial. Do not marry a celebrated beauty, because your home will become as frequented as a confectioner's shop... Avoid writing about the faults of a great person, as your correspondence will be intercepted. And lastly, always avoid disputes about religion.' Aubrey devised an entire educational system whose schools should include teachers of Rhetoric, Mathematics and Logic. Mingled with the pupils were to be ten or twelve Swiss, Dutch or Scottish boys who would broaden the horizons of English students. Such schools were to be

◁ Henry Purcell; an engraving by Closterman, after the sculpture by White. Born probably in 1659 and probably in London; joined the Chapel Royal as a choirboy, and in 1673 was made assistant keeper of the King's instruments. Charles's composer-in-ordinary from 1677, and organist at Westminster Abbey from 1679. Wrote at least twenty-nine celebration odes for State occasions. His great operas – Dido & Aeneas, King Arthur, The Fairy Queen and The Indian Queen – were written after Charles's death, but they owed their genesis to the King's forceful encouragement of music as one of the noblest arts. Under Charles, there was a steady improvement in vocal and instrumental techniques, and in 1672 one John Banister, previously master of the King's own band, began the first ever series of public concerts in Europe; there was to be a concert every afternoon, admission price a shilling. Charles sent a promising young composer called Pelham Humfrey to study under Lully in France, and persuaded Purcell to adapt religious forms for secular use. Organ building began, and most educated households possessed a spinet. Like Wren, Purcell understood that music had a State function; his most famous song, "Lillibulero", is against the Irish and popery. It was said that half the nation could sing it. Purcell died in 1695; he was only thirty six.

organized nationally; the home education of the rich was condemned. Private and privileged education, argued Aubrey, allowed the young to be flattered by servants and dependants; thus, when they entered the world, they would be more likely to give offence.

Paradoxically, the universities at Oxford and Cambridge appear to have been jealous of the newer establishments. Although many university students continued to make a considerable mark – such men as Newton, Wren, Pepys, and Evelyn – as institutions, the universities seem not to have contributed much to this intellectual vigour. Evelyn records that the Oxford orator indulged in 'some malicious and indecent reflections on the Royal Society as underminers of the University.' Oxford continued to be immersed in more traditional questions, no doubt of vital importance to the early fourteenth century but irrelevant to the mid-seventeenth. The essay subject for the University Prize in 1669, for example, had been whether Duns Scotus wrote better Latin than Cicero. Little has changed.

*   *   *

The artistic bustle which Charles stimulated provides an essential clue to his age. If its achievements do not finally stand comparison with those of Elizabeth, or of his father, or even those of Cromwell, they demonstrate a remarkable vitality and modernity of outlook. Encyclopedias of the arts and sciences proliferated, while periodicals ran columns of useful projects and information; item, a haunted house in Cherry Tree Alley where the ghost appeared sometimes as a man and sometimes as a dog: item, houses and shops to let: item, time-tables of stage-coaches: item, horses stolen or strayed. And although the various news-sheets, a public manifestation of this thirst for knowledge, led dangerous lives, they developed a knack for survival. The closely printed official newspapers, on the other hand, were dull and predictable, and important government servants such as Pepys often preferred to brief themselves in the growing number of coffee-houses. But even if they seem limp and ill-informed when read alongside Addison's *Spectator* of thirty years later, these newspapers were still a revelation to Charles's curious public. Henry Muddiman's *Parliamentary Intelligencer*, a weekly summary of news first distributed in 1659 at £5 per annum, popularized the demand for a free Parliament. Arlington began his entire career as a government lackey publishing the bi-weekly *Oxford Gazette*, later renamed the *London Gazette*.

Perhaps the most significant illustration of this developing concern for learning was the increase in literary criticism. A determined effort was made to evaluate both current literature and its inheritance from the past. Dryden's *Essay on Dramatic Poesy*, published in 1668, was written 'chiefly to vindicate the honour of our English writers, from the censure of those who unjustly prefer the French before them.' Thomas Rymer thought that 'the tragical part

236

[of Othello] plainly none other than a Bloody Farce, without salt or savour.' Shakespeare's style, he wrote, is 'so pestered with figurative expressions, that it is as affected as it is obscure.' The Royal Society had set up a committee in 1664 to 'improve' the English language, 'to return back to the primitive purity'; only recently English poets had learned to 'mould their thoughts into easy and significant words; to retrench the superfluities of expression.' A plain and direct prose style emerged, later to become the weapon of Defoe, Addison and Swift.

Charles's 'Merry Gang' were not dependent on the Royal favour, of course, but gained inevitably because of it. They lived at a time when traditional beliefs and accepted moral standards were being questioned. Their exuberance created an atmosphere of intense excitement; they were curious about everything, and believed in nothing, at least, not for its own sake. They were against the 'Kingdom of darkness', they were for life itself and reason, 'the light of Nature', in which they 'blazed out their youth.' They knew that educational opportunities were not open to all. They worried that their society was not tolerant, even in the sense we dimly perceive it today. 'There is a difference of degrees in men's understandings, apprehensions and reasonings', noted Locke, 'to so great a latitude, that one may, without doing injury to mankind, affirm that there is a greater distance between some men and others in this respect, than between some men and some beasts.' The purpose of education was not to 'perfect a learner in all or any one of the sciences, but to give his mind that freedom, that disposition, and those habits, that may enable him to attain any post or knowledge he shall apply himself to.' Such freedom was embodied by the very existence of this Merry Gang, as much as it was openly and richly expressed by them, as much as it reveals today an inner strength to the reign of Charles II.

Chapter Twelve
Whose arse is blackest?

If Charles's religious problems were partly exorcised during the Popish terror, his difficulties with Parliament were not. The Plot had steadily carried away much of Charles's support at Westminster; 'I will not say who started the game', wrote Shaftesbury, 'but I am sure I had the full hunting of it.' Shaftesbury and his cronies had hoped to destroy the Cavalier Parliament by subjecting it to waves of violent anti-Papist emotion.

But Shaftesbury, like so many before him, had underestimated Charles. The King had not tolerated a proposed address designed to exclude the Queen from Court, and through Danby had even managed to insert a clause in the latest Test Bill excluding James from its provisions. When the Commons had voted the disbandment of the army and introduced a Bill to raise the militia, Charles had refused to give his assent, claiming that it was an infringement of his prerogative. Shaftesbury, furious, had redoubled his efforts. If he could not bully Charles, he would destroy Danby instead, using every device of espionage, perjury and thuggery. But when, as we have seen, the Commons had finally impeached Danby in December 1678 on the evidence of secret letters sent to Ralph Montagu, the ambassador in Paris, Charles had also been implicated. The phrase 'I approve this letter' was appended to the text of Danby's letters in Charles's own handwriting, although whether these words had been added later or forged was hotly disputed. Charles had bought time by proroguing both Houses, telling them he had 'not been well used by them', and assuring the Mayor and Aldermen of London that he would bend every sinew to 'preserve peace, the Protestant religion and trade, and would presently pay off the army to show the world he intended to rule that way.' Through Danby, he had also tried to appease the Country Party by offering numerous compromises, such as disbanding the army and summoning Parliament in return for a promise of extra funds. James was convinced that a 'new parliament would act in a milder strain and would not fly so high.' Charles was not so sure.

Changes in the government were now announced; former Members of

Parliament who had held office and yet voted against the Court were removed, and the Solicitor-General who had been active in urging Danby's impeachment was dismissed. James was told to go abroad, and Charles declared formally that he had never been married to any woman other than the Queen, thus excluding Monmouth from his claim to the throne. Then, after an informal deal with the Opposition whereby Danby would be saved in return for fresh elections, Charles dissolved Parliament. It had sat for eighteen years.

The subsequent campaign in February and March 1679 was a scramble. Although not conducted along party lines, it was clear that partisan feeling was strong. An anonymous pamphlet entitled *England's great interest in the choice of this new Parliament* was the first statement of 'party policy' placed before the electorate. Choose men of 'large principles', it urged, men who will maintain civil rights; above all, choose sincere Protestants. Another pamphlet, probably written by William Penn, outlined the aims of the Opposition. Legislation was to be adopted for securing frequent Parliaments; evil counsellors were to be brought to justice; pensioners of the previous Parliament were to be punished and further discoveries of the Plot pursued; and measures should be introduced for the ease of Protestant Dissenters.

Pamphlets apart, the usual electoral influences were at work. Barrillon asked Louis to send money for beer; Charles wrote to all the Lords Lieutenant informing them who was the government nominee. Shaftesbury exercised unusual restraint, warning electors not to return bribe-takers or voluptuous persons, since these were inevitably agents of the Crown. His confidence was justified; when the results of the election were analysed, 302 of the new members were for the Opposition, only 158 for the Court. Barrillon reckoned that Charles could count on only 40 votes; the influence of the earlier cabals was over. Charles was not unhopeful, however, of Members' support. He wanted national unity, he told them, 'and I resolve it shall be your faults, if the success be not suitable to my desires.' He listed all he had done to achieve this unity; he had ended the Popish Plot, including the 'execution of several ill men upon the score of the plot'; he had disbanded as much of the army as he could with the cash he had been given; he had sent James abroad. He needed money to continue his good work, he said, observing: 'There can be no man that must not see how fatal differences amongst ourselves are like to be at this time, both at home and abroad.'

The Houses listened patiently. They resisted Charles's attempts to impose upon them a Speaker of his persuasion, yet did not insist on their own candidate, accepting an impartial nominee, William Gregory. But they were not to be diverted from other matters, reaffirming their belief in the existence of a widespread conspiracy. Charles, foreseeing disaster, advised Danby to resign, offering him £5,000 a year for life and the doubtful benefit of becoming a Marquis. Alas, news of this arrangement leaked out and Charles found himself accused of wilfully deceiving Parliament. He pleaded that he had pardoned

Buckingham and Shaftesbury in much the same way, but the Houses were not impressed, especially when it was discovered that Danby was to be replaced by two friends and appointees. The pardon was voted illegal. The Lords wanted Danby banished, the Commons favoured a Bill of Attainder; both Houses convinced themselves that Danby himself had raised an army as a 'limb of popery' to destroy Parliament. Publicly, Charles assured Parliament that Danby was innocent of the charges against him; privately, he urged Danby, as he had done Clarendon, to go into hiding or else flee abroad. But Danby was tougher than Clarendon, and threatened Charles that, if he were abandoned to the Commons, he would reveal information damaging to the Court. He asked Charles's permission to surrender to Black Rod; reluctantly, Charles agreed. Danby presented himself at the bar of the House of Lords on 16 April 1679, and was committed to the Tower where he stayed for five years. 'My God, how I am ill-treated', Charles remarked. 'But I must bear it and keep silence.'

With Danby's removal, the floodgates opened. 'I am here in my old station', reported Ormonde, 'pulled at on all hands. Time was when I was believed to be an enemy to French and Papists; now I am said to be absolutely at their service. But I feel myself just as I was.' Danby was jeered and pelted as he was taken down the Thames to the Tower; 'I never saw any man more sensible of the miserable condition of his affairs than I found his Majesty upon many discussions with him', recorded Temple in his memoirs. The Commons brought in another Bill against Popery, and Edward Cooke observed that if Christ himself were still on earth He would find himself labelled a Papist. To be called French or Papist, Cooke wrote to Ormonde, were 'two terms of art in every malicious mouth, completing revenge on whomsoever either can be pinned. And considering the easy credulity of this uncharitable age, it seldom fails to stick.' On 27 April, the Commons voted that the only way to preserve the King's safety was to ensure the succession did not fall into the hands of a Papist, since James himself had obviously been the cause of the Popish Plot.

Danby, meanwhile, was feeding Charles advice from the Tower. He urged the King to seize control of the army, the navy and the garrisons, and then appeal direct to the country against the unreasonable behaviour of the Commons. Charles should again dissolve Parliament, Danby told him, summoning a new assembly to meet outside London. But Charles preferred the suggestion of Temple's that he form a Council including a Lord President, the princes of the blood, fifteen officials, ten Lords and five commoners to guide the King (Charles told Parliament) on 'weighty and important' affairs. Its purpose, of course,, was to bring the leaders of the Country Party into the Royal counsels, thus enabling Charles to govern without resort to the constant bickerings of Parliament. Shaftesbury was offered the post of President; 'he might do as much mischief as any', if he were left out. For James, now in Brussels, it seemed as though a republic was about to be established. For Charles, the Council soon followed a familiar pattern. 'God's fish, they have put a set of men about me but they shall know nothing', he told Bruce, adding, characteristically, 'but keep this to yourself.'

Despite the new Council, Parliament seemed determined to force the issue of succession. Charles offered another compromise whereby he would agree to certain constitutional limitations in the event of a Roman Catholic monarch, provided the succession remained intact. Perhaps Charles had no intention of accepting such a scheme, but it was a neat suggestion; if the Opposition rejected it, the responsibility for whatever followed would be theirs. Shaftesbury opposed the plan in Council, but agreed to present the idea in Parliament. At first the Commons seemed sympathetic but one Member, Thomas Pilkington, wanted James impeached for High Treason, while another, Richard Hampden, son of the parliamentarian, John Hampden, introduced a Bill to exclude James from the thrones of England, Scotland and Ireland. The Duke of York, the preamble read, had been seduced by the Pope's agents to enter the Church of Rome and thus advance the power of the French King to the hazard of these kingdoms. He was thus 'disabled' from the succession. The Bill was passed unopposed, or at least those against it would not stand up to be counted and so 'yielded the question.' Ten days later, its second reading was carried by 207 votes to 128 and bonfires were lit outside the various Whig clubs at Temple Bar in celebration.

The Commons were in no hurry to move its third reading, however, fearing (probably rightly) that the Lords would reject the Bill. Meanwhile, a host of other business had crowded in; again the Commons voted an address to remove Lauderdale from Scotland; the Archbishop of St Andrews had been murdered by some drunken Covenanters; Charles was still urging the Commons to vote him supplies for equipping a fleet to combat Louis, lately so successful at Nymegen. Not for the first time, Charles decided enough was enough. On the advice of Halifax and Sunderland, and without bothering to consult his new Council, he came down river to Westminster, settled whatever outstanding business he could, including giving Royal assent to the Habeas Corpus Act, and prorogued Parliament until August, hoping thereby to avoid further confrontation. The Habeas Corpus Act only survived the Upper House because the tellers, in jest, had counted one particularly fat Lord as ten and then forgotten to adjust the figures.

Charles felt a great burden had been lifted from him. His resolve was strengthened. 'I shall find means to pay the fleet and manage economically', he said. 'It will be difficult and uncomfortable for me, but I will submit to anything rather than endure the House of Commons any longer.'

The loss of Danby had been bitter; 'nothing he said to me moved me more', remembered Temple, 'than when he told me he had none left with whom he could so much as speak to them in confidence, since my Lord Treasurer's being gone.' Danby, like Clarendon or Arlington or Clifford, had been essential to Charles's notion of stable government. Their responsibility, as Charles understood it, was to handle the day-to-day administration of the Kingdom and thereby manage Parliament. The wider concerns of foreign affairs and defence remained matters for the King. Charles had always been his own Prime Minister and President; he *was* the executive. Social welfare and political reform were not the principal concerns of Parliament, which existed to administer the laws as handed down by Charles.

But this notion depended upon the co-operation of Charles, his ministers and Parliament; its weakness was that Charles rarely chose his ministers from within Parliament. Rather, they were mostly ennobled careerists who had to rely for their Parliamentary influence on agents. By default, therefore, Parliament was able to make notable constitutional advances. It established a right to appropriate supply, and began to dictate its will in matters of foreign policy and defence. That these changes were achieved without the dubious benefits of revolution owed much to Charles's skill as a politician and everything to his wisdom as a man.

*   *   *

The possibility of a coup d'état was emphasized when Charles fell ill in the summer of 1679. 'Good God! What a change would such an accident make', recorded Henry Savile. 'The very thought of it frightens me out of my wits.' James was recalled from Brussels, but told to come in disguise amid fears of general unrest. Charles alone was unmoved. 'The King has contributed much to his recovery', Sir Robert Howard wrote to Ormonde, 'by that extraordinary calm temper that he has shown in all his sickness; and in those fits, which are of great pain and uneasiness, he never changed from that calmness he had in health.' Charles knew he must prepare for a traumatic confrontation, now made unexpectedly worse by fresh troubles in Scotland which Shaftesbury blamed on Lauderdale, believing that Charles would be forced into recalling Parliament. But Charles sent the Duke of Monmouth north with sufficient forces to crush the rebels, which he did, efficiently and ruthlessly, at Bothwell Brig. Monmouth returned to London in triumph, the darling of the army and the Saviour of the nation. Was *this* the Protestant Messiah who could save the country from Papist domination?

Monmouth was now thirty. His beauty, indeed overt sexuality, had made him increasingly popular; 'the new Adonis', Gramont called him, 'the universal terror of husbands and lovers.' He was good at sport and valiant in battle; his military skills had won praise from Marshal Turenne, lately one of Louis's most trusted generals. He had boundless enthusiasm for any task which his father gave him, 'always in action', Pepys said, 'vaulting, leaping or clambering.' Once, it was rumoured, this skittishness had resulted in a night of drunken violence during which Monmouth had hacked to death a watchman on his knees begging for mercy. As Charles's eldest bastard, however,

The Duke of Monmouth, young Monmouth, in a miniature by Samuel Cooper. The beautiful, illegitimate son of Lucy Walter, born 9 April, 1649, in Rotterdam. Known variously as James Scott, Fitzroy, or Crofts. The Protestant Duke, as he became known, beloved of the Whigs, beloved of Charles, was vain and, notwithstanding his manifold qualities, stupid. Although Charles was consistently loyal to his recalcitrant eldest son, no man ever tried harder than Monmouth to usurp the throne. He worshipped publicly in St. Martins-in-the-Field, courted Nell Gwyn, talked openly of insurrection and assassination (of Charles), maintained himself and his entourage in a semi-Royal state near to wherever Charles was lodged, and blatantly scorned the legitimate claims to the throne of Charles's brother, James. Monmouth's uncle eventually had his revenge; following an abortive rebellion, James had Monmouth beheaded on 15 July, 1685. The key to Monmouth's failure, apart from his own character, was that although Charles doted on him and the public adored him, there was never any question of his succeeding to the throne. The Crown would not overlook the lessons of 1649, nor would the men of property forget 1646–60. Political or constitutional opposition might have its place; but it could never be extreme otherwise civil war and anarchy might result, and no-one wanted that. "What does it matter who serves his Majesty," Sunderland would ask, "so long as his Majesty is served?" Monmouth never grasped this fundamental principle of Charles's success.

Monmouth attracted that same aura of legend which Charles himself still used to advantage.

The son of Lucy Walter, Monmouth had been entrusted to the care of William Crofts just before the death of his mother in 1658, and for some years had been known as James Crofts. Although brought up in the Protestant religion, he had not been allowed into England until the summer of 1662, whereupon he had been received by Charles with the utmost favour. A marriage was arranged with the wealthiest of Scottish heiresses, Anne Scott, Countess of Buccleuch, with James created Duke of Monmouth. A host of other honours had followed; the Garter, the additional title of Duke of

243

Buccleuch, Captain of the King's Own Troop of Guards, Duke of Orkney, member of the English Privy Council and of the Scottish Privy Council, Commander of the British forces seconded to France during the Second Dutch War, Master of the Horse (in succession to Buckingham), Chancellor of the University of Cambridge, Captain General of all the armed forces in England, and later Captain General of all the armed forces in Scotland. In both his person and his offices, Monmouth seemed the epitome of all that a worthy successor to the throne should be. When, in the mid 1670s, he had embarked on a series of Royal progresses, he had everywhere been hailed as the great Protestant Duke. Monmouth, Shaftesbury hoped, would be susceptible to Shaftesbury's control.

But James too had his supporters, not the least and most determined of whom being Charles himself. And when Sunderland, Essex and Halifax – the latest of the King's cabals, this known as the Triumvirate – persuaded Charles to dissolve Parliament again and thus forestall any attempt by Shaftesbury to use Monmouth as a focus for any new exclusionist movement, Shaftesbury protested vigorously. Charles told him that dissolving Parliaments was a matter for the Royal prerogative, and that was that. Although Charles's skill at dealing with this latest exclusion crisis has sometimes been exaggerated – his nerve seems to have failed him more than once – in this instance, the King had clearly foreseen Shaftesbury's plan. When only four members of the Council agreed with the dissolution, Charles quite arbitrarily overruled the rest. Temple's constitutional experiment thus collapsed.

The subsequent election campaign went badly for the Crown. Again Charles sent letters to the Lords Lieutenant instructing them to secure a majority favourable to the Crown; again he asked the French ambassador if Louis would consider giving a little cash to help. A subsidy of £500,000 was suggested, although the price was negotiable. James, in separate dealings, appears to have guaranteed England's submission to Versailles for a mere £170,000 a year, although he was never authorized to make such an offer. As it became evident that another exclusionist House of Commons would be returned, Parliament found itself prorogued before it had even met. Charles persuaded James to leave the country once more, suggesting that, for the moment, he went to Scotland as Royal Commissioner. In the hopes of making any alliance with Shaftesbury less attractive, Charles deprived Monmouth of his recent Commissions and told him to go abroad. Shaftesbury was ordered to stay out of London. So James went to Edinburgh, Monmouth to Holland, and Charles to Newmarket – 'in good health and very good humour', reported Ormonde.

London was not so merry. Shaftesbury, still nominally Lord President of the Council, sneaked back to Westminster and summoned the Council without telling Charles. The proposed appointment of James in Scotland, Shaftesbury announced, was 'the worst counsel that was ever given to the King, and the

The Solemn, mock Procession of the Pope, Cardinals, Jesuits, Friars, etc., through the City of London, 17 November, 1679. A contemporary engraving. "Pope burnings" were not invented by the Whig Green Ribbon Club, nor confined to London, as is sometimes believed, although the London processions of 1679 and 1680 were financed by the Whigs. The Pope was burned in Oxford in 1678, in Edinburgh in 1679, in Taunton and Salisbury in 1680. Bonfires and fireworks in London on 5 November were recorded by Pepys in 1600 and 1661; in 1673, a large Pope was burned and shot in the Poultry. The burnings were not so much political demonstrations, as excuses for a party in response to undue anti-Catholic propaganda. Ale and wine was sold in abundance, and a room with a view in The Temple cost £10. The pageant of 1679 (as above) was particularly spectacular. It was said to have cost £2,500; a statue of Queen Elizabeth, clutching Magna Carta, was erected. The Pope, of course, had to bow before it. Two hundred porters were hired to carry torches at two shillings a man. Fireworks exploded all over the place as two hundred thousand people lined the streets. The idea that "the mob" influenced or frightened Charles, however, as it had done his father, is nonsense.

Council ought to have been consulted.' Charles also returned to London and, in an act of some political courage, told Shaftesbury to mind his own business and dismissed him, informing a group of peers who petitioned the King to summon another Parliament that he wished everyone took as great a care of the nation as he did. Charles wrote to William of Orange that he had become convinced the Commons 'would have his Crown.'

Shaftesbury accepted the challenge in what he anticipated would be one last, bloody fling. His Green Ribbon Club set up its headquarters in Aldersgate Street, and organized. According to Henry Sidney, the annual pope-burning was attended by more than a third of the population of London. Among the exhibits were a 'Jesuit giving pardons very freely to those who would murder Protestants', and the Pope himself 'preceded by silk banners with bloody daggers painted on them for murdering heretical kings, and behind him his counsellor the Devil.' Shaftesbury was everywhere:

> Restless, unfixt in principles and place:
> In power unpleased, impatient of disgrace:
> A fiery soul, which, working out its way,
> Fretted the pigmy body to decay.

Many thought there would be revolution before the end of the year. Monster petitions began arriving on Charles's doorstep; 30,000 Wiltshiremen signed a declaration demanding a new Parliament. 'Imagine that you see the whole town in one flame', a pamphlet warned, 'occasioned this second time by the same Popish malice which set it on before. At the same instant, fancy that amongst the distracted crowd you behold troops of Papists, ravishing your wives and daughters, dashing your little children's brains out against the walls, plundering your houses and cutting your own throats.'

Shaftesbury sent Justice Warcup to plead with the King for a sensible resolution of the present troubles. Then Monmouth reappeared in London, presumably at Shaftesbury's suggestion. Charles lost his temper, ordered his son out of the country again and stripped him of all his offices. But Monmouth would not go, and continued on his Royal progress to great acclaim. Shaftesbury distributed pamphlets which 'can only serve to manifest the factious and seditious spirits of those who promote them', as well as 'raise tumults and disorders in the city and discontent against his Majesty's government.' Failure to concur was inadvisable. 'The King', reported another, 'seems to have staved off the evil day as far as he is able, and now I fear it will come upon him with the utmost calamities we can apprehend; he seems to all ends and purposes an undone man.'

Charles reacted with appropriate cynicism. In defiance of the Privy Council, he announced on Christmas Eve that under no circumstances would he allow Parliament to meet again until the following November, and then went on to a milk diet 'to abate the sharpness of some humours.' Quietly he removed those advisers who had favoured appeasement or otherwise spoken against James; Essex, for proposing to recall Parliament, was replaced as chief commissioner at the Treasury by Charles's brother-in-law, Clarendon's younger son, Lawrence Hyde; Halifax and Temple were persuaded to retire, temporarily; Henry Coventry was dismissed as Secretary of State, the job being given to Sunderland. Sidney Godolphin, 'never in the way and never out of it' according to Charles, was brought in to assist Hyde. Together, because of their youth, this group became known as the 'Chits'.

In retaliation, Shaftesbury's principal supporters, among them Russell and Cavendish, threatened their resignations, which Charles gleefully accepted. He then dispatched Sunderland's uncle, Henry Sidney, to Holland; after all, the Prince of Orange was an impeccable Protestant with stronger and more legitimate claims to the throne than Shaftesbury's Monmouth. Sidney wrote enthusiastically to London that, after lengthy discussions with William, he had come to the conclusion that the Prince 'had an abundance of good qualities', whereupon Charles, feeling increasingly confident of his authority, invited James back to London provided there were no special celebrations. The Aldermen of London decided they too had had enough of Shaftesbury, and on 8 March 1680 entertained the Royal brothers at a splendid feast to celebrate their reunion. Charles, much pleased, returned to Newmarket.

The battle, however, was far from over. Rumours began to circulate that a mysterious black box containing the marriage deeds of Charles to Lucy Walter (Monmouth's mother) had been discovered in the possession of the Bishop of Durham, who, being dead, could not deny it. Charles, irritated, returned to London and issued a denial that such a marriage had ever taken place. But the suspicion remained. Shaftesbury then encouraged rumours of an Irish plot; hordes of Irish cattle-thieves 'with bad English and worse clothes' who, 'hearing that England was disposed to hearken to good swearers', were said to be pouring into England. He also secured the election of two new Sheriffs for the City of London, Cornish and Bethell; being known Republicans, they would ensure that all London juries returned verdicts pleasing to Shaftesbury.

News came that the garrison at Tangier was in danger; Charles was forced to send supplies and ships for its assistance, thus weakening his resources at home and forcing him once more to consider an alliance with France. 'If he [Louis] will put me [Charles] in a state of showing my gratitude to him', Charles told ambassador Barrillon, 'no one will be more attached to his interests.' 'It will be very difficult to explain to your Majesty', a puzzled Barrillon wrote home to Louis, 'what is the real design of the King of England and his ministers.' Shaftesbury was having nightly meetings with Charles; England had signed or was about to sign a treaty of mutual union and defence with Spain; there was talk of an alliance with Holland. It was all most confusing.

In fact, it was all quite straightforward. As Charles explained to Barrillon: 'I act out of necessity. I must pacify the English and do my best to prevent the outbreak of war. That is my only aim.' 'The King', observed William Temple, 'looks better in health than I have known him since his sickness last year.' Charles went off to Windsor, then back to Newmarket, where he amused himself dictating for Pepys's benefit his own version of the escape from Worcester. A further bout of influenza in May prolonged his convalescence, and he became despondent about the large number of courtiers who seemed to be deserting him. He had quarrelled with Louise de Kéroualle – she had declared for the exclusionists, hoping that her son, the Duke of Richmond, would become a candidate for the throne – and their love affair was no more. Shaftesbury had presented Louise to a Middlesex grand jury as a prostitute; James was accused of being a popish recusant.

James was strangely taciturn; with Charles, he spent much time 'fishing or walking in the park.' Shaftesbury's continuing attempts to provoke trouble fell increasingly on deaf ears, as if the country was now bored by the excitement. Sidney was once more in Holland talking with William, and Charles was confident that, such was his personal support in the country, all could wait until the next meeting of Parliament which, he announced, would convene at the beginning of October. Tactically, the delay was a shrewd move. It would keep Shaftesbury's venom bottled up in London and prevent its poison spreading throughout the country, which a dissolution might have risked. James was sent back to Scotland, and Charles returned to London.

As preparations for the new Parliament began, however, Charles's ministers were noticeably less sanguine than the King. Holland had rejected the draft treaty with England, while the Privy Council was divided about the succession. A proposal that Charles be given £600,000 plus the right to nominate his own successor, provided he accept James's exclusion, was dismissed. Bribes again flooded in from France, although Barrillon was unsure for whom they were intended. In July, Barrillon reported that he was for Monmouth; in August, he was not; in November, he was to favour Monmouth. In December, he believed that the principal aim of French money was to divide Charles from the country; the following February he urged Louis to support the monarchy. All depended, he said, on the new Parliament. The power of the Opposition had never seemed stronger; terrorized by Shaftesbury's gangsters, the 'brisk boys' from Wapping, the London mob was the muscle on which the Opposition would rely for support.

When Parliament finally assembled in October 1680, thirteen months after its election, the tension was considerable. James, confident of support in Scotland, certain that Louis would come to his aid, and boastful that at least half the English nation would rise in his favour, made it clear that if Parliament removed his rights he would take to the battlefield. 'All Europe have their eyes on this Assembly', Charles told both Houses. 'The several prorogations I have made', he went on, 'have been very advantageous to our neighbours and very useful to me.' Such fresh alliances as he had negotiated were 'the best measures that could be taken for the safety of England and the repose of Christendom.' He referred darkly to 'our divisions at home', but promised to give the fullest attention to the security of the Protestant religion as long as it was consistent with 'the succession of the Crown in its due and legal course of descent.' He appealed for unity, 'a perfect union among ourselves', and for money to defend the trading colony in Tangier. 'Let us take care that we do not gratify our enemies and discourage our friends by any unreasonable disputes.'

The speech went down like a lead balloon. Lord Russell shouted that it was absurd to consider such trifles as the problem of Tangier when the life of every Protestant gentleman in the country was at risk. Dangerfield, although discredited, was brought to the Bar of the House accusing James of having bribed him to invent his (Dangerfield's) stories of a plot. The Commons decided that it was and always had been the right of English subjects to petition the King for the calling of Parliaments; to represent such petitioning as seditious was a denial of liberty. Charles was angered but equally determined, 'and immediately fell upon the proceedings of Parliament with great heart.' He told Reresby: 'Do not trouble yourself. I will stick by you and my old friends, for if I do not, I shall have nobody to stick by me.' Inevitably, with its considerable opposition majority, the Commons brought in another Exclusion Bill. It not only debarred James from the throne, but accused him of High Treason should he ever return to England after 5 November 1680. Only three members dared speak against it, Hyde, Seymour and Secretary of State Jenkins. Jenkins, in a quietly reasoned speech, argued that the Bill was contrary to natural justice since the accused had not been heard, contrary to the Protestant religion since it dispossessed a man simply because he disagreed with the majority, contrary to the oath of allegiance which had always implicitly included James as heir presumptive, and contrary to the very notion of Kingship since the effect of the Bill would be to make the monarchy elective. Jenkins was shouted down. The Bill was then physically taken to the Lords by Russell, accompanied by a horde of Parliamentarians and a procession including the same Lord Mayor and Aldermen of the City of London who had so recently feasted the Royal brothers. It was in the Lords, as Charles realized, that the crucial battle would be fought.

The debate began at eleven. Shaftesbury led the attack, supported by Monmouth himself who declared he had been profoundly hurt by Charles's rejection of Lucy Walter's reasonable marital claims. 'The kiss of Judas', Charles was heard to murmur as Monmouth rambled on. Halifax, on behalf of Charles, rose sixteen times to reply. He cited the Duke of York's credit in Ireland and with the Fleet; he emphasized the dangers of civil war; he berated Monmouth for his conduct. Tempers mounted. Several peers drew their swords. Halifax had to be protected from attack. But his persistence won the day and, just short of midnight, the Lords rejected the Bill by 33 votes. Shaftesbury could not believe it. The Commons were speechless. But there were no riots in the streets. Charles had doubled the guard as a precaution.

Next day, Halifax attempted to press home the advantage. He proposed that, in the event of a Popish King, strict constitutional limitations could be placed upon his authority. Shaftesbury shrieked back that Charles must divorce Catherine, because she was barren, and then procure a wife capable of producing a Protestant heir. The Commons, meanwhile, voted to remove Halifax from the counsels of the King, accused Scroggs of misconduct, impeached Lord Justice North, and homed in on the senile Lord Stafford, one of the five Catholic peers accused during the Popish Plot and still in the Tower. 'To talk of the condition of Tangier now', observed Colonel Titus, 'is like Nero when Rome was on fire, to fiddle.'

Halifax offered to resign. Charles refused to accept. Stafford was less resolute, as we have seen, and on 7 December 1680 was found guilty of treason by a majority of the Lords. Charles said he would not have hanged a dog on the evidence presented. But Parliament had gone mad for a victim. Russell wanted Stafford hung, drawn and quartered, but Charles refused and commuted the sentence to beheading. It was to be the only successful impeachment in Charles's reign, and almost certainly strengthened his determination to stop Shaftesbury.

Parliament continued squabbling. The Lords discussed various Bills for securing the Protestant religion: should James ever succeed to the throne, he was to have no veto and only the legal capacity of a minor. The Commons discussed legislation to guarantee frequent Parliaments, to make the illegal exaction of money High Treason, to ensure that Charles appointed judges favourable to Protestantism, and hinted that Charles's acceptance of exclusion might be their price for supplying Tangier. Both Houses obviously believed that Charles could be frightened into agreeing, but while the Commons were hotly debating 'whomsoever should advise prorogations of Parliament was a betrayer of the Kingdom', Charles arrived at the Lords and did just that. 'I daresay the King will never be brought up to it', the Countess of Sunderland had written to Henry Sidney, 'for you and I know what a spark he is at going through with anything.' She was deceived; Charles had waited long enough. By refusing to prorogue Parliament thus far, Charles had forced Shaftesbury into open support of Monmouth through the introduction of another Exclusion Bill, while allowing time for the country to become exhausted by the crisis. Now, as Parliament stood amazed, he strengthened the army in the City (again), temporarily retired Halifax (again), dismissed Sunderland and Temple (the principal advocates of exclusion apart from Shaftesbury within the Privy Council), and dissolved Parliament, informing Members that a new Parliament would meet in two months' time, but in Oxford, 'the retreat of Kings in time of war and pestilence.' In vain, petitions were hurriedly presented urging that the new Parliament must be held in Westminster; Essex offered a 'loyal address', but for his pains was stripped even of his Lieutenancy of Hertfordshire; Salisbury threatened to withdraw from the Council should Parliament be called to Oxford. Charles took him at his word and 'ordered his Lordship's name to be struck out of the Council book.'

But why Oxford and why so soon? Some reckoned that Charles wished to demonstrate the uselessness of Parliaments, others that a new Parliament was

The Sheldonian Theatre in Oxford, in a contemporary engraving. Designed in early 1663, the foundation stone was laid in June 1664, and the first ceremony held there in 1669. Commissioned by the Bishop of London, Gilbert Sheldon, formerly Warden of All Souls College, as a secular hall for enacting university ceremonies, it was Wren's first major architectural undertaking. He modelled the building on the Theatre of Marcellus in Rome, a drawing of which by Sebastiano Serlio was contained in an Italian pattern book circulating in the 1660's. The Sheldonian soon housed the Clarendon (or University) Press; thus, the ceiling painting was thought to be curiously appropriate as it showed allegorical figures depicting the Triumph of Truth and the Arts.

necessary if only to avoid civil war. But Charles must have known that a fresh general election would not reduce the numbers or the determination of the Opposition. After all, Shaftesbury's murky activities were now reaching their zenith. A fresh plot involving Charles, the Queen and James was unearthed, while in Paris it was being reported that Charles had been besieged in the Tower and poisoned. Charles did what he could to contain Shaftesbury, dismissing from local office such deputy Lords Lieutenant and commissioners of peace as were known to be Whig fanatics, although such was Shaftesbury's grip that some country Tories were afraid to stand against the local Whig nominee. The Whig organization had grown considerably since the last election, with loyal addresses and pamphlets urging the merits of exclusion being distributed by the thousand.

Nonetheless, Charles sensed that Shaftesbury had overreached himself.

Respectable Anglican country gentry had begun to resent being allied to a bastard pretender and a Republican fanatic who condoned dissent. Militancy was becoming uncomfortable, especially when confronted with a ruthless monarch. Danby's untrustworthiness, originally a cause of their agitation, had long been forgotten; the fear of war had not. Charles had nightly conferences with Chiffinch who briefed him on the latest feelings in the City; before leaving for Oxford, he attempted to make London secure by strengthening the defences of the Tower and appointing himself Commander of the volunteer London Artillery Company. The Earl of Craven, a veteran Royalist, was given specific instructions to kill anyone who disturbed the peace during Charles's absence. On the road to Oxford, Charles passed several armed gangs clustered round Whig politicians. Everywhere, hundreds of quasi-military uniforms were topped with blue ribbons and 'No Popery' badges; a military coup must have seemed a distinct possibility.

Although Shaftesbury's organization had increased, however, it did not anticipate the outburst of pro-Royalist sentiment that welcomed Charles on his arrival in Oxford. The University greeted him with a loyal address: 'You are the blessed father of our country', it read, 'and under the shadows of your royal protection we enjoy all our rights, religious and civil.' 'Remember your Royal father and keep the staff in your own hands', one supporter shouted. 'Ay, by God, I will'. Charles replied, 'and the sword too.' Shaftesbury, having established his headquarters at Balliol, scarcely raised a smile. Charles received yet another Bible and was hailed by a speech from the public orator. He had brought with him the Queen, Nell Gwyn *and* Louise, so, pleased with his reception, he went off to Witney for a little hunting. Hawking in the Cotswolds the following day and a merry dinner at Campsfield passed away the weekend, together with 'the pleasing business of the night.' Nell Gwyn found her coach surrounded by a crowd one afternoon and shouted, 'Pray, good people, be civil. I am the *Protestant* whore.'

Parliament met on a bleak Monday morning. Monmouth paraded over Magdalen Bridge, chaired by thugs whacking great leaden flails, supposedly for beating out the brains of recalcitrant papists. Charles was defiant. 'I, who will never use any arbitrary government myself, am resolved not to suffer it in others', he began. Referring to the 'unwarrantable proceedings of the last House of Commons', which had caused him (temporarily) to abandon Parliament, he chastised Members for their behaviour, warning them he could tolerate it no longer. The honour of the Government had been brought low. 'It is as much my interest, and it shall be as much my care as yours, to preserve the liberty of the subject', he told them. Without the dignity and safety of monarchy, neither religion nor property was safe. 'They support each other', Charles affirmed. Exclusion, therefore, was utterly abhorrent. The King was willing 'to remove all reasonable fears that may arise from the possibility of a Popish successor's coming to the Crown', but he would not be blackmailed, nor deterred from his duty, nor depart from 'the known and established laws of the land, which neither can nor ought to be departed from nor changed by Act of Parliament.' No doubt Charles feared that unless some accommodation with the Whig Opposition could be found, civil war might result; but he was resolved. If this was to be his sternest test, he knew it, and by general agreement his opening speech was a 'subtle and crafty one.'

Instead of replying directly, Parliament launched into what was almost routine business. The Commons agreed as a test case to impeach one Edward Fitzharris, recently exposed as an Irish informer employed by the Court against the Whigs, although actually a double agent working for Shaftesbury. Jenkins refused to carry the impeachment to the Lords until bludgeoned into doing so. Meanwhile, Thomas Littleton, acting on behalf of Halifax, suggested a new solution to the exclusion problem. If a Roman Catholic succeeded to the throne, a regency could be established to protect the monarchy. In the case of James, the regents would be William and Mary. Some reckoned this constitutionally unthinkable, since the King would be effectively divided from his power; anyway, James would never agree to it. Sir Thomas Meres reminded the House that their main business was religion; something must be done to quieten the fears about Popery, he told them. Accordingly, yet another Bill was brought in to exclude James.

Parliament's belligerence was short-circuited, however, by an extraordinary event in the Lords. The Commons were being told that the Lords, sitting in the Geometry School, had refused to accept the impeachment of Fitzharris, when news came of a startling confrontation between Shaftesbury and Charles. Shaftesbury, it seems, had asked the Marquis of Worcester to hand Charles an anonymous note stating that the only way in which the country could be saved from civil war was an immediate declaration of Monmouth as the successor. Charles said gently that such a declaration would be contrary to law and justice. 'If you are restrained only by law and justice', Shaftesbury had replied sneeringly, 'rely on us and leave us to act.' Parliament, he said, would pass a Bill legitimizing the Duke of Monmouth.

The insult was clear. Charles had long ago realized that Monmouth would make neither a strong King nor an effective politician; he was too vainglorious to be taken seriously, much though Charles loved him. His enthronement would almost certainly bring about the very civil war which Shaftesbury said the country feared. With Shaftesbury's pointed insult, Charles knew that the moment had come to confront Shaftesbury and the exclusionists. Usually an unimpressive public speaker, Charles had begun: 'Let there be no self-delusion; I will never yield and will not let myself be intimidated. Men ordinarily become more timid as they grow old. As for me, I shall be, on the contrary, bolder and firmer, and I will not stain my life and reputation for the little time that perhaps remains for me to live. I do not fear the dangers and calamities which people try to frighten me with. I have the law and reason on my side. And there is the Church' (pointing at the Bishops), 'which will remain united with me. My Lord,' Charles had concluded to Shaftesbury's face, 'she and I will not be divided.'

The Lords had been stunned, so the reports went. But the Commons were even more amazed, and started complaining *inter alia* about the cramped quarters they had been given (Convocation House) and in which they were being expected to conduct their business. Very well, said Charles. Let them move into the new Sheldonian Theatre just completed by his Surveyor General, Christopher Wren. While they busied themselves settling in, Charles went to the Lords in his day clothes with everyone assuming that he had at last seen sense and gone to surrender. Unnoticed, he had brought his robes and Crown in a separate sedan chair, and entered the Chamber in full regalia. Smiling, he said: 'My Lords and Gentlemen. That all the world may see to what a point we are come, that we are not like to have a good end, when the divisions at the beginning are such: therefore, my lord Chancellor, do as I have commanded you.' Accompanied by a regiment of cavalry, Black Rod went to the Commons, now locked in a ferocious debate about Fitzharris's impeachment. 'It is His Majesty's Royal pleasure and will', Black Rod announced to the assembly, 'that this Parliament be dissolved.' Members were aghast. Before they had time to reply, Black Rod concluded: 'This parliament is dissolved.'

Parliament was understandably shocked; there were 'dreadful faces' and 'loud sighs' from Members. 'Though I have seen the distractions and dejections of routed armies, a prospect dismal enough', Colonel Cooke wrote to Ormonde, 'yet nothing ever equalled this day in this place at the surprising dissolution of Parliament.' 'I am now a better man than you were a quarter of an hour since', Charles told one young member. 'You had better have one king than five hundred.' Charles had judged the mood correctly; to Shaftesbury's disappointment, there were no uprisings in London, not even a single demonstration. Charles returned immediately to Whitehall to be assured by Craven that all was quiet; in Oxford, many of the Opposition feared that Charles would call up the guards and 'pull them out by the ears', so fled in disarray to their country homes. The price of horses doubled overnight, and the roads from Oxford were packed with Whigs scampering for their lives.

Charles published his own account of the Oxford Parliament a week later, which he ordered to be read in all churches the following Sunday during Matins. The King explained that he could never have consented to exclusion out of 'honour, justice and conscience.' He apologized for having found it necessary to dissolve Parliament again, but the Houses had caused him 'exceeding great trouble.' Nonetheless he regretted having to dismiss them 'without more benefit to our people by the calling of them.' Parliament had been impossible, he said, threatening 'arbitrary orders for taking our subjects into custody . . . [and] strange illegal votes . . . without any order or process of law.' If anything, Charles had rescued his people, he told them, from civil war, anarchy and from 'the restless malice of ill men who are labouring to poison our people.' The reaction to Charles's apparently heartfelt declaration confirmed his victory. Only the Common Council of London voted its disbelief at the 'untimely dissolution of Parliament'; Whitehall and Windsor, where Charles had gone to rest, were inundated with loyal addresses thanking the King for having saved the nation.

Charles failed to mention, however, yet another secret agreement he had made with Louis. Although nothing was put down on paper, he had promised ambassador Barrillon the day before the dissolution not to call another Parliament for three years in return for a £400,000 subsidy from Louis, and an assurance that he, Charles, would disengage himself from all treaties that were inimical to France. This verbal, informal agreement was not, of course, the reason for the dissolution; the £400,000 spread out over three years – assuming it was ever paid, and many subsidies promised before had not been – was trivial compared with Charles's overall needs. But its existence undoubtedly gave Charles moral support at a crucial moment. Louis fell for the old bluff. Charles had some more pocket money, and mysteriously failed to keep his word.

Toward the Whigs, however, Charles kept his word with a vengeance. 'I will not let myself be intimidated', he had told them. The Whigs had already begun to circulate anti-Charles pamphlets, including *The True Englishman speaking Plain English*, which argued that since Charles was as guilty as James, he ought to be deposed. One informer reported that Major Wildman, an ex-Leveller, had said 'we had enough of a King and such a one as this is, and it was no sin to cut him off.' But it was the informers themselves, hitherto so deviously manipulated by Shaftesbury, who were the first to desert. Charles found himself beseiged by 'honest witnesses' in search of employment. They were to be disappointed; Secretary Jenkins told one of them that the Government was for 'truth, not designs.' The business of Fitzharris was quickly concluded. Shaftesbury argued that since the Commons had voted for impeachment, Fitzharris could not be tried by any ordinary court of law. Alas, the Commons were no longer sitting. Fitzharris said he wanted a private interview with the Lord Chief Justice at which he would tell all – about the Queen, James and Danby. But Chief Justice Pemberton, who had replaced Scroggs, called Fitzharris's bluff and challenged him to declare in open court. Fitzharris then offered some feeble evidence for his claims but failed to produce supporting witnesses. He was found guilty of treason and perjury, convicted and hanged.

And then, on 2 July 1681, at six in the morning, Charles arrived at Whitehall from Windsor. Shaftesbury, still in his bed, was arrested and brought before the Council; his papers were seized, and his person dispatched to the Tower. His application for bail under the terms of his own Habeas Corpus Act was refused. The Tower, it was said, lay outside the jurisdiction of the judges.

Throughout the country, on one excuse or another, corporations were forced to surrender their Royal charters for 'revision'. Lords Lieutenant and their deputies, known to be in the pay of Shaftesbury, were dismissed; recorders and town clerks were removed. This systematic replacement of local officials was much facilitated by the discovery among Shaftesbury's papers of two lists of local magistrates, one of 'worthy men', the other of 'men worthy' to be hanged. It gave Charles considerable pleasure to evict Shaftesbury's 'worthy men', and put in their place 'men worthy.'

Pamphlets appeared urging Shaftesbury's case. *The Growth of Popery, The Perplext Prince* and *The Whore's Rhetoric* were just a few. Dryden replied that the name of Shaftesbury was now 'to all succeeding ages curst'.

> Bart'ring his venal wit for sums of Gold,
> He cast himself into the Saint-like mould . . .
> But, as 'tis hard to cheat a Juggler's eyes,
> His open lewdness he could ne'er disguise.

Charles was more succinct. 'At Doomsday', he observed, 'we shall see whose arse is blackest.'

Amid the furore, William arrived from Holland. Louis, taking advantage of Charles's pre-occupations, had persuaded his smaller neighbours to join a political and economic union with France against Holland. William wanted Charles to declare war for their mutual defence. But Godolphin had already warned William that the good understanding which once existed between the King and his nephew 'will be quite lost at last if your Highness will not please to make use of all your prudence and all your temper.' Charles was still displeased at William's disloyalty during the exclusion crisis, and when William suggested that Charles recall Parliament and ask for supplies, Charles asked him: which did he prefer, exclusion, or parliamentary control of the Militia, the Fleet and the Judiciary? William replied feebly that he did not know England too well. As Arlington wrote to Ormonde: 'The Prince of Orange is returned, as the discontented party says not well satisfied with his negotiations here, but this advantage he hath had . . . that he hath clearly seen the hands of both sides playing our great game.'

There remained the question of what to do about Shaftesbury: 'I hear [he] is to be tried speedily', Peter Shakerley wrote to his father. But for Shaftesbury to be tried by his fellow peers, which the law demanded, it was necessary first to prove that a genuine case existed. Such proof would have to be accepted by a grand jury, chosen in Middlesex, the county in which the alleged crimes were supposed to have taken place. Yet Middlesex was a notorious Whig strong-hold, and none could be found to speak out against their leader. 'It is a hard case', Charles ruefully observed, 'that I am the last man to have law and justice in the whole nation.'

Shaftesbury, by now ageing and weak (he was sixty), petitioned Charles to be released on grounds of health. Charles allowed the Earl to take coach rides with his wife, but otherwise kept him locked securely in the Tower for nine months. Shaftesbury even offered to retire to Carolina, the American colony of which he was a proprietor. Charles refused. 'If it were anybody else', he remarked, 'though he knew he were guilty and could prove it upon him, he would grant what he desires.' Shaftesbury was brought to trial at the Old Bailey on 24 November 1681. 'A great rabble' packed the court house and tried to shout down the judges. Despite pleas from Lord Chief Justice Pemberton that the jury should do its patriotic duty, they returned a verdict of 'ignoramus'. Witnesses for the prosecution were later stoned and bonfires lit to celebrate Shaftesbury's acquittal. One supporter set up a stall and forced passers-by to drink Shaftesbury's health, in dog urine.

At first, Charles refused to release him. Monmouth offered to stand bail, but Charles ordered the publication of all the evidence he had accumulated against Shaftesbury, including a damning list of those who were to have been destroyed for opposing exclusion. Charles knew, if only from the mass of loyal addresses that were still arriving daily expressing outrage at Shaftesbury's hitherto unpublished and secret designs, that public opinion was swinging in his support at last. With Charles determined to govern without Parliament, at least for the present, the Whigs lost their rallying ground and public forum. 'The Court was everywhere triumphant', Burnet reported. Charles redoubled his efforts to control local government, and Halifax occupied himself 'revising' local charters, thus earning himself the nickname, as he boasted, of the 'trimmer'. There was a darker side to this control. In a misguided burst of patriotic fervour, orders were given to tighten up the penal laws against Dissenters. The persecution was fierce and the gaols were full. The King's sudden ruthlessness was a dangerous expedient, but for the moment it provoked no reaction.

Charles relaxed. He accepted and enjoyed the gift of two lions and thirty ostriches from Morocco. He laid the foundation stone of Wren's new hospital in Chelsea. 'The City is at this time very quiet', Jenkins wrote to Ormonde. 'The restless spirits, which are not near so many as they would be thought to be, are indeed working to unsettle men's minds in order to disturb the peace. But the wealthier sort among them know when they are well.' Charles 'went a-hawking in the mornings, to cock matches in the afternoons (if there were no horse races) and to plays in the evening.' No one knew whether this was a lull before the storm, with bloody rebellion just around the corner, or the much-longed-for peace at last. Reports then began to come in that Monmouth was proposing to set out on a 'progress' of the north. His sponsor, no less, was Shaftesbury.

Chapter Thirteen

Far-distant regions

In April 1660, Charles had promised at Breda 'a liberty to tender consciences.' Yet, after twenty years of struggle, he had begun to despair of finding a peaceful solution to the religious squabbles which surrounded him. Although this was only one cause of the immense colonial expansion that occurred during his reign, for Charles it was perhaps the most significant. Six of the original thirteen States of America were founded or established during his reign, and it is surely no accident that many of their administrators were not only close personal friends of the King, but Catholics, Quakers and assorted Dissenters.

William Penn, the founder of Pennsylvania, for example, had presented Charles with a systematic and thorough exposition of religious toleration entitled *The Great Case of Liberty of Conscience*. The son of Charles's most trusted Admiral during the Dutch wars, Penn had preached frequently on this text in the streets of London, and been arrested and tried for his activities at the Old Bailey in 1670. The jurymen had refused to bring in a verdict of 'guilty', however, and been fined and imprisoned; whereupon the then Chief Justice Sir John Vaughan, on Charles's instructions, had declared that a judge 'may try to open the eyes of the jurors, but not to lead them by the nose.' The ruling was a landmark in English jurisprudence, since it established beyond question the independence of the jury. Penn had written up the trial in a pamphlet entitled *The People's Ancient and Just Liberties Asserted*, and during the next decade had travelled throughout Holland and Germany preaching on religious toleration.

Hoping to construct an ideal Christian commonwealth, loyal to Charles, Penn and eleven other Quakers bought the proprietary rights to East New Jersey at a public auction in 1681 for £3,400. Three months later, the three 'lower counties', now Delaware, were added. Penn wrote to a friend already in America: 'There may be room there, though not here, for such a holy experiment.' In his 'Frame of Government', Penn legislated that neither he nor his successors should have 'power of doing mischief, that the will of one man may not hinder the good of a whole country.' Freedom of worship was to be absolute. As he had written in his most famous tract *No Cross, No Crown*, 'true Godliness don't turn Men out of the world, but enables them to live better in it, and excites their Endeavours to mend it', a sentiment not dissimilar from Charles's own belief that 'mercy and indulgence is the best way to bring men to a true repentance. It will make them good subjects to me, and good friends and neighbours to you.'

In his *Some Account of the Province of Pennsylvania*, Penn advertised the 'attractions' of his territory as being complete religious liberty and easy terms for land. He specified the kind of person he needed and gave detailed instructions for the journey, which details were translated into French, German and Dutch, thereby gaining wide European circulation. Although the majority of his early emigrants were English and Welsh Quakers, a cosmopolitan atmosphere was soon established. The already existing colony of New Sweden was absorbed, and within three years the population exceeded 9,000. Welsh Quakers founded Radnor and Haverford; German linen weavers from Crefeld settled Germantown. By 1684, Penn could write to Charles with pride: 'I have led the greatest colony into America that ever any man did upon a private credit, and the most prosperous beginnings that were ever in it are to be found among us.'

Although he appointed a resident Deputy Governor, Penn himself supervised the colony's early growth. His political constitution provided for a Governor, Council and Assembly who were to enact Penn's Great Law, a code of jurisprudence founded on the English example but notable for its explicit belief in liberty with obedience and liberty of conscience. By the eighteenth century, Pennsylvania was to be regarded by many as the ideal state in which a man could lead the good life without monarchy, feudalism or religious uniformity.

Maryland had had comparable beginnings. Named after Charles's mother, it too had been intended primarily as a refuge from religious persecution, in this case for English and Irish Catholics, although Maryland's proprietor, Lord Baltimore, insisted that non-Catholics be given equal justice. 'Suffer no scandal or offence to be given to any of the Protestants', he wrote to his brother, the Governor, 'whereby any just complaint may hereafter be made.' In no other Catholic colonial province, such as those of France, Spain or Portugal, were Protestants allowed to exist, let alone acquire land or hold office. But in Maryland, Protestants were to be treated 'with as much mildness and favour as Justice will permit.' Baltimore was so determined to achieve religious toleration that he requested Catholics and Protestants to worship in the same church, and even appealed to Rome against three over-zealous Jesuits who insisted on bullying 'offenders' with canonical law. The Jesuits were sent home. 'The Anabaptists have little to say here; [only] the Adamite, Ranter and Fifth Monarch Men, Maryland cannot digest within her liberal stomach', one eyewitness reported.

In New York, a similar atmosphere prevailed. In May 1664, Charles had granted his brother James the largest territorial gift ever bestowed by an English sovereign. It included not only the present state of New York, but the entire region between the Connecticut and Delaware rivers, as well as Long Island, Nantucket, Martha's Vineyard and half the present state of Maine. The Duke had appointed Richard Nicolls his Deputy Governor, and instructed him to sail into the Dutch-owned New Amsterdam harbour and demand its surrender. The local Dutch Governor, Peter Stuyvesant, pleaded with the inhabitants to resist but, having become discomfited with Dutch rule, they surrendered without firing a shot. An encampment further up the Hudson called Fort Orange was captured and renamed Albany, Fort Casimir on the Delaware renamed Newcastle, and New Amsterdam itself re-christened New York in honour of its new owner. Besides English-speaking Puritans, James inherited Scottish Presbyterians, Swedish Lutherans, Dutch Protestants, French Huguenots and German Quakers. Toleration was essential to secure political stability. Nicolls set the pattern by refusing to interfere with the Dutch constitution and language in Manhattan. In fact, he was ordered not to do so by James, who told Nicolls that the Dutch were to be treated with 'humanity and gentleness.'

Although it would be wrong to conclude that all those to whom Charles granted proprietary rights in the Americas were inspired by high ideals – many simply wanted to make their fortunes, either from land speculation or from trade – and although it would be wrong to believe that Charles encouraged the settlement of these colonies in the exclusive hope of achieving religious toleration, it is curious how often his 'colonial policy' seemed to be one of rewarding loyal friends who subscribed to the notion of religious freedom. Apart from Penn, there was John Winthrop, who had obtained his charter for Connecticut in 1662 and knew Charles through fellowship of the Royal Society. Dr John Clark, to whom Charles had granted a charter for Rhode

A facsimile of The Constitutions of Carolina, as drafted by Locke in his handwriting. Charles ▷ did not have what could be described as a colonial policy, at least not one which was consistent. Nonetheless, he identified colonial property with trade and the opportunity for religious freedom. In 1662, Anthony Ashley Cooper, General Monck, Clarendon, Sir John Colleton and four others applied to Charles for a grant of "Carolina", the area between Virginia and Spanish Florida. Charles issued a Royal Charter in 1663. Locke was Ashley Cooper's secretary. "The Fundamental Conditions of Carolina" is a bizarre document; it is reactionary in that it created a nobility based entirely on the purchase of land – 20,000 acres entitled its owner to become an hereditary landgrave; but it is also revolutionary in that it guaranteed liberty of conscience to all settlers. The common people could elect a house of commons, ut no bill could become law unless it met with the approval of the barons & etc.; yet Locke's constitution, adopted by the proprietary board in 1669 and rejected by the colonial assembly the following year, outlined many of the "self-evident" truths later adopted by Franklin, Jefferson and others for a more conspicuous charter. "Reason", Locke said, "must be our judge and guide in everything." Except that, by reasonable Locke meant what seemed reasonable to men of his own class. Ten years after its foundation, Carolina's population was only 450.

Our Soveraigne Lord the King
having out of his royall grace
& bounty granted unto us ye Province
of Carolina with all ye roialtys
Proprietys Jurisdictions & priviledges
of a County Pallatine as large & ample
as ye County Pallatine of Durham
with other great priviledges. for ye
better settlem̃t of ye Governm̃t of ye
sd Place & establishing the interest
of ye sd Proprietors with equality
& without confusion & yt ye Governm̃t
of this Province may be made most
agreeable unto ye Monarchy under
wch we live & of wch this province
is a part & yt we may avoid erecting
a numerous Democracy. We ye true
& absolute Lords & Proprietors of ye
Province aforesd have agreed to his
following forme of Governm̃t to
be perpetualy established amongst
us unto wch we doe oblidge our
selves

Island in 1663, was another close friend. Albemarle was a proprietor of Carolina; so was Clarendon. The earliest grant of land in Carolina had been made to Sir Robert Heath as early as 1629, but the first Royal Charter was not confirmed until 24 March 1663. Shaftesbury and Albemarle were also among its eight proprietors, each contributing £25 capital. They were given land between the 31st and 36th parallels, and told to concede liberty of conscience to the settlers and by this advantage expect that 'ingenious and industrious persons' would settle. Although the Church of England was to be established by law, any group of at least seven members would be accorded the rights of a Church. Any man not belonging to a Church was to be ostracized, but not persecuted. The territory was to be divided into counties, each having eight seignories, eight baronies, and twenty-four colonies of 12,000 acres. The proprietors retained the prerogative of summoning parliaments, vetoing the acts of that parliament and pardoning offences. The Governor and the Assembly, however, were to be elected by popular choice. 'We have no other aim in the framing of our laws', Shaftesbury had written in 1671, 'but to make everyone as safe and happy as the state of human affairs is capable of.' The laws were to be the 'equallest' that a state could have; no mention was made of trade, or of any financial obligation to the Crown. The author of this radical scheme was John Locke.

In New Jersey, the 'Concessions and Agreements of the Proprietors', issued by Charles in 1665, had also guaranteed 'freedom of conscience'; Clarendon had even wanted to secure religious toleration by insisting on the right of appeal from colonial tribunals to the supreme court in England. How he imagined this right could have been enforced is not clear. In Virginia, although most early Virginians observed strict Anglican rules, religious worship was free. Free schools multiplied, illiteracy was almost unknown and dice were banned, as was travel, business and the loading of ships on the Sabbath. There was a fine of fifty pounds of tobacco, the equivalent of a week's wages, for missing church on Sunday. Surplices were rarely worn, and there was frequently no altar or altar cross, with the congregation preferring to sit round a table as in a Puritan meeting.

Paradoxically, the colonies of New England to the north, established during the reigns of Charles I and James I specifically to provide religious freedom, savagely persecuted those who did not agree with the ruling sect. John Dunton wrote to a friend in England: 'they [the New Englanders] are generally . . . great censors of other men's manners, but extremely careless of their own.' Charles hated them, and they were openly defiant of his attempts to amend their ways. 'It is not unknown to you', wrote one English agent to Charles, 'that they [the New Englanders] look on themselves as a free state . . . there being too many against owning the King, or their having any dependence on England.' Boston had not proclaimed Charles as King until August 1661, and only then with a noticeable lack of enthusiasm.

In April 1664, Commissioners had been sent to the four New England states, Massachusetts, Plymouth, Connecticut and New Haven, to discuss outstanding problems. Their presence alone had been regarded as a breach of the colony's privileges, and Charles had been obliged to appoint a committee of the Privy Council to enforce his authority. The colonists replied in phrases that were later to become a battle-cry throughout the thirteen states; 'we humbly conceive', they wrote to Charles, 'that the laws of England are bounded within the four seas, and do not reach America. The subjects of His Majesty here being not represented in Parliament, so we have not looked at ourselves to be impeded in our trade.' By way of appeasement, the colonists had offered Charles a gift of 'ten barrells of cranberries, two hogsheads of special good samp, and three thousand of codfish.' But when Charles sent out a customs collector to levy tax, the local courts acquitted every single 'illegal trader' whom he arrested.

*   *   *

Many of these far distant regions had been originally acquired for exploitation by trade, of course, and for Charles customs levies were an important source of income. In 1664, Charles had written to Minette: 'You will have heard of our taking of New Amsterdam, which lies just by New England. 'Tis a place of great importance to trade . . .' Shrewd alliances with increasingly prosperous businessmen, therefore, ensured that the trading colonies, those wherein various merchants initially owned the land, received maximum Royal protection. In December 1660 Charles had appointed a Council of Trade and Plantations which included representatives of all the great Incorporated Companies; its members had been directed to inquire into the various existing charters, advise about new ones, consider trade, production and emigration, and obtain such information as would enlighten the policy of the Crown.

The activities of this new Council were fully documented and reveal an astonishing energy which indicates the new and important role that such affairs had begun to play in English society. (Later, in 1696, the Council was to become the Board of Trade, which it remained for over 250 years.) That Charles hoped some of his colonies would fulfil his dreams of religious and political toleration does not detract from their venal foundation. Apart from the Americas, Charles acquired Tangier, Bombay, and a string of other trading colonies in the East, including Madras, Calcutta and Bantam in Java. There was also Guyana in South America, as well as the Bahamas and Jamaica, Barbados, Tobago, and the Leeward Islands with Antigua. The basis of what became known and feared as the British Empire was mapped out during Charles's reign.

Jamaica, for instance, a Crown Colony or territory wherein Charles initially owned the land, supplied England with sugar, coffee, ginger and pepper, whilst offering an expanding market for English manufactured goods. By 1670, the population had grown to 15,000 who, between them, worked 57 sugar refineries, 49 indigo plants and 47 cocoa walks. Barbados was still more prosperous. By 1668, its trade was being carried by 10,000 tons of shipping; its 100,000 acres, worth over £20 per acre, provided a staple crop of tobacco. Later the island changed to sugar, which proved to be a mistake since it found itself in the midst of fierce competition from the neighbouring French and Portuguese colonies and the resulting glut caused the price of refined sugar to fall catastrophically. Nonetheless, by 1680 the island supported about 20,000 white planters, serviced by 40,000 negro slaves brought over by the Royal African Company, whose dividends had trebled between 1660 and 1675.

Elsewhere, the Bahamas furnished England with tobacco and cedar wood; the Leeward Islands sent sugar and tobacco. In Newfoundland, a trading colony, it was estimated that the fisheries, if properly managed, might produce £50,000 per annum in customs duty, while giving employment to over 10,000 sailors. In 1671, the Privy Council drew up a list of regulations by which the Newfoundland fishing industry was to be administered. English sailors were to have freedom of fishing in all the harbours and rivers of Newfoundland to the complete exclusion of 'aliens', especially the French. The season was to extend from 1 March to 1 October only, and no fisherman was to remain on the island in winter. All inhabitants were expected to pay a customs duty of five per cent on exports to England, while an Act of 1673 had imposed various other local taxes payable to the Crown, the first such direct charges apart from customs dues not initiated by colonial legislation. Regular payments were sometimes incorporated thereafter into Royal Charters as conditions of ownership, such as a fifth part of all precious metals found in the soil.

Some territories had been gained through victory in war, some by diplomatic manoeuvre, some by robbery. Sir Henry Morgan, for instance, a Welshman and acknowledged boss of the West Indian pirates, had sacked the headquarters of Spanish trade in central America in 1668, destroyed an Armada sent against him, and made off with 250,000 pieces of eight. Two years later, he was causing such havoc off Cuba that he was voted an official thanks by the Council of Jamaica who were hoping to acquire the island. Morgan then turned his attentions to Panama, landing repeatedly on the isthmus, plundering everything he could find and systematically destroying a chain of Spanish forts. Next he marched into Mexico, seizing prisoners, and putting them 'to the most exquisite tortures imaginable' to reveal their hidden treasures. In seven years, Morgan sacked eighteen cities, four towns and endless villages, to the considerable inconvenience of the Spanish. That England was nominally at peace with Spain seems not to have disturbed anyone, except the Spanish, and a grateful Charles appointed Morgan Lieutenant Governor of Jamaica in 1674.

But it was the Crown Colonies on the American mainland that interested

Charles most; apart from anything else, they appeared to have immense commercial possibilities. From Virginia, the largest of all the American settlements, by 1678 11.5 million pounds of tobacco was arriving in London per year worth an annual levy (for the King) of £100,000. The system was not quite as profitable for the actual trader. The standard practice was that a planter selected a London or Bristol merchant and made over his entire crop in return for the next year's provisions. The merchant then sold the tobacco in England for whatever he could get, charging the planter a commission. Should his sale price amount to less than the cost of the provisions (and there was little incentive to make it more), the planter was obliged to sell his next year's crop in advance to the very same merchant. Not that this economic servitude prevented various settlers from prospering; one Robert Carter became so wealthy that he was known as 'King' Carter. Another was William Byrd, the son of a London goldsmith, who had arrived in Virginia aged nineteen in 1671. Elected to the House of Burgesses, he had bought a plantation named Westover, built a mansion, a shop, a warehouse and a fleet, and begun exporting grain to the West Indies and importing sugar, rum and African slaves. When he died in 1704, he was widely regarded as the first gentleman of Virginia, and all thanks to tobacco.

Most of the crop was processed into pipe tobacco and snuff; the cigarette had not been invented, and the cigar not widely used outside the Spanish Empire. All prices and salaries, even those of priests, were expressed in pounds of tobacco. Prosperity was such that several roads out of James Town, the capital, were soon under construction, the first being built to the Governor's plantation. It was dead straight, so that it could be used for horse races.

Surprisingly, the non-Crown colonies were not always as valuable as their merchant owners had expected. Tangier, for example, acquired as part of Queen Catherine's dowry, had been prized as an entrée into the rich Barbary trade of corn, oils, copper and gold. But it needed a garrison of 2,000 men for its protection, and cost about £70,000 per annum to maintain. The civilian population was a ragbag of some 600 criminals and political scapegoats; it might have been to everyone's advantage, it was suggested, to people the colony with Scots, a solution not greeted with much enthusiasm north of the border. The first governor only survived for a year; the second was killed in a skirmish with the Arabs. Entirely dependent on provisions sent from home, Tangier attracted few 'men of credit.' The port, although it had strategic advantages, was frequented more by men-of-war than trading vessels, and this in itself discouraged commerce. A heavy Arab siege in 1680 had left most of the fortifications in ruins; in 1682, Charles tried to sell Tangier to Louis. Louis did not want it. Charles offered it back to Portugal. The Portuguese did not want it either. So, in August 1683, Charles evacuated the place, leaving it to the Arabs after all.

Bombay, also acquired as part of the marriage treaty 'with all rights, profits,

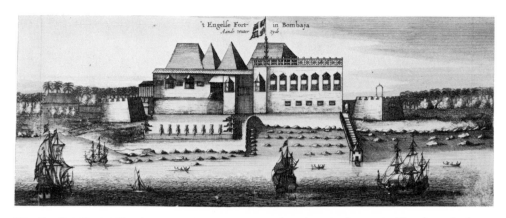

The English Fort at Bombay; a contemporary engraving. Acquired as part of the eleventh clause of Charles's marriage treaty with Catherine of Braganza, Bombay was a pain. It cost the Crown more than it provided, and was sold to the East India Company on 27 March, 1668, for £10 per annum. Even then, it was one of the more unhealthy places on earth; its palm trees were manured by rotting fish, its swamps infested with snakes and ants. Gerald Aungier, the city's first governor, opened a hospital, established a High Court, and built the fort as above. By 1677, Bombay claimed to be "Urbs prima in Indis". As the home of the East India Company, however, it rapidly acquired another significance. Since the Company was frequently pressed into lending the Crown large sums of money, it was able to extract privileges to its advantage. It set up its own courts whose authority rested on the royal prerogative alone; it exported bullion to finance its needs, thus establishing a gold standard in commerce; and it used the excise to build forts and prepare for future military conquests. For £10 a year, Charles sold a troublesome settlement, although he acquired for the Crown the beginnings of a British Empire.

and territories thereto belonging', was an even bigger headache. The Portuguese no doubt hoped that an English base in the East Indies would enrage the hated Dutch, who were busy acquiring their own trading empire in that area to the disadvantage of everyone else. In March 1662 an English fleet with 500 troops had been sent to take possession of the new colony, but the expedition finished up on the island of Anjediva where half of it died of malaria. As a result, a furious correspondence ensued between the Portuguese and English governments as to the actual meaning of this particular clause in the treaty. Portugal offered to buy Bombay back. Clarendon thought the suggestion sensible, but demanded an additional £109,000 to cover the expedition's expenses. The Portuguese refused, and England was stuck with Bombay. In 1660, the cost of its ammunition and provisions alone had been £11,498. Its rents, by comparison, including the revenue from customs, amounted to a mere £6,490. Nonetheless, Bombay, together with the neighbouring islands, provided a base for the East India Company, re-licensed by Royal Charter, 1661. But the decline of the Mogul Empire soon necessitated an increasingly military defence of the Company's property, and by 1684 it was thought essential to fortify Bombay. The various settlements in Bengal were also strengthened, with their administrative centre constantly moved in search of better protection; eventually, an appropriate site was agreed and the foundations laid for the modern Calcutta.

266

At Bantam in Java, where it was hoped to develop the spice trade, the Dutch expelled the English from the fort. In St Helena the Dutch were expelled by the English. Guyana was captured by the Dutch during the Second Dutch War, recaptured by the English, and then ceded to the Dutch by the Treaty of Breda. Cayenne was occupied by the English, captured by the Dutch, and finally given to the French. Such comings and goings were obviously not conducive to regular trade, or profit.

*   *   *

Peopling these colonies also proved haphazard. Most of the English settlers in the province of New York, for instance, were transported criminals, 'his Majesty's seven-year passengers.' Young boys and girls were spirited on board colony-bound ships by 'trapanners', and sold in America as 'servants' to recoup the costs of transport and the kidnappers' fees. One such girl was immortalized in a popular ballad called 'The Maydens of London's Brave Adventures', which promised 'merry London girls' untold riches from the gold and silver mines of Virginia.

Lord Baltimore had set up a more respectable arrangement. He had opened an office in the City of London to interview prospective landlords and servants. The 'servant' had his passage paid, and in return was expected to work for a particular landlord for an agreed number of years. Unfortunately, the applicants were few, as they were for a similar scheme in Maryland. Attempts to persuade people to live in Carolina also encountered difficulties. Two vessels fitted out in England during the summer of 1669 had been wrecked in passage, while a third had not reached the mainland until the following spring. Commanded by Captain Joseph West, the ship had finally sailed up the coast until it reached a large bay watered by two rivers. These he had named Ashley and Cooper, after his demonic proprietor, and there he established a township named after the King who had originally inspired the expedition, Charles Town. But, after three years, only about 450 people had settled in the entire province. Worse, a severe winter frost ruined many expectations. Shortage of provisions led the settlers into debt and a slave trade developed, capturing Indians and selling them back again to their families.

The disappointing response to legitimate colonization encouraged a slave trade throughout the American colonies. The Portuguese had been the first systematic dealers in negro slaves from Africa, although the need for cheap labour soon overcame whatever moral objections might have been felt by the English. Charles's own brother, a prominent shareholder in the Royal African Company, had been granted exclusive rights in 1662 for the trading of slaves along the west coast of Africa, from Morocco to the Cape of Good Hope. The Company had built a chain of forts, and paid rent to the local negro potentate who also supplied the local negro slaves. By 1673, black slaves had outnumbered the white population in Jamaica two to one, and by 1680 5,000 slaves were arriving every year from Africa. By 1700, the number grew to 25,000. Paradoxically, the subsequent identification of the black man with manual labour led to a gradual stultification of invention and industry. As a result, the West Indian colonies never benefited from that grim determination which characterized the colonies on the eastern seaboard, and which enabled the mainland, ultimately, to prosper so spectacularly.

Although not harshly treated, the slaves had few rights in law. When the constitution of Maryland mentioned the 'Advice, Assent and Approbation of the Freemen', it referred exclusively to white men; indeed, in 1664 the Maryland assembly had passed a 'black code', affirming that a negro was a slave for life because of his colour. Earlier, it had always been assumed, both in Maryland and in Virginia, that a black man was a slave until baptized. Now, Maryland legislated that neither baptism nor conversion could affect a black man's freedom. In 1765, the blacks would number one-third of the total population in the Americas.

*   *   *

It might be argued that to doubt the moral worth of Charles's empire because of its slave population is anachronistic; but there can be no disguising the reactionary nature of much of its local government. 'The Fundamental Constitutions of Carolina', far from creating 'equallest' laws, established a landed Carolinian aristocracy. Anyone who purchased 3,000 acres could become a baron and lord of the manor. Anyone who purchased 20,000 acres, acquired the German title of Landgrave. Although the less fortunate were allowed to elect their own House of Commons, no Bill became law unless consented to by the majority of the barons. About forty such landowners, many of them absentees, finished up calling themselves by a variety of silly names and holding all the power. The Carolina House of Commons survived until the 1688 Revolution, but failed to make its constitution work in a pioneer society. Men boasted how, for a bowl of punch, they could secure the election to Parliament of whomsoever they chose, and North Carolina soon became the acknowledged hide-out for racketeers from all over America.

Even Pennsylvania, apparently the model state, was less than it seemed. Numerous crime waves caused its authorities to become so tough that the English Privy Council had to intervene and modify their more repressive legislation. Maybe the authorities had taken a lesson from William Penn himself, or at least, his family. Penn's agreement with the Indians from whom he took his land, 'under the elm tree at Shackamaxon', was the only treaty in history, according to Voltaire, not ratified yet never broken. It asserted that no man could claim or buy more land from the Indian than he could walk in a day and a half. Penn's brother Thomas interpreted this maxim in a way that became all too familiar for the Indian. The younger Penn chose a good, clear trail, and hired three of the fastest runners in the province. Accompanied by pace setters on horseback, plus a few Indians to ensure fair play, the runners set off at a cracking speed. By noon on the first day, the Indians had given up in disgust. 'No sit down and smoke', one of them said later, 'no shoot squirrel, just lun, lun, lun all day long.' One of the three runners quit, a second fell into a river and drowned, but the third kept going. In this manner, and without further payment, half a million acres of Indian cornfields and hunting grounds came into the Penn family.

*   *   *

Apart from the prospect of financial gain and the possibility of religious toleration, it is not clear how involved Charles was or became with his Empire. His apparent neglect of the North American colonies, for instance, is usually held to be yet another example of his laziness in government; certainly, the absence of any general administrative policy in England toward this irregular collection of overseas territories, suggests the lack of any guiding principles in their government. The extent to which the laws of England applied in the Crown Colonies of America, let alone the numerous mercantile outposts around the world, was never clearly defined, even when the initial grant of land or trading rights had been made on condition that such laws be upheld. The High Court in London remained undecided throughout Charles's reign, and the matter was left unresolved. Increasing legal autonomy, moreover, encouraged fiscal autonomy, to the obvious disadvantage of the Crown.

In fact, Charles intervened only once in any colony, in Massachusetts Bay, and that after his Commissioner Edward Randolph had discovered that Boston was harbouring regicides, violating the Navigation Acts, refusing to administer the oath of allegiance, denying legal appeals to England, and putting Quakers to death because of their religion. Charles ordered that the colonists send representatives to England to explain their behaviour, and in particular their uncompromising attitude toward those religious sects whom they persecuted. But the colonists refused, and further evasions and delays so infuriated Charles that he cancelled their charter in 1684 and brought their territories directly under the Crown's control. But no Royal troops ever defended the colonists against the Indians or the pirates, no Royal bounty helped feed the settlers when they were starving, and no Royal subsidies bolstered the price of colonial products.

By contrast, Canada, a province of the French colonial empire, was governed absolutely by the French monarch, Louis. All its chief officers were Royal appointees, public meetings were forbidden and criticism of the ecclesiastical, civil or military powers suppressed. Emigration was strictly controlled by the King, trade was restricted to private monopolies, and the cultivation of land, including what was to be sown, regulated by French law. In Louisiana, another French province, but to the south, a man could not even sell a cow without an order from Paris.

Direct administration of the English colonies, however, would have presented Charles with impossible problems. When he became King, half of these territories were already inhabited, with embryonic constitutions providing for local government. As to the rest, Charles had neither the power nor the resources to impose anything approaching the French model. It would have been uncharacteristic, moreover, to have exerted an absolutism which elsewhere he found repugnant. Nonetheless, attempts to police this empire, although ineffective, encouraged the development of England as a world naval power.

Dealing with the American Indians was a further problem. Until 1675, there had been only one serious conflict; a short, sharp and brutish suppression of the Pequot tribe in 1637, which had frightened the Indians into submission. Missionaries such as Richard Bourne, John Cotton and John Eliot had made considerable efforts to encourage literacy among the Indians, training native preachers and printing the Bible in various Indian dialects. About a quarter of all the Indians in southern New England were 'converted', and over twenty 'Praying Indian Towns' established in the neighbourhood of Cape Cod alone.

But the increasing numbers of English settlers, and the inevitable demand for land, gave the Indians cause to feel they were being squeezed out. They never understood ownership in the English legal sense; for the Indian, the exchange of a piece of paper in return for a specified number of axes, kettles and mackinaws, was for partnership or rent, to be repeated if necessary, but not interpreted as a final and irrevocable payment. Three unconverted tribes eventually refused to accept further payments, the Nipmuck of central Massachusetts, and the Wampanoag and the Narragansett who inhabited eastern Rhode Island. On 24 June 1675, these Indians attacked Swansea, a frontier settlement in Narragansett Bay, led by their chief Metacom, called Philip by the English King. The immediate cause of their uprising was the execution by hanging of the Indian murderers of one Sassamon. (Sassamon was a Harvard-educated Indian, once Philip's secretary, subsequently in the pay of Governor Winslow of Plymouth.) Ironically, the jury which found the Indians guilty included Indians, a fact which does not seem to have concerned King Philip by the English. The immediate cause of their uprising was the man in battle, or even torture him to death as punishment. But to hang a man after trial offended his sense of morality.

Encouraged by their plundering of Swansea, the Indians now pillaged other frontier settlements. The New England confederation declared war, although by autumn all the westernmost settlements of Massachusetts Bay and Plymouth had been wiped out, and two military expeditions sent against the Indians badly mauled. The Indian could afford to wage total war, whereas the farmer–settler, who needed to plough, sow and reap in order to survive at all, could not; it began to look as if the English in New England might be driven into the sea. Only in far off Dublin was the hat passed for contributions to the war effort. The Quakers preached that the attack was retribution for the harsh treatment of Quakers; Governor Berkeley of Virginia wrote to Charles that the New England Puritans were being punished for their erstwhile support of Cromwell; others blamed the young who wore long hair, drank rum and fidgeted during sermons.

Philip was an unpleasant character, whose taste for the high life of Boston was usually paid for by the sale of more of his lands. Luckily for New England, the Indians thought him a fool. Despite his initial successes and a deal of subsequent warwhooping, Philip failed to unite the Indians against the settlers. Indeed, a large number of the 'Praying Indians' actively helped the English, both as scouts and fighters. Philip had no concerted plan of action and was a poor match for the military Governors, some of whom had been trained by Cromwell. Eventually, despite the onset of winter, Winslow, the Governor of Plymouth, raised an army of over 1,000 men and surrounded South Kingstown in Rhode Island where 3,000 Narragansetts had camped. The fighting was desperate and bloody, but Winslow triumphed, killing or burning to death over two-thirds of the enemy. Philip was knifed, while on the run, by a member of the Pocasset tribe who had tired of the fighting. Some Indians escaped westwards, but most surrendered or were captured. The women and children were sold as servants, and the contumacious warriors enslaved in the West Indies. Brief though the war had been, its devastation was immense. It would be twenty years before all the destroyed villages were resettled, forty before the frontier advanced. Throughout all the fighting, no help whatsoever had come from England.

Urgent requests from Virginia for protection against the Indians had also been ignored. The Virginian policy had long been to enclose the Indians in small reservations which, needless to say, were being constantly encroached by the whites. By 1675, only 3–4,000 of these Indians remained. Envy of Indian lands had been further aggravated by the increasing economic and political hardship of the white working classes. Under the Virginian system, the ruling classes were tax-exempt. There had been no elections for fourteen years, and by the mid-1670s the one-crop tobacco settlements around Chesapeake Bay were suffering an all-time low in the price of their goods. Inevitably, the Governor, Sir William Berkeley, was blamed for the Indian presence.

When three settlers had been murdered by Indians in August 1675, the local militia was finally called out, led by Lieutenant Colonel John Washington, ancestor of the first President of the United States. Washington surrounded the Indians on the north bank of the Potomac. Five chiefs came to parley; after angry exchanges, the Indians were murdered, whereupon the embittered tribe fought their way out of Washington's blockade and began to attack every

Penn's Treaty with the Indians, made 1681 without an oath, and never broken; the foundation of religious and civil liberty, in the U.S. of America. Visualised by Edward Hicks. Penn, born London, 1644, the son of Admiral Sir William Penn, the conqueror of Jamaica, was expelled from Oxford University for Nonconformity. He became a Quaker, and published "Truth Exalted" (1667) in which he attacked Anglican and Roman Catholic doctrines. "No Cross, No Crown" (1669) asserted his Quaker beliefs, for which he was imprisoned the following year. The province he acquired and named Pennsylvania after his father, was obtained from the Crown in return for the cancellation of a considerable debt which Charles owed the Penn family. Penn's "holy experiment" resulted in the predictable exploitation of Indian hunting grounds and cornfields. In fact, the agreement – "under the elm tree at Shackamaxon", immortalised later in a painting by Benjamin West and praised by Voltaire – was a myth. No such meeting ever took place.

Virginian settlement in their path. A familiar pattern emerged. If the white man could not find the right Indian to punish, he killed any Indian, feeling instinctively that the fewer Indians the better.

Still resenting Berkeley's comparative inactivity, the men of Charles Town Council organized themselves into a volunteer force under the command of one Nat Bacon. The Governor ordered Bacon's troop to disband, but it refused.

Technically, Berkeley said, Bacon and his troop were now rebels, although this did not deter Bacon from leading a successful foray against the hitherto friendly Occaneechee Indians. Berkeley denounced the action as being one inspired by 'Oliver Bacon', and announced a new assembly. Bacon issued a counter-manifesto, entitled the *Declaration of the People of Virginia*.

Berkeley begged Charles to send him military support; he knew Bacon intended to arrest him and transport him back to London, there to stand trial for his apparent failure to protect the colonial frontier. Within months, Bacon was master of all Virginia except the eastern shore; encouraged by a similar uprising in Maryland, he also tried to form an independent state out of Virginia, Maryland and North Carolina, allied with the Dutch and French, against the English. But the planters became weary of the fight, and desertions began. In October, at Yorktown, Bacon caught dysentery, 'the bloody flux', and died. His rebellion collapsed. Berkeley court-martialled and hanged all Bacon's supporters, although only just in time. Within days of the executions, a fleet arrived from Charles carrying instructions to find out what was wrong in Virginia, as well as a general pardon for the rebels. Berkeley was summoned to explain his conduct. Charles was not persuaded by Berkeley's pleading; 'that old fool hath hang'd more men in that naked Country', he said, 'than he had done for the murder of [my] Father.'

*　　*　　*

Whatever the difficulties, and however neglectful he may have been, Charles never doubted the financial possibilities and religious importance of his overseas territories. Josiah Child, much trusted by Charles, noted in his *Discourse on Trade* that the Dutch 'have, in their greatest councils of state and war, trading merchants that have lived abroad in most parts of the world.' What was the point, asked Child, of 'exporting men', and establishing plantations if not to benefit the mother country? A colony is an investment by the State of men and money in a venture across the oceans.

Preoccupation with the trading interest, however, frequently rankled both the colonists and Charles. The Governor of the Caribees had written to Charles in 1667: 'Whoever he be that advised His Majesty to restrain and tie up his colonies in points of trade is more a merchant than a good subject.' And Charles's own attitude was perhaps best summed up by one of his more loyal subjects who wrote to him with pride of the new horizons opening up before seventeenth century England. They symbolized 'freedoms untold, extending to those far distant regions, now become a part of us and growing apace to be the bigger part, in the sunburnt Americas.' That subject was the ancestor of another patriot, and shares his name, Winston Churchill.

Chapter Fourteen

Entirely beloved

Charles's authority in the closing years of his reign was increasingly secure and his government more firmly established than any administration during the previous eighty. 'He wanted not money', Thomas Bruce was to write. 'He was free from Parliaments that so greatly disturbed him, the succession was settled in the due line, he had a good ministry, he was out of intrigues with France . . . and he gave no countenance to loose and buffooning persons that flourished so in former years. In fine, his heart was set to live at ease, and that his subjects might live under their own vine and fig tree.'

The King mopped up, quite systematically, the remains of Shaftesbury's disintegrating opposition, although the old man tried again to rouse a mob on Guy Fawkes Day 1682 in one last bid for revolution. But London was sick of Shaftesbury and his threats. 'The Whigs come over to us daily', noted one Tory gleefully. 'You can hardly find six at High Exchange in the City.' Men burnt their Whig sashes or hid them for fear of prosecution. All that the City Sheriffs could find to arrest from Shaftesbury's once feared and once so numerous army, were 'a parcel of equivocal monsters, half-formed like those fabled of the mud of the Nile. Legs and arms scattered about, heads undressed and bodies unheaded.'

Charles's policy of obtaining Tory control over local government was bringing its rewards. By Michaelmas 1682, London had a Tory Lord Mayor and two Tory Sheriffs; it was conceded that 'the King has mastered this great beast, the City.'

Monmouth attempted a reconciliation with Charles assuming, as many others had done before him, that Charles could be appeased. He could not, and gave orders that the Court was to ignore Monmouth. Monmouth then challenged Halifax to a duel, accusing him of subverting Charles against a Protestant successor; Charles ignored the challenge, exonerated Halifax, and told Monmouth to mind his own business. So Monmouth began urging Shaftesbury to force another exclusionist Parliament; but Shaftesbury was afraid, whereupon the Duke launched into another Royal 'progress' of the north, hoping to find that same enthusiasm he had encountered two years earlier. Charles promptly had his son arrested for disturbing the public peace, and brought him back to London. He allowed his son bail, but exiled him from Court. 'The Duke of Monmouth was an unfortunate man', Shaftesbury said, 'for God hath thrice put it in his power to save England, and make himself the greatest man in Europe. But he had neglected the use of all these opportunities.' Shaftesbury, hearing rumours that fresh warrants were out for his own arrest, fled in disguise to Holland. There, less than two months later, broken, outmanoeuvred and out-politicked by Charles, he died.

Monmouth's existence was sufficient to inspire a new conspiracy against Charles, however, although its details were not discovered until three months after the plot was supposed to have taken place. According to an informer the Court spies unearthed, the plan had been to murder Charles and his brother as they travelled by coach from Newmarket to London. The place chosen had been at a junction in the road eighteen miles north of the City, overlooked by a large house owned by a one-eyed drunk called Captain Rumbold, and named the Rye after a nearby meadow. Forty or fifty men were to have been employed on the job, each armed with a blunderbuss. Unfortunately for the conspirators, a fire at Newmarket had caused Charles to come south earlier than expected.

The discovery predictably unleashed an abundance of rumour about plots and counter-plots, in the confusion of which it became difficult to take any particular piece of information seriously. So when Josiah Keeling, a bankrupt dyer, offered his story about the Rye House Plot to Secretary Jenkins, Jenkins was sceptical. Keeling then reappeared with other witnesses to confirm his story, which convinced Ormonde. As the complications of the Rye House assassination attempt were unravelled, moreover, they seemed to indicate another and more sinister stratagem. Rumbold mysteriously fled, but West and Romsey, two of the other conspirators named by Keeling, gave evidence that for nearly a year now a Council of leading Whigs, including Monmouth, Russell, Essex, Algernon Sidney (brother of Henry), John Hampden (grandson of the hero of Charles I's reign) and Lord Howard, had been planning a countrywide insurrection. Princess Anne, Charles's niece, was to be placed on the throne and married with some 'honest country gentleman' to raise 'a Protestant brood of princes.' The excitements at Rye House were to have been the first step.

Although West's story seemed as wild and inconsistent as anything Oates had manufactured, Charles saw in it an opportunity to implicate the Whigs. Charles would be able to demand yet more patriotic fervour in support of the Crown, and thereby purge the remnants of Shaftesbury's party. Many fled before they could be arrested; Monmouth hid at Toddington near Bedford in the house of his mistress, a reward of £500 being offered for his recapture; Howard, found hiding in a chimney, turned King's evidence; and Essex, having been sent to the Tower and fearing that whatever he may have done would somehow prove him guilty of whatever he was to be charged with, cut his throat. By chance, Charles was in the Tower the day Essex committed suicide, thereby giving the impression he had authorized Essex's murder. The King was much moved: Essex's father had died on the scaffold for Charles's father. 'My Lord of Essex needed not to have despaired of mercy', Charles recorded sadly, 'for I owed him a life.'

Judge Jeffreys, recently appointed Lord Chief Justice, was not so merciful. Sidney rested his defence on the plea that the incriminating papers shown to the Court had been written many years ago, and thus had nothing to do with the present charges. Jeffreys replied: 'A man convinced of those principles and that walks accordingly, what won't he do to accomplish his designs?' Sidney was executed on Tower Hill in December 1683. Toward Russell, Charles was equally ruthless, revealing a feminine capacity for revenge that shocked many of his advisers. He refused to listen to any plea for mercy, including a last minute intercession from Louis. Attempts to bribe the Crown were scornfully rejected. As he told George Legge, Lord Dartmouth: 'If I do not take his life, he will soon have mine.' Politics for Charles had become, albeit temporarily, a personal vendetta. Russell was beheaded, and the crowd which gathered dipped their handkerchiefs in his blood. Hampden was given a crippling fine, and only Monmouth escaped Charles's steel fist.

Charles's spies eventually discovered where Monmouth was hiding, and the King sent Halifax to bring his son back to London. Halifax told Monmouth that his father 'would never be brought to believe that he [Monmouth] knew anything of that part of the plot that concerned Rye House. But, as things went, he must behave himself as if he did believe it.' Halifax then showed Monmouth two letters Charles had already drafted, in which Monmouth humbly begged Charles's pardon and that of his uncle James. Monmouth signed, and was brought secretly to London, where his confessions were duly published in the *London Gazette*. Charles then drafted another statement for Monmouth to sign, as *quid pro quo* for the abandonment of all legal proceedings, in which Monmouth was to say: 'Your Majesty and the Duke know how ingenuously I have owned the late conspiracy; though I was not conscious of any designs against Your Majesty's life, yet I lament the having had so great a hand in that other part of the said conspiracy.' Again Monmouth signed.

Monmouth's supporters became alarmed that he was about to betray them all, and urged him to withdraw. Monmouth vacillated, and then asked for the documents back. Charles lost his temper and told his son to go to hell, that is to leave the Court, if he valued his life. Taking the hint, Monmouth left for the Spanish Netherlands, there to be joined by his mistress; together they went on to Holland, where they were well received by William. James wrote to his daughter, Mary, William's wife, telling her that 'it scandalises all loyal and monarchical people here to know how well the Prince [William] lives with,

276

George Jeffreys (1679), in a portrait attributed to W. Claret. Born 1645 in Acton, Denbighshire; educated at St. Paul's, Westminster, Trinity College, Cambridge, and the Inner Temple. A man of little learning but with an exceptionally loud voice and foul temper; he was knighted in 1677 and became Recorder of London in 1678, Chief Justice of Chester from 1680, and was appointed Lord Chief Justice of the King's Bench and made a member of the Privy Council in 1683 at the age of only 38. James II raised him to the peerage; in return Jeffreys executed over two hundred of Monmouth's rebels; in return James appointed him Lord Chancellor. Much recent scholarship has emphasised that in Stuart England the Chief Justice was not required to administer the law impartially; he was an instrument of political repression. Thus, Jeffreys's well documented outbursts merely reflect his loyalty to the Crown. They also reflect his desire to please. He profited from the misfortunes of others by accepting bribes and letting it be known that a heavy sentence could be readjusted, for a consideration. He ignored evidence, screamed abuse at witnesses, and told his juries what verdict would be appropriate. In this, he was not unusual for his time; a verdict was thought to be the collective agreement of judge *and* jury. The revolution of 1688 forced Jeffreys to flee, but he was captured in the attempt and sent to the Tower where he died in 1689, of gallstones.

and how civil he is to, the Duke of Monmouth . . . and in this affair methinks you might talk to the Prince (though you meddle in no others) . . .' But no doubt William reckoned that, as Monmouth was one of his chief rivals in the struggle for the English succession, the safest place for the Duke to be was next to William.

Monmouth returned only once during Charles's lifetime, and his departure represented for the King another problem resolved. Indeed, Charles's generosity toward his glamorous son caused many to question the existence of a plot; had the rumours been propagated merely to discredit the Whigs? Or had there been a substantial attempt by Protestant extremists to remove all possibility of a Popish successor? If so, why? Fear of persecution? 'The King is informed', Barrillon reported to Louis, 'that in most parts of England people are beginning to doubt the conspiracy, and the King's friends are astonished at the impunity enjoyed by Monmouth.' Charles dismissed such conjectures; he knew the truth.

Europe, meanwhile, seemed on the brink of fresh hostilities. The Turks were said to be assembling a huge army in preparation for an attack on the Hapsburg Empire; the Swedes, allied to William, were threatening war with the Danes; the Elector of Brandenburg had allied himself with Louis against the Emperor Leopold; the Hungarians wanted war with the Austrians. The only monarch who was at peace was Charles. By marrying his niece Anne to the Lutheran Prince George of Denmark, a subsidized ally of France, he prevented Anne being used, as Monmouth had been used, by any future Whig Council. He could therefore claim that, despite his alliance with William, William was no longer the sole inheritor in the family of Protestantism.

For William, the marriage was 'a slap in the face', and caused much ill-feeling. The Turks duly arrived at the gates of Vienna and the Emperor fled; the Spaniards declared war on France and offered Charles money to assist them; Louis reluctantly paid over the subsidy agreed at Oxford. As Lord Preston, the English ambassador to Paris in 1682, noted: 'The great aim of the allies is once to engage him [Charles] in a war, and then to give him as little assistance as they can. For their great maxim is that England is rich, and that it ought to bleed in its turn as well as other estates.'

But Charles had no intention of being dragged into another war. To every overture, he replied courteously that he could not afford the expense of battle and had no intention of recalling Parliament for the extra money. His countrymen were enjoying an unusual degree of prosperity, both in trade and the arts, neither of which he intended to disturb. His diplomatic efforts, he said, would be directed toward securing peace. William was foolish, Charles told him, to imagine he could again persuade his fellow Dutchmen to enter a financially crippling war; the Spaniards, Charles told them, were equally foolish. They had started the war in the first place, and had even wanted to recruit mercenaries in England against the King's nephew which, inevitably, had been refused. They should both, therefore, conclude a settlement with Louis. Eventually, both agreed. William thought the peace infamous, but Charles who had conveniently ignored his treaty with Spain, 'liked it well.' 'The King of England', Barrillon reported, 'feels pleased with his conduct up to the present, and recognizes more and more every day that his understanding with Your Majesty [Louis] is very advantageous to the good of his affairs.'

To suggest that this indicates Charles to have been 'psychologically dependent' on his cousin, or that Charles could only 'stand aside' while Louis 'strengthened his grip' on Europe, thereby frustrating England, is an exaggeration. Charles hoped that his good works would dissuade Louis from granting trade concessions to the Dutch which might threaten England; he had never forgotten the humiliations he had endured at the expense of the Dutch. Now Shaftesbury had fled to Holland. So had Monmouth. And the various Dutch trading colonies still treated their English rivals with contempt. To reassure Louis, Charles openly renewed his affection for Louise, a passion the French thought long dead. Louis was persuaded; 'Ma Cousine', he wrote to Louise, 'I have learnt with pleasure of the continuation of the kind feelings you bear me. I am convinced that the choice he [Charles] has just made in [re-]appointing Lord Sunderland to the post of Secretary of State will contribute very much to my perfect understanding with the King of Great Britain . . . and that he owes his re-establishment to some extent to your good offices.'

Although Charles used Louise as he used others, he retained some nostalgic affection for his French mistress. He had, after all, taken her with him to Oxford during the exclusion crisis and, during one of the worst moments, had written to her: 'I should do myself wrong if I told you that I love you better than all the world besides, for that were making a comparison where 'tis impossible to express the true passion and kindness I have for my dearest, dearest Fubbs.'

In the summer of 1682 he bought a new yacht, christening it *The Fubbs* in honour of Louise. Her patronage of foreign artists continued to provoke his admiration, and, as Osmund Airy later pointed out, she alone among Charles's mistresses had a conception of *la haute politique*. Her annual income was considerable; by 1681 it was estimated to be £138,000. Despite her advocacy of Sunderland and others, on most issues she was scrupulously loyal; it was suspected she had the same cynical view of affairs as Charles. 'She bows to no one', observed Madame de Sévigné, 'and I believe that in her heart, she laughs at this tyranny.' When Louise fell ill in November 1684, Charles never left her apartments. When he died the following February, jealous factions rumoured that she had murdered him with a cup of chocolate laced with poison. Others believed the Queen had poisoned Charles with a jar of dried peas, evidenced by the fact that, after death, his tongue swelled enormously. Neither accusation was true.

Thomas Bruce, afterwards Lord Ailesbury, considered these last years of

Charles a golden age. 'We breathed nothing but peace and happiness, and God knows that was the last year [1684] of our enjoying my good and great King and master.' Dryden had set the tone in an address at the opening of the Oxford Playhouse in March 1681, just before Charles's last Parliament. He wrote:

> From hence you may look back on Civil Rage,
> And view the ruins of the former Age,
> Here a New World its glories may unfold,
> And here be sav'd the remnants of the old.
> But while your days on public thoughts are bent
> Past ills to heal, and future to prevent;
> Some vacant hours allow to your delight,
> Mirth is the pleasing business of the night,
> The King's prerogative, the people's right.

Charles made it clear he had no intention of recalling Parliament, in spite of the provisions of his own Triennial Act which specified that parliaments should meet every three years. He kept the army permanently outside the gates of London as a reminder to the Whigs of the King's power, and applauded the denunciation of Whig pretensions by the University of Oxford. James was left more or less isolated in Scotland after the dissolution of the Oxford Parliament, and Hyde sent to Ireland with instructions to strengthen by whatever means necessary the authority of the Crown. Godolphin, now head of the Treasury, began to regulate government expenditure with fanatical efficiency. Charles suspected that Monmouth and William might still between them contrive a Protestant coup d'état, so assured Barrillon that 'the friendship of the King of France was more necessary to him than ever.' Some thought Charles had become childish in his old age, rushing after Louise like a young lover and tolerating ministers less sophisticated than their predecessors; Sunderland, Louise's 'man of business', was thought mean and insolent. But everyone agreed that Charles needed watching even more carefully than before. The belief that he had lapsed into 'petulant senility' was dangerously naive.

A feeling of prosperity abounded. 'We had no generals to march themselves at the head of superfluous armies', remembered Bruce, 'nor had we one penny raised on land tax.' Charles felt secure enough to release Danby on bail after nearly five years' imprisonment. He instructed Chief Justice Jeffreys to be more generous with those Roman Catholics who had been imprisoned as a result of the popish plots, and encouraged James to bring his libel suit against Titus Oates. He also informed the Council that James was to be restored in fact if not in name to his old position of Lord High Admiral, forfeited earlier because of the Test Act. Relations between the Royal brothers, once so close, had cooled during the exclusion crisis. But Charles admired the resourceful manner in which James governed Scotland, although he remained suspicious of his brother's following. That James's court seemed predominantly

Anglican, in calculated defiance of those who had accused him of being exclusively Catholic, amused Charles. No doubt James's public affection for Monmouth was in part to tease his brother. Charles objected, however, to James's constant advice: 'Brother, you may travel if you will', Charles told him. 'I am resolved to make myself easy for the rest of my life.'

There was an assortment of minor political changes; Sunderland replaced Jenkins as Secretary of State, and Lawrence Hyde, created Earl of Rochester (the poet Rochester had died in 1680), became President of the Council. No undue political significance should be deduced from these changes – Jenkins resigned primarily because he was old and ill, the others had commended themselves because of their efficiency – except that they were all friends of James, who returned from Scotland in May 1682 through the intercession of Louise. Determined to revenge himself on those who had earlier opposed his legitimate succession to the Crown, and anxious to establish his own future authority, it was James perhaps, rather than Charles, who, as the effective chief minister of the Crown, now punished the Whigs so relentlessly.

Charles, it was said, preferred to be eclipsed rather than troubled, although this was always a foolish assumption when assessing the King's motives. Increasingly, Charles 'was not much disposed to be drawn from his divertisements.' He went frequently to Winchester, observing impatiently the progress of his new palace there, but enjoying the 'hunting and hawking and French plays at night.' He adored Newmarket, although he was too old now to ride the horses himself; he visited a cut-glass factory at Lambeth which Buckingham had started. He wandered quietly by the river, and sailed occasionally to Woolwich and Sheerness to inspect the new ships being built in the naval dockyards. He avoided London as much as he could, although each Sunday travelled to Hampton Court for a meeting of the Council; he preferred walking the downs or visiting the Isle of Wight. 'He loved planting and building', noted Evelyn, 'and brought in a polite way of living.' Charles was quite aware these were his last summers – 'a year was a great time in [his] life', he remarked. He was not concerned for of the future, although he worried about its peacefulness: 'I am weary of travelling and am resolved to go abroad no more', he wrote. 'But when I am dead and gone, I know not what my brother will do. I am much afraid that when he comes to wear the crown, he will be obliged to travel again. And yet I will take care to leave my kingdoms to him in peace, wishing he may long keep them so. But', he added with utter realism, 'this hath all of my fears, little of my hopes, and less of my reason.'

*   *   *

When Charles died, many were quick to dismiss the achievements of his reign. For some, Charles's last years were, as Evelyn described them with undaunted humbug, little more than a time of 'gaming and all dissoluteness, and as it were total forgetfulness of God.' The moral imperatives, or apparent lack of them, during Charles's reign had become a scandal; it was thought that honesty, virtue and integrity were qualities no longer to be admired. The high hopes frequently expressed at the Restoration had been frustrated. Evelyn said that God had become 'incensed to make his [Charles's] reign very troublesome and unprosperous by wars, plagues, fires, loss of reputation, by a universal neglect of the public for the love of a voluptuous and sensual life, which a vicious court had brought into credit. I think it with sorrow and pity, when I consider how good and debonair a nature that unhappy prince was: what opportunities he had to make himself the most renown'd king that ever swayed the British sceptre.'

Charles's reported promiscuity was legendary. But much of the information about the King's lechery came primarily from Clarendon and Evelyn, both notorious prigs; although sympathetic to Charles, they despised his sexual prowess. Pepys, who gives the impression of being as sexually adventurous as his master, delighted in every last detail of Royal scandal. And in an age which enjoyed, if not approved, the 'loyal libel', it was believed that the more scurrilous the gossip, the more prestigious the libel.

Parliament chastised Charles for his sexual extravagances, though it was not the women that were objected to, but their cost. The King's mistresses also fulfilled much the same function as members of the various cabals had done during Charles's complex negotiations with Louis; they provided an essential camouflage. Amid disaster after disaster – plague, fire, the Dutch invasion, the stop of the exchequer, war, endless rumours of plot, counter-plot and revolution – the ladies, by their conspicuous presence, provided an element of farce in what might otherwise have become a doom-laden atmosphere. It was assumed, from Charles's apparently libidinous behaviour, that affairs of state interested him little; as a result, politicians at home and abroad consistently underestimated his ruthlessness. The antics of his mistresses were a diversion, while the dirtier business of politics was accomplished efficiently.

The ladies were not his only diversion, although certainly his most exotic. It would be wrong to assume that Charles's interests were limitless, but they do seem to have covered a remarkable range of activities, from sailing to chemistry, from poetry to horse racing. There was hardly a significant or influential figure in his reign, from Wren to Gibbons, from Dryden to Marvell, from Pepys to Milton, from Purcell to Locke, from Bunyan to Halley, from Boyle to Hobbes, who did not owe some measure of their success to the encouragement and involvement of Charles. Today we look askance at a President or a Prime Minister who indulges his hobbies, suspecting that the work of politics is being sacrificed to the pleasure of sport. Charles invited similar criticism.

He had a prodigious memory, however. He disliked speaking in public, yet could be an eloquent and persuasive conversationalist. He longed for intellectual stimulation which he rarely found with politicians; for their graft and cheating, he had only contempt. Such men were overshadowed by Charles and spitefully played down his achievements in their memoirs. Often these memoirs came from those who felt themselves frustrated by Charles, politicians such as Clarendon or Halifax. To their cost they realized that Charles could not be shaken from what he interpreted as his inherited prerogatives; nor could he be diverted from governmental decisions he thought correct. It was grudgingly acknowledged that, when he felt the need, Charles could display a ferocious mastery of politics. He refused to accept Monmouth as successor, for instance, partly out of fraternal loyalty, but essentially because he believed that James was the proper, constitutional successor. He prevented Danby from being impeached, and probably saved Clarendon from execution. When he exerted himself to destroy the Whig leadership, he demonstrated a political ruthlessness more devastating than that of all his ministers combined.

He alone seemed unafraid of the threats and counter-threats from his opponents; by comparison, James was terrified at the prospect of another civil war, and Danby had urged Charles to imprison his opponents. It was believed that, as the exclusion crisis worsened, Charles would sacrifice James for peace. He did not. As young comrades, they had fought side by side at Edgehill, suffered the deprivations of war-time Oxford and the perils of flight and exile. Charles had no illusions about James's temper or stubbornness, nor about his political ineptitude in proclaiming Catholicism so loudly. They had frequent rows, with Charles reminding James that brotherly love was not the only consideration in good government. As Danby said, Charles 'denied almost nothing to the Duke, [but] did not really love him.' Yet he never wavered from loyalty to his brother, however great the provocation, nor from the ideals which that family loyalty entailed.

In his youth Charles had been dominated by a father for whom the virtues of family life were paramount, and throughout both exile and reign, he had struggled to recreate an atmosphere in which those virtues could flourish. He resented his mother, not just because she was a bully, but because he came to understand the part she had played in his father's murder and the consequent disruption to their family life. In exile, he had sought refuge with his widowed sister Mary of Orange; as King, he had come to rely for emotional reassurance on his youngest sister Minette. Their deaths, both before they were thirty, had shaken him profoundly, and his affection for William of Orange, Mary's son, was in part gratitude to his sister.

His devotion to Catherine, whom he thought ugly and spoilt and by whom he felt entrapped in a marriage against his will, was remarkable. He had to endure with her the bitter disappointment and political nightmare of having no legitimate children, but he never abandoned her even when advised to do so for his own safety. He teased her affectionately, rose in the middle of the night to clear up the mess after she had been sick all over the bedclothes, wept and cared for her during her frequent illnesses, and told her gently she had given birth to 'a very pretty boy' after she had screamed hysterically following yet another miscarriage. For each and every one of his children, he was a loving father, and no one has ever been able to count his mistresses; he had at least thirty-nine, who produced in all fourteen acknowledged bastards. From them, Charles derived the peace and contentment denied him by affairs of state; Barbara Castlemaine, for all her bossiness, and Louise, for all her social climbing, were better company than those who called themselves politicians. Amid the worst crises, they and their children provided comfort for a man who found friendship rare and affection irritating, because it made demands. Catherine's greatest offence, probably, was to have fallen in love. The dominance these ladies achieved over affairs of state was less than they imagined, although some made outrageous claims. Even Louise, the noisiest of all, was kept totally ignorant of the many negotiations between Charles and Louis, and especially of the secret treaties of Dover. Charles was pro-French not because of any persuasion from Louise, nor out of admiration for the French King, nor because he was part French himself, nor even because of the endless bribes which Louis offered Charles. The total 'subsidies' Charles managed to extract from Louis throughout the whole of his reign, were less than one year's income from other sources. Charles was pro-French out of necessity.

Charles's foreign policy is usually represented as lacking coherence or purpose, the major result of which was an England 'humiliatingly lowered in prestige.' At the beginning of his reign, Charles had found himself involved in a war against the Dutch primarily because Parliament had voted supplies for it. The navy was ill-equipped, and when the English fleet had twice been defeated by the Dutch, Charles came to feel that Parliament had bungled the whole operation. He saw that his personal fortunes, in terms of the income he

Charles in later years; a portrait attributed to Hawker. He played tennis, walked and rode out ▷ at dawn to follow the hawks. He sailed when he could, urged Wren to hurry with his plans for the new palace at Winchester, suitable for the new capital of his Kingdom. He took communion with his three tall sons by his side, and entertained the Quaker William Penn. When Penn rather ostentatiously kept his hat on in the Royal presence, Charles with a twinkle removed his, observing that it was the custom for only one person to remain covered in the company of a King. He drank only for thirst, worked frequently in his chemistry laboratory, and worried about Louise. Yet, at the same time, Charles skillfully played off one politician against another, kept his brother James – of whom he talked with bitterness, blaming him for many of England's recent troubles – in check, preventing him from taking over the government after his return from Scotland in May 1682, and icily dismissed the pretensions of Tory/Anglicanism to absolute rule. He never failed, moreover, to review his troops (the last occasion was at Putney Heath), or celebrate the Queen's birthday (15 November, 1684 was marked with fireworks and water pageants with the Royal initials linked in letters of fire), or dote upon his children. "Be assured that I am your kind father", he wrote to his daughter, Charlotte Lichfield. For Charles, as for his people, the family, with the King at its head, was the most important unit in the kingdom.

285

hoped to derive from customs and excise, as well as the country's prosperity, depended on an expanding and vigorous trading empire. And since it seemed likely that the French would align their interests with those of the Dutch, either by treaty or conquest, Charles's principal objective became to prevent any alliance which would threaten English expansion. Either the Dutch had to be subjugated, or Charles had to obtain better trading concessions from the French than he could from the Dutch.

This policy was complicated by another factor, not of his seeking, but one which he could hardly ignore. Throughout his reign, Charles had to contend with violent anti-Papist feelings which, being unpredictable, were perilous. Suspecting that Charles was, by inclination, a Catholic, Louis constantly implied that his price for advantageous trading concessions was that Charles should either now or at some time in the future declare himself. To do so, as both he and Louis knew, would be to risk civil war; consequently, Charles found himself drawn closer and closer to Louis for military aid and moral support. Not that Charles ever relied on Louis; he fully understood why Louis, with his grand European designs, was so willing to offer Charles encouragement. To invoke French military support in the event of trouble, moreover, could only be a last resort; but the failure of the Whig Lords to bully Parliament into accepting exclusion increased the possibility of revolution. Charles's only protection, apart from Louis, was a small army whose loyalty was uncertain, against which was the determined and Protestant fanaticism of Shaftesbury and his gang, the glamour of Monmouth, and an unknown horde of discontented Cromwellians who still lurked in the countryside.

Charles's Catholicism has to be understood, therefore, in the context of these political manoeuverings. An obvious attraction of Catholicism, if that is what it was, lay for Charles in its doctrines supporting the authority of Kings. It was to be claimed, after his death, that he had received the sacrament on his death bed, and in 1686 James was to produce two documents supposedly written by Charles (they certainly appear to be in Charles's handwriting) in which he affirmed his belief in the Roman Catholic religion. James showed the papers to Pepys, who also seems to have been convinced.

Yet, when Louise told Barrillon that 'at the bottom of his heart the King is a Catholic', it must be remembered it was in Louise's interest to reassure the French ambassador that she alone had the confidence of Charles; and when Barrillon said later that, with his own ears, he had heard Charles say 'aloud from time to time' he would welcome 'with all my heart' a Catholic priest, being Louis's ambassador it was very much in *Barrillon's* interest to reassure Louis that Charles had died a Catholic. In other words, 'the fact' of Charles's last minute conversion was promulgated most assiduously first by those who, diplomatically, needed to convince themselves or their masters about Charles's true inclinations, and second by his Catholic successor, James, in an attempt to justify and secure his position as a Catholic monarch. All the eyewitness accounts of Charles's apparent 'conversion', moreover, have one thing in common; they were all written by those who had most to gain from Charles's declaration, Catholics. What no one seems to have appreciated is that Charles would have *said* almost anything, had he judged it politically expedient to do so.

Charles's declaration in the original Secret Treaty of Dover, of which both James and Pepys were ignorant, that he 'was convinced of the truth of the Catholic religion', was part of the devious game he played with Louis. Charles was too much a politician to commit irrevocably to one course or another. The hypocrisy of all established religions never ceased to amaze him; the torment which the Scottish Presbyterians had subjected him to in his youth; the violence that the established Churches inflicted on those who disagreed with them. Cutting off people's ears because of a particular belief, as happened to the Quakers, was repulsive to Charles. Admittedly, a Catholic priest was to be summoned to his deathbed, though by whom is none too clear. By the time the priest was called, Charles had known for some while he was dying. Although barely conscious, it is plausible that, as he commended himself to Queen and mistresses alike, he realized the supreme irony of destroying the selfish designs of those who had frustrated his hopes for toleration, namely the Anglican hierarchy who even now were begging him to receive the Sacraments of a Church of which he was nominally the head. As a final cynical gesture, his 'conversion' would have been quite in character with the actions of a man who had so successfully manipulated the complex spectrum of ambitions it had been his misfortune to inherit. He was to be buried in the chapel of Henry VII at Westminster Abbey. According to his wishes, he was interred at night; there was no lengthy burial service, no mourners, no inscription, and no monument. Prince George of Denmark, Charles's nephew by marriage, represented the family. James took no part in the ceremony, which was Anglican.

Charles's political success is sometimes attributed to little more than his ability to lie and lie convincingly. No one trusted him; Louis knew that a stack of secret treaties would not hold Charles to his word if the occasion demanded otherwise. Charles's shifty eyes made it difficult for his closest confidants to know his true purpose. It is possible, of course, that he lacked true purpose, merely stumbling from crisis to crisis; his skill was luck, or mere opportunism. Yet his choice of ministers, for instance, was far from haphazard. He surrounded himself with first-class administrators such as Danby, Clifford, Clarendon, Shaftesbury, Jenkins and Arlington, choosing them not just because they were skilful in government, but because they were as unscrupulous as he was. Being his direct appointees, they owed everything to him; not one thought himself above the King, not even Shaftesbury. Charles never expected their gratitude, and never hid his disregard for their professed morality. If he lied, he did so because he knew it was safer than to imagine he told the truth. Truth in politics was, and still is, a flexible concept; Charles's father had regarded it as quite legitimate to promise anything that came into his head, if he thought such promises would secure the throne. The Scottish Presbyterians had made it a condition of Kingship that Charles accuse his father of being a murderer and his mother a witch. They had also made him swear, as King, to a covenant which he 'hated in his heart.' It seemed to Charles no less dishonest, and just as irrelevant, to make one set of promises to the Scots, and a completely opposite set to the Irish. Publicly he told Parliament how much he loved them; privately he said he found them burdensome. Eventually, he deliberately abandoned them while maintaining that 'he loved [them] most dearly.'

Loyalty, and thereby honesty and integrity, were virtues he suspected were false. Yet, having survived innumerable public crises in which these virtues had been conspicuous by their absence, it is astonishing how loyal Charles remained in private toward those for whom he felt affection; Monmouth, in spite of a conservatism at odds with Charles's own personality and present needs; James, in spite of his being an ill-tempered bigot and political liability; the Queen, in spite of his not loving her and her proving barren. To these and many others Charles remained a devoted, if saddened friend. To those who served him well, he could be an unswerving advocate, except and until they made it impossible for him to continue being so. As to comradeship, there have been few rulers of their country so much loved by so many different sorts of men. It was not simply that his interests were breath-taking in their scope, nor that his acquaintances were more numerous than those of any other rich or well-informed dilettante. Rather, he seems to have genuinely worried about the burdens of his people, not least because he had experienced many of those burdens himself when in exile. Whether racing on the heath at Newmarket, or fighting the Fire in the front line; whether supervising the distribution of bounty after his Restoration, or personally instructing his justices to alleviate the sufferings of Dissenters, Charles seemed everywhere. He was accessible, and kind. Above all, he cared.

Charles's constitutional importance is also discounted because of the apparent collapse of his policies during the subsequent and short reign of his brother. At home, he failed to establish the religious tolerance about which he said he felt so passionately, and failed to establish a *modus vivendi* between the Crown and Parliament, thus merely postponing an inevitable conflict. Real wages fell, despite a growth in trade. Rigid censorship was imposed, although not always to much effect. Grammar schools were shut because they were widely believed to have caused the Civil War. Abroad, England was defeated in both wars against the Dutch, and achieved neither trading hegemony nor naval supremacy. His contribution to the Navy, about which he boasted so often, was less than triumphant; from Cromwell, Charles had inherited 156 warships. By 1684, in spite of an immense expenditure, he had only 162 warships. Admittedly, the two Dutch wars had sunk or damaged a considerable number, but for a monarch with a declared love of the sea it was a dismal record. Only three years after Charles's death, James desperately needed a fleet to protect England from invasion by William of Orange. There was none, or at least none of sufficient strength, to counter the Dutch.

But, in spite of all, Charles managed to inspire his country with a remarkable energy, both in the richness of its life and in the workings of its constitution. He was a relentless political tactician, one of the most astute ever to have governed England. It is possible that, just as in his dealing with the Royal Society where he was obsessed by the gadgetry of science without fully comprehending the implications of scientific theory, he never grasped the need for long-term political strategy. Yet, when he died, a republic had been converted into a constitutional monarchy, wherein a two-party system of government complemented the Crown. This 'revolution' was achieved, moreover, without disturbing the fundamental laws of the land, and it is still only one of two occasions in history when such a transition has occurred, and peacefully.

A spirit of intense enquiry dominated men's actions, whether in science, the arts, sport or politics. If the execution of Charles's father had been the most important political event of the century before 1660, then the restoration of his son was the event which augured best for the future. Under a less good-humoured, less intelligent, less tolerant, less skilful ruler, it is possible, indeed probable, that despite the outpouring of pro-Royalist sentiment in 1660, the monarchy would have been swept away. Yet the monarchy not only survived, but its constitutional importance and emotional significance in the political and social life of its territories was immeasurably enriched by the personality of Charles. The people of England were made to feel they had a leader who was on their side; they were allowed to fill the Matted Gallery at Whitehall and watch Charles at dinner; they were encouraged to approach him as he walked in the park, and he evidently enjoyed their company when they did. To his people, with his many and varied interests, he seemed omniscient, 'debonair, easy of access, not bloody nor cruel', above all, the consummate gentleman. Englishmen identified with the financial struggles which curtailed the King's freedoms; Charles called them his prerogatives. They sympathized with the apparent loneliness of a man who seemed without a family, although yearned for the happiness of family life. By the autumn of 1670, one brother, two sisters, his mother and an aunt were all dead. His childhood hero Prince Rupert was still at Court, but the two had little in common.

His sense of humour, usually at the expense of unpopular ministers, never failed to please. He invented nicknames, which received wide circulation, for all his main protagonists. Titus Oates he called the Salamanca Doctor; Buckingham was Alderman George; Shaftesbury was Little Sincerity; the Duke of York was Squire James. Monmouth he called Prince Perkin, the

Queen was Lisbon Kate, himself Old Rowley. Once, after he had been publicly rebuked by Parliament, Charles replied: 'tell Dr Frampton that I am not angry for to be told of my faults, but I would have it done in a gentlemanlike manner.' Criticism, if justified, he never minded. 'What account will you give at the Day of Judgement of all the idle words in that book?' he asked a courtier who was pressing on Charles a copy of his plays. 'Why truly', came the reply, 'I shall give a better account than Your Majesty shall of all your idle promises which have undone many.' Charles merely shrugged, and smiled. 'Matters are in a very ill state', another of his advisers told him 'but there is a good, able man that if Your Majesty would employ, all would soon be mended.' 'And who is that?' Charles inquired. 'This is one Charles Stuart', came the reply, 'who now spends his time fucking about the Court. But if you were to give him this employment, he would be the fittest man.'

Charles's informality was famous. He told Judge Jeffreys: 'It is a hot summer, and you are going the circuit, therefore I desire you will not drink too much.' To another he said: 'You have but thin shoes. Get a stronger pair to prevent getting cold.' He hated pomposity; he remarked about Louis XIV: 'He will not piss but another must hold the chamber pot.' He mocked himself; one night, during a performance of Macbeth, referring to his own black periwig as compared with the sandy coloured one of Shaftesbury, he said in a loud voice: 'Pray, what is the reason that we never see a rogue in a play, but Oddsfish! they always clap on him a black periwig, when it is well known the greatest rogue in England wears a fair one?' So gracious and great in his expressions was he thought to be 'that he could send away a person better pleased at receiving nothing, than those in the good King his father's time that had requests granted them.' Defending his religious policy, Charles remarked once that he had no wish 'to be the Head of nothing.'

Maybe his approach to Kingship itself, a brilliant mixture of charm, laissez-faire, wit and steel resolution, preserved both the institution of the monarchy and Charles's own particular dynasty. Throughout his reign, we witness the sudden, almost premature, birth of the modern world; the essentially two-party system of democracy, the delicate balances within a constitutional monarchy, the foundations of a world-wide trading empire the extent of which had not been seen before, as well as a flowering of the arts and sciences unequalled hitherto in direct English Royal patronage. Charles's tastes were initially French, but nothing pleased him more than to boast to foreign ambassadors of the achievements of his English architects and poets. Newspapers, coffee-houses, a rudimentary transport system, the election to Parliament of members whose frequent attendance led to the development of full-time politicians; such were the fundamentals of a system of parliamentary representation which, notwithstanding Charles's personal control, became more vigorous in its democracy than any which had preceded it. It was a long way from the doubtful merits of equal franchise, but it was a beginning.

The winter of 1684 was long and cold; a magnificent display of fireworks on the Thames at Whitehall had celebrated the Queen's birthday. 'The Court had not been so brave and rich in apparel since [the King's] restoration', noted Evelyn contentedly. Charles had trouble with his legs which prevented him taking his daily three-mile walk; foolishly, he ignored the advice of his doctors, preferring to treat himself with his own home-made drugs. But, to everyone's delight, he still had an excellent appetite, including 'one thing very hard of digestion – a goose egg or two.' At the beginning of February 1685, Evelyn caustically observed how the Court at Whitehall was full of 'inexpressible luxury and profaneness', with Charles 'toying with his concubines.' The King was in high spirits, chatting through the night with Louise and his men-servants Bruce and Killigrew. Charles told them excitedly of the new palace he was building at Winchester. 'I shall be happy this week', he told them, 'as to have my house covered with lead.'

The following morning Bruce remarked that, unusually, Charles had tossed and turned in his sleep. 'Lord, that is an ill mark', observed one of the royal grooms, Robert Howard, 'and contrary to his custom.' Charles woke, but was unable to speak. He managed a few words in broken French, as if to someone not present. His face was ashen white. Abruptly, he went alone into his closet where he remained for some minutes. Now alarmed, Bruce sent Chiffinch to bring Charles back, saying it was time for him to be shaved. The King returned obediently, apparently not being too sure where he was. As he was being attended by the barber, he fell back into Bruce's arms, his mouth foaming 'and screwing horribly upwards towards a white, pupil-less eye.' Bruce ordered the Royal physician Dr King to bleed Charles, which he did, clumsily. Charles lost fifteen ounces of blood, while Bruce ran to fetch James who arrived with a shoe on one foot and a slipper on the other. The bleeding was stopped, and Charles put to bed. A variety of purgatives were forced down his throat and he came round at midday. He asked for the Queen, who was by now kneeling at the foot of the bed rubbing his feet. He took Bruce's hand and told him: 'I see you love me dying as well as living.'

The bedchamber was soon crowded with fourteen doctors and twice as many courtiers. The doctors prescribed a diet of manna, cream of tartar in thin broth and barley water, together with a little light ale made without hops; Charles said that, as a result of this revolting mixture, he felt as if a fire burned within him. James ordered all ports to be stopped lest rumours of Charles's illness should reach Monmouth. A huge crowd assembled outside the Palace, silently awaiting news. Mercifully, Charles fell asleep.

The following morning the immediate effects of his heart attack were beginning to wear off. 'About seven this morning, he began to talk of the way he took his disease very cheerfully', the Earl of Moray recalled later, 'to the unspeakable joy of all present.' Charles complained that his throat was sore, and a pain bit into his arms and shoulders. 'The King continues to grow better and better', noted John Drummond, Earl of Melfort. On Wednesday morning, he seemed much recovered, and later that day the Privy Council issued a bulletin saying the King was out of danger. Throughout the City, bells were rung in celebration.

But it was not to be. By evening, Charles fell into a sweat. Again the gates of Whitehall were shut. By Thursday, it was clear the King was dying. Only Charles himself remained cheerful. 'He was very sensible of his condition all that Thursday', noted James Fraser, 'and spoke very freely and said many good things.' 'But', he added, 'for nearly two hours the report was His Majesty could not recover out of it, which made all persons of all ranks and degrees melt into tears and fall a-crying.'

A drama of more ominous character was being played out meanwhile in the French ambassador's apartments between Barrillon and Louise. The Anglican bishops were already crowding round the dying monarch, urging Charles to take the last rites of the Protestant Communion. 'It is time to speak out', pleaded Sancroft, the Archbishop of Canterbury, 'for your Majesty is about to appear before a Judge who is no respector of persons.' Yes, yes, there was time enough, replied Charles. Across Whitehall, Louise was not so sure. With extraordinary temerity, she launched into a long and urgent harangue with Barrillon. 'I am now going to tell you a secret', she began (according to Barrillon's own statement written later), 'although its public revelation would cost me my head. The King of England is in the bottom of his heart a Catholic, and there he is surrounded with Protestant Bishops! There is nobody to tell him of his state or to speak to him of God. I cannot decently enter his room. Besides, the Queen is now there constantly. The Duke of York is too busy with his own affairs to trouble himself about the King's conscience.' According to Barrillon, he then hurried to Charles's bedroom and drew James aside into the Queen's room. There, he told Charles's brother of what Barrillon considered to be his (James's) duty. After a pause, James replied: 'You are right, there is no time to lose. I will hazard everything rather than not to do my duty on this occasion.' He returned quickly to Charles's bedside. After bidding the assembled company stand back, James whispered in Charles's ear: 'Do you wish to see a priest, sire?' The courtiers strained forward for the answer. In a faint voice, Charles replied; 'Yes, with all my heart', but begged James not to do anything which might endanger himself. James returned immediately to Barrillon, and told him that the King had consented.

The problem remained to find a priest. Of the Queen's Portuguese monks, not one could speak a word of English. Eventually, a seventy-seven year old priest called Father Huddleston was found. By a strange twist of irony, it was believed to be the same Huddleston who had assisted Charles after Worcester over thirty years before. More recently and in gratitude, Charles had prevented Huddleston from being rounded up (it was said) after the Popish Plot. Huddleston agreed to do what James said Charles required, and was told to go through the private entrance of the Queen's apartments with 'all things necessary for a dying person.' From there, disguised in an Anglican cassock and a black wig, he would be smuggled in by Chiffinch.

The deathbed was lit by candlelight; to his horror, Huddleston discovered that, in his haste, he had forgotten the Host. Desperately, one of the Queen's monks was told to go and get it. James ordered everyone to leave Charles's room, except for Bruce and the Protestant earls of Bath and Feversham. Huddleston was then brought in, still empty-handed. James whispered to Charles: 'Sire, here is a man who saved your life and is now come to save your soul.' Charles replied, also in a whisper: 'He is very welcome.' Huddleston knelt by the bed. 'What service can I perform for God's honour and the happiness of your Majesty's soul at this last moment, on which eternity depends?' There was a long pause. And then, as if summoning all his remaining strength, Charles replied in the 'appropriate manner.' 'I desire to die in the faith and communion of the Holy Roman Catholic Church', he said softly. 'I am most heartily sorry for all the sins of my life past, and particularly for that I have deferred my reconciliation so long . . . with all my heart I pardon my enemies, and desire pardon from all those whom I have in any wise offended.' Huddleston then spoke the Sacrament of Penance. Charles made his confession, repeated after Huddleston the Act of Contrition, and was absolved. Huddleston then asked the King if he would now receive the Host. 'By all means', replied Charles.

But Huddleston still did not have the Host, and had to reply feebly: 'It will be brought to your Majesty very speedily.' He then anointed Charles. Just as he was finishing, the Host arrived at last. Charles struggled to get up. 'Let me meet My Heavenly Lord in a better posture than in my bed', he cried out. But Huddleston told him to lie still. 'God Almighty, who sees your heart, will accept your intention.' Huddleston administered the Sacrament, saying: 'Your Majesty hath now received the comfort and benefit of all the Sacraments that a good Christian, ready to depart out of this world, can have or desire.' Holding a crucifix before Charles's eyes, Huddleston concluded: 'Lift up therefore the eyes of your soul to your sweet Saviour here crucified, bowing down His head to kiss you . . . in the name of the Father, of the Son, and of the Holy Ghost.' There was silence, save the ticking of the clocks. Huddleston was in tears. James thanked him, and he left.

The mob that had gathered outside the bedroom door shuffled in. It was now ten in the morning. Charles was conscious and seemed at peace. James knelt by the bedside, also crying. Bruce held Charles in his arms. At noon, Charles rallied and began to give James instructions. 'Gentlemen', he told the crowded room, 'I have suffered very much and more than any of you can imagine.' He spoke with affection of the Duke of Richmond and gave his blessing to his children by Barbara Castlemaine, the Dukes of Grafton and Cleveland and the Duchess of Northumberland. Nell Gwyn's son, the Duke of St Albans, also received Charles's blessing. Charles asked after Louise. 'I have always loved her', he murmured to James, 'and I die loving her.' A little later he said, 'Do not let poor Nelly starve.' He never mentioned Monmouth. The Queen became hysterical, and fled to her own apartments. She sent a message by Halifax begging forgiveness. 'Alas! Poor woman', Charles replied. 'She asks my pardon? I beg hers with all my heart.' His breathing became erratic, but he lingered on into the night. 'My business will shortly be done', he said. The doctors bled him again. In considerable pain he told James how sorry he was that he had ever seemed unkind to him, but whatever he had done he had been forced into. James was by now in a state of collapse. All night the vigil continued. The Bishops asked Charles to bless his Kingdom and people, which he did. He longed for death, and for an end to suffering. 'I am sorry', he told everyone, 'to be so long dying.'

As dawn broke, he said: 'Lift me up that I may once more see the day.' He gave James the keys to his cabinet and wished him prosperity. 'This was so like a great, good prince', noted one observer, 'and the solemnity of it so very surprising, as was extremely moving.' Charles listened to the sounds of his beloved river. At eight he said: 'That clock must be wound tomorrow.' He sank back but was propped up by pillows. His breathing became more spasmodic. He was bled again. Just before noon on Friday, 6 February 1685, he died. He was only fifty four.

Appendices

Charles II's Principal Ministers:

Lords Privy Seal

1660	Viscount Saye & Sele
1661	Lord Robarts, afterwards Earl of Radnor
1669	Commissioners: Sir Edward Dering, Sir Thomas Strickland, Robert Milward
1673	Earl of Anglesey
1682	Marquis of Halifax

Lord Chancellors & Keepers of the Great Seal

1658	Sir Edward Hyde, afterwards Earl of Clarendon
1667	Sir Orlando Bridgeman, lord keeper
1672	Earl of Shaftesbury
1673	Sir Heneage Finch, afterwards Lord Daventry, lord keeper
1675	the same, now Earl of Nottingham & lord chancellor
1682	Sir Francis North, afterwards Lord Guildford, lord keeper

Lord Treasurers

1660	Commissioners: Sir Edward Hyde; George Monck, afterwards Duke of Albermarle; Earl of Southampton; Lord Robarts; Lord Colepeper; General Mountagu; Sir Edward Nicholas; Sir William Morice
1667	Commissioners: Duke of Albermarle; Lord Ashley; Sir Thomas Clifford; Sir William Coventry; Sir John Duncombe
1669	The same without Sir William Coventry
1672	Lord Clifford, in commission
1673	Earl of Danby, in commission
1679	Commissioners: Earl of Essex; Lawrence Hyde; Sir John Ernley; Sir Edward Dering; Sidney Godolphin
1684	The same without Dering and Godolphin

Secretaries of State

1660	Sir Edward Nicholas (south)	Sir William Morice (north)
1662	Sir Henry Bennet, afterwards Lord Arlington (south)	
1668		Sir John Trevor (north)
1672	Henry Coventry (north 'til 1674, south 1674–80)	
1674		Sir Joseph Williamson (north)
1679	Earl of Sunderland (north 'til 1680, south 1680–1)	
1680	Sir Leoline Jenkins (north 'til 1681, south 1681–4)	
1681		Lord Conway (north)
1683	Earl of Sunderland (north 'til 1684, south 1684–8)	
1684		Sidney Godolphin (north)

Presidents of the Council

1679 Lord Ashley
1679 Earl of Radnor
1684 Lawrence Hyde, Earl of Rochester
1685 Marquis of Halifax

Archbishops of Canterbury

1660 William Juxon
1663 Gilbert Sheldon
1677 William Sancroft

Lord High Admirals

1660 James, Duke of York
1673–84 various commissioners

Principal French Ambassadors in London

1661 Gaston, comte de Cominges
1664 Honoré de Courtin
1665 Henri de Bourbon Duc de Verneuil   (supplementary)
1667 Henri de Ruvigny
1668 Charles Colbert de Croissy (brother of Jean Baptiste Colbert)
1677–1685 Paul Barrillon
1678 Henri de Ruvigny (son of 1667 ambassador, as supplementary)

Charles II's mistresses by whom he had surviving children

Lucy Walter or Barlow (1630–58)
James Scott, Duke of Monmouth (1649–85)

Lady Shannon
Charlotte (born c.1650)

Catherine Pegge
Charles Fitzcharles, Earl of Plymouth (c.1650–80)

Barbara Palmer, Countess of Castlemaine, Duchess of Cleveland (1641–1709)
Anne Fitzroy (born 1661), married the Earl of Sussex
Charles Fitzroy, first Duke of Cleveland (1662–1730)
Henry Fitzroy, Duke of Grafton (1663–90)
Charlotte Fitzroy (1664–1718), married the first Earl of Lichfield
George Fitzroy, Duke of Northumberland (1665–1718)

Nell Gwyn (1650–87)
Charles Beauclerk, Duke of St. Albans (1670–1726)
James Beauclerk (1671–80)

Louis de Kéroualle, Duchess of Portsmouth (1649–1734)
Charles Lennox, Duke of Richmond (1672–1723)

Moll Davis
Mary Tudor (1665–1705), married the Earl of Derwentwater

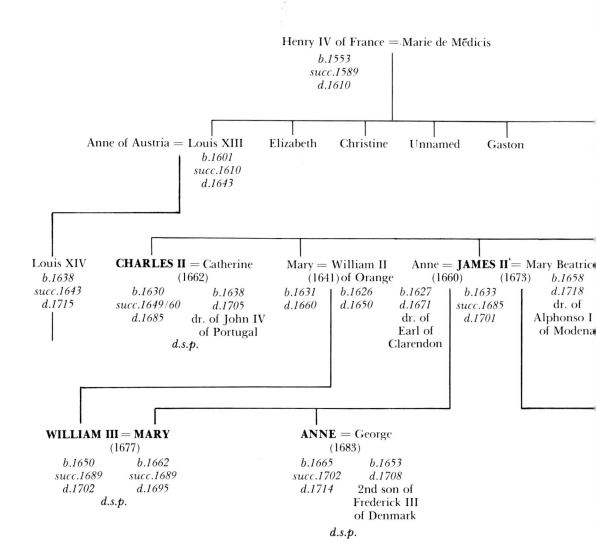

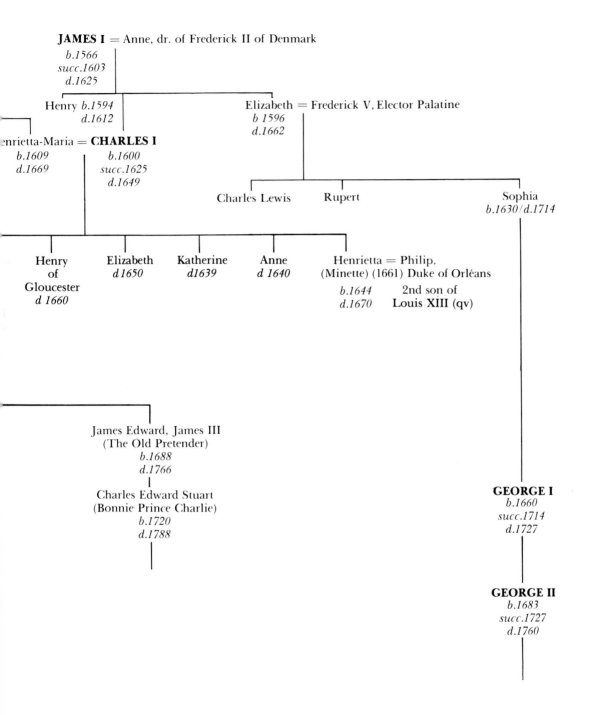

JAMES I = Anne, dr. of Frederick II of Denmark
b.1566
succ.1603
d.1625

Henry *b.1594*
     d.1612

Elizabeth = Frederick V, Elector Palatine
b 1596
d.1662

enrietta-Maria = **CHARLES I**
b.1609   *b.1600*
d.1669   *succ.1625*
                      d.1649

Charles Lewis   Rupert   Sophia
                                                      b.1630/d.1714

Henry   Elizabeth   Katherine   Anne   Henrietta = Philip,
of   *d 1650*   *d1639*   *d 1640*   (Minette) (1661) Duke of Orléans
Gloucester   *b.1644*   2nd son of
d 1660   *d.1670*   **Louis XIII (qv)**

James Edward, James III
(The Old Pretender)
b.1688
d.1766

Charles Edward Stuart
(Bonnie Prince Charlie)
b.1720
d.1788

GEORGE I
b.1660
succ.1714
d.1727

GEORGE II
b.1683
succ.1727
d.1760

299

Select bibliography

Among the works consulted were:

ACTON, Lord   *Secret History of Charles II* (publ. 1907)
AILESBURY, Earl of   *Memoirs* (1890)
AIRY, Osmund   *Charles II* (1901)
                     English Restoration and Louis XIV (1888)
AKERMAN, J.W.   *Money received and paid for secret services of Charles II and James II* Camden Society (London 1851)
ANDREWS, Allen   *The Royal Whore* (1971)
ASH, Bernard   *The Golden City* (1964)
ASHLEY, Maurice   *England in the 17th Century* (1952)
                     Charles II, Man and Statesman (1971)
AUBREY, J.   *Lives* (ed. Clark)
BARBOUR, V.   *Henry Bennet, Earl of Arlington* (1914)
BATE, F.   *The Declaration of Indulgence, 1672* (1908)
BAXTER, S.B.   *The Development of the Treasury 1660–1702* (1957)
BELL, W.G.   *The Great Plague in London* (1916)
                     The Fire of London (1920)
BEVAN, Bryan   *Nell Gwynn* (1969)
                     Charles II's French Mistress (1972)
BOSHER, R.S.   *The Making of the Restoration Settlement* (1951)
BOXER, C.R.   *The Dutch Seaborne Empire 1600–1800* (1965)
BRAILSFORD, M.R.   *The Making of William Penn* (1930)
BRETT, A.C.A.   *Charles II and his Court* (1951)
BROWNING, Andrew   *Thomas Osborne, Earl of Danby* (1944–51)
BRYANT, Arthur   *King Charles II* (1931)
                     Restoration England (1934)
                     The Letters, Speeches and Declarations of Charles II (1935)
                     Samuel Pepys (1933–8)

BUNYAN, J.	*The Pilgrim's Progress* (Folio Society edn. 1962)
BURNET, Gilbert	*History of His Own Time* (1823)
Calendars of Domestic State Papers 1683–85	(intro. F. Bickley, HMSO, 1933)
CARTWRIGHT, Julia	*Henrietta-Anne, Duchess of Orleans* (1894)
CHAPMAN, H.W.	*The Tragedy of Charles II* (1964)
CHRISTIE, W.P.	*Life of Shaftesbury* (1871)
CLARENDON, Earl of	*The History of the Rebellion and Civil Wars in England* (ed. W.D. Macray 1888) *Life* (1851)
CLARK, G.N.	*Science and Social Welfare in the Age of Newton* (1937)
COBBET, W. (ed.)	*State Trials* (1809–28)
COKE, R.	*Discourse of Trade* (1670)
COLLIER, Jeremy	*Short View of the Immorality of the English State* (1680)
COLLINS BAKER, C.J.	*Lely and the Stuart Portrait Painters* (1912)
COSMO, Grand Duke of Tuscany	*Travels* (1821)
CRAGG, G.R.	*Puritanism in the Period of the Great Persecution 1660–88* (1957)
CRANSTON, M.	*John Locke* (1947)
CRAWFURD, Raymond	*The Last Days of Charles II* (1909)
CUNNINGHAM, W.	*Alien Immigrants to England* (1897)
DARBY, H.C.	*The Draining of the Fens* (1940)
DASERST, A.I.	*Nell Gwyn* (1924) *Private Life of Charles II* (1927)
DAVIDSON, Campbell-	*Catherine of Braganza* (1908)
DAVIES, Godfrey	*The Restoration of Charles II* (1955)
DAVIS, Ralph	'English Foreign Trade 1600–1700' *Economic History Review* II vii (1954)
DEFOE, D.	*Journal of the Plague Year* (1722)
DERING, E.	*Parliamentary Diary* (ed. Henning 1940)
DRINKWATER, John	*Mr Charles, King of England* (1926)
DRYDEN, J.	*Writers and their Background* (ed. Earl Miner 1972)
EVANS, F.M.G.	*Secretaries of State 1558 to 1680* (1923)
EVELYN, John	*Diary* (ed. de Beer 1955)
FANSHAWE, Lady	*Memoirs* (ed. B. Marshall 1893)
FARLEY-HILLS, David (ed.)	*Rochester, the critical heritage* (1972)
FEA, Allan	*King Monmouth* (1902)
FEILING, Keith	*British Foreign Policy 1660–72* (1930)

FEILING, Keith	*History of the Tory Party 1640–1714* (1924)
FIRTH, C.H.	*Life of Newcastle* (1886)
FORD, Grey	*Secret History of the Rye House Plot* (1754)
FOX, George	*Journal* (1924)
FRASER, Lady A.	*Cromwell* (1973)
FRASER, P.	*The Intelligence of the Secretaries of State and their Monopoly of Licensed News 1660–88* (1956)
FOXCRAFT, H.C.	*A Character of the Trimmer* (1946)
GARDINER, S.R.	*Charles II and Scotland in 1650* (1894)
GREEN, M.A.E.	*Letters of Queen Henrietta Maria* (1857)
GREY, Anchitel	*Debates of the House of Commons 1667–1694* (1769)
GROSE, G.L.	'Louis XIV's financial relations with Charles II and the English Parliament' *Journal of Modern History* I (1929)
HALEY, K.D.H.	*The First Earl of Shaftesbury* (1968)
HALIFAX, Marquis of	*Works* (ed. Raleigh 1912)
HAMILTON, Anthony	*Count Grammont at the Court of Charles II* (ed. and trans. Nicholas Deakin 1965)
HARDACRE, Paul H.	*The Royalists during the Puritan Revolution* (1956)
HARRIS, William	*Historical and Critical Account of the Life of Charles II* (1766)
HARTING, J.H.	*Catholic London Missions* (1903)
HARTMAN, C.H.	*La Belle Stuart* (1924)
	The Vagabond Duchess (1926)
	Clifford of the Cabal (1937)
	The King my Brother (1954)
HAY, M.V.	*The Jesuits and the Popish Plot* (1934)
HENDERSON, G.D.	*Religious Life in 17th Century Scotland* (1936)
HILL, C.	*The Century of Revolution 1603–1714* (1961)
HOOKE, Robert	*Diary 1672–80* (ed. Robinson & Adams 1935)
HUDDLESTON, Father	*Short and Plain Way: A brief account of Particulars occurring at the Happy Death of King Charles II* (1687)
JONES, J.R.	*The First Whigs* (1961)
	'Shaftesbury's "Worthy Men"' *Bulletin of the Institute of Historical Research* (1957)
JORDAN, W.K.	*The Development of Religious Toleration in England* (1932–40)
KEETON, G.W.	*Lord Chancellor Jeffreys and the Stuart Cause* (1965)

KENNEDY, W.	*English Taxation 1640-1799* (1913)
KENYON, J.P.	*Robert Spencer, Earl of Sunderland* (1955)
	The Stuarts (1960)
	The Stuart Constitution (1966)
	Halifax – Complete Works (1969)
	The Popish Plot (1972)
KING, Gregory	*Natural and Political Observations upon the State and Condition of England* (1696)
KNORR, K.E.	*British Colonial Theories 1570-1850* (1944)
LANE, Jane	*Titus Oates* (1949)
LEE, Maurice	*The Cabal* (1965)
L'ESTRANGE, Roger	*Brief History of the Times* (1688)
LISTER, T.H.	*Life and Administration of Edward, First Earl of Clarendon* (1838)
LOCKE, John	*Two Treatises on Government* (ed. P. Laslett 1960)
LOTH, David G.	*Royal Charles* (1931)
MACRAY, W.D.	*Notes which passed at meetings of the Privy Council between Charles II and Clarendon 1660-67* (1896)
MAGEE, Brian	*The English Recusants: a study of the post-Reformation Catholic Survival* (1938)
MARVELL, A.	*Growth of Popery* (1677)
MATHEW, David	*Catholics in England* (1955)
MATTHEWS, William	*Charles II's Escape from Worcester* (1967)
MILLER, John	*Popery and Politics in England 1660-1688* (1974)
MILWARD, John	*Diaries 1666-8* (ed. Caroline Robbins 1938)
MONTPENSIER, Mlle de	*Mémoires* (ed. A. Chervel 1889)
MORISON, S.E.	*Oxford History of the American People* (1965)
NORMAN, Charles	*Rake Rochester* (1955)
NORTH, Roger	*Lives of the North* (ed. Jessopp 1890)
OGG, David	*England in the Reign of Charles II* (2 vols 1934)
OLLARD, Richard	*The Escape of Charles II* (1966)
PEARSON, Hesketh	*Charles II, his life and likeness* (1960)
PEPYS, Samuel	*Diary* (ed. by R.C. Latham and W. Matthews 1968-78)
POLLOCK, John	*The Popish Plot* (1903)
POWELL, J.R.	*The Navy in the English Civil War* (1962)
REDDAWAY, T.F.	*The Rebuilding of London after the Great Fire* (1940)
RERESBY, J.	*Memoirs* (ed. A. Browning 1936)
ROBB, Nesca	*William of Orange* (1966)

Select bibliography

ROGERS, P.G.	*The Dutch in the Medway* (1970)
ROTHENSTEIN, Sir J.	*Introduction to English Painting* (1933)
The Rules of Civility (1678)	
SACKVILLE-WEST, V.	*Life of Duchesse de Montpensier* (1959)
SCHLATTER, R.B.	*The Social Ideas of Religious Leaders 1660-88* (1940)
SCHOFIELD, Seymour	*Jeffreys of the Bloody Assizes* (1937)
SCOTT, Eva	*The King in Exile* (1905)
	The Travels of King Charles II 1654-60 (1907)
SCOTT, Lord George	*Lucy Walter, Wife or Mistress* (1947)
SEWELL, W.	*History of the Quakers* (1725)
SIDNEY, H.	*Diary of the Times of Charles II* (ed. R.W. Blencowe 1843)
SITWELL, Sir G.	*The First Whig* (1894)
SPRAT, Bishop	*History of the Royal Society* (1683)
TEMPLE, William	*Works* (1814)
THIRSK, Joan	'The Restoration Land Settlement' *Journal of Modern History* **XXVI** (1954)
TREVELYAN, G.M.	*England under the Stuarts* (1904)
TUKE, Samuel	*A Character of Charles II* (1660)
TURNER, E.R.	'The Privy Council of 1679' *English Historical Review* (1915)
TURNER, F.C.	*James II* (1948)
UNDERDOWN, David	*Royal Conspiracy in England* (1960)
WALTER, J.	'Censorship of the Press during the reign of Charles II' *History* **XXXV** (1950)
WESTFALL, R.S.	*Science and Religion in 17th Century England* (1958)
WHINNEGE, M.	*Wren* (1971)
WILLEY, B.	*The Seventeenth Century Background* (1934)
WILSON, C.	*Profit and Power* (1958)
	The Dutch Republic (1968)
WILSON, J.H.	*Nell Gwyn, Royal Mistress* (1952)
	Court Wits of the Restoration (1954)
WOOD, Antony	*The Life and Times of Antony à Wood* (5 vols ed. Clark 1891-1900)
ZEE, B. & H. van der	*William and Mary* (1973)